FINANCING INDIA'S IMPERIAL RAILWAYS, 1875–1914

Perspectives in Economic and Social History

Series Editors: Robert E. Wright
Andrew August

Titles in this Series

13 Sex in Japan's Globalization, 1870–1930: Prostitutes, Emigration
and Nation Building
Bill Mihalopoulos

FORTHCOMING TITLES

Energy, Trade and Finance in Asia: A Political and Economic Analysis
Justin Dargin and Tai Wei Lim

Violence and Racism in Football: Politics and Cultural Conflict in British
Society, 1968–1998
Brett Bebber

Meat, Commerce and the City: The London Food Market, 1800–1850
Robyn S. Metcalfe

Welfare and Old Age in Europe and North America: The Development
of Social Insurance
Bernard Harris (ed.)

Markets and Growth in Early Modern Europe
Victoria N. Bateman

Policing Prostitution, 1856–1886: Deviance, Surveillance and Morality
Catherine Lee

Respectability and the London Poor: The Value of Virtue
Lynn MacKay

To Lynne, Thomas and Elizabeth, for everything

FINANCING INDIA'S IMPERIAL RAILWAYS, 1875–1914

BY

Stuart Sweeney

Routledge
Taylor & Francis Group

LONDON AND NEW YORK

First published 2011 by Pickering & Chatto (Publishers) Limited

Published 2016 by Routledge
2 Park Square, Milton Park, Abingdon, Oxfordshire OX14 4RN
711 Third Avenue, New York, NY 10017, USA

First issued in paperback 2015

Routledge is an imprint of the Taylor & Francis Group, an informa business

BRITISH LIBRARY CATALOGUING IN PUBLICATION DATA

Sweeney, Stuart, 1963–
Financing India's imperial railways, 1875–1914. – (Perspectives in economic
and social history) 1. Railroads – India – Finance – History. 2. Railroads –
Social aspects – India-History.
I. Title II. Series
385'.0954'09034-dc22

ISBN-13: 978-1-138-66435-7 (pbk)
ISBN-13: 978-1-8489-3047-6 (hbk)

Typeset by Pickering & Chatto (Publishers) Limited

CONTENTS

Passepartout, on waking and looking out, could not realize that he was actually crossing India in a railway train. The locomotive, guided by an English engineer and fed with English coal, threw out its smoke upon cotton, coffee, nutmeg, clove and pepper plantations...

Jules Verne, *Around the World in Eighty Days* (1873; Puffin: London, 2004), p. 66,

INTRODUCTION

By 1908 Britain had invested £274 million of capital in Indian railways, making it the largest single investment programme ever undertaken in the British Empire.[1] Railways made up 80 per cent of Britain's industrial investment in India, relying on Indian taxpayers to fund construction and early operations. The size and prominence of this public works project has prompted a continuing scholarly debate on the motivation and results of Indian railways, since Lord Dalhousie's original railway minute of 1853. However, most of the analysis has focused on the earlier period of railway construction up to 1875. Like much historiography of the colonial Indian period, analysis has been characterized by subjective responses to British Imperialism. For example, Daniel Thorner's work on government provision of early Indian railway guarantees complemented Indian nationalist writing on railways, as part of the 'drain' debate. To be fair, Thorner was sensitive to the difficulty of pursuing development policies in British India given the political landscape at Westminster. After all, the India Office was not unique in guiding colonial enterprise towards dependence on manufacturers and financiers at the metropole. In contrast, the 'new Imperialist' scholars, reinterpreting British railway policy as liberal, sensible and benign have ignored the most compelling aspects of Indian nationalist critique. Dutt, Naoroji, Ranade and Wacha may have overstated their case at times, but the complaint that Britain pursued railways in isolation from other legitimate development concerns has never been rebuffed.[2] The opportunity cost of railways, in a balanced budget environment, in terms of irrigation, sanitation and education expenditure foregone was considerable.

Indian railways have been criticized for absorbing more than their fair share of India's tax receipts. They have also been seen as stifling industrial development and wealth creation in India. It is true that nationalists underestimated the challenges in converting India's eighteenth-century artisan textile businesses into western-style industry. Nevertheless, India's industrial stagnation in the nineteenth century is an awkward fact for apologists of Empire. The British neglect of Indian industry after the fall of the Company is beyond debate, but the extent to which this was understood to place limits on India's growth potential is still discussed. Even Keynes had seen the terms of trade moving in favour of India's agricultural base over time.[3] Modern globalization theory has stressed the benefits of rigorous international specialization. Victorian railways in India were constructed to accelerate that process but, uniquely, India became a major railway power without benefiting from the normal accelerator and multiplier effects of capital investment. The cataclysmic famines of the 1870s and 90s were the most dramatic evidence of the failure of the Raj to create economic growth and combat extreme poverty in India. Over 1875–1913, for example, China generated comparable economic growth to India, without a railway network, while both countries underperformed the average for developing nations.[4] At the same time, the British focus on overseas capital exports, of which Indian railway bonds and equities made up a significant share, created longer term problems for the UK economy, which suffered from the opportunity cost of capital directed at 'rentier' empire pursuits, rather than new domestic industries like electricity, chemicals and motor cars.[5]

During the late nineteenth century the British were prepared to question the benefits of rail investment at public committees and commissions. However, by 1909, in a memorandum detailing the achievements of the Raj in the half-century since the Mutiny, self criticism had ceased. Railways were emphasized as one of the great achievements of the period since the abolition of the East India Company (the Company). Aggregate gross earnings were £30 million and the benefits of the railways were estimated at a spectacular £100 million per annum, incorporating savings in transport fares per mile travelled but excluding additional benefits of spared time. The railway network employed some 525,000 people of whom 508,000 were Indians. Railways had produced a return that year of 4.33 per cent. Like modern scholars of the Imperialist school, the report failed to consider alternative uses of the enormous capital expended. Indeed, the report pointed to returns of some 8 per cent on more recent irrigation expenditure on an aggregate capital programme of only £32.5 million. These were returns unheard of in the Indian railway sector, outside the Bengal regional monopoly, the East Indian Railway (EIR). The India Office/GOI had over previous years channelled ten times as much capital into the lower yielding railway business in a policy which ignored considerations of market-based returns.[6] One aim of this monograph is to explain the strength of support for this railway investment programme across large sections of British decision-makers without resorting to a partisan view of the rights or wrongs of the project.[7] To do so it is necessary to look in detail at debate surrounding the three rationales used by the British to justify prioritization of Indian railways: trade and commerce, famine protection and relief, and military/strategic benefits for the defence of India. The triumvirate of early rail enthusiasts, W. P. Andrews, Macdonald Stephenson and John Chapman used all three aspects in promoting Indian rail projects.[8] These three rationales provide a helpful framework for interpreting the period after 1875 when similar arguments persisted.

The commercial rationale for railways had been called into question by 1875. The first generation of government-guaranteed companies, with the exception of the EIR and Great Indian Peninsula Railway (GIPR), had failed to meet their 5 per cent guarantees and absorbed large GOI subsidies. This prompted a shift to direct state funding under the Liberal Viceroy Lawrence, a decision reversed in the early 1880s in an attempt to move railways off the government's balance sheet. The second generation of guaranteed companies provided ample opportunities for City underwriters, financial advisors, stockbrokers, rail promoters, managing agents/traders, shippers and insurers to generate service industry revenues. This was achieved in parallel with large manufacturing orders for locomotives, wagons, steel railings, steel lines, bridge contracts and general engineering products. The extent to which Indian railways could act as a counter-cyclical source of demand during the 'great depression' of the later nineteenth century was much discussed at the parliamentary commission hearings on the depression of trade. Sheffield, Glasgow, Manchester and London Chambers all had significant representation in parallel with the Indian chambers. The book will attempt to disentangle these different interest groups, to draw conclusions on the relative strength of service industry and manufacturing lobbies. This should contribute to the active debate on gentlemanly capitalism which has developed in recent years.[9]

Given that India made up over 80 per cent of the population of the British Empire by 1900, Cain and Hopkins made clear that 'no plausible explanation of the purpose of empire-building can afford to stumble over the sub-continent'.[10] This makes the sub-continent's largest industrial project central to any critique of the 'gentlemanly capitalism' paradigm. Indeed, Dumett criticized the lack of attention paid by the two authors to railways and shipping across the British Empire. He saw their references as 'brief' and argued that the writers failed to link transport technology to 'the wider industrial revolution'. Further, he questioned positing a close relationship between the City and politics, apart from the prominent Bank of England/Treasury relationship (where the requirements of public funding brought them together). There was a lack of 'representative examples' where City people had demonstrably influenced 'overseas political, military and naval operations' or 'the building of new colonies and the extensions of empire'.[11] Indian railways provide a test case for these gaps in gentlemanly capitalism's historiography. Equally, scrutiny of British manufacturing lobbies, which pressed railways, should allow consideration of Clive Dewey's view that manufacturing influence in British India was declining by the late Victorian period. Dewey argued that the 'eclipse of the Lancashire [cotton] lobby' could be traced back to 1870. Lancashire's success in overriding 'infant industry' protection for Indian textiles was said to disguise longer-term weakness. This reflected the 'decline of the provinces in British politics, and the emergence of a highly-centralized class-based political system', in line with Cain and Hopkins assertions.[12] This was a bold statement which would be strengthened if the largest Imperial industry was seen to benefit only British service industries. Further, the overwhelmingly Greater London investor base for the bonds and equities originated by Indian railway companies may give support to the Cain and Hopkins emphasis on the middle-class elite of the South East of England. Certainly the demographics of that investor base differed from the non-guaranteed British railway companies up till the 1840s, which had attracted savings from the regions where they were located.[13]

The trading and commercial aspects of Indian railways occupy a central position in the debate about 'economic imperialism'.[14] W. J. Macpherson took a benign view of the influence of British commerce and finance on the India Office and GOI, including public lobbying by the 'cotton barons'. He largely ignored the informal advisory arrangements between prominent bankers and the India Office, and lobbying activity by Indian Chambers of Commerce. Like Dewey, Macpherson was sceptical of the influence of manufacturers on the dual government. While steel railway lines and sleepers became an important source of demand for British manufacturers he concluded that 'the output of the iron industry, whether British or Indian, was an effect rather than a cause of the construction of lines in India'. He could detect no bias in the tendering process in favour of British manufacturers, and argued 'if anything the bias was towards India, but price was the ultimate determinant'. In short, Macpherson rejected accusations of 'economic imperialism' in Indian railway administration, seeing little evidence of efforts 'to exploit the ryots'. He gave an exhaustive description of 'the new issue market for Indian railway securities' but little insight into the advisory function of City bankers. He was satisfied that the underwriting fees charged on debentures and stocks were reasonable, highlighting the tendency to distribute stock to existing shareholders and so dispensing with underwriters altogether. In support of this contention, he quoted F. Lavington who had characterized railway investors as being motivated by steady returns rather than speculation.[15] Macpherson's research focused on the earlier period up to 1875 but, beyond that, the volume of construction and financing increased, making the stakes for British suppliers greater. Similarly, the extent to which foreign competition could expect to win manufacturing and financing business heightened as other countries industrialized and competed more effectively with Britain. Hence, Macpherson's assertions about the impartiality of the dual government in allocating contracts demand added scrutiny in the period beyond 1875.[16] It is surprising that the period of 'High Imperialism' has received so little attention in the historiography of Indian railways.

The famine prevention rationale for Indian railways prompts equal controversy to that surrounding commerce and trade. The failings of railways to protect against famine in the disasters of 1896–97 and 1899–1900 created heightened resistance from Indian nationalists, but little re-examination of government investment priorities. Irrigation and education expenditure still lagged behind, despite assurances at the subsequent famine commissions that this would change. Scholarly analysis of famines and Indian railways has mainly consisted of static regression analyses by Michelle McAlpin and John Hurd, using famine commission data to prove links between food price equalization across regions, and railway investment. However these models could not cope with the complexity of the matter, where high clearing prices for food often worsened matters by spreading famine wider. Cross correlations between variables in simple regression analysis make the pro-railway conclusions problematical.[17] The opportunity cost of scarce resources devoted to railways in the late nineteenth century was significant, but such costs did not become a focus of economic theory until the early twentieth century. McAlpin's confident assertion that railways had played no part in worsening famine conditions in the late nineteenth century requires further research through accounts of the time, to supplement crude price data. This detail is accessible through the voluminous famine commission accounts of Indians present in the affected regions. Furthermore, the extent to which railway transportation was imposed as an isolated government policy, which shocked grain and rice markets without countervailing adjustments in terms of relief food supplies or export bans, is ignored in McAlpin's work. She asserted that railways 'permitted the import of grain into regions of harvest failure and thus helped to limit the mortality from such disasters'.[18]

This rather heroic picture of British famine relief and prevention ignores the impact of failed monsoons in the 1870s and 90s, which resulted in unprecedented mortality figures of 13–16 million. Something clearly went wrong although the British account of the period, written in 1909, boasted of rising agricultural prices relieving peasant poverty through wealth accumulation. True, wages rose eventually leaving people less vulnerable to increased grain prices, but in the short term railways wrought rising prices and encouraged Malthusian fatalism amongst officials.[19] It seems reasonable to ask whether policy makers were aware of the dangers of what Amartya Sen subsequently named the the problem of 'exchange entitlement'.[20] Equally, with well over £200 million of railway investment sunk into a food distribution network by the advent of the late 1890s famines, one might have expected a better mortality outcome than that suffered in prior famines. Debate on the relative severity of these famines versus prior experiences, in that sense, is missing the point. Again, famine commission testimony should provide insight. Finally, the assertion that famine disappeared after the 1899/1900 crisis, proving the potency of railways in combating hunger, ignores the more consistent public health concerns in colonial India. Ira Klein attempted to widen debate on the failings of British infrastructure in improving sanitation and disease control. Statistics in Northern India from the first census of 1871, for example, showed stagnant population due to a rising death rate. The death rate reached an unprecedented 5 per cent by 1908. Too much focus on famine outbreak risks diverting attention from the role of railways in disrupting 'traditional socio-economic institutions ... hampering older modes of agrarian production, and ... impoverishing the soil'. In 1905, for example, by which time the Raj boasted that famine had been eradicated, Klein pointed to failed crops, 25 per cent price rises, and famine/disease related death rates comparable to that suffered in 1879. Within two years, wheat prices had risen by a further 50 per cent, and had pulled up prices of cheaper grains to worsen disease-related mortality rates in the region.[21] In contrast, the Raj's 1909 memorandum stressed the immunity of the Central Provinces and United Provinces to the drought of 1907, where higher grain prices had improved peasant wealth, allowing the avoidance of another catastrophic famine. The Raj tended to view high prices as reflective of a buoyant agricultural sector, perhaps as a rebuff to Dutt's accusations of overbearing land assessments.[22] Officials' inability to trace links between railway development in isolation, high prices and general susceptibility to famine and disease needs further explanation. It also encourages consideration of the extent to which British policy was underpinned by Malthusian fatalism on the prospects for India's supposed population problem, notwithstanding the static population over those years.[23]

The third rationale for Indian railways, the military and strategic benefits in the defence of India, was emphasized by W. J. Macpherson in the period after 1870.[24] The experience of the Indian Mutiny, coupled with increasing tensions on the North West Frontier was said to have reinforced the requirement for railways to despatch troops and materials rapidly. Railways had become the technology of choice for military strategists by the 1870s, based on experience in the American Civil War and Franco–Prussian War. However, it is far from clear how the thinking of Friedrich List and Prussian General Von Moltke was absorbed by the India Office and Calcutta. The expense and engineering challenges implied in constructing even narrow-gauge railways into the Himalayas, to meet the challenge of Russia from Central Asia, presented great difficulties for military planners. It was evident that the low cost military railways built by the Russians were not achievable by the British on the North West Frontier. However, the defence of India placed British military planners in a theatre of war akin to continental wars. This made India less suited to the traditional dominance of the Royal Navy. The British Army was constrained by lack of conscription and the requirement, post-Mutiny, to shift away from native troop concentration. Railways may have been the most suitable solution to the unique challenges of Russia's railway capacity, but the existing historiography fails to examine the method by which this came to be accepted. The quality of British strategic analysis of Russia's Transcaspian and Orenburg–Tashkent Railways requires consideration. Not all observers were convinced that Russia could readily turn her Central Asian network into a platform for an invasion of British India. Indeed, by 1904 the shortcomings of the Transiberian railway for Russian troop movements were evident for all to see against the Japanese. However, even after the Anglo–Russian concordat of 1907, military railway expenditure in India continued at a high level, casting doubt on whether Russophobia fully explains the phenomenon. Certainly, British India's strategic position was complicated by the 'buffer states' in the North West (Afghanistan and Persia) and North East (Burma). Railway strategy in these states appeared to differ according to the attitude of indigenous rulers and the opposition of local tribes. Relationships between Britain and Russia, as the Great Powers, and buffer states need to be dissected, to understand the dynamics of railway building. The enthusiasts for frontier railways often pressed the commercial and trading benefits of these lines as added benefits though the commercial attributes of Afghanistan, Baluchistan, Persia and Burma were doubtful. It is reasonable to ask whether the construction pattern represented an early version of what Eisenhower would much later christen the 'military industrial complex'. The role of energetic military railway planners in the ICS and India Office warrants further examination. They gave evangelical sponsorship to private guaranteed strategic lines, then the consolidated/nationalized North Western Railway, the largest loss-making institution in Indian railway history.[25]

This thematic analysis is intended to explain the single-minded investment policy in railways pursued by the dual government, despite anti-railway agitation by nationalists. Indeed, Ambirajan identified unanimity in British India's 'interest in the construction of public works and utilities', but differences over 'execution' of such policy. This 'execution' overlapped with official's ideological attachment to 'laissez faire and Classical theory of economic policy'.[26] In assessing the practical implementation of policy, it is helpful to examine case studies of specific Indian railway companies spanning the spectrum of the private to the public sector. This approach serves to identify common ideological themes in the financing and management of companies, and elucidates the extent to which the process was more arbitrary and chaotic. India operated without a written constitution and with limited regulation from Westminster, so one might expect officials in Calcutta and Whitehall to have operated with discretion. This might not lead to corruption in dispensing contracts and concessions, but would involve challenges for modestly remunerated government officials dealing with powerful and well funded counterparts in the private sector.

The hybrid ownership and management of guaranteed railway companies, with private London boards tempered by India Office appointees, make them a suitable case study for examining the workings of India's early mixed economy. The debate and negotiation between government officials, railway promoters, financiers, lobbyists, railway executives, diplomats and provincial representatives might be expected to reveal much about the consistency and transparency of politics and business. The process was dynamic with government accounting and administrative rules changing over time, offering opportunities for nimble traders, manufacturers and financiers to benefit from links to government and information on the tendering process. Private papers at the India Office Library, and elsewhere, should give insight into the intimacy of these relations. In the detail of deals negotiated it is possible to assess the benefits that private individuals extracted from these relationships. Technical expertise might allow informal advisory functions for financiers and managing agents, or membership of government commissions on railway matters, and related currency, famine, trade, military and expenditure forums. This area of research has attracted little attention in the 'gentlemanly capitalism' debate. A representative study of Indian railway companies gives insight into the preponderance of these 'experts' on the board and share registers of businesses. The tendency for ex-officials to switch from 'gamekeeper' to 'poacher' profile will be examined. The case studies are intended to cover a substantial share of the asset base of Indian railways, a diversity of private/public ownership/management structures, and a geographic spread across regions touched by railway development. Of course, the choices are partly constrained by the availability of research material to recount the company's narrative in sufficient depth.[27]

In presenting a picture of the largest Empire investment programme over a period of almost forty years, the underlying political, strategic and financial landscape of Britain and her Empire impinges. This was a period of relative economic decline for Britain. The so-called 'Great Depression' of the 1880s, when price deflation afflicted domestic consumer confidence, made export markets like India more important for British industrialists. SB Saul has identified the central position of India as a customer for British manufactures and services/ capital, and a Trojan horse for exports into protected markets like France and USA.[28] Railways played a prominent role in facilitating this foreign trade on British terms, but suffered from London's need to administer India without net British contributions. The costs of the Second Afghan War and the annexation of Upper Burma, coupled with declining opium revenues and arguments with Manchester over the legitimacy of Indian tariff revenues, put pressure on the Viceroy's Finance Member to balance his books. While House of Commons scrutiny of administration remained slight, the requirement of the Secretary of State to lay before Parliament an annual budget statement for India created some check and balance. The Indian railways present a clear picture of early attempts by government to finance and manage businesses within draconian budget conditions. Off balance sheet financing structures resemble modern government financing methods, like Private Finance Initiatives in health and education. It is important to understand the extent to which creative public accounting was viewed as controversial at the time.[29] Equally, Indian railways wrestled with many of the same problems of pure private British rail companies operating in markets, where damaging price competition could undermine financial integrity and deliver poor value to both shareholders and customers.[30] The case studies should demonstrate the extent to which industrial combination and regional monopolies were courted by Indian decision-makers, paralleling moves towards railway amalgamation in Britain. At the same time, the lack of democracy amongst Indian taxpayers made the advent of a railway rates controversy comparable to that in Britain unthinkable. Further, more covert methods of state support for joint stock companies need to be examined. Critics of the time, like Sir George Campbell, saw the companies as benefiting from multiple gold plating provided by the India Office. Case studies should serve to clarify the existence of government subsidies, regional monopolies, land gifts and off-market acquisitions. Widespread efforts to disguise state support would suggest greater requirements amongst government officials to maintain a façade of laissez-faire. This has been a controversial debate for scholars, with the extent of British India's adherence to free markets much disputed.[31] As ever, the particulars of financing discussions bring these pressures most clearly to the fore, as officials wrestled with financing and refinancing deadlines.

Finally, the scale of the Indian railway project, in the context of malleable laissez-faire, gives a unique insight into the extent to which late Victorian India represented a meaningful first attempt at a national development plan. In the 1850s Marx had highlighted the potential of railways to create a more dynamic Indian economy, warning of the risks to Britain in creating something of a 'Frankenstein's monster'. He predicted in the 1850s that railways would encourage Indian assertiveness since 'when you have introduced machinery into the locomotion of a country, which possesses iron and coals, you are unable to withhold it from its fabrication'.[32] However, in reviewing Indian railways, Ambirajan was sceptical about the coherence of the Raj as a platform for development. He argued that 'development' policy was exclusively targeted at agriculture and 'was to be achieved through individual initiative without *direct* government assistance'. Public works were to combine with legal and monetary systems, business entrepreneurs, and education as a platform for agriculture-focused government assistance. However, departures from laissez-faire in Smith and Mill allowed 'carte blanche to the Raj' with pursuit of development where it wished.[33] Daniel Thorner went further arguing that London-listed Indian railway companies had ignored considerations of development since it was 'simply not their concern'. He expressed sympathy for fellow American Leland Jenks' assertion that in their first seventy-five years, the Indian railways had 'destroyed more occupational opportunities than they opened'.[34] Thorner saw a deliberate effort to maintain the 'buy British' approach towards railway equipment, which explained part of the underperformance of the Indian economy. This was facilitated by the charging of low freight rates on Indian exports to ports and British exports from Indian ports. The policy was aimed at deepening 'the country's economic dependence on the United Kingdom'.[35] More recently, Tirthankar Roy pressed the legacy of the railway network bequeathed to India as representing a valuable resource for future economic development, but characterized the British motivation for building the infrastructure as 'governance rather than development'. The government's share of the Indian economy by the early twentieth century was only 5 per cent, meaning economic growth was still overwhelmingly dependent on the private sector (primarily agricultural).[36]

In reviewing British railway policy over these years it will be possible to assess the extent and sophistication of British development policy in India. Juland Danvers as India Office Public Works member, for example, was pressing in the 1860s to have more rail material produced in India, but the shift to Indian railway line and locomotive manufacture never really occurred. The British maintained a control of railway equipment manufacture in their 'formal' Indian Empire, in a manner which they failed to achieve in 'informal' Argentina.[37] By the first committee dedicated to Indian rail finance in 1908, Danvers's ambitions had been suppressed. A study of individual companies, their financing and governance may give insight into the abandonment of industrial development, as a policy pursued even indirectly in India. Moreover, the activities of James Mackay and his managing agent/City associates at the railway-related committees should give more colour to the view that there was a consistent opposition from business to government development. The role of James Mackay, himself, in participating in different Indian council committees and chairing the 1908 railway committee demands attention. Scrutiny of his committee, and the extent to which he was able to choose members/witnesses and choreograph events, should reveal much about the extent of the India Office's development ambitions and the dominance of commerce/trading elites up to the end of our period. While Dewey presented Mackay as a bastion of business independence, who opposed Curzon's 'new industrial policy', his activities on Indian railway finance may suggest a more symbiotic relationship with Whitehall.[38]

The Mackay railway committee supported the continuation of London-based boards, managing railway assets from a distance of 6,000 miles albeit with India Office interference on overall capital expenditure budgets. John Stuart Mill had questioned the efficacy of shareholders holding management to account in the context of mid-Victorian joint stock companies (the modern principal-agent problem). The extent to which guaranteed London shareholders in Indian railway companies could really be expected to maintain private-sector discipline on ex-ICS/India Office railway directors must be open to doubt. Again the activities of these executives in the practical running of their companies will add to this debate. Mackay and fellow committee members like Sir David Barbour doubted the capacity of Bengali or Bombay entrepreneurs to run railway companies, even as Acworth positioned the industry for nationalization in 1921. The veneer of private-sector efficiency and shareholder accountability, which the hybrid financing arrangements allowed, gave these businessmen immunity to criticism from government officials although they shared the same paymaster in the Indian taxpayer. In the same way that Mill struggled to applaud laissez-faire in his writings, while providing entry points for government intervention in almost any industry, the contradictions of Indian railway policy may well have delivered the worst of all worlds. We must ask whether the accumulation of minor scandals and inefficiencies allowable in India's hybrid companies represented an inferior alternative to a more rational planned approach, pursued for a time by Viceroy Lawrence. At the same time, the level of scrutiny achieved may have been just rigorous enough to constrain industrialization through a stifling of private sector dynamism. As Clive Dewey characterised the failings of Curzon's 'new industrial policy':

> 'Few countries have ever industrialised...in which entrepreneurs have been unable to corrupt the state, exploiting taxpayers and consumers far beyond the limits set by proper tolerance...'[39]

1 'PRODUCTIVE' INDIAN RAILWAYS, 1875–1914: SPACE FOR GENTLEMANLY CAPITALISTS AND INDUSTRIALISTS IN A MIXED ECONOMY

Introduction

When J. R. Seeley posed the question 'cui bono?' in the context of British annexations in India, his own answer was 'English commerce'.[1] J. Hobson tackled the same question later, focusing specifically on 'the investor' and the 'speculators or financial dealers' who 'constitute ... the gravest single factor in the economics of Imperialism'. Hobson proceeded to highlight that 'every railway or mining concession wrung from some reluctant foreign potentate means profitable business in raising capital and floating companies'.[2] The representatives of commerce and finance who attracted the attention of Seeley and Hobson were to become the focal point for a new debate on the motivation and outcome of British Imperialism, through Cain and Hopkins's paradigm of 'gentlemanly capitalism'. British commerce and industry were to be pursued, where possible, in the private sector (off the government's balance sheet). However, Indian railway finance never escaped from the intrusions of government support, either directly through state lines or indirectly through government guarantees. The long-running debate on laissez-faire versus state ownership and management of railways continued over the late nineteenth and early twentieth centuries, with gentlemanly capitalists and industrialists equally involved. While many participants may have had ideological concerns about excessive state involvement in the process, it was obvious that the relative poverty of India made most of the railway lines unattractive investments, short of state support. Equally, industry could benefit from a government-directed 'buy British' policy pursued over the years. British commerce and finance would extract commission from a rising volume of foreign trade, albeit under the guise of India's 'deindustrialization'. In short, Indian railways provided opportunities to keep all British capitalist groups on side, but necessitated pragmatism on matters of political economy. Dissecting the importance or motivation of individual groups in this process is complicated but it is possible to identify consistent ambitions for the Indian economy, which united state and private sectors, operating in a 'mixed economy'.

Evolution of Indian Railway's 'Mixed Economy'

As early as the 1840s, the commercial rationale for government support for Indian railways was illuminated by John Chapman, chief promoter of the Great Indian Peninsula Railway (GIPR)[3]. Chapman was an industrialist, financier, radical writer and Baptist deacon. He had absorbed the liberal political economy of the earlier nineteenth century, but faced the practical challenge of raising scarce capital for his 'Chapman Line'. Chapman asserted that English capital would have been available without government support in the mid-1840s had the investment proposition been more clearly explained.[4] However, the granting of Government guarantees to the EIR in Bengal was a damaging precedent which curtailed private capital. The guaranteed EIR stock crowded out investor demand for non-guaranteed GIPR equities and bonds. Earlier, the granting of railway guarantees in Jamaica and Ceylon under British guidance and subsequent guarantees of 4 per cent offered in France, had made resistance to guarantees in Bengal and Bombay problematic.[5] In a private note, dated January 1849, Chapman produced a quantitative justification for the involvement of private companies in Indian railways. The note provides insight through a rare attempt to quantify the efficiencies of private over state enterprise, albeit without much analytical rigour. Chapman made a series of laissez-faire assertions about the inefficiency, lack of incentive and general tardiness of state-run industry which might have come from the pages of J. S. Mill's *Principles of Political Economy*. Private companies were predicted to save an arbitrary amount of 30 per cent on all construction and operating costs relative to the public sector. Equally, their marketing efforts would generate some 30 per cent more in terms of 'receipts per mile per annum'. These assumptions translated to a return on capital for a private railway company of 16 per cent against a meagre 4 per cent for railways constructed and operated by the government.[6] In fact, the period of private management and ownership with guarantees from 1853 to 1869 failed to realize returns comparable to Chapman's projections for private sector railways. Indian railway prospectuses from Chapman's period assumed freight charges at English rates, but by 1866 the government's annual report on railway performance complained of Indian freight and passenger fares 'still ... low as compared with European rates'.[7] On the cost side, Chapman had projected £4,000 per mile for GIPR construction in 1845. However, average construction costs over the 1850s and 60s were a burdensome £18,000 per mile.[8] The inability of private management to realize these ambitious expectations for high revenues and low costs was to be explained, under Chapman's laissez-faire thinking, by the contagion effect of guarantees. By 1853 he described such guarantees, which he had fought for, as 'a effectual quietus to [shareholders] ... they care nothing about how fast or how slowly the works go on.'[9]

Viceroy Sir John Lawrence's railway minute of January 1869 was a reaction to the failings of guarantees, but departed further from laissez-faire, as the state took on an increasing burden in India's military dominated 'mixed economy'. Lawrence emphasized the benefits of Indian railways to 'traders and travellers'. This he quantified at more than £5 million per annum, even after the inflated cost base. Transport costs were halved by railways and the public would save on transport costs what they paid in taxes to fund the project. For the 'commerce' of India, the benefits were much larger than commonly understood. However, this did not justify average costs of construction over 1854–68 at an unacceptable £17,000 per mile. This bore no relation to the modest costs of production in India. It was reflective of the high import component from England, coupled with a tendency to over-engineer lines and stations. Lawrence could not imagine state-sector railways replicating these inefficiencies. Management of Indian railway contractors by distant London boards had been poor. The Viceroy struggled to identify a single example of action undertaken by a London board, which had given rise to benefits for India's railway network. Lawrence quantified the additional cost of using the private companies, favoured by Chapman, at no less than £5,000 per mile. Hence, the next 5,000 miles of state railways might be constructed at about £12,000 per mile over the next fifteen to twenty years. This implied a cost of 'laissez faire' capitalism on construction alone of some £25 million. Of course, cost per mile might have been expected to fall under any ownership, as technology became tried and tested.[10] Financing costs under state ownership were also lower. This was manifest in trading prices for India's sterling stock against the best-rated railway company.[11] Equally, private companies had inflated their capital budgets to originate more guaranteed securities and avoid taking costs to the profit and loss statement. This allowed them to massage upwards distributable profits for shareholders. However, in times of difficulty (war or 'political danger') in the financial market, these rail companies needed help from the government to raise more guaranteed money. In the previous monetary crisis, the GOI had stepped in to bail out a number of companies. The burden on the Indian taxpayer was doubly great, since half the excess profits of companies were paid out as surplus earnings. Hence, while the GOI was owed some £13.5 million of guaranteed payments up to 1869, the companies would have to earn £27 million to repay the advances.[12]

Secretary of State Argyll argued that the private sector should keep profitable commercial lines, while loss-making 'political lines' should stay with the state. This was said to be necessary to prevent an overhang of unpopular securities which 'weighed down' the market for Indian railway investments. In this,

Whitehall was more sensitive to the needs of its near neighbours in the City than was Calcutta. Viceroy Lawrence worried that leaving the GOI with all the loss making enterprises would impact the reputation of the public sector for prudent financial management. This was an astute concern.[13] Moreover, experience in England showed the extent to which performance at commercial railways in India might be improved. By 1869 English railway lines numbered twenty-seven against nine for the Indian subcontinent, with gross receipts per week per mile at £64, against £26 in India. Revenues would be constrained by India's less developed manufacturing base (which arguably railways would further suppress), and the extent to which Indians were less 'addicted to commerce' than the British. Lawrence set out detailed plans for each region of India. The aggregate rail mileage under state control should rise from 5,000 miles to 15,000 miles over a thirty-year period, at a growth rate of 300 miles per annum. This would reflect the economic needs of the subcontinent. In fact, by 1900 total route mileage was some 24,000 miles or almost double the mileage recommended by Lawrence. In spite of this accelerated build programme, at substantially above the targeted £12,000 per mile, there was little sign of India overriding Lawrence's observations about her meagre industrialization and limited appetite for 'commerce'.[14] Nevertheless, the old 5 per cent guaranteed companies, left in private ownership, had their contracts amended to be still more attractive to shareholders. According to Daniel Thorner, this gave 'the companies a new lease on terms even more favourable to them than before'. This seems to have been an initiative of the City-friendly India Office and opposed in Calcutta.[15]

The arguments surrounding Lawrence's railway minute of 1869, announcing the abandonment of private company finance, were widely debated within the India Office at the time.[16] Secretary of State Argyll encouraged contributions from different sides of the public/private debate, with differing opinions on the motivation and effectiveness of private financiers/promoters, and the advantages to be reaped from exercising government buyback options. Military advisor, Sir Henry Rawlinson, was sceptical on the merits of private guaranteed companies. He reserved particular criticism for the Western Indian GIPR. The company was cosseted by 5 per cent guarantees, but guilty of 'faulty execution' and 'notoriously bad conditions'. Under government ownership, the excesses of these companies would have been curbed. Construction costs might have been pruned to £10,000 per mile, against the £20,000 per mile incurred. Rawlinson quantified the unnecessary costs of these private companies at a minimum of £50 million (5,000 miles at £10,000 waste per mile). Added to this was the share of surplus profit channelled to shareholders above the 5 per cent guarantees. Moreover, had the India Office pursued state funding from the outset, it might have raised rupee loans directly in India. The Indian public were comfortable about investing in rupee government loans and would have seen railway loans as their equivalent, had 'construction and maintenance' of lines been the government's responsibility. While the EIR buyback option (exercisable at 1874) offered an opportunity to reverse guaranteed arrangements on the largest line, the terms of that buyback were so advantageous to shareholders as to make it impossible to justify on 'economical arguments alone'. However, the management and performance of Chapman's GIPR was so poor as to justify a repurchase of its stock at almost any price, even on a hostile basis.[17] Further, the cost of leaving the GIPR, Madras and Bombay Baroda companies under private management was high. In another India Office contribution, the member concerned registered that he had dissented from Whitehall's decision to waive the buyback options on those railway securities at 1870. This decision had been made without any communication with Calcutta and was to be regretted. The cost of purchasing GIPR stock at market price on a nominal £22 million outstanding (about 120 per cent of par) was far less than the surfeit of coupon on the 5 per cent dividend plus profit share, plus the 'extravagant expenses of the Home Boards'. The latter he estimated at not less than £50,000 per Railway Company per annum.[18] Such costs were widely agreed to be out of kilter with the benefits to be derived from locating in London. Over time, it was hoped that mergers and consolidations of private companies might reduce overall administrative expenses. In a memo which pointed to the later strategy of Lord George Hamilton, Sir F. Currie pressed for this 'consolidation' process to begin. Like Hamilton's efforts to encourage well-capitalized 'private sector' railway cartels in India, this approach risked building monopolistic lines immune to any price tension.[19]

Juland Danvers, Public Works member at the India Office, adopted a pragmatic approach to state/private sector arguments. Without the guarantee system, the network of India would have been much smaller than the 5,000 miles reached by 1869. The rail companies had raised capital of some £82 million, which in crises like the Mutiny would have been redirected to other purposes had railway finance come out of general government financing. In general, private sector discipline had placed curbs on the excesses complained of by sceptics, who lobbied Argyll for state control. It is certainly possible that the wastefulness of £20,000 per mile on construction costs would not have been replicated in operating expenses. After all, each £1 million of capital costs produced £1 million of guaranteed 'gentlemanly capitalist' securities for the investing public, while out of control operating expenses limited surplus profit payments. However, in contracts like the Southern Mahratta, where surplus payments came out of profit before interest, there were no incentives for operating cost controls. Further, certain railway companies practised 'creative accounting' by taking expenses to the 'capital account' of the financial statement, rather than through the profit and loss statement, so massaging distributable profits upwards for the guaranteed shareholders. The GOI was urged to monitor these financial statements more closely.[20]

This confidence in the overall approach to railway finance was rejected in another memo, written by Sir C. Mills. He saw rail finance as unsatisfactory under either state or private ownership. Governor Generals were said to press railways and other public works for a time, to demonstrate qualities of statesmanship and 'promote the prosperity of India'. Initially, Secretaries of State in Whitehall might go along with that, but any financial problems would prompt them to abandon the exercise. This made long-term approaches under government funding impossible, and pushed government towards the private company solution, delegating the decision to someone else. However, the cost of private finance was made even more expensive by that time through the requirement to compete with 'high yielding' Russian and Canadian railway securities.[21] Weighing up these different contributions, Argyll, as Whig appointee of Gladstone, concluded that the cost of company financing was prohibitively expensive. Moreover, the role of agency for private companies (later stressed by Strachey) brought no benefits in terms of efficiency. Government was at least as well positioned to contract business to engineers and construction firms as a board of directors, seated 6,000 miles away from the business they were managing.[22]

Earlier, Lawrence had been warned by Tory Secretary of State Cranborne (later Lord Salisbury) that, if the state failed to attract funding for public works programmes, there would be renewed pressure from private promoters to own and manage the railway lines. The minute of 1869 had been an attempt to see off such pressures and rise to Cranborne's challenge 'to save India from being devoured by private companies'.[23] Salisbury's own involvement in British private railway companies positioned him well to understand this danger. By 1884, Salisbury's concerns were proven prescient as the India Office and GOI prepared to revert to guaranteed private companies. A timely pamphlet was published in Calcutta which reasserted the benefits of Lawrence's public-sector approach. The author tried to quantify the costs of private companies against state railways, using Rothschild's Bengal Central as an illustration. While Bengal Central financed itself at 5.5 per cent on a perpetual basis, an 'Imperial loan' could be raised at 3.5 per cent. In present value terms this involved an 'immediate present' to the private sector of £3,500 for each £10,000 mile of railway line constructed, assuming Bengal Central was nationalized at the first repurchase date. If the Bengal Central stock were left outstanding, the additional cost rose to some 38 per cent. In this example the cost of initiating private finance was hugely expensive, while effecting buybacks later on was too late. While the involvement of a firm of the 'high standing and reputation' of N. M. Rothschild (underwriter on Bengal Central) might prompt greater investment than the state would allow, the cost of private capital was prohibitive. Each company would need to employ its own engineers in India and England, many of which would be poached from the government, which would oversee their training. The profits generated by the railway companies were out of kilter with the benefits derived. Not atypically, the author highlighted GIPR as an inefficient company, run exclusively for shareholders. There had been a bitter legal battle between GIPR and the Bombay Chamber of Commerce, demonstrating conflicts between chambers and railway companies. GIPR made profit margins of some 10 per cent on the transport of grain in western India, which left almost no money for food exporters. India's food exports, the British believed, were necessary for India's economic prosperity, and GIPR was constraining export growth. In 1884 when the EIR reduced rates by 20 per cent, their turnover increased, but profits hardly moved. Under private company management there was no incentive to make changes which were profit neutral and EIR abandoned the experiment. At the very least, the author suggested, the state needed to involve itself in regulating the excesses of private monopolies like GIPR. This would involve state inspections, maximum tariff rates, standard gauges and repurchase rights at regular intervals.[24]

Companies like Bengal Central and GIPR raised concerns about private funding. However, by the early 1880s, the financial burden of the Second Afghan War, famine relief expenditures and declining opium revenues placed enormous pressures on state funding. The government sought to control railway expenditure by placing limits on different categories of investment. 'Productive' public works could be funded by state loans up to £2.5 million. These railways needed to offer returns of 4 per cent per annum within five years (with capital including capitalized land value, pensions and leave allowances). Separately, 'protective' rail expenditure was a debit item from the 'famine insurance grant' or the general revenue account, and taken to the Profit and Loss statement of the GOI. By 1879 this item was fixed at £500,000 per annum. State funding was being pursued at a level which failed to meet the ambitions of key advisors like Evelyn Baring, Louis Mallet and Theodore Hope (all ideologically attached to laissez-faire). They put pressure on Secretaries of State Kimberly and Hartington to return to the old guarantee system, with the principal of guaranteed loans placed off balance sheet. Liberal Viceroy Ripon was supportive of Baring's arguments, but only in the context of famine protection where the social costs of famine overrode laissez-faire ideology. By 1881 Ripon pressed for moderate guarantees with a limited life to attract 'private capital'. However, Baring quickly widened the role of guarantees to encompass commercial lines that while 'not strictly speaking protective will be more likely to prove remunerative'. Commercial lines might not pass through famine regions, but could be expected to facilitate 'development of the country' which would indirectly provide famine protection. This was a wide definition of 'protective' railway and opened up guarantees to all manner of promoters.[25] These changes were formalized at the Parliamentary Committee of 1884, which removed the distinction between the protective and productive categories, encouraged longer-term budgeting, and placed the decisions on increases to the £2.5 million per annum ceiling with the Secretary of State. The committee specified that additional taxation should not be raised in India to bring this about. Of course, borrowings needed ultimately to be repaid partly from taxes unless the railways became self financing (which failed to occur until the beginning of the twentieth century). The emphasis was on private-sector capital being raised, preferably without guarantees. Any guaranteed interest payments would be taken from the revenue account of the GOI. This was a check and balance on the aggregate level of guaranteed payments, but placed the principal amounts owed on guaranteed railway companies off the GOI's balance sheet. This was justified on the basis that these guarantees had a limited life, but ignored the explicit or implicit 'put' protection to investors. Indeed, Evelyn Baring in his financial statement of 1881 pressed the limited life and low interest rate on the new guarantees. Excess profits might be expected to 'fructify' in the pockets of private individuals to more advantage than with government. Baring attacked the £2.5 million per annum ceiling on productive railways as inadequate. While non-guaranteed private sector finance was more attractive than new guarantees, he stressed the more prudent structure of second generation guarantees. Baring's budget for state-line expenditure for the ensuing five years was £19 million against £11.25 million for companies (substantially all of which would be given guarantees, meaning that only the interest portion uncovered by profits would appear in the annual borrowings).[26]

While Baring pressed new guaranteed issues, the state began repurchasing 'old' guaranteed bonds and equities. This began with the EIR buyback in 1880, and culminated in the delayed GIPR buyback in 1900. The rationale for these changes in financing policy was almost always cost, but government displayed reticence to elucidate clear principles on how to minimize costs. It was difficult to reconcile buybacks of old guaranteed companies, at inflated prices, while new companies were floated at modest prices. Under the terms of the 'old' guaranteed bond and share prospectuses the Secretary of State was not obliged to buyback the securities but had an option to do so, usually at twenty-five and fifty years. The cost effectiveness of doing so was open to doubt, since the option was not exercised at par as one might have assumed, but at the market price of the securities. This meant that British investors were being compensated for the loss of the high yielding security which was paying at 5 per cent (a huge surfeit over the yield on consols) in the form of a buyback price which reflected this generous return. Moreover, the securities issued to finance the buyback would themselves be raised at a significant spread to the underlying government security, so that Indian taxpayers were paying twice for the cost of their funding – the buyback cost of the old credit spread and the new credit spread required to refinance. After these buybacks, the government had heightened control, but through leasing many of these assets back to the 'new' private companies they had not effected much change in operational or financial discipline. Doubts about whether the new financing system would be cheaper than the old were explicit in the bills drafted to facilitate buybacks. A bill drafted in 1888, for example, to allow the Secretary of State to raise £10.3 million to purchase bonds and equities in the Oude and Rohilkund Railway Company, stated that the rationale for the refinancing was that the 'charge on the revenues of India ... *might* be less if such moneys were raised ... on the credit of the revenues of India' rather than 'through the agency of such companies'.[27] There was apparently little confidence that this would be the case. Indeed, by the following year, the *Economist* lamented the state of Indian finance in general, by which time the spread between Indian debentures and comparable UK consols had widened out to 1 per cent.[28]

The subtleties of the distinction between these old and new guarantees were highlighted by the Welby Commission, which sat from 1896–7 to consider the 'administration of the expenditure of India'. Sir Stephen Jacob, comptroller and auditor general to the GOI was cross-examined on the differences which seemed opaque to committee members. Jacob responded that railway assets of the old businesses were 'the property of the companies', while the newer assets were government-owned but 'leased for a certain number of years to the companies that work them'. Later in his testimony, Jacob pointed towards additional costs to the GOI in the buyback process as having been due to a drafting error, in the original bond and equity prospectuses. He referred to a clause in the original documents which allowed for government calls on the securities at par, being overridden by the put provision on the part of investors which allowed them to claim the full market value in the 'repayment of its capital'.[29] This unnecessary GOI financing cost was present in nationalist discourse on the railways at the time. As the sole Indian committee member on Welby, Dadabhai Naoroji declared the premium on the railway shares to be 'artificial' being due to 'the government guaranteeing a high rate of interest'.[30] In the case of the largest repurchase (EIR), the government was obliged to pay the average market price of securities over three preceding years. This gave a premium of 25 per cent to investors over original purchase price, in addition to the 5 per cent per annum, plus surplus profits enjoyed up to that point. On the equities alone, this involved an outlay of an additional £6.55 million at the call exercise.[31] If this 25 per cent 'drafting error' were applied routinely across the bonds and equities of the 'old' guaranteed companies, one could easily arrive at a number in excess of £25 million of 'drain' paid across to the 'gentlemanly capitalists' of London on the exercise of the put/call options. This money was incurred to facilitate a degree of heightened state control that was so subtle that the witnesses and committee members of Welby struggled to articulate its significance. By way of comparison, the additional cost of over £25 million compared to a total expenditure on irrigation projects in India of only £45.1 million in the period up to 1920.[32]

By 1895, an advisor to Liberal Viceroy Elgin, admitted that in spite of best endeavours, successive governments had failed to dispense with government guarantees, and raise real private sector capital.[33] Bengal–Nagpur, Indian Midland and Assam–Bengal all illustrated the failings of laissez-faire finance, with their multiple levels of government support. The Bengal Central had been constructed without explicit government support but, as soon as it faced financial difficulties, the Secretary of State under enormous pressure was made to 'take it over'. Equally, the Bengal NW was rescued with an advantaged leasing of the Tirhoot line which made the business profitable through an effective government subsidy. At the time Bengal NW was behaving like an 'independent line' in pressing for further concessions outside its articles of association, while failing to acknowledge its failings as a private enterprise. Further, the Delhi–Kalka line had begun as an independent business, but over time demanded waivers on rental payments due to the state owned military North West line. Further subsidies were paid by Government, as Delhi–Kalka demanded the redirection of government traffic onto their lines. These subsidies were often opaque and it is only rarely that we get an insight into the extent of hidden government support. Elgin's advisor mocked Robert Millar's attempts, on behalf of the Bengal Nagpur, to further government support. The controversial recipient of famine insurance moneys was bidding with another group to gain control of the key East Coast line, and Millar affected an interest in the 'prospects of the line'. To Elgin's advisor, Millar's interest in the business was nothing of the sort, but simply a wish to acquire more guaranteed assets. A 3 per cent guaranteed return would attract unlimited investors in such an undertaking, even if it were a 'railway to the moon'.[34] True, Millar's activities might be expected to create some competition for Strachey's monopolistic EIR in Bengal, and open up access to Calcutta. Railway promoters might even feel compelled to moderate rates in their pressure to win concessions. However, the process was dominated by 'capitalist pressure brought to bear on parliament'. This gave rise to railway construction that was misconceived and wasteful.[35] The frustrations were echoed by the railway engineer and government advisor, Horace Bell. Bell placed responsibility at the door of Elgin himself, who had allowed the mixed economy to create unfair competition between state and guaranteed railway companies. The state lines had financing advantages, and were free from many of the delays which affected private promoters. In order to tempt private capital into Indian railways, the state businesses needed to be disbanded. In effect, the mixed economy did not work.[36]

British Beneficiaries of Commercial Railways

The evolution of British India towards a 'mixed economy' in railway finance displayed little clear ideological purpose or long-term planning. Rail promoters like Chapman, Andrew and Stephenson had early on influenced events on the cusp of the private/public sectors. Their successors continued to do so though, with the dual government system, it was often difficult to pinpoint exactly where decisions were being made. Although London constitutionally oversaw India, a weak Secretary of State combined with a strong Viceroy might allow Calcutta to dominate.[37] Public finance was a frustration for administrators and lobbyists alike, but the rewards for British manufacturing and commerce from the Indian railways were such as to encourage a permanent period of lobbying over 1875–1914 for more railways. British manufacturers, whom Dewey and others saw in decline from the 1870s onwards, were omnipresent in these discussions. They were motivated by a wish to sell locomotives, iron and steel railings and other materials. Once built, the accelerated transport system encouraged the increase in other British exports, notably cotton textile goods, to be transported from Bombay, Karachi and Calcutta to the interior of the country. Manchester industrialists and MPs pressed for increased raw cotton production in Western India, as an alternative to the southern USA, and for the enhancement of rail communications to distribute Lancashire product. This Manchester lobbying prompted House of Commons debates by 1870, involving all former Secretaries of State for India, and the only living former Viceroy, Sir John Lawrence. Manchester MP and spokesman for Lancashire cotton interests, Sir Thomas Bazley applauded Lawrence's new policy of state-owned and constructed railways, believing that greater mileage would be constructed. He even pressed state repurchases of all existing guaranteed railway lines. India was compartmentalized as a primary producer, prompting Bazley to call for a powerful Indian agricultural department which would link with the railway construction.[38] However, Bazley's commitment to public sector development was less than consistent. During the long-running tendering process by rail promoters wishing to access the Southern Mahratta region, Bazley had put himself forward as prospective Chairman of a Karwar-to-Hubli private railway company. This was eventually superseded by Sir Douglas Forsyth's alternative Goa-based project, but showed Manchester representatives pushing railways in the private and public spheres simultaneously.[39]

By 1886 the so-called 'Great Depression' had prompted the setting up of a royal commission to discuss means of increasing the demand for British goods from overseas. The Indian market, which in population terms dominated British Empire demand, was a focal point for discussion. While the extension of railways in Britain might facilitate better distribution of goods at home, it was recognized that India and China offered far more potential for expanding trade. Moreover, tariff walls in other large countries like the USA, Germany, France, Belgium and Russia, made Britain's free trade arrangements with India indispensable.[40] For Sheffield steel manufacturers, for example, building more railways to facilitate Indian trade was expected to increase exports in a period of dampened world demand. Extensions of Indian railway lines through Burma to the Chinese border would link the world's two largest populations for selling Sheffield steel. The same lines could be used on return journeys to increase imports of cheap Indian food, which reduced reliance on the USA whose trade surplus was causing concern. Preferential rail rates favouring British exports to India might also be pursued. By way of comparison, the German railway system was envied for its preferential tariffs, supporting domestic product.[41] Sheffield's concerns were understandable, since the depression in British iron-making was acute. Capacity utilization amongst manufacturers of iron-rails was said to be less than 50 per cent. India was viewed as offering attractive growth opportunities. This could be realized if Indian railway companies were persuaded to buy iron sleepers in replacement for the more common wooden sleepers, although this would increase railway costs for Indians.[42] Crucially, to facilitate this railway-led business, free trade should be maintained with India, and various employers and industrial associations were cited as having lobbied against tariff impositions and in favour of rail construction. This followed a period of free trade lobbying in the early 1870s.[43]

While Sheffield had much to gain from India's burgeoning population, Manchester continued to play a prominent role in lobbying for cotton carrying railways. This was not always successful. A Director of the Manchester Chamber of commerce, for example, complained in 1886 that he had pressed a Commons committee on railways for greater mileage. This had resulted over the previous two years in the sanctioning of only 500 miles of Indian Midland Railway. In the meantime, the attraction of Indian raw cotton as an input for Lancashire cloth had increased. The development of GIPR and Bombay Baroda's infrastructure allowed cotton presses to be sited near cotton fields, away from Bombay. This facilitated closer monitoring of crops by buyers and more rigorous quality control. Similarly, the 1863 Indian Cotton Frauds Act had restricted the adulteration of Indian cotton with water. Yarn sales from India to continental Europe would be short staple and would not cannibalize Manchester manufactured product. Iron manufacturing would be stimulated with cotton-related demand for British locomotives, rails and rolling stock, suggesting a unity of purpose between Manchester and Sheffield. Even India's economy would share in these benefits, through increased consumption of Indian coal and wood, coupled with employment for 200,000 natives on the railways. However, the importance of railway/cotton industry expansion in India was so great as to be 'not a question for Lancashire, but a question for England'. It was not felt to be a question for India. Further, these advantages could only be reaped with generous 3.5 to 4 per cent government guarantees, offered to private rail companies. The Manchester chamber's representative waved a promotional letter to the members of the commission, pressing the urgency of government support for the Bengal–Nagpur line. He professed support of an ex-Governor of Bombay, now Manchester MP, who argued that Britain would benefit generally through cheap silver-priced

Indian wheat. Chinese trade would be enhanced through extensions of the Bur-mah railway to SW China, via the Siam line. Both Bengal Nagpur and Burmah railway extensions would shortly be pursued by the India Office, supported by government guarantees.[44] Predictably, Manchester Chamber testimony was complemented by a memorial from Sheffield Chamber. Sheffield was driven by large iron-related orders from railways, and foresaw benefits for British trade. This was an area that had received too little attention from successive govern-ments, according to the Sheffield lobbyists.[45]

While Manchester and Sheffield lobbied for the British benefits of Indian rail-ways, Secretary of State Kimberley was prepared to challenge their more extreme attempts at 'economic imperialism'. Steel manufacturers were accused of press-ing Indian railways solely to achieve employment for English labour and capital. Bombay and Calcutta merchants were equally self serving. Kimberley pointed to the cost to India in terms of funded guarantees, and challenged the Chamber of Commerce argument that railway development was free for the British.[46] Oth-ers in the India Office argued that benefits from the investment would be more evenly shared in the future with India. For example Juland Danvers, India Office Public Works member, declared as early as 1860–1 that 'as the lines approach completion, the amount of materials sent from this country will diminish'.[47] It was clear to Danvers that the key areas for industrial development, to allow growth through railways, were 'coal and iron'. Danvers acknowledged the blight of deindustrialization by holding up the prospect that 'India may again become a manufacturing as well as producing country'.[48] However, by 1868 the Danvers annual rail report registered a rise in English sourced materials for the year to £4.05 million (from £1.59 million in 1861), against a fall in Indian domestic inputs from £4.96 million to £2.98 million. Indeed by 1882 Danvers lamented the lack of progress on Indian coal and steel manufacturing: 'There are coal beds of considerable extent which have as yet been untouched, and to which access by railway is only required ... iron ore may be found ... for the manufacture of iron...'.[49] In fairness, India's coal industry developed after that point and by 1905 domestic coal usage for the Indian railways was 2.67 million tonnes, while British coal was a marginal source at 148,000 tonnes.[50] This had the beneficial effect of reducing costs through reduced shipping and insurance charges on domestic coal against that transported by steamship from Britain. However, the drain to Britain continued through managing agency groups like Andrew Yule, which controlled large reserves of domestic coal through intricate ownership structures.[51]

While coal was mined in Bengal, progress on developing India's steel loco-motive/ component manufacturing was slow.[52] British efforts to protect this lucrative business were aggressive and successful. Though foreign competition for these contracts was intense, the India Office responded to the pressure from Northern England and the Midlands. In 1874 for example, a frustrated Mr

Fowler, a British commercial agent working for a Belgian locomotive manufacturer, wrote to his India Office contact Richard Strachey, pressing the merits of Belgium's 'powerful locomotives' on a 5'6" gauge for famine relief purposes. Three years later, after *The Times* highlighted the plight of starving peasants in Southern India in the face of poor transportation, Fowler tried to shame Strachey into following his advice to invest in Belgian engines. By purchasing stocks of old engines, which sat in a French warehouse, savings could be made. Locomotives which had cost £3,600 per unit in 1870 were available for only £2,400 by 1874. No such decline in locomotive prices, reflecting an overhang in supply, was discernible in the British locomotive purchases for India during this time. However, the India Office was sufficiently concerned by Fowler's onslaught to demand an explanation from their railway department on why they failed to 'buy Belgian' even at discounted prices. Belgian manufacturer's standard design was apparently inappropriate for the irregular Indian railway gauge system, where a tailor-made approach to locomotive manufacturing was necessary. Instead, a famine relief-related order for Southern India had been placed with the Glasgow firm of Major and Dubbs. Secretary of State Salisbury, in further correspondence with Fowler, was characteristically dismissive of accusations of unfair tendering for these contracts.[53] However, Salisbury received further complaints about the 'buy British' approach from a London observer who had visited India in 1857. This observer identified the benefits of encouraging Indian manufacturers of railway materials, as the Mutiny raged, to allow the 'full development of the resources of India'. These laudable aims were shelved after the rebellion of 1857/8, presumably on the basis that suppression of Indian economic independence helped maintain Indian political dependence on Britain. By 1878, Salisbury was reminded that British iron railing and materials were still being purchased extravagantly in India, while the cost of replacing rails in England had been much reduced. If manufacturing of Indian iron product was still some way off, at least the Indians could follow the English in using the iron from worn-out railings to keep costs down. Again, there is no evidence in the correspondence that Salisbury or any of his colleagues took such economies seriously. Indeed, further evidence of 'extravagance' in railway purchases is apparent in the export of iron sleepers to India. By 1879 an audit report on the performance of EIR, just prior to government repurchase, calculated that the cost of 100,000 plate iron sleepers for the railway was approximately £52,000, against creosoted timber sleepers at £27,500. The latter were said to have identical properties in terms of durability, but orders of British ironwork for this purpose continued. Further, the transportation cost of iron sleepers 'up country' from Calcutta was far greater, though presumably by train. These iron import costs were taken to the capital account of EIR, leaving surplus profits unaffected for distribution to London shareholders.[54]

Given the importance attached to the Indian market for railway-related exports in the Depression of trade committee hearings, it is not surprising that little advance was made on Indian industrial development. Danver's earlier promises about increased domestic production failed to materialize. Over the period 1884/5 to 1888/9, British railway plant and rolling stock exports to India rose from £1.6 million to £2.5 million. This was despite sterling appreciation against the rupee, which made such imports more expensive. Even the 'Great Depression' failed to dampen this important source of demand for British manufactures. By the 1908 annual 'review of Trade of India', the report was able to boast of accelerated line openings leading to record exports of railway material. Indeed, the period 1903/4 to 1907/8 saw a spectacular rise of 74 per cent in these British exports, from £3.8 million to £6.6 million. Equally, railway goods traffic rose impressively, demonstrating buoyant British–Indian trade, with the accompanying profits for Britain's 'gentlemanly capitalists'. Over 1902–7, ton miles of Indian railway trade had risen by some 54.5 per cent .This was encouraged by the almost unique zero tariff level imposed on British railway material and coal (used to power the railways) exported to India.[55] The advantages of railway construction, pressed by British chambers of commerce in the midst of a trade depression, appeared to have been proven. By 1912, even Chancellor Lloyd George pressed the importance of British foreign trade through Indian railways. That year saw plentiful rainfall in India with a vibrant export sector, allowing the country to purchase 'an increased amount of our goods'. This purchasing power was partly financed by the allocation of British capital to India, targeted at the railway sector. In 1909 Britain's 'great Dependency' had received some £16 million of capital but, by the first half of 1912, Lloyd George boasted that this had risen further. Britain was able to export railway items on both current and capital account to India, secure in the knowledge that India would balance her books with the USA and Europe.[56] The size of these contracts remained impressive, explaining the ferocious lobbying by Chambers of Commerce and managing agents around the Mackay Committee of 19⁰⁷⁸ (centred on additional wagons).[57] In line with Mackay's recommendations, by 1918 the Sheffield firm of Cammell Laird was able to conclude a large contract with Robert Miller's Bengal Nagpur Railway. It was to provide the guaranteed company with up to 9,000 wagons of different specification over a ten-year period. Only the first 720 wagons had a fixed price element. After the delivery of the original batch, price increases would be allowable on the basis of cost increases in labour, materials or 'any other cost of production'. This gave ample scope for padding of profitability on the lion's share of the order. The initial batch of items was priced at £467,000 with a declared profit of 15 per cent or £70,000. Hence, over the life of the contract, profits of at least £875,000 for the Sheffield manufacturer, and probably much more, might be anticipated. This represented a contract for a modest sized railway company. Extrapolating such business over the entire network would imply profitability in the tens of millions of pounds, with related British employment opportunities. It is hardly surprising that Lloyd George felt bound to emphasize its importance.[58]

In winning these contracts, British manufacturers had strong lobbyists operating on their behalf. None was more persistent than Sir Alfred Hickman representing Wolverhampton-based steel interests, who pressed Secretaries of State Churchill and Hamilton to purchase British locomotives. In 1885 Hickman lobbied Randolph Churchill on the benefits of further Indian rail expansion, which would facilitate handsome British export markets and cheap food for British workers. He seemed confident that Churchill shared his views on these advantages.[59] By the turn of the century, Hickman was defending British exporters against fierce American competition. The Burma Railway Company had placed large bridge, locomotive and railway material orders with Pennsylvania Steel Co. and Maryland Steel Co. The American Bridge Building Company had also benefited from large orders, including a £100,000 project to construct the Gokteik Viaduct. Hickman was keen to rubbish the quality of American workmanship. Locomotives bought by the railway company had already shown signs of deterioration, but Hickman accused railway officials in Burma of blindly pushing American orders. This 'disloyalty' to British manufacturers had its roots as far back as 1867/8, when EIR had the temerity to place an order for thirty locomotives with a German firm. Hickman found a willing ally in the Conservative Imperialist, Hamilton, who declared his intention to fight to allow British manufacturers to 'regain their monopoly' on locomotive sales. Hamilton was sensitive to the competitive advantages stolen by American firms over the later nineteenth century, through better research, technical education, advanced industrial organization and capital investment. Nevertheless, with standardization of British product, and greater productivity, American competition might be seen off. British manufacturers needed to imitate the American approach using trade 'combination'. Firms were to be encouraged to work in unison, to create cartelized markets. The London-based Indian railway company boards had always been willing 'to give the preference in contracts to British manufacturers'. Hamilton assured Hickman that short of an enormous difference in 'price, quality, and delivery' the British firms would be given the business in future.[60]

The incentive for British Chambers of Commerce to lobby on Indian railway construction is clear in a pamphlet produced by William Birkmyre 'of Calcutta and Port Glasgow'. He delivered the paper to the Glasgow Chamber of Commerce in 1886. Indian railways were a universal concern which had 'occupied the attention of all the leading commercial chambers in the United Kingdom'. This had prompted the parliamentary committee of 1884 to enquire into East Indian railways, with limitations on borrowings by individual companies. These restrictions had constrained the growth of railways unnecessarily. Much concern focused on Indian railway groups borrowing in Britain in gold-backed sterling, to finance their silver rupee denominated assets. Indian nationalists had argued that railways themselves prompted currency depreciation, through heightening India's reliance on British manufactured imports. Birkmyre took a different view. Indian exports would increase through expanded railways, as would demand for silver since Indian's might readily transport and hoard the specie. Indian absorption of silver was estimated at more than £5 million per annum over 1879/80–1884/5, and of gold at £3.3 million. Indian exports were sold for gold, which in turn would be converted to silver at an attractive rate of exchange, so maintaining silver demand and the value of the rupee. Similarly, India's rice, wheat and other grain exports had increased by almost 130 per cent over the decade 1873/4 to 1882/3. By 1883/4 Finance Minister Evelyn Baring had predicted a doubling of wheat exports to 40 million cwt, through cultivation in Punjab, Burma, Assam and Central Provinces.[61] However, the focus for Birkmyre's Glasgow audience was the capacity to increase British exports and pay British investors. Lord Cross, as Under Secretary of State was applauded for his summary of the arithmetic. For each £1 million sunk into Indian railways by government and other investors, an annual 'remittance home' of £35,000 was affected, which absorbed the annual produce of 25,000 acres of Indian land. Had this relationship held for the duration of the nineteenth and early twentieth centuries, an investment programme of £300 million would have required the dedicated export of food from some 7.5 million acres of scarce Indian agricultural land, a very high price to pay. Finally, Birkmyre pointed to Britain's profits and expanded employment in shipping, iron production, mills, factories, dye works and print works in Lanarkshire and Yorkshire. British iron producers would benefit most directly, but all Indian trade was interdependent and British 'capitalists and traders' would see enormous opportunities. This would extend to areas 37 miles either side of rail tracks, all within the trading area of the enhanced network. Birkmyre pointed his Glasgow manufacturers towards 'a new industrial America' in India, achievable through the railways. Already, the efforts of Manchester lobbyists in pressing Indian railways had been handsomely repaid with Indian cotton manufacturing imports rising by an impressive 41 per cent over the ten years to 1882/3. Shipping tonnage had seen a remarkable increase of 2.25 million tons over the same period.[62]

While the Manchester, Liverpool, Glasgow, Middlesborough and Sheffield Chambers of Commerce lobbied for cotton, shipbuilders/shipping, iron and steel and locomotive, and rail manufacturers; the City of London, traders and 'gentlemanly capitalists' were supported by the London Chamber of Commerce.[63] The East India and China section of London had frequent discussions on Indian railway matters, from the 1880s to the early twentieth century. In 1886, financiers and railway promoters pressed the merits of guaranteed railway companies to the India Office. At the same time, London's Chamber combined with the Iron and Steel Association to send a joint delegation to the India Office arguing for rail expansion. This evoked internal disagreements about trade sections combining with steel manufacturers, showing dislocation between commercial and manufacturing interests. There was less concern about joint initiatives with other commercial organizations in India. When the Calcutta Chamber of Commerce wrote to their London counterpart to solicit support for railways between Calcutta and Upper India, London agreed and offered backing for any 'feasible plan for railway development of India'. The London Chamber's members were content to pursue 'active measures' to bring about further construction.[64] By the late 1880s/early 1890s the distinction between manufacturing and trading oriented chambers was again clear. The Blackburn, Bradford, Birmingham, Liverpool and Glasgow Chambers of Commerce had all passed resolutions supporting an extension of the Burmah–Shan China Railway. This would allow Burma to be used as a connection between British India and China for the transport of British manufactures to the largest market in the world. London's interests did not coalesce with these northern pressure groups, and the Chamber avoided joining forces. Earlier, appeals from the Karachi Chamber of Commerce attracted more enthusiasm. The Punjab Chamber had lobbied the Viceroy for rail links between Karachi and Rajputna, to allow growth in the northern port. London was keen to lend its weight to memorials in favour of the 'Sind Rajputna and Punjab Railway'. Trading links between Indian ports and the interior of the subcontinent were an obvious source of potential business for London's traders. Perhaps added competition for the 'duopoly' ports of Calcutta and Bombay was also welcomed.[65]

The London Chamber met in 1895 to discuss the importance of Indian railways for London commerce. Eminent sources were quoted to create enthusiasm for the Indian railway companies. Archbishop Walsh had argued that greater rail mileage would support Indian exports while transporting English goods to the interior. At the same time the cleric stated his confidence in the famine protective attributes of the investment. Lord Lytton, former Viceroy, was invoked. He lauded the Indian railway assets as 'a vast and annually growing property'. As the opium revenues of British India declined, Lytton looked to railways to compensate. Indeed, the financial prospects of India depended on the growing rail and canal system. For the London Chamber, the enthusiasm for the project was coupled with short term pricing advantages. In the midst of the 'great depression', rolling stock, steel rails and sleeper prices were much reduced. Supplies from Europe were plentiful, and there was strong competition amongst large numbers of 'skilled contractors' to work on railway projects in India. While manufacturing interests in Britain might not welcome this, for the City's shipping, insurance and trade representatives this was encouraging news. Lower input costs made projected railway company returns more attractive, encouraging government guarantees. From these financings would follow more British/Indian trade, and investment opportunities in guaranteed trustee stock.[66]

By the first decade of the twentieth century, with the Robertson committee and the subsequent Mackay committee on railway finance, there was much emphasis on defining suitable investment targets for Indian railways. Many of the same individuals, who appeared as witnesses at the Mackay Committee, played prominent roles at the London Chamber of Commerce. Sir Patrick Playfair, of managing agents J. B. Barry and sons, moved to organize a delegation from the Chamber to the Secretary of State for India, lobbying for increased railway grants to purchase railway materials. The delegation included W. B. Gladstone (of Gillanders, and son of the former Prime Minister) and David Sassoon (head of a powerful managing agency). In line with Mackay, the need for more railway wagons was emphasized. Meanwhile a representative from the powerful Indian trading house of Ralli Bros complained that Karachi trading business was being constrained by lack of rail capacity. This risked losing growth opportunities from the embryonic manganese industry in Punjab, and related trading opportunities. In certain cases, industrial and commercial interests were allied. Manufacturers of railway wagons would have welcomed Playfair's initiative in Whitehall, even if the impetus was coming from the London-based service industries. In that sense, extrapolating gentlemanly capitalist activities from manufacturing industry becomes problematical.[67]

Other familiar faces from government commissions lobbied through the London Chamber up to the outbreak of war. Sir Felix Schuster, for example, had been a member of Mackay in 1907/8. He and David Sassoon complained of wagon shortages in the west of India, where Sassoon's business was based. Pressure mounted to set up a specialist India section of the Chamber. By 1912, there was a direct overlap between India and London, with Charles Cambell Mcleod holding chairmanship of both the East India section of the London Chamber and the Bengal Chamber of Commerce. Not surprisingly, Bengali railway matters were prominent in London discussions over succeeding years. In particular, Indian railway company ownership of Bengali collieries became a focal point. There were frequent complaints that railways operated inefficiently in transporting coal cheaply and efficiently. Mcleod and a senior representative of Ralli Bros lobbied the Secretary of State on behalf of the London Chamber in support of state ownership of the mines. The hybrid state/private attributes of guaranteed rail companies were seen as the worst of all worlds. Continued government restrictions on wagon and line expenditure made profit-oriented companies ineffectual in achieving their investment budgets. Perhaps pure private companies would have fared better. While it was pointed out that the coal trade had increased from one million to 12 million tons since 1881, railways had concentrated on cannibalizing business from the canals, rather than opening up new regions. With greater competition between railway companies coal prices might be kept low. Mcleod operated in concert with the Calcutta Mining Association, pressing for government expenditure to be increased from £12 million to at least £15 million, rising to £30 million over time.

Secretary of State Crewe encouraged the London Chamber to give their views on rail and the coal industries. However, he complained that their demands were unrealistic. Producing budgets for rail expenditure was a perilous task, given the volatility of Indian government revenues. Even in countries with pure private railway companies, similar tensions existed between traders and railways. Government was always being pressured to intervene in the market and the Indian system was no worse. While diversified railway companies appeared to manipulate transit prices, Crewe argued that any government controls on railways integrating into coal mining were impractical and illegal. Given vast government support for such rail companies, this seemed unconvincing. Indeed, Indian rail companies were directed to use their coal internally, and precluded from selling onto the market.[68] This was condemned by Mcleod's associates in the Bengal Chamber of Commerce, who complained that coal demand was consequently reduced by 25 per cent in the presidency. Bengal operated with the Indian Mining Association and Bengal coal proprietors in this protest. The Secretary of Bengal's chamber roundly condemned Indian railway companies, which he saw as GOI properties, with stifling inefficiencies. In coal mining, for example, the companies relied on purchases from distant South Africa at inflated prices to compensate for low domestic produce. Meanwhile such companies were being given greater control of Indian coal mining, leaving reserves under exploited. In short, the chamber observed that Indian railway's 'shortcomings have been almost ceaselessly in evidence for the last eighteen years'.[69]

C. C. Mcleod, with senior positions in London and Bengal, symbolized the overlap between British and Anglo-Indian trading interests. London and Calcutta were more likely to act in concert than Sheffield and Calcutta, since the Northern English chambers were motivated more by manufacturing orders than trading volumes. Birkmyre as a representative of both manufacturing Glasgow and trading Calcutta appeared to be an exception. Indian chambers were dominated by the so called 'managing agent' breed of trader and entrepreneur, concentrated in Calcutta and Bombay.[70] The importance of these chambers and their British equivalents were manifest in their being lobbied by Macdonald Stephenson to support his 'International Railway'. The ambitious project was to connect London with Calcutta, via domestic and international railway networks. As one of the triumvirate of early promoters, Macdonald Stephenson had a remarkable pedigree in Indian rail development.[71] In 1850, he had lobbied Lord Palmerston on the 'International Railway'. With Palmerston's blessing Stephenson visited European crown heads and heads of state, including King

Leopold of Belgium, Prince Metternich and Aali and Fuad Pashas in Constantinople to lobby support. Each European government expressed willingness. Stephenson argued that the 'political significance and importance' of the project 'can scarcely be overrated'. In his correspondence to all the major Anglo-Indian and British chambers, he pressed that without their lobbying power the British political will would prove inadequate. Akin to the lobbying approach used for military railways in India, Stephenson looked for commercial attributes of his project, to allow governments to see strategic benefits as an adjunct to sound 'private sector' enterprise.[72] Stephenson's 'international line' was to pass through Asiatic Turkey, Persia and Afghanistan. The project was on a grand scale with 1,500 miles contemplated in Europe, the same in India and International cooperation on a 3,000-mile intermediate section. The journey time from Britain to India travel was to be reduced to six and a half days. The project involved building 2,400 miles of line from Constantinople to Herat at £8,000 per mile, requiring £26 million. By 1884, when lobbying had stepped up, the project's promoters boasted that an Indian population of 300 million with a rail network of 15,000 miles would be connected to European equivalents of 200 million and 80,000 miles. The scale of such an undertaking would produce vast benefits to all sectors of the British economy, according to the Chairman of the 'International Railway Committee', Major-General Sir Lewis Pelly.[73] Like the Suez Canal project, which attracted scepticism initially, doubters needed persuading. Those benefiting would include 'the mercantile and manufacturing interests of the country', whose business would attract 'permanent advantages'. Pelly promised business for gentlemanly capitalists in financing and trade-related business, and for manufacturers in the supply of materials. Stock and debentures issued for the project, presumably guaranteed, would offer attractive minimum returns of 4 per cent with a small partly paid requirement of 5s. for each £20 share to give investors an option for further investment. Returns of 16–18 per cent on the initial investment were to be expected, based on profitability at the four largest Indian railway groups. The extent of the business for British manufacturers would include at least £5 to 10 million of new orders for British iron and engineering works, mostly railway materials and rolling stock. Pelly emphasized that the project would give still greater benefits to the 'commercial and trading interests' of Britain.[74] Manufacturers and gentlemanly capitalists in England, and traders/managing agents in India would benefit. They would form a potent political force. However, even for the most pro-commerce Indian Secretary of State, Randolph Churchill, the project represented such a drag on India's budget that the commercial benefits to Britain were deemed inadequate. Churchill ridiculed Macdonald's obsession with the project and his 'monomaniac' tendencies.[75] The extent to which Indian taxpayers could safely be obliged to pay for Britain's 'addiction to commerce' was limited. However, the request for GOI support on an 'international railway' continued. By the early twentieth century, when Britain was offered a shareholding in the Baghdad railway (spanning part of Stephenson's route), it was assumed that Indian taxpayers would pay at least 50 per cent of the cost.

Indian Chambers were understandably keen to promote Stephenson's International Railway, since it would increase trade links between India and Europe. On Indian domestic trunk railways, they were less assertive at first. They argued that financiers needed to take a more prominent role in realizing the Dalhousie's plans. However, by the 1870s they were more active. The Bombay chamber argued that Western India had been underrepresented in the build out of railways. Calcutta had benefited as administrative capital, with rail links towards the North West, and trunk lines completed to Lahore. In contrast, Bombay lacked efficient links to Hindustan or the North West. By 1896, Bombay was presenting memorials to Viceroy Elgin, prompted by Calcutta's improved trading links to Karachi. Even Western India was vulnerable to Calcutta's railway hegemony. This had been complicated by the Government of Bombay's disagreements over railway gauges. Sir Richard Temple's governorship was criticized for his backing of narrow gauges, where he was allied with the Calcutta-friendly Richard Strachey. The latter was described as the Bombay Chamber's 'chief bugbear...an inveterate champion of the narrow gauge'. Strachey had demonstrated antagonism towards Bombay, which he saw as demanding profligate government railway-spending of £20 million per annum. The aggressiveness of Bombay's demands masked a sense of unease within the Presidency about their prospects in the railway age. Bombay operated as the lowest cost Indian port as late as the turn of the century, receiving support from the 1903 Robertson Committee and its centralizing Railway Board. However, Bombay was likely to lose ground to Calcutta through this work in progress on railways. By 1902, railways under construction would direct 69 per cent of associated trade to Calcutta, against a paltry 2 per cent for Bombay. Two years later, Bombay's share of India's foreign trade was a dominant 35 per cent, while her share of rail grants for the next three years was a marginal 11 per cent.[76]

The Bengal Chamber's lobbying methods were more successful. They were opportunistic in their dealings with government and private companies. The EIR was initially a powerful ally and, working in concert with EBR and South Eastern Railway, the Chamber boasted of early achievements. In 1865 the GOI sanctioned £100,000 to double the width of the line north of Luckerasam after 'numerous representations to the authorities'. Bengal won credibility with their GOI neighbours for their 'vigilance and ...intimate knowledge of local trade requirements'. The Chamber played a prominent role in pressing the needs of Bengal and Assam tea planters, spurred on by growing competition from Ceylon. By contrast, on coal production, the Chamber found itself in conflict with the EIR after the government buyback in 1880. The Chamber used 'laissez-faire' rhetoric, absent when pursuing government assistance themselves, to attack the partly nationalized company as an instrument of central government. EIR's control of valuable coal fields allowed it to undermine private mines by initiating 'state trading in competition with private enterprise'. While coal mining and railways were mutually dependent, the EIR pursued monopoly profits. The Chamber claimed success in curbing EIR's dumping of coal by 1891, but these complaints continued. However, the Chamber's disaffected mine-owning members were far from pursuing perfect competition, but rather a cartelized coal market with price leadership to be exercised by EIR. In parallel, the Chamber pressed the potential for iron production and engineering businesses with rail development, leading to the founding of the Engineering and Iron Trades Association by 1900. The Chamber professed to operate in an even-handed manner in encouraging Indian and British manufacturers, but their intimacy with the London Chamber displayed a continuing 'buy British' trading bias.[77]

The Bengal and Bombay Chamber's opinion on how best to organize rail companies was difficult to characterize. The shortcomings of both state and private sector rail initiatives were clear by the late nineteenth century. The underlying problem of poverty and lack of tax base for Indian finance was unlikely to be solved, given the policy of using railways to maintain an agricultural focus. In 1884, at the Select Committee on East Indian railways, called to examine the state/private emphasis, the Bengal Chamber of Commerce contributed a memorial which encouraged state and private railways to operate 'side by side'. The volume of business was said by the Calcutta trading community to be large enough to sustain both state and privately owned/managed railways. Such pragmatism was applauded by the parliamentary commission, and contrasted with more aggressive lobbying by the Bombay chamber. As ever, laissez-faire ideology was less important to Calcutta than maximizing rail mileage and trading volumes.[78] Later, at the AGM of the 1908 Bengal Chamber of Commerce, the members debated the question of 'state versus company management'. The President of the committee, Ernest Cable, who played a prominent role on that year's Mackay railway committee, pressed the advantages of state railways in centralizing administration. The challenges of increasing rail traffic were too great to be handled by a complicated web of independent companies, according to Cable. In contrast, his fellow committee members argued that the existing system of 'agency' by private companies could be preserved, allowing private-sector involvement in the contracting and financing aspects of railway construction and management. These members had confidence that, with railway finance separate from the general budget of the GOI, the problems of erratic government support for private companies would disappear, allowing the 'agency' function dependable public-sector support.[79] Cable's Bird and Company managing agency might be expected to benefit from an enlarged railway network, through expanded foreign trade.

Foreign Exchange and Trade Policy

With sustained lobbying on railways and the boom in British manufactures which it encouraged, India was saddled with a protracted balance of payments deficit with Britain by the late nineteenth century. Indeed, even before that time her trade surplus had been eradicated by the so called 'drain' or 'tribute' paid to Britain in home charges. This drain was heightened over time as the size of sterling-denominated railway bond coupons and equity dividends paid from India to Britain increased. These Indian railway securities provided an attractive asset class for the 'gentlemanly capitalist' investor base of South East England, which looked for low risk/medium return investments. The liquidity and demand base for the securities was significantly enhanced with the passing of the Trustee Act of 1893, which allowed any financial trustee to invest in debenture stock of an Indian rail company, provided it was guaranteed by the Secretary of State or common stock with a guaranteed fixed or minimum dividend from the same. This placed Indian railway stock and annuities on the same footing as 'Government securities of the United Kingdom', but offered a more attractive yield.[80]

The advantages of this status for the Indian railway companies and their investors was clear in appeals made in 1912 by representatives of the Canadian railway companies, seeking to achieve comparable status. A Lazard banking representative argued to the British Treasury that Canadian railway debentures enjoyed a comparable quality of guarantee on both principal and interest, supported by a first mortgage over the railway. In contrast Indian rail securities had interest alone guaranteed.[81] The addition of Canadian securities to the pool of trustee stocks would have increased the market of £2 billion by no more than 1 per cent. Nevertheless, the request was declined by the British Treasury who argued that the pool of trustee stock was large, which risked making trustee investors too powerful in the market. By 1912 the consol market was vulnerable to price falls, and supply concerns were important. While the Dominion status which Canada had enjoyed a more privileged political and trading relationship with Britain than that given to India, the relative importance of railways in India for trade and investment purposes was seen to be pre-eminent.[82] The lack of formal guarantee on principal, or perfected security on the underlying assets, seems not to have been of concern to Indian rail investors. Indeed, the general level of sophistication of these 'gentlemanly capitalist' investors must be subject to some doubt. Lord Rothschild informed the Mackay committee in 1908, for example, that investors rarely read the prospectuses of these securities, so that they would be unlikely to make rational investment decisions. One insurance company, the financier recalled, was surprised to discover a call option in the fine print of their security and surrendered their asset (thankfully by now at par) to the Government of India. This investor warned Rothschild that he would never invest in another Indian rail security. In such an opaque market there were presumably good opportunities for the more sophisticated City investors, like Rothschild himself, to identify hidden value in little understood securities, and enhance their earnings accordingly.[83]

While London investors may have been ignorant of the details of the Indian railway assets in which they invested, they were aware of the dangers of running foreign exchange risks on their financial assets. In arranging sterling-denominated financings for the railway companies, City financiers passed this risk on to the companies themselves, and ultimately the taxpayer. With the closing of silver mints in 1893 and the phased introduction of the 'gold exchange standard' from 1898 the foreign exchange risk of sterling liabilities was eradicated for companies, but at the cost of an uncompetitive exchange rate which made exports to silver-based Japan and China problematical.[84] The focus on a British investor base, by the India Office and City, while understandable given the undeveloped nature of banking and capital accumulation in India, was expensive. This was highlighted by Dinshaw Wacha in his testimony to the Welby Commission in 1897. He pointed out that any tendency for the rupee to depreciate against sterling could rapidly override the anticipated benefits of borrowing at 3 per cent in sterling against the alternative of 4.5 to 5 per cent, which might be necessary to tempt Indian rupee based investors into the market. Given that a depreciation of 1.5 per cent to 2 per cent in the rupee was quite common in these years, Wacha's analysis was highly relevant.[85] However, Lord Welby as Chairman failed to grasp the subtlety of Wacha's point and responded in paternal fashion, cautioning that Wacha should be aware that 'the advantage of the English market' needed to be borne in mind.[86] Later Welby went to great lengths to discredit Wacha's testimony in general by recalling Stephen Jacob to the witness stand and drawing attention to small mistakes in numbers used in some of Wacha's previous contributions.[87] In fact, Wacha's concerns about the focus on sterling denominated finance for a company which was primarily rupee-based in terms of assets and revenues, was highlighted much earlier by the English. In 1880 Juland Danvers in his annual railway report for 1860 complained that for every £1 million of capital raised for the railways at that time, some £976,000 was raised in sterling in England. Danvers looked forward to 'a more normal state of things' where 'India is again in a position to furnish the Home authorities with the funds required for their expenditure in this country'.[88] While this remained a stated aim of railway financing policy, the results were disappointing, and the impression left in many of the committee discussions was that Indian investors preferred much higher yielding and speculative investments if they were to be persuaded to abandon hoarded wealth. The rich maharajas and rulers were pre-pared to invest in their own state railways, but the savings base elsewhere was limited and these investors were not tempted by low-yielding Indian govern-ment paper. It is unclear to what extent this opinion was tested in the market, and it seems likely that at interest rates which would have proven cheaper, after the foreign exchange moves alluded to, a much larger volume of finance might have been achieved in rupees. Examples like Delhi–Umballa–Kalka Railway's rupee funding in 1889, using a rupee denominated contract from the EIR to support rupee liabilities, showed some investor demand. Elsewhere, the volume of such finance appears to have been limited. A proposed rupee financing for the Bengal Nagpur Railway Company was abandoned because it was feared the security would interfere directly with state loan operations in rupees.[89] Sourcing indigenous rupee-based finance proved a difficulty for Indian Railways up to independence. Even by 1938–9, while the complexity of the financing system makes it hard to attain accurate numbers, it has been estimated that £236 mil-lion of the £550 million invested in Indian railways came from Britain.[90] Of course the listing of Indian railway companies in London, with annual reports produced in sterling terms, created a façade of sterling as the 'home' currency. Some military, famine protective and commercial revenues might have been easily paid in sterling, to justify some sterling denominated debt as a 'transac-tion hedge'. However, the 'buy British' strategy on railway materials created off setting 'payables' to counteract such currency exposure. Overall, there was little effort to match assets and liabilities in the same currency.

In the formal debates on currency reform which characterized late Victo-rian Indian affairs, railways were a prominent theme. Interested parties in the railway industry were never far from the forefront of parliamentary sessions. Indeed, at the royal commission on the 'relative values of precious metals' in 1888, railways were listed as one of three major influences which had tended to support the value of the silver rupee by attracting demand for silver in India. The expenditure of 'large amounts of capital in that country' meant a requirement for greater silver to pay for the domestic costs of production. This ignored the high sterling import aspect of this expenditure, paid for in gold. The American cotton famine of the mid-1860s stimulated Indian cotton exports, albeit for a short period, to increase silver demand, as had the earlier Mutiny, which for a short while involved Britain making silver remittances to India. These effects had all ceased to have any supportive effects on silver by 1888, whose value was in free-fall against the more popular gold based currencies. The analysis in the report seemed not to grasp the structural weakness of silver. The abandonment of silver by France and other countries in the 1870s, and their embrace of the gold standard, sent the rupee into long-term decline against sterling. This had long-term effects on the efficacy of Indian railway companies borrowing in gold against rupee denominated assets. However, the commission did highlight the tendency of railways to widen India's trade deficit with Britain by opening the country up to British manufactures, so pushing silver prices lower. This, coupled with the removal of import duties in India and protectionism in some of India's key export markets, risked widening India's trade deficit worldwide to unacceptable levels. Here, the depreciating rupee did at least make Indian exports more competitive, to offset some of the effects. In short, under this analysis, a depreciating currency was a necessary adjunct to the flooding of India with British exports through the railways.[91] This made railway company's sterling borrowings and stock doubly crippling. Further, the cost of building the railways had been inflated by what the commission identified as 'a time of great speculative activity' prior to 1873, when British coal and iron prices had been forced up on markets through frenetic demand. Speculators were active in the state loans provided to finance these railways which led to great price volatility. The boom and bust effect of these arrangements affected confidence in state loans as speculators saw securities prices falling again. This contributed to Evelyn Baring's reluctant move to seek guaranteed private company loans by the early 1880s. It illustrates that speculators were able to make money under all financing regimes, given the scale of the railway programme.[92]

However, the impact of currency speculation on India's railway programme was challenged by Alfred Marshall, Professor of Political Economy at Cambridge. Marshall gave wide ranging testimony to the commission, suggesting that railways in India were not burdened by a depreciating rupee. The wheat export market, which financed Indian imports from Britain, depended on railways, and the gradual lowering of freight charges as the network was extended. In classical economic terms, the decision by a railway company to borrow in sterling now rested on the prospects of the railways rupee revenues, not on guesswork as to where the gold/silver exchange rate might be in the future. These railway revenues were attractive, since the regulatory regime gave companies the flexibility to move rates up or down (within reason) to capture the maximum overall profits. Australian railway companies, also borrowing in sterling, faced similar dilemmas to Indian companies, but made positive financing decisions. Marshall made little effort to consider the longer term prospects for gold/silver rates, given the tendency of countries to shift to gold, but argued such long-term matters were unknowable. Longer term benefits from railway development would be forthcoming through a reduced deficit for the GOI (assuming state ownership) and an increasing tax base through improved agriculture. In true classical terms, the price mechanism would work favourably to allow optimal long-term outcomes. Externalities, resultant of the uncomfortable state/private balance, were ignored by Marshall.[93]

The subsequent Herschell currency committee of 1893 (he had also chaired the 1888 royal commission) faced an escalating crisis in the value of silver.

Uncertainty on the capacity of Indian assets to pay back gold denominated securities to London gentlemanly capitalists was a focal point. Notwithstanding Marshall's earlier confidence in railway fare flexibility, this applied to railway securities equally (these were, after all, the lion's share of British 'private sector' investments). However, the confidence level of British investors in Indian securities might not be enhanced by a shift to the gold standard for the subcontinent. An overvalued gold rupee might engender price deflation in India, akin to the 'great depression' in England, which would make investment returns on railways and elsewhere equally precarious. Equally, the status quo, with India required to buy-in depreciating silver to meet her obligations, was unsatisfactory since the country immediately crystallized enormous losses. The problem seemed to be beyond the committee members to solve, but the discussion was as ever rooted in concern for the short-term prospects of English investors, rather than long term solutions to India's poverty.[94] Further, over the proceeding six years, the bi-metallic debate gathered momentum in India. In an era of deflation, any shift to a wider currency base and broader money supply might have been applauded. It would have dampened the effects of deflation accompanying a full gold standard for India, which had been warned of at Herschell, and would have prevented a further collapse in hoarded silver prices.[95] For railways, a 'middle way' might have avoided crippling foreign exchange losses, without placing the economy on an overvalued currency.

At the Fowler currency committee of 1899, City representatives with railway interests worked hard to persuade the committee that bi-metallism was an unnecessary evil. Sir James Mackay, director of the EIR, and later chairman of the 1908 railway committee, produced tables illustrating that revenues from railway and irrigation companies had not been affected by the closure of India's silver mints and the move to the 'gold exchange standard' after Herschell. Lord Rothschild, disarmingly modest as ever, professed that with his 'small knowledge of India' he would not venture to advise the GOI on the implications of a gold standard for India. Notwithstanding this lack of knowledge, he proceeded to recommend a highly technical approach to currency management for India. The priority was to curb the influx of silver into the country, which was tending to push up supply and undermine the closing of silver mints. A loan should be raised by the GOI in England to buy and hold gold as a reserve against silver backed notes. Gold exchange standard reserves would be enhanced, and India could be expected to trade her way back into solvency through concentrating on agricultural exports. Rothschild was encouraged by India's export potential in cotton, jute, indigo, wheat and tea. However, the most exciting opportunities lay in the burgeoning opium exports to China, which closed off the British trade deficit with that country. Railways would facilitate British manufactured exports, and the knowledge that railway construction was helping manufacturers would encourage London investors to purchase the bonds and stocks. There was little doubt that Lord Rothschild intended India to raise the London loan, nor the firm best positioned to purchase the gold bullion for the GOI.[96]

By the Mackay Committee of 1907/8, a direct link was identified between currency management and railway construction. Some £1 million of the profits from the minting of gold-backed rupees would be applied to purchase what the committee had seen as desperately needed English wagons. By Austin Chamberlain's finance and currency commission of 1914, some 50 per cent of coinage profits were channelled to railways. The committee was told that this application of government moneys (several millions) had been 'strongly criticised in India'.[97] Lionel Abrahams, chief architect of the gold exchange standard and member of Mackay, lamented the failure of railways to produce their promised returns for GOI. Railway budgeting at the GOI was problematical when profits were liable to come in £3–4 million below projections. At least the committee could feel assured that all locomotives, rails and bridgeworks would be purchased in England. It was noticeable how the British had become more transparent about the 'buy British' approach since the days of Juland Danvers in the 1860s, when the affectation was maintained that Indian manufactures would be encouraged. Equally, rhetoric about the railway's drive to borrow in rupees had disappeared. Abrahams pointed out that while the Secretary of State had been pushing for the railway companies to raise rupee loans, the liquidity of the sterling market was such as to allow long term funding at yields less than 4 per cent. Mcleod, of the London and Bengal Chambers, applauded the superior liquidity provision in India itself through the state-run Presidency Banks, which were by 1914 able to lend against the security of all Indian railways, with or without guarantees. London investors could feel comfortable that railway securities were underpinned by this further liquidity. Meanwhile, the financial secretary to the India Office made a forlorn attempt to push the longer-term prospects of Indian manufactured rolling stock and steel rails one day usurping British manufactured product.[98]

Consistent with the Raj's ambivalence towards industrial development, an agricultural focus for India attracted consensus support, from railway executives and leading managing agents to John Maynard Keynes.[99] There was little debate about the 'deindustrialization' of India in the commissions and correspondence of the time. It was realized that India must remain solvent as a trading partner, and the European, Asian and North American agricultural exports were expected to allow her to 'meet her obligations to her English creditors'. In addition to providing protection for British manufactured exports, this allowed British traders and consumers to access cheap agricultural product and raw materials from India. With the outbreak of the American Civil War in 1861 the main raw cotton supplies to Lancashire were cut off. In the years running up to war, enormous lobbying of the India Office by Manchester representatives took place. While Secretary of State Charles Wood was determined to withstand these pressures, the influence of the cotton lobby was significant. However,

Indian short staple cotton was ill suited to the Manchester machinery, meaning that at the end of the war Lancashire manufacturers shifted back to American long staple and higher quality Egyptian cotton.[100] India had been pushed into greater cotton cultivation to provide an insurance policy for Lancashire manufacturers. When British demand switched back to Alabama and Louisiana in the mid-1860s, Bombay's speculative cotton bubble burst, prompting stock market and banking collapses.[101] With the removal of British demand, Indian raw cotton was targeted at Continental Europe, which by 1907 accounted for 70 per cent of revenues.[102] The export market in Indian foodstuffs and agricultural cash products became a more controversial matter as the acute famines of the late nineteenth century took hold. Many Indian administrators felt compelled to play down the extent to which India was exporting cheap wheat and rice, and switching acreage to cotton, jute, salt and opium production.[103] Nevertheless, for the Indian Chambers of Commerce, the façade was maintained that Indian poverty could gradually be eradicated by agricultural specialization. In reality Calcutta and Bombay, and the railways themselves benefited from two way trade with manufactures out from England, and raw materials back to England.

Conclusion

Viceroy Lawrence's assertion that Indians did not share the British 'addiction to commerce' was a departure from the basis of Dalhousie's liberal vision of Indian railways. What Thomas Metcalf has called 'the confidence that India could somehow be made over in the image of Britain' was a consistent attribute of the British approach, but was used selectively, like so many other tenets of British thinking, to the advantage of the controlling power.[104] The commissions and parliamentary debates on financing the railways, showed the British united in the opinion that British commerce would bring to India a facility that the population themselves struggled to provide. This justified a fatalism about Indian manufacturing industry and financial markets which implied the need for sterling finance and British locomotives. While Lawrence in his railway minute was attempting to escape from the excesses of 'sham private enterprise', with a focus on state railway financing, this fatalism left India vulnerable to British interest groups which claimed to provide surrogate commercial expertise.[105] The opportunities presented by the vast Indian rail project went far beyond Cain and Hopkins narrow vision of 'gentlemanly capitalism'. Through its different financing stages, whether more public or private oriented, manufacturers, traders and financiers were normally pushing at an open door with Whitehall and Calcutta. Without the commitment or desire to pursue wide ranging economic development in India, British policy became focused on crude railway mileage. This was a simple and attainable target, which transcended the ideology of laissez-faire and allowed effective memorials by all those in Britain who shared an 'addiction to commerce'.

2 INDIAN RAILWAYS AND FAMINES, 1875–1914: MAGIC WHEELS AND EMPTY STOMACHS

Introduction

In 1899 Secretary of State Hamilton complained of the 'see-saw' policy pursued by successive Indian governments on famine prevention and relief. Administrations from the 1870s onwards had been criticized for being too frugal or generous. The cost of famine relief had risen dramatically, while budgets were constrained.[1] By the early twentieth century, the financial burden of the South African War had imposed further economies on Indian expenditure. Hamilton resisted parliamentary pressure for 'free grants' to India and a grain export ban in the midst of the most acute and widespread famine of the Raj. British sympathy and charitable contributions were best targeted at the soldiers fighting in South Africa, rather than India's starving peasants.[2] However, the last 'famine relief/ protection' item be trimmed were railways. Viceroy Curzon declared after the appalling famine of 1899/1900 that he was not 'frightened' of adding to the 'bogey' of Home Charges through rail expenditure. Long-term trade benefits from railways overrode all short term considerations.[3] At the India Office, there was consensus that long term rail investment would pay off in more efficient famine relief efforts than achieved in earlier famines of 1896–7 and 1876–8. A network had been constructed which could transport grain and rice from sea ports to major interior cities via trunk lines, and from there to more remote areas by branch lines. That investment programme had given benefits through the equalization in food prices, as railways allowed rapid movements of grain to the areas where prices were highest. The state railway lines constructed for this purpose, and the larger infrastructure of 'company lines' many of which performed some 'protective' function, benefited the GOI financially, even if their dividend returns were disappointing. It was expected to save on future famine costs so that the enormous cost of previous famines would be avoided.

The Nationalist Complaint on Railways as
a Panacea for Indian Famines

Many nationalists argued that railways impoverished India through the associated tax burden. This lessened resistance to famine.[4] Most nationalists could see the longer term benefits of railways as part of a development programme. However, by the 1880s rail expenditure was out of kilter with irrigation and industrial investment. Romesh Dutt distinguished between early trunk lines for trade and economic development and those since 1878 which had been driven by 'capitalists and speculators'.[5] By 1897 he was calling for irrigation to enhance agricultural yields, in preference to superfluous railways. Railways increased land tax payments, with rising wheat and rice prices which 'steadily added to her land revenue', while leaving growers impoverished.[6] High food prices left even poor farmers paying higher taxes and unfortunate non-agricultural workers suffering a crippling deterioration in their terms of trade.[7] Sensitive to such criticism, Curzon collected comprehensive data to prove that the percentage land assessment burden had fallen over the nineteenth century. He was loath to admit that other industrializing countries would have seen more dramatic falls, helped by railways. In fact India's rail investment bred complacency amongst policymakers that levels of famine protection were sufficient. Such complacency was taken to task by Naoroji in his correspondence with Juland Danvers, the Public Works member at the India Office. Danvers had written obliquely of the 'railway wealth' engendered by increased grain prices. From an accounting perspective rising food prices expanded India's nominal national income. Naoroji mocked what he saw as accounting sophistry with the riposte that 'if the mere movement of produce can add to the existing wealth, India can become rich in no time. All it would have to do is to go on moving its produce continually ... the magic wheels of the train wealth will go on springing till the land will not suffice to hold it ...'[8] Those 'magic wheels' were intended to push India towards specialization on agriculture. Danvers was technically correct that there would be short term benefits, but longer term the lack of diversification and volatility of production probably worsened poverty.[9] Moreover, in his assessment of India's national income, Danvers failed to consider the impact of lesser volumes of food through the GOI spending finite resources on railways rather than irrigation. By 1943 Nehru pointed to the failings of British railway policy in protecting against famine. The catastrophic Bengal famine of that year showed India's reliance on railway transported Burma rice and grain had left the food supplies in other parts of the subcontinent vulnerable to drought.[10]

1876–8 Madras/Bombay Famine and 1880 Famine Commission

Hamilton was sceptical about the 'so called famine of 1874' when the GOI spent millions of pounds gratuitously on famine protection. The expenditure was a reaction to Orissa's famine of 1866 when 'a million or more people had died' (or 25 per cent of the population), partly through government negligence.[11] By the time a more serious and widespread famine broke in the Madras Presidency in 1877, the Conservative Viceroy Lytton had been placed by Disraeli at Calcutta. Criticism of 'lavish' famine relief at Bengal and Bihar three years previously, prompted government caution.[12] Sir John Strachey writing four years later estimated the cost of the 1874 Bengal famine at £6.75 million. However, despite further expansion of protective railways and Lytton's frugality, relief costs of the Madras/Bombay famine rose to £9.25 million.[13] While taxpayers funded relief, the railway companies benefited from famine-related business around Madras and Bombay. Receipts on the guaranteed and state railways rose over 1875/6 to 1876/7 from £8.7 million to £12 million, with government directed business benefiting shareholders. In fairness, the railways were performing the role expected of them. They transported at least 80 per cent of grain reaching famine areas with an average journey of about 500 miles but, despite these impressive operational characteristics, the human and financial costs were oppressive.[14] The experience of these consecutive droughts prompted GOI to plan for recurrences. Famines were no longer to be viewed as 'abnormal and exceptional calamities' but instead accounted for as 'ordinary charges of the state'.[15]

This institutionalization of famine relief had its roots in the Raj's unquenchable appetite for government surveys, data collection and commissions. Lytton responded to the Madras famine by appointing Sir Richard Temple as senior observer of the crisis. Temple, in characteristic ICS style, produced rafts of statistical analysis, with large sections of his reports focused on the performance of the railways in food transportation. He travelled vast distances through famine affected regions. Government funding of some £16 million over the 1874 to 1879 famine period, supported by a further £1 million contribution from the Lord Mayor of London's famine funds was viewed as generous.[16] Railways played a dominant role in food distribution and providing plentiful opportunities for relief works. Indeed, Temple identified the key advantage possessed by famine victims in British India, over those in the native states, as being 'the possession of railways an advantage unprecedented in the history of Indian famines'.[17] Temple's optimism seemed at odds with the failings of this food distribution and low-paid work in preventing fatalities. Indeed, some years later, in a heated House of Lords debate on the subject, the sceptical Lord Kinnaird mocked the optimism of Temple and others about famine railways. By 1877, he reminded his audience, grain prices had multiplied by some five to eight times making food too expensive for even agricultural workers. The India Office confidently asserted that food supplies remained plentiful, but by the later stages of the 1876–8 famine there were some twenty-three distressed 'taluks' across Madras and Bombay. Kinnaird observed that no less than 855,000 persons of a population of less than five million were missing. Nevertheless, the GOI and India Office refused to spend money importing grain into South India to relieve the extreme conditions.[18] Perhaps anticipating these concerns, Temple challenged the links between famines and crude mortality numbers. The Madras conditions had extended unexpectedly into 1878, prompting epidemics of cholera and infant smallpox, which were only indirectly linked to famine. The contemporary method of calculating famine deaths compared actual population against projected population, using expected demographic growth rates which exaggerated fatality numbers. In fact, the exodus of people from flood areas meant that birth rates had collapsed and population rises were naturally lower. Temple seemed keen to reconcile the expense and expectations of his protective railways and railway relief works with the crude numbers compiled by the GOI. Without such expenditure, the death rate would have been still greater, he argued, though this was unproven.[19] The authorities had suffered peculiar bad luck in the later part of the 1876–8 famine. Drought gave way to 'excessive' rainfall destroying new crops and spreading cholera, influenza and malaria epidemics. Rats laid large areas of the Deccan to waste, eating whatever crops survived. According to Temple 'the concatenation of calamities is to be remembered, when the mortality is computed'. In fact famine relief had worked in combination with railways, akin to the experience of Bengal and Bihar in 1874. However, the administration of the relief was poor, lacking 'adequate supervision, either by European officers, or by Native officials of status and capacity'. The situation in Madras and Bombay was marred by corruption and theft. While the density of population in Bihar made food distribution by rail efficient, in Madras and Bombay many of the most vulnerable lived in inaccessible hills and valleys. In desperation, large numbers of the rural poor fled to Madras and nearby religious centres to take advantage of the 'western and southern Indian ... habit of giving and receiving alms'. The energy expended in such migrations led to further deaths. However, Temple failed to look at the extent to which this was worsened by the tendency of peasants to move towards railway termini in search of food.[20] His enthusiasm for railways was stretched to extremes when he attempted to present, unconvincingly, that the 1874 and 1877/8 famines had positive legacies in the form of 'the northern Bengal railway' and 'the Behar branch railways'.[21] Apparently the existence of such tools of famine relief was compensation for their failure to deliver anticipated results.

While Temple's correspondence kept the GOI and India Office alert to the detail of famine in Madras, the British public were able to read detailed reports in newspapers. This coverage helped to encourage the Lord Mayor of London's fund raising, which *the Times* reported had reached the sum of £38,000 by August 1877. City firms with prominent Indian business were keen to have their names associated with this modest charitable contribution. These included Rothschild, Baring, Sassoon, Arbuthnot, Morgan, Fleming and P&O.[22] However, charitable contributions from India were resisted by the GOI, since they were said to distort private-sector famine policy. *The Times* reported that Viceroy Lytton's attitude to domestic charity was met with 'regret' and appeared to be 'a mistake' since it was 'difficult to see how that aid would interfere with Government plans'.[23] While the Madras famine was calculated to have cost the government £8 million by August 1877, increasing by £0.5 million each month, 'the importation of grain would be left to private trade'. In contrast the GOI would actively 'reinforce the railways' and 'arrange for tramways where cart power failed'. Lytton's priorities were evident in his personally travelling to Poona to chair a conference with Temple on improving railway links. Meanwhile the affordability of food made this initiative questionable with grain at 'ruinous prices'. Even in the midst of the crisis, with the price mechanism breaking down, the GOI's priority was for the Great Indian Peninsula Railway Company (GIPR) to place a huge order for sixty locomotives. As ever, this was to be paid for by the Indian taxpayer and constructed in England. It is difficult to imagine that the engines would have arrived in time to provide any relief.[24] Government-guaranteed 'private sector' rail companies were left to facilitate grain and rice deliveries while the GOI gifted them rolling stock, locomotives and additional revenues through famine relief. Private charitable contributions were blocked, while grain price speculation was allowed to continue in a seemingly arbitrary mixture of laissez-faire and mercantilism. The sense that railways were delivering grains to the areas afflicted, but at prices outside the purchasing power of the natives, was clear in *The Times* reporting. A Public Works Department employee had described how 'carts laden with rice travel about and [godowns] are stored but no thefts of the food take place'. Instead of outrage at the anomalous situation, an ICS witness railed against the 'apathy displayed by the people' who were indifferent to 'death and suffering' since '[for them] life has no charm'.[25]

The debate over rising prices and affordability of foodstuffs transported by rail was accompanied by anxiety about the volumes of food exports which India was sending overseas at a time of acute scarcity. Prior to the worst of the Bengal famine in 1873, Sir George Campbell (Lieutenant Governor of Bengal) pressed for a prohibition on the export of rice from Indian ports. This radical departure from laissez-faire was rejected by Viceroy Northbrook in favour of discreet rice purchases for peasants, as and when required. Banning exports was said to 'derange trade'. It could create large liabilities for the GOI through compensation claims by rice traders and exporters. This thinking was expanded in a 'laissez-faire' pamphlet of the time. The rise in food prices was a necessary evil, according to the author, to allow the market to reallocate resources for longer term efficiency. The government had no legal right to intervene in the activities of grain traders. Were they to legislate on forced sales of foodstuffs to peasants the government would lose large amounts. To provide relief to peasants they would be forced to sell at prices below that at which they purchased from grain traders. Their activities as large buyers on behalf of the distressed poor would hike prices more, implying even greater losses on the discounted sales. As ever, the role of railways as a government-sponsored shock to the market was conveniently ignored, while laissez-faire amongst middlemen was to be preserved at all cost.[26] Nationalist writers condemned Northbrook's actions, arguing that the tradition of self insurance, where stocks of food were held in reserve by farmers in case of famine, was undermined by railway exports. Digby, for example, highlighted that in the pre-railway period Indian regions were required to be self sufficient in foodstuffs, and to plan beyond one year for the possibility of drought. This gave rise to effective 'self insurance' so that grain and rice were stored in years of bumper harvest to tide peasants over the poor years, when there might be a shortage. Of course, self insurance had its limitations, since foodstuffs would perish over time, and droughts had often continued for more than one year. Railway enthusiasts seized on this. They argued that railway distribution would end the waste observed in many parts of India, where piles of rotting food were not uncommon.[27] Nevertheless, Digby warned of the collapse of a regional support system built up over centuries, which had evolved to meet the difficulties of failing monsoons. It was to be replaced by British orchestrated modernity in the form of Naoroji's 'magic wheels'. Temple, who did seem more aware than most of risks in the abandonment of self insurance, saw the longer term advantages of moving to a western system as counteracting any shorter term inconvenience. He expressed admiration for his predecessor as Lieutenant-Governor of Bengal, Sir George Campbell, but lacked Campbell's commitment to reform.

Indeed, Temple's denial of the practical shortcomings in the famine railway policy was manifest in his summation of the crisis. Food had been 'despatched by private enterprise with regularity and promptitude ... by the railways ...' Further, the subsequent Indian Famine Commission provided 'a repertory of all circumstances and suggestions relating to famines'. Temple's faith in the government observation and pragmatism was unlimited.[28] The Famine Commission Report of 1880 was a long document, with evidence collected in all regions affected by recent famines. The report's main section lauded the performance of railways in the 1876–8 famine. Two million tons of grain had been imported into Madras, mostly by rail, allowing twelve million people to be kept alive for twelve months. While the mortality rate had still been unacceptably high, this showed that India needed more railways and telegraphs for rapid distribution and communication. Railways offered the most compelling evidence that 'the trade of the country may be confidently left to provide for the supply of food in times of scarcity'.[29] The new transport dominated the section of the report on 'measures of protection and preservation'. In places the report had more to say on railways than famine. With Richard Strachey as President of the Commission, soon to be Chairman of EIR, this was unsurprising.[30] The report argued that returns to British railway financiers and others were handsomely repaid to India through the benefit of the infrastructure for famine and other purposes. This contradicted early nationalist 'drain' theorists who viewed the surplus of Indian exports over imports, including railway payments, as money wasted by India in the form of the 'tribute' to England.[31] The commission pressed for a further 10,000 miles of rail line on top of the 10,000 already constructed, or in the process of construction, at 1880. The cost of this new rail construction was expected to be far cheaper than that incurred by the first generation of guaranteed railway companies. With a projected costing of £6,000 per mile, the additional 10,000 miles of famine railway would imply £60 million over 25 years, or £2.5 million per annum. Relative to the historical cost of famines, this would provide good value for money, assuming it solved the problem, and that the cost estimates were fair. On the former point the report had few doubts proclaiming that 'railways may be confidently relied upon to meet all possible demands ... for the distribution of food in times of scarcity'.[32] On the cost estimates, given that India had returned to a system of guarantees similar to the 1850s and 60s, the cost per mile might have been expected to bear some similarity to past experience. Sir Arthur Cotton, in a wide ranging pamphlet, estimated past Indian railway costs at £19,500 per mile for the first 7,000 miles constructed (or £23,000 per mile including debt). While the second generation of state railways had lower guaranteed coupons/dividends and a reduced profit share, and state railways were cheaper, anticipating cost reductions of up to 70 per cent relative to past experience was optimistic.[33]

However, the commission did identify areas where famine railways might improve. There was a need for greater rolling stock to cover emergencies and for an accelerated build out of branch lines from existing trunk lines to target distribution. Further, rail tariff rates were discussed with some unease, since this seemed to be the preserve of the companies themselves. In the famines of 1868 and 1873 an expensive subsidy system had operated so that railway companies were fully compensated on all reduced tariff transport, notwithstanding the increase in volume of traffic which this generated for the companies. By 1877 in Madras this subsidy system was abandoned, and grain was transported at market price. The commission report argued that one way or another government would be involved in subsidizing the business, through control of relief wages which it 'regulates ... in proportion to the cost price of food at the relief works'. The extent to which compensation was being paid to the grain dealer or railway companies in these circumstances was said to be 'a matter of secondary importance'. This seemed to avoid the issue since payments of subsidy had different implications for government borrowing, when made to partly state-owned railway companies as against independent grain dealers. Moreover, it was admitted that in setting tariff rates 'the interests of the public ... are ... not altogether identical with those of the railway companies'. While government sought to encourage the highest volume of grain transport at the lowest cost, their capacity to make judgements on price and volume, in volatile food markets, was limited. The suspicion that rail investors were still benefiting from the misery of the Madras/Bombay famine victims persisted, though curiously prompted no scrutiny of rail company profits or share prices. With the buyback of the EIR stock then imminent, on a trailing average share-price basis (transacted in 1880), and discussions on other share buybacks like GIPR at the forefront of India Office policy, this was surprising. The solution, as ever, was to build more railways to engender 'a sufficient degree of competition' which would 'prevent any such evils'.[34]

Government attachment to laissez-faire was further seen in their refusal to insist on rail companies transporting food crops over the more profitable cash crops in times of famine. This reflected a wish to minimize 'the inconvenience experienced by merchants' in delays over their non food deliveries.[35] Captain Bisset applauded the delivery of food in the Bengal famine of 1874, but criticized the handling of the Madras famine of 1877. Madras had proven more demanding due to longer distances and the need to cross more railway company lines, but Bisset called for greater consistency across the different companies.[36] A more serious criticism was given in a telegraph note by Bisset from Raichore in the Madras Presidency during the famine, where he warned that 'open preference is given to cotton and linseed over grain and other seeds'.[37] Madras in 1877 had seen resources reallocated towards cash export markets in a manner warned of by the nationalist writers. In his testimony to the 1880 Commission, Bisset complained of regions like Nagpore, where grain dealers were at a disadvantage since they were given less priority than the valuable cash crops like cotton and linseed.[38] This was the same Nagpore region whose Bengal–Nagpur railway was given generous contributions from the famine insurance fund only five years later. In contrast, the generally maligned GIPR line was rated most highly by Bisset on food delivery during the crisis. The capacity of trains to deliver vital foodstuffs could be increased with wide rather than narrow gauge. Bisset calculated that a ton of food would feed 2,000 people for a day, and that wide-gauge railways could deliver twice the volume daily.[39] This placed Bisset at odds with Strachey and Temple in the so called 'battle of the gauges'. Bisset was supported in this 'battle' by Theodore Hope, public works member of the Viceroy's council, but for different reasons. Hope warned one of his close promoter 'friends' that the Bengal–Nagpur famine railway should resist Strachey's pressure and expend (famine insurance) moneys on wide-gauge lines to avert 'the outcry' of 'the Calcutta and Bombay commercial public'.[40] This Anglo-Indian commercial pressure was presumably for greater volumes of British manufactures and food exports rather than famine rations. For Hope and others, the added costs of famine railways like Bengal Nagpur implied 'no risk' to the GOI since the charge would simply be made to the 'famine insurance grant'.[41]

The cost of famine railways was a long-running discussion, and the Famine Commission's recommendations added to possible expense. In 1873, Secretary of State Argyll had complained to Viceroy Northbrook that he had been promised for years that expenditure on railways would be trimmed, but was being asked for a further £16 million on railways, inflated by wide-gauge famine lines to ease shortages in Bengal. This was long-term investment targeted at the short-term problem of remedying 'the deficiency of a single rainy season'. Argyll pressed for more focus on the cheaper irrigation alternative of 'the storage and distribution of water', rather than over-engineered rail lines designed to combat 'a mere military inconvenience'.[42] These cost complaints were most easily overcome for all 'protective' railways by promising other revenues. Seasoned 'orientalist' and railway enthusiast Sir Henry Bartle Frere pointed to military and famine rationales in declaring that 'war must be declared on famine'.[43] Temple accepted that early guaranteed railway companies had been constructed 'upon a scale too grand for the resources of the country'.[44] With better cost control (narrow gauge where possible) railway construction and famine relief costs could justly be added to India's national debt 'sometimes by special taxation'. In that sense, famines might be financed in a manner comparable to war.[45] To set against the costs of famine railways, Temple provided a calculation of the benefits to Famine Commission President, Richard Strachey. Temple compared the cost of passenger and freight transportation in India using road and canals, against his preferred rail method. Cost per mile was reduced by a factor of three to four times. Spread over the entire country, given a present revenue base of £9 million for the railways, the total benefit of railways was about £28 million. While railways speeded up transportation, the 'fully loaded' amortized cost was much higher, so that Temple's analysis was incomplete. However, Strachey responded enthusiastically to Temple's testimony. His brother John, after all, had calculated the gain from railways overall at no less than £40 million.[46] Further, Temple pointed to 'indirect benefits' which were said to be more significant 'materially and morally'. These unspecified public benefits justified the taxpayers' funding burden 'much as taxation is to be deprecated'.[47] The commission heard no comparable analysis on the overall benefits from canals, which would have included irrigated food production as well as distribution. The opportunity cost of building famine railways rather than canals was ignored, but Temple's analysis was more balanced on the environmental externalities of railways. The deforestation which occurred as a result of railway building and the burning of wood as fuel (before local coal resources were exploited) caused concern. In his Madras famine correspondence in 1877, Temple worried about deforestation affecting rainfall levels and worsening the famine.[48] He relayed these concerns to the commission in 1881, admitting that the links between climate and forestation were uncertain. Indian forests might 'promote condensation' but even if not, they did at least 'retain and distribute moisture in a meaningful way'. By planting more trees to compensate, households might abandon the use of manure as fuel, using it instead to enhance crop yields and pre-empt famine.[49] As ever with Raj analysis, the tools to create a more balanced picture appeared to exist, but in the effort to create uncluttered policies the information was often ignored.

The commission report pressed the benefits of two-way trade between India and England. Indian nationalists, who saw British trade policy as consciously seeking to accelerate Indian 'de-industrialization', would have been alert to encouragement for cotton textile imports from England. Unlike other forms of transport, argued a representative from North-Western Provinces, rail protected the English cargo in a manner which avoided 'the risks of road or water conveyance'.[50] Most commission representatives would have argued that the encouragement of two-way trade, and exploiting of comparative advantage, would enhance Indian wealth and alleviate famine. In this vein, the Bombay Chamber of Commerce contributed a long memorial on the importance of further railway expansion for the Bombay economy. The Chamber followed Bisset in pressing for the additional expense of wide-gauge railways, and devoted a large portion of their report to promoting the Bengal–Nagpur railway, and 'tributary lines' which would fully open up the 'granary of India'.[51] The Bombay Chamber's emphasis was exclusively on promoting trade rather than facilitating domestic deliveries of foodstuffs. Criticism of GIPR's fare structure, for example, was aimed at making that company more accommodating to British trading interests and removed from humanitarian concerns. The commission's report was equally trade focused. Railways were applauded for maximizing wheat exports from British India to England during the period of the famine. Total exports of wheat from British India, they boasted, had risen from 1,069,076 cwts in 1874–5 to 6,340,150 cwts in the famine years of 1877–8.[52] This support for international specialization was inconsistent with concerns expressed in the document about excessive dependence on agriculture as a cause of Indian poverty, and in turn the inability to withstand droughts.[53] The Bombay Chamber had no such doubts. India might grow and relieve poverty through a Ricardian focus on agriculture and trade. In Central India, for example, only one third of the cultivatable land was sown, so that with railways expansion and access to markets it would be possible for 'the ryot to better his condition'.[54] Constraints on land assessment in Western India were needed to improve cultivation further. In attacking the GOI's revenue base, Chambers of Commerce and Indian nationalists forged an unlikely coalition.

Much of the questioning of regional representatives at the commission was choreographed to solicit responses in line with commission member's thinking. Witnesses were asked to comment on the extent to which lines had helped to 'equalise prices and stimulate trade'. Such equalization was presented as an undoubted benefit. Witnesses were not encouraged to consider the overall impact of railways and alternative approaches to feeding their populations. In fact, there was great consensus on the price effect of railways. Observers from the Punjab, North-Western Provinces and Oudh, Bengal, Central Provinces, Bombay, Sind, Madras and Mysore all identified price convergence in wheat and rice prices across their regions. Railways were seen to have acted in concert with other influences in this process. At Lucknow, for example, 'the railway, river, good bridged roads and the fall of the value of silver as regards its value to gold' were all seen as important. In Bombay, railways were seen to have been slow to promote the trade required to homogenize food prices, but grain traders had purchased food further away to counteract local shortages. These traders had been 'amazed at the result'. Only once this enforced purchasing had begun did people start to understand 'the value of the railway'.[55] However, when the regional witnesses were asked to look at different public works which might provide direct benefits to the famine relief programme, irrigation, canals and the building of tanks were stressed ahead of railways. General Sir Arthur Cotton wrote prolifically on the subject of irrigation in place of railways, and his opinions permeated a number of the Anglo-Indian communities at the time of the commision. In a pamphlet written in 1878, Cotton observed that it was 'far easier' to persuade the India Office to look at a £4 million rail investment for famine protection than a £40,000 irrigation scheme. With some famine railways costing £20,000 per mile, the costs were out of kilter with the value of food and other goods being transported. It cost as much to send a bushel of wheat 1,000 miles from inland to Calcutta as it did to ship it 7,500 miles from Calcutta to London. Even in the North West Provinces, where the terrain made canal building difficult, Cotton's arguments held sway. Colonel Brownlow told the commission that 'canal or reservoir projects provide the largest proportion of work best suited to the employment of famine labour'. In contrast railways had significant shortcomings through 'involving a large proportion of expenditure in Europe, [being] burdensome to the finances and quite useless for relief of distress in India'.[56] This was an indictment of the main focus of famine relief activity in the 1876–8 Famine. It was unusual for an Anglo-Indian to point to the problems of enforced British suppliers, and the implied tribute within railway expenditure. The comparison between railways and irrigation, in terms of potential demand for British goods, was compelling. Government papers revealed that over the two years 1885–7, for example, manufactured 'stores' imported from England to India for military railways alone was £2.84 million, against a comparable figure for irrigation at a negligible £6,130.[57]

However, Cotton failed to convince a number of prominent ICS representatives of the merits of irrigation. Most prominently, Secretary of State Salisbury declared to a Bradford audience in the middle of the Madras famine that irrigation spending would simply burden Indian taxpayers with more costs and heightened poverty. He claimed to have been the target of overblown promotion of irrigation for India over many years, with projects failing to attain their expected returns. It is notable that Salisbury declined to apply such rigorous performance hurdles for the much larger railway budget. Instead, Salisbury pressed a return to traditional peasant values of 'frugality' with added emphasis on self insurance and protection from the 'grasp of moneylenders'. Of course railways made all these improvements of what Salisbury termed the 'social and moral condition' of Indians less attainable. Self insurance was abandoned, and moneylenders and grain traders benefited from food-price inflation. Even Manchester's John Bright, with a constituency in the middle of the cotton textile region of Lancashire, was able to declare by September 1877 that had only £30 million of public works moneys been targeted at canals 'millions of the population' who had perished in famines might have been saved.[58] The irrigation versus railways debate continued into the new century, prominent in the testimony of the different famine commissions, but it did little to change the spending patterns of the India Office on famine relief.

While these government commissions were intended to highlight topical concerns in the administration of India, some consistent monitoring of India policy was facilitated by the annual Indian budget debate in the House of Commons, and the accompanying financial statement produced by the GOI. In the late 1870s and early 1880s, when the social and financial aspects of Indian famine had come to the fore, GOI budget reports devoted much space to railway matters. The combination of state, guaranteed and subsidized railways had by this time made railways a major line item in revenue and expenditure. By Auckland Colvin's budget statement in 1883–4, failings of the railways in delivering famine relief were highlighted. In spite of enormous investment, wheat transportation rates were much higher than other exporting countries, notably the USA. Evidence to a recent Royal Agricultural Commission had praised the achievements of the American railroad in reducing wheat distribution costs to ¼*d.* per ton per mile. Indian costs were a multiple of this, inflated by the GIPR and EIR regional monopolies. This must have created anxiety in Calcutta, given the expense incurred in repurchasing EIR stock a few years before. However, the requirement to repay borrowings for the buyback may have compromised the GOI's efforts to steer EIR away from monopoly profits, which were a tax on consumers. While it was confidently expected that EIR would soon follow the Bombay, Baroda and Central Railway with an 18.5 per cent reduction in wheat rates, this would still leave Indian wheat producers and consumers at a significant disadvantage to their American equivalents. Further, the inflating of wheat prices in India was complicated by the existence of a profusion of middle men in the distribution process. The budget report complained of a complicated route for wheat distribution where, after rail haulage, supplies were bought and sold by numerous grain merchants, storage and shipping agents. This inflated costs and made delivery time longer. These superfluous agency roles would have benefited both Anglo-Indians and middle-class natives. The system was per-haps representative of famine protection/relief devised by other agents, notably the managing variety in Calcutta and Bombay. Unsurprisingly the report had few concrete recommendations on how to simplify matters, but professed that free trade attributes of British India more than accommodated for the trans-port disadvantages of the locals. The USA consumer by contrast, suffered from diminished purchasing power due to the unwieldy level of tariffs imposed on foreign imports. Indian wheat exporters and consumers would override railway tariff problems through the liberating effect of free trade.[59]

However, this vision of India as recipient of benign British liberalism was taken to task the following year in a wide-ranging attack on 'Indian Railways and Indian Wheat', presented to the Statistical Society. Indian free trade was simply a 'synonym for the abolition of cotton duties'. Government interven-tion was prominent all over the Indian economy, not least in the 'protectionist principles applied to railway construction'. The Americans had a far more robust attachment to laissez-faire, which included cheap railway transport through companies whose tariffs were low, reflecting their anticipated profits on land trading. This was far removed from hamstrung guaranteed regional monopo-lies in India. With the threat of Indian wheat exports to Europe undermining American sales, America's 'western farmers' might be expected to pressure their federal government to abolish wheat tariffs. The author suggested that the Eng-lish might be using Indian rail guarantees in that context 'as a weapon of war ... to frighten America into free trade'.[60]

1896–7 Northern India, Bengal, Burma, Madras, Bombay and Central Provinces Famine and Indian Famine Commission Of 1898

In the midst of the wide-scale famine of 1896–7 Lord Kinnaird told Parliament of the human suffering. Accounts of distressed regions reached England through newspapers and GOI/India Office correspondence, but the crude statistics were shocking to the House of Lords. The loss of life in Madras–Bombay in the 1870s had been 5.8 million out of a regional population of 27 million. Now, in a more acute famine affecting a population of some 40 million, Kinnaird applied a simi-lar mortality rate, to arrive at a horrific estimate of 8 million deaths. No one on the government bench felt confident in challenging Kinnaird's analysis. His assumption that the per capita mortality rate had failed to improve undermined the view that rail infrastructure had improved famine protection since 1878. In fact, Kinaird quoted sources normally sympathetic to rail expansion to highlight the mixed effects of modern transport. The price of food by 1897 was far above the inflated levels existing in 1874 or 1866, according to the Bengal Chamber of Commerce. Meanwhile, the British India Association called for direct government intervention through the import of grain to 'outlying districts'.[61] Kinnaird's criticisms were dismissed by the government, which argued that by that time prices in the Punjab and North West Provinces were falling. In any case it was impossible to make generalizations about what was a dangerous price level for grain, beyond which it became unaffordable, since conditions varied from 'district to district'. There was no denying that high prices caused exchange problems, but despite the vast information gathering under famine codes, there was fatalism about the GOI's ability to intervene through want of price knowledge.[62] Further, Secretary of State Hamilton told the House that he would resist all Imperial aid, despite the rising deficit of the GOI. As ever direct intervention in food markets was avoided, while intervention through railway building would 'carry on without interruption or postponement'.[63] Private correspondence on India's fiscal position showed the strain on finances which Hamilton's commitment to rail expenditure implied. In December 1896, for example, Hamilton wrote to Viceroy Elgin complaining that the famine 'had been most inconsiderate in the date of its reappearance'. Famine costs placed him under pressure from the finance department to 'curb rail expenses' as he attempted to meet the budgeted payments. The currency depreciation, which made rail financing in sterling more expensive, gave the India finance minister a further excuse for rail cutbacks. Nevertheless, despite the increased foreign exchange cost of the railways and escalating famine costs, Hamilton concluded that they were 'justified in pushing on'.[64] With such a single-minded set of financing priorities, it is unsurprising that Bipan Chandra charted the beginning of nationalist agitation on the question of irrigation against railways as lying in the 'disastrous famine of 1897'.[65]

The subsequent 1899 Famine Commission, under the presidency of Sir James Lyall, was set up as a response to the emergency. It had a less wide-ranging remit than Strachey's 1880 commission. Lyall's commission was asked to focus on the extent to which famine code guidance had been followed and recommendations for future famines.[66] The report again lauded the expansion in railways, reduced sea freights and export growth which continued to homogenize grain prices across India. Many of the concerns mentioned in the 1880 report recurred in testimony to the 1898 commission, suggesting that progress had been slow. The optimism that railways were in their infancy and over time would relieve the problem of failed monsoons had faded by the end of the century. By 1898 price equalization together with the silver rupee depreciation continued to raise grain prices, seemingly permanently. It was crucial to discover whether the rise in Indian consumption (population related) had engendered an increase in demand unmatched by supply from new cultivation, or improved productivity. This represented 'a factor of the greatest importance as regards the future'.[67] Population outstripping production was viewed as creating a long-term upward movement in food prices, with Malthusian implications. In contrast finite railway development and currency depreciation (now curtailed by the closure of the mints) were one off inflationary pressures on food. Given the continued lobbying for more railways, the distinction with population growth was overstated. In fact, the report concluded that while railways equalized prices they tended to 'widen the area of scarcity' while 'lessening the intensity elsewhere' of the famine.[68] The optimistic interpretation of the railway was, as ever, to see it producing greater economic growth and wealth, so making increased prices affordable. The impoverished, in drought conditions, would feed on imported food.

Some of the witnesses, on whose evidence the 1898 report was supposedly based, did not agree. One Indian observer in Central Provinces and Berar, for example, stated that 'railways made it possible that we were starved to death as well as our neighbours', while at the same time making it 'very unlikely that we both be saved'. In contrast, without these price rises and redistribution of grain, only one of the two parties was at risk.[69] The railways had allowed improved living standards through trade and growth, but this had been accompanied by rising 'rates and taxes payable', according to another witness from the province. Railways had decimated the storage of grain, which was now exported, thus undermining self insurance.[70] Grain price rises in the Central Provinces were an intolerable 50 per cent to 100 per cent over recent years. The 'famine protective' Bengal–Nagpur railway, for example, had accelerated price increases in areas like Sambalpur to the extent that locals could not cope. That same district showed net exports of food during the famine. The export trade brought new demand and pushed grain prices higher, while the depreciating rupee made Indian grain relatively cheaper to the English and other foreigners.[71] Remarkably, for a terminus on a major famine protective railway, Nagpur suffered 'grain riots' in the middle of the famine, due to inflated food prices. In Dongargarh the experience of Nagpur was narrowly averted with the threat of severe punishment if problems arose. While the bordering state of Nandgaon attempted to override the price problem by fixing grain prices, the merchants and traders elected to transport their grain over the border to Dongargarh (presumably by rail) to enjoy unregulated prices. State intervention was undermined by transportation. The witness concluded fatalistically that any 'attempt to fix the prices causes famine, but does not diminish it'.[72] Regulating prices across the borders of British and Princely State India was problematic. In the Sagar (Saugor) district of the same 'famine protected' railway region, the population increased by 18 per cent, cultivable area by 48 per cent over 1865–95, but the new product was sent overseas, with wheat exports by rail rising from 40,000 maunds to an unsustainable 758,000 maunds over 1887–97.[73] A Calcutta agent told the Bengal hearing that railways had proven of much less use in the 1896/7 famine than its Madras/Bombay predecessor. The more recent drought had affected many more regions, so that better distribution failed to tackle low production across a wide region. Many areas fought to cling on to their scarce food supplies.[74]

Further, a number of witnesses complained that rail fare structures kept transportation costs higher than necessary, so failing to encourage required distribution. In this respect the findings of the 1880 commission had not been followed. Gujarat, for example, had suffered hugely in the recent famine through the starvation of cattle impoverishing livestock farmers. The hay required to keep animals alive was uneconomic to transport, given the railway company fare structure.[75] Further departures from laissez-faire policy were demanded from those in the worst affected regions. A witness from North Western Provinces and Oudh complained that no tariff reductions were made by the rail companies when famine was raging. Government could easily manipulate prices downwards by importing grain from overseas. More dramatically, a British missionary in Central Provinces/Berar argued that demand might have been tackled to reduce prices, by 'allowing the people to migrate freely to other provinces'. This dovetailed with the underlying British conviction that India suffered from a debilitating density of population, notwithstanding the evidence to suggest that India's overcrowding was less extreme than most of western Europe, including Britain.[76] However, the same Bishop C. F. Pelvert of Nagpur observed that in the Nagpur area, where peasants attempted to flee to railway stations to escape the worst of the famine, thousands of the desperate émigrés met 'untimely deaths' through the strain of the journeys on so little food. Had they been encouraged to stay in their districts with subsidized food, mortality figures in Nagpur would have been lower.[77] The promotion of railways in rural areas had been successful, but the effect of the new technology affected many aspects of famine relief. The implementation of railway-led relief was poor, and railway development in isolation was insufficient to ease poverty.

On a similar theme, little had been done constrain grain traders, who benefited from the railways. This was a pre-occupation at the time amongst policy makers.[78] It was suggested that 'banjaras' or local grain merchants had lost power in recent years to the larger merchants.[79] Elsewhere, in the district of Banda in NW Provinces/Oudh, a resident missionary complained that 'the middlemen, the banias, brokers, dalals and agents' had all benefited from the rise in wheat prices. The cultivators were so indebted to moneylenders that income from price rises went to moneylenders to pay off accrued interest which they had accumulated under lower prices, to avert foreclosure. Overall, the railways in that district had not proven 'a panacea for the evils' of famine. In Bengal, by contrast the 'middleman' was marginalized by the ability of cultivators to deal directly with end customers via the railways. The effect of such export business was seen as harmful since 'India was permitted to send away what she needed for her home use'.[80] Further, the other corporate beneficiary of famine insurance fund moneys, the Indian Midland Railway, was said to have prompted large wheat price rises in districts where the working population attained no offsetting rise in income. These included, 'the small shopkeepers, artisans ... professional classes just above them'.[81] Similarly, the larger group of unemployed agricultural workers lacked any 'hedge' against rising prices. This distorting role of grain merchants was attacked by another observer in NW Provinces/Oudh who saw grain merchants holding back grain supplies, with a view to dumping product when prices reached distressed levels. Meanwhile government failed to curb 'the free play of private trade' with marginal reductions in rail freight charges, and small loans to grain dealers. A number of other witnesses testified to the effectiveness of the system such that 'when crops fail and prices go up, private trade freely makes up the deficiency by imports'.[82] Witnesses from different regions gave nuanced reports on the role of middlemen and their effect on grain prices. Generalizations were difficult, as ever, in such an enormous land mass, but it was clear that railways had made prices more volatile, giving opportunities to speculators. Longer term, the classical economist might argue that these agents would accelerate equilibrium in the food market, but in the shorter term it made resource allocation more difficult. As in so many Indian commission reports, the detail of real testimony on these matters did not appear to find its way into the conclusions and summary report. In the distillation of the material a pro-railway bias was always present.

Many witnesses demanded more direct famine relief, through government-controlled supply, outside the control of the private railway companies. The shortcomings of laissez-faire were discernible at the start of the famine in 1896. Loveday pointed to food price rises not compensated by income rises, leaving India vulnerable to further famines.[83] Direct government intervention was required to overcome the income shortfall. Indeed, the 1898 Famine Commission had concluded that areas of highest relief saw lowest mortality.[84] However, the report broke down famine relief expenditure against railways and irrigation, to reveal the extent of railway bias. Over the period 1881–96, total famine relief expenditure was a modest Rs 3.13 million (£208,000), against £6.79 million on protective railways, and £1.21 million on irrigation. A further £3.55 million was credited to debt repayment, which appears to relate to further guaranteed 'protective' railways financed off balance sheet (in particular the controversial Southern Mahratta system).[85] Loveday's preferred direct relief had absorbed less than 2 per cent of famine-directed government expenditure.

In the same year, the Indian Charitable Relief Fund, a centralized charitable fundraising vehicle, published its first annual report highlighting government resistance to private contributions. The fund was founded on the basis that it was 'in a position to act with knowledge of the local circumstances'. The GOI lent support to the fund, conceding that it possessed the size and expertise to complement GOI and provincial government famine codes. However, by 1898 the relief fund was openly critical of the extent of direct GOI intervention and the complacency brought about through their faith in railways. The GOI hoped its famine code would allow government to take 'the place of [the] landlord to the agriculturalists', which was unrealistic. More damagingly the GOI's construction of 'a series of protective railways' across areas vulnerable to drought, which had occurred since the 1876–7 famines, meant that the 'danger of food-supply running short was not apprehended'.[86] The GOI may well have regretted allowing the charitable fund to go ahead given the level of criticism it gave to government. Calcutta had, after all, shunned domestic and overseas contributions. Nevertheless, some British public sympathy was pricked by newspaper coverage, growing socialist/radical comment and the British Committee of the Indian National Congress, leading to a modest charitable effort through the Mansion House funds of 1896–7.[87] Overseas charitable funding was opposed more stridently by Calcutta and Whitehall, concerned about foreign intervention in Empire matters. This came to a head with the Kaiser's support for Indian famine victims in 1900/1, in the context of German antagonism over the Boer War.[88]

1899–1900 Punjab, Rajputana, Central Province and Bombay Famine and Indian Famine Commission Of 1901

Lovat Fraser, editor of the *Times of India*, produced a heroic picture of British famine policy and railway building. Viceroys Elgin and Curzon were said to have competed with each other to leave the greatest legacy to India, in terms of railways sanctioned and constructed. This included significant railway investment in the native states, so that famine protection should have been improved across the subcontinent.[89] Looking back on the costly famine of 1899–1900 from the perspective of 1911, Fraser argued that it was impossible to understand how 'a single sensible Englishman' could criticize the famine protection and relief policies of that famine, or subsequently. The system, which had evolved for mitigating risks and effects of famine, was said to be 'admirable in conception, almost automatic in its operation, and unfailing in its efficacy'. While the Indian population had increased by over 100 million over the previous forty years, the railways had 'immensely simplified' food distribution over India.[90] However, the drought of 1899 occurring so rapidly after the prior famine tested even Fraser's optimistic assessment of famine protection. It affected an area of over 475,000 square miles, housing a population of 25 million in British India and 30 million in contiguous native states. Crops and water distribution failed, leading to cattle fodder shortages in areas like Gujarat. Viceroy Curzon wrote of the annihilation of 'the working capital of the agricultural classes'. Railway construction in the native states seemed not to have lessened the effects there, since Fraser identified vast emigration to British India where famine relief was more generous and better organized. The assumption that famine in India was a facet of distribution alone, rather than improved production and irrigation across the country was contradicted in Fraser's account. Lack of water supply (presumably accentuated by a inadequate investment in tanks and canals) had helped produce conditions across large regions of India 'of scarcity' turning to famine.[91] On closer examination Fraser had limited confidence in the competence of a technocratic ICS to handle famine.

The very occurrence of famine in 1899, within two years of the last, undermined confidence. The famine commission of 1880 had used precedent to predict an average of one drought every twelve years.[92] In appointing another famine commission so quickly after the last, Viceroy Curzon was alert to the need to avoid repeating analysis carried out so recently. He pressed the new commission to report speedily while memories of the famine were still fresh in people's minds.[93] As famine-protective railways were coming under the spotlight again, with drought across large areas of India, Curzon was wrestling with the intractable problem of railway administration, in setting up the Robertson Committee of 1901. Typically, Curzon had immersed himself in the detail of the subject, and argued that a technocratic 'railway board' might create consistency and objectivity in state protective railways. Curzon's contentment to focus on the detailed administrative matters of an Indian Railway Board was consistent with the conclusions of the Indian Famine Commission of 1901. That commission stated impressively that railways had now rid India of the 'final horror of famine', which was a shortage of food in large regions. While certain outlying mountains and valleys might still be inaccessible to locomotives, it was impossible to conceive of wide ranging scarcity on the level of 1876–8 or 1896–7. Perhaps as a riposte to the nationalist complaints about railway's role in undermining the old 'self insurance' system, the report applauded the contribution of such transport to 'the policy of famine insurance'.[94] In Darwinian terms, the report declared that any famine resultant of the loss of food to the export market would be part of the 'change in the habits of the people ... a regular attendant of progress ... a transient phase of a great economic movement, which makes for national prosperity'.[95] Famine relief would be used to tide Indian peasants over this 'transient phase' by which time the general level of wealth in the economy would be bolstered by trade and division of labour, as predicted by Adam Smith a century before. Such long-term analysis was an alternative to Hamilton's 'see saw' policy, but contradicted the earlier assertion that famine was a thing of the past (as did later shortages, notably the Bengal Famine of 1941).

However, some of the witnesses at the commission identified problems with rail distribution, which defied long-term solutions. Railways had, after all, been promising much since the 1870s. By 1900 cattle still perished in Gujarat because the cost of delivering hay by rail was simply too high in the Central Provinces. The Central Provinces were suffering badly by 1900 with a fall in population of some 8 per cent, and a mortality rate five times the projected level. This may have been compounded by the large export of grain by rail from the region over the previous five years. The report suggested that such grain traffic had been reversed in the face of the desperate situation, but in aggregate over that five-year period exports had exceeded imports by 20 per cent. In the summary findings the people of the Central Provinces, notwithstanding the high mortality rate being suffered, were said to have abandoned their view of railways as 'an aggravation of their ills' and to see them instead 'as their salvation'. Those who focused too much on grain exports rather than the more recent imports were forgetting the losses of 1837, 1866 and 1877 when millions died 'owing to the want of railways'.[96] The report failed to explain why millions were still dying despite railway infrastructure, especially in the Central Provinces. More railway capacity was always the solution proffered. Rolling stock was urgently required to increase the imports of food, and this would be paid for by the peasants themselves through their 'famine insurance grant'.[97]

These witnesses from the Central Provinces found support in the later account of Loveday. The historian pointed to the failure of fodder and grain crops by 1899 as more extreme than in the previous crises, and highlighted the unacceptable price of imported fodder. While famine relief in 1897 had met the challenge of 'the unwillingness of the hillsmen' to travel to the relief areas, by 1899–1900 the benefits of such relief were better understood. Now the perennial attempt to keep a lid on costs, especially while India was paying to station her troops in South Africa, came to the fore. There was a general 'lack of preparation' and the authorities could not cope with the number of peasants who 'flocked to them'.[98] In general the starvation levels were extreme over an affected population of some 59.5 million people, suggesting that the 'final horror of famine' was still very much present.[99]

While the authors of the report might have been premature in signalling the end of famine, they did at least appear to have paid attention to the pro-irrigation polemic of Cotton and Digby. However, in reaffirming a commitment to shift the focus of protective public works from railways to irrigation, they were only following the 1898 commission recommendations, which had been ignored.[100] Digby declared in 1901 that 'the members of a select committee of the House of Commons which, in 1878, conducted an inquiry into Public Works (East India) are primarily the authors of the recent famines'. These members had ignored Sir Arthur Cotton's advice of 1878, focusing on rail rather than irrigation. While the railways had allowed grain to be transported to famine districts in the 1900/1 famine, the price of the product had risen so high that millions could ill afford 'a daily sufficiency of food'.[101] Further, Digby seized on a speech by Horace Bell, former consultant to the GOI's state railways, widely reported in the Anglo-Indian newspapers in 1901. Bell's controversial speech highlighted the 1898 famine commission observation that the food production of British India was in deficit of 18 to 19 million tons over the years 1896–7, and suggested that 'an even greater deficiency' must have existed over the period 1898–1900 across the country.[102] This contradicted the assertion that Indian famines were distribution rather than production problems. The cost of importing grain from overseas was seen as uneconomic, without significant government support. Within India itself only Burma could offer significant foodstuffs (grain and especially rice) but the shipping and rail costs from that region made the likely grain/rice price 'prohibitive'.[103]

Bell failed to highlight that despite the expense of Burmese imports, some 95 per cent of the famine relief budget for Burma in the previous famine of 1896–7 had been spent on the Meiktila–Myingyan Railway, with 'labourers ... drafted from long distances to this work'.[104] That railway employed some 19,333 people on earth and ballast workings at a benefit to the company of £55,000. The timing of this cheap labour and additional revenue could hardly have been better for Burma Railway Company whose stock was floated one month before.[105] It begs the question as to why any famine relief was being paid to the Burma railway company, in a net food exporting region, while railway transportation costs stayed prohibitively high.[106] In fact, Lower Burma was exporting rice to Europe, dissatisfied by the profitability of the Indian market, including presumably Upper Burma.[107] Nevertheless, Bell took a more positive view than Digby on the benefits of railways. He had after all spent his whole life working in the industry. Bell's emphasis was closer to George Campbell, in calling for grain export bans during famines, and a return to self insurance. A system of railways 'without collateral safeguards' (like Burma Railways) was in Bell's view 'not an unmixed good'.[108]

While debate continued in the pages of British and Indian newspapers, parliamentary debate on Indian famine became more heated. By 1900 Hamilton admitted that, even with railways, the scale of famine problems were far worse than either 1876 or 1896. Notwithstanding the protective railways, the number on famine relief by July 1900 was a crippling 6.1 million, against relief payments to 3.3 million in July 1896. The most vulnerable region was Gujarat, which had not suffered drought for 100 years.[109] Everywhere the harvests had been decimated, with Bombay food production falling by £15 million. To balance the appalling news, Hamilton offered the distasteful 'silver lining' that the 'railways have given a very good return, nearly half a million in excess of the estimate'. Given that much of that return went to guaranteed bond and stockholders, this profit was unavailable for famine relief.[110] Hamilton was aware of the extent of price failure in the grain market, concluding that the crisis was 'not a famine of food, but a famine of wages'.[111] In fact it was both. Remarkably, given the evidence to the contrary, a Barnsley MP contributed to the debate with a eulogy for the railway system. According to Joseph Walton, the House needed to recognize the rail extension and irrigation investment served to 'increase the prosperity of India' and largely protected against 'the recurrence of famine'. Given that India was in the middle of a widespread famine, and poverty was necessitating extensive famine relief, both assumptions were questionable. The rhetoric was so inappropriate that the speaker of the house asked Walton to curb his acclaim for the Indian railways.[112] In the later debate, Samuel Smith, MP for Flintshire, distinguished between the two forms of public works. Had a portion of the £300 millions invested in railways over the previous fifty years gone to irrigation 'a great part of India would by this time have been beyond the reach of famine'. With investment targeted at rail, the land had been unable to yield enough to meet high land-tax assessments and a profusion of small cultivator bankruptcies had resulted. This was compounded by the laissez-faire sensibilities of the GOI, which left middlemen to prosper everywhere in the food production and distribution system. According to Smith, the usurious agricultural moneylenders would charge up to 3 per cent per month (or more than 36 per cent annually).[113]

Conclusion

Three major famines with the loss of between thirteen and sixteen million lives afflicted the Indian subcontinent over the period 1875–1914.[114] The exhaustive famine commission reports, supported by provincial famine codes, showed the capacity of the Raj to gather vast swathes of data and extract conclusions which reflected the underlying pressures to which the India Office and GOI was exposed. In the case of Indian famines this was, to a limited extent, the parliamentary and private outrage felt in Britain at the scale of these tragedies, and increasingly a nationalist voice which charted the links between poverty and famine and rebuked the British for failing to tackle the causes of poverty in India. More than this, there was a consistent wish to keep Indian finances outside the remit of the Imperial government, so that the India Office could remain 'gloriously detached' in a way that the Colonial Office, for example, could never attain.[115] Free grants from Westminster were resisted by Hamilton, as the GOI struggled to balance its books during the 1896–7 and 1899–1900 famines. Overseas charity, and even domestic charity, was discouraged. Meanwhile railway expenditure continued with little need to justify the vast expense or document the contributions made to famine relief. The annual reports of the second generation Indian rail companies devoted no space to famine relief, and there was little questioning of senior rail executives during the extended hearings for the three famine commissions. Even after the resistance mounted by Salisbury to irrigation had fallen away, and the 1898 commission followed Cotton in pressing canals and water tanks ahead of more railways, nothing happened.

The Bombay Chamber of Commerce memorial to the 1880 commission was long and revealing. It focused exclusively on the encouragement of trade through railways. The link with reduced poverty and eventually famine protection/relief was oblique and unproven. The railways themselves practised a buy-British approach and were supported by the Chambers precisely because they transported Lancashire cloth quickly and safely to the interior of India, and exported food and raw materials to the coast. This is what Bipan Chandra has termed the transformation of India 'into an agricultural colony of Britain'.[116] Beneath the surface of the famine commission discussions, and British thinking on Indian famines was a suspicion that the culture of India was to blame, and that the density of population in the country was reflective of 'moral' shortcomings. Even when it was admitted that Britain itself had a higher density of population than India, the defenders of British policy pointed to Britain's enviable ability to import half her foodstuffs from abroad. In this context, the modernizing power of the railway sat comfortably with the view that India would transform herself economically and 'morally' in the long term. Short-term irritants like grain traders, moneylenders and spiralling grain prices could be safely ignored as Naoroji's 'magic wheels' rolled forward. Unfortunately, modernization through railways was not instantly transferable into India. In testimony to the Bombay section of the 1898 famine commission, a witness remembered problems amongst the Khandesh people, who resisted transportation by rail to reach food, for fear that they would be slaughtered and their fat used for 'greasing railway carriage wheels'.[117]

The railways were presented by the British as a self-contained solution to famine and underlying economic poverty. In fact neither of these related problems could be tackled in such an exclusive manner. Without the multiplier and accelerator aspects of railway investment which benefited the other railway powers of the time, little was done to relieve poverty and Amartya Sen's exchange problems remained. While the British did start to channel more money into irrigation after the famine of 1899/1900 and a catastrophe on that scale was avoided again until the Second World War, the opportunity cost of railway investment had delayed that industrialization.

3 MILITARY RAILWAYS IN INDIA, 1875–1914: RUSSOPHOBIA, TECHNOLOGY AND THE INDIAN TAXPAYER

Introduction

According to W. J. Macpherson, in his succinct assessment of Indian railway investment over the period 1845–75, the Government of India (GOI) wanted railways for 'social, economic, and perhaps mainly military reasons'. The stimulus for strategic railways in Macpherson's earlier period was the trauma of the Sikh wars and crucially, the Indian Mutiny. Inadequate troop transportation was said to have made the British response to the Mutiny slow and inadequate.[1] Over time the strategic rationale for railway construction shifted from Indian security concerns to the external threat of foreign invasion. This prompted continued expenditure on strategic railways, with a focus on the Afghan and Persian border areas, where the Russian threat was most prominent. Further, Burma presented concerns about the prospect of joint Russian/French incursions, especially after their alliance of the 1890s, requiring railways to transport troops and supplies.[2]

While the GOI sought to distinguish between 'productive' railways, which would meet financial targets, and 'protective' lines which had military or famine-protective qualities, the distinction was less clear cut. Private-sector rail companies generated revenues from troop and material transport, paid for by the army, while state-owned military railways performed a 'development' role in the north of India. Indeed, over the period 1889–94, only 8.5 per cent of revenues from government-defined 'military railways' came from military traffic. In times of peace, the railways had no need to transport troops and provisions.[3] The commercial attributes were stressed to justify escalating military budgets. By 1906 Viceroy Minto argued that plans to scale back 'strategic' railways in northern India risked delaying economic growth by ten years.[4] Hence, segmenting the nearly £300 million aggregate Indian rail investment between defence and commercial/famine aspects is problematical. However, in the period 1875–1914 strategic concerns were heightened, prompting greater focus on military mobility. Britain fought a second Afghan war and annexed Upper Burma.[5] Meanwhile, in 1885, Russia attacked Afghans at Pendjeh and proceeded with its 'step by step' colonization of Central Asia.

With the technology of warfare changing, as shown by the US Civil War and Franco–Prussian Wars, there was concern about Russian railway construction deep into its new Central Asian empire. The construction of the Russian Transcaspian and Orenburg–Tashkent Railways in the late nineteenth century was a cause for disquiet at the India Office, GOI, Foreign Office and War Office.[6] However, the differing reports produced in different British government departments suggest a consistent failure to evaluate the strategic significance of Russian railways. Exaggerated claims were made about the rapidity of potential Russian troop movements to the border of India, while limited attention was paid to Russian financial constraints. Analysing the threat of Russian incursions through Afghanistan or Persia made it difficult for British strategists to consider all the permutations of Russian railway war. The role of Afghan and Persian natives and border tribes in Central Asia was uncertain. Joint Russian and French intentions on the Burmese border complicated matters, as did the complexity of 'Great Power' politics around the Baghdad Railway. With uncertain intelligence and so many variables the capacity within British and Indian military circles to agree on a 'forward' or 'wait and see' policy was limited. Strong personalities like Salisbury, Curzon, Roberts, Kitchener and Balfour brought their own subjective judgements on railway matters. They struggled to distinguish commercial from military railways on the Russian side, and were subject to enormous pro-railway bias from the press and general public at times of heightened Russophobia. Even after the Russian defeat to Japan and the Anglo–Russian entente, suspicions remained about the Russian railway infrastructure, by then state controlled by Sergei Witte.

W. P. Andrew and the Move from Internal to External Strategic Focus

William Patrick Andrew was one of the three key promoters of Indian railways in the mid nineteenth century. He wrote prolifically on the subject, and played an active role as Chairman of the Scinde and Punjab Railway Company.[7] While Andrew saw significant commercial and cultural advantages in the spread of efficient communications through the subcontinent, he viewed the internal and external security benefits of railways as primary. This followed Lord Dalhousie's original railway minute of April 1853, which had promoted military trunk lines between Presidencies. Andrew developed Dalhousie's arguments, pressing the strategic benefits of new white settlement from Britain, facilitated by railways. With 100,000 Europeans safely settled in the foothills of the Himalayas, connected and supplied by rail, all 'native treason' and 'Russian aggression' could be controlled. Only the cooler climates of the higher altitudes could be expected to encourage such emigration from Britain. The mountains would be accessed by railways.[8] Further, in 1857 at the height of the Mutiny, Andrew criticized the failure to realize Dalhousie's ambitious rail links. Had trunk routes between Calcutta and Delhi, and between Karachi and Lahore, been in place, railways would have prevented the insurgency. The ability to deliver troops 'with vigour and promptitude' rather than 'after eleven months of exhausting marches' would have been decisive.[9] However, the normally supportive *Railway Times* disagreed, arguing that insufficient loyal troops would have been available to exploit railways.[10] Railways were seen as requiring additional military resources, in contrast to Andrew who viewed enhanced troop mobility facilitating lower troop numbers. In Andrew's support, the *Lahore Chronicle* in 1857 had called for 10,000 soldiers with rail infrastructure, in preference to 30,000 travelling on foot.[11] Indeed, Marx had argued that Indian 'railways will afford the means of diminishing the amount and the cost of the military establishments'. Food and other supplies would be shipped in more regularly, and storage of essentials lessened. The health of East India Company troops would be improved, since they could be accommodated in areas less subject to disease, moving in and out as required, so reducing the cost of the army.[12]

Andrew saw that many opportunities, highlighted by Marx, had been missed. The failure to invest liberally in railways before the Mutiny risked being repeated on the North West Frontier of the 1870s. Russian armies alone, or in concert with Persians, could move rapidly to the North West Frontier via Russia's new strategic lines. The Russians were building offensive rail capability covertly, under the guise of commercial transportation. Andrew pressed government support for his own Indian railway company as a means of pre-empting the Russian advance. In 1879, a special commission was set up to report on army reorganization and expenditure in India. This gave further support to Andrew's polemic. The army commission stressed the primacy of transportation in effecting concentrated and rapid troop movements around India when internal and external problems occurred. This would avoid the problem of exhausted soldiers being made to march vast distances on foot. Again, the mutiny had taught lessons. The move to Delhi by Indian army troops was said to have been seriously delayed at Umballa in May 1857, when insufficient 'carriage' was made available. The army failed to deliver the required 'sharp, prompt blows' to gain momentum over the rebels.[13] By contrast, the railway programme had improved the ability to concentrate troops around a terminus. This could be done more efficiently than in Britain, where the government was required to use the Army Regulation Act of 1871 to requisition commercial railways for military purposes. In India that power was permanently vested in the GOI. However, transportation from rail terminus to 'local disturbance' was equally crucial. Reports produced in response to the 1879 commission focused on this problem, with detailed discussions on camel and elephant transportation, and concerns about the difficulties of transporting carriage animals on railways. Elephants, which had previously provided much of this carriage, were too large to travel by train. The GOI expressed concern about a slump in elephant prices as now redundant elephants would be 'dumped' on the market.[14]

While Andrew received strong support in his efforts to maximize railway mileage (both trunk and local), there was less consensus on railway gauges. In the long-running 'battle of the gauges', Richard Temple and Richard Strachey promoted one metre gauges, which were cheaper and easier to construct. Andrew pressed for the more robust 5' 6 inch width. Proponents of the wide gauge argued that avoiding having to change locomotive on long military journeys was imperative, to achieve the speed and reliability needed to access points of conflict. The matter became prominent in political debate, with Gladstone promising the House that the question would not be settled until a full Commons debate had occurred. By 1873, the dual government was split, with Viceroy Northbrook supporting Andrew's call for universal wide gauge, while Secretary of State Argyll (with an eye to economy) called for a narrow military gauge on construction beyond Lahore. Gladstone was urged to meet with Andrew to be made aware of the military implications of Argyll's decision. Many years after his early publications, Andrew was still the acknowledged authority on all strategic railways in India. He responded with a lengthy memorial to Gladstone setting out the impressive list of supporters for his somewhat arcane concern.[15] Argyll held firm and was able to secure Gladstone's support for flexibility in the use of narrow and wide gauges. Ironically, within four years, the military combatants motivating Andrew's concerns would discover for themselves the problem of transporting troops on inconsistent railway lines. Russian locomotives struggled to overcome the defences of Turkish narrow gauges when approaching the border from their own Russian broad gauge.[16]

By 1889, two years after Andrew's death, a joint memorandum of the India Office and War Office was produced for the British Cabinet, concerned with the new Russian Transcaspian Railway. The report argued that military planners should now focus on external matters since a repeat of the Indian Mutiny was 'no longer within the region of probability'. Railways and telegraph communications had 'facilitated strategical concentrations', and the Arms Act had removed weaponry from 'the civil population'.[17] However, without robust defences against Russian strategic railways, another Indian Mutiny might recur. Russian domination of Afghanistan or Persia, through extended Central Asian railways, might allow the rival Great Power to spread discord into Northern India or the plains of Punjab.[18] By that time, the scale of construction required pushed strategic railways beyond the resources of entrepreneurs like W. P. Andrew, even supported by government guarantees. The newly merged/nationalized North

Western Railway Company was expected to protect Indian taxpayers against the inefficiencies of the private sector in the context of defence.

The North Western Railway Company

Andrew's military railway grouping in the North West of India commanded enormous support as a panacea for related matters of internal and external security. Over time, under the beneficial guarantee arrangements, his business was protected by the India Office/GOI and allowed to develop a regional monopoly on transportation. Such regional monopolies became more widespread over time, amongst famine-protective and commercial railways. By the early 1860s the Scinde Railway Company controlled the steam navigation business (Indus Flotilla Company), together with the Punjab Railway and Delhi Railway companies, all under an agency arrangement. As ever, such government-sponsored 'agency' arrangements allowed centralized control with capital being provided by other people. In 1869, while Viceroy Lawrence moved railway finance towards state funding, Andrew's military lines were left under private control. Instead, river competition was removed with the closing down of the Indus Flotilla. Railway assets were merged into the Scinde, Punjab and Delhi Railway Company. This private/government-guaranteed ownership remained for a further sixteen years until a generous state buyout of the amalgamated line was implemented. In 1886 the North Western State Railway Company was formed, with Andrew's businesses being merged into smaller state controlled regional lines.[19] In the twenty years to 1901, the North Western Railway Company (North Western) had amalgamated most of the military lines in the Punjab and border regions, absorbed £33 million of capital from the government, and produced losses of half that amount. The total absorption of taxpayers' money in North Western and its predecessor organizations was £50 million. Nationalist Dinshaw Wacha complained that these costs were kept outside the military budget of the GOI, residing as a hidden military expenditure in the Public Works Department.[20] The North Western by then held all pure military/strategic lines, so that losses were bound to be greater than those incurred by other guaranteed or state lines. However, Wacha's complaints about lax accounting and financial controls were pertinent, given the size of the undertaking. Indeed, prior to partition, North Western made up 26 per cent of the mileage of the Indian rail network, and subsequently 34 per cent of Pakistan's rail capacity, within the Pakistan Western Railway.[21]

The 'pure' military business therefore absorbed somewhere between a quarter and a third of railway resources over the period. This was carried out under guaranteed and later state arrangements in a manner which attracted some criticism. In a wide ranging attack on the military lines of the North West Frontier, written in 1896, an ex-employee of North Western gave concrete examples of inefficiencies and unnecessary costs in construction, financing and operations. The Scinde–Punjab had been granted a government guarantee of five per cent in the 1860s, but struggled to attract London investors. All Indian related businesses had become unfashionable after the trauma of the Mutiny, and financiers like Overend Gurney (later victims of the bank crisis of 1866) resisted subscribing for additional stock. Scinde Punjab's military characteristics and modest financial prospects made it more vulnerable to 'bearish' sentiment. Financiers, working with the company, placed buy requests for the stock in the London press to create a false sense of demand for the new 'scrip' issue, while Overend was employed to buy the stock as agent of the company. As the stock rose quickly from £76 to £84 pounds, all banks and investors in the company-sponsored consortium dumped their securities in the market, to leave smaller investors holding the overhang of new stock at rapidly declining prices. The company's behaviour was described as 'culpable negligent extravagance' and reputedly left a number of Anglo-Indian families on 'the verge of ruin'.[22]

The tensions between 'military men' at the company pressing for completion of strategic lines, and financiers within and without the company were plain. A group of ex-Bengal Artillery officers plotted retribution against City speculators, and sent one of their colleagues to the City to better understand City practices. This was likened to sending an 'honorable player' to compete with 'a card-sharper and his pals on Epsom downs on the Derby day'. The visitor to London was refused entry to the Royal Exchange, but was able to revive the fortunes of the Punjab and Delhi Railway by talking up their prospects.[23] The manipulation of stock market sentiment might help to raise some new finance but cost inefficiencies, which blighted all guaranteed Indian railways, were prominent at North Western and its predecessor organizations. The author highlighted lead and 'petty' contractors on military railways. All construction passed through such 'agents', who were protected from criticism by engineers, within the intimate Anglo-Indian community. It was unlikely that a superfluous agent would incur complaints from an engineer with whom he had just shared 'breakfast or tiffin'. The contractors working on North Western were an elite group who had created indispensable links with the company. Many had worked as engineers on the 'Sind-Pishin' or 'Bholan' lines, before moving into agency functions.[24]

In fact, North Western's average construction costs of approximately £20,000 per mile compared to Russia's strategic railway spend of only £4,500 per mile, suggesting that British Indian rail defences were an expensive method of combating Russian incursions into Central Asia.[25] North Western's contractors struggled to avoid fraud and overcharging on contracts. Railway sleepers presented particular opportunities for 'sharp practice' on the part of suppliers. The North Western paid for 80,000 sleepers, only receiving 50,000 on one occasion. Another time, the quality of the sleepers provided was inadequate, prompting

North Western to sell the sleepers for a negligible sum only to buy the same product back at full price. The guaranteed railway companies had no incentive to enforce stricter purchasing methods and there was immense loyalty amongst these thieves. Moreover, guaranteed companies like Scinde–Punjab were no worse than the state lines like Punjab Northern State Railway. The latter's construction on lines from Lahore to Peshawar were likened to laying 'a sheet of silver, the thickness of a rupee' over the entire distance. Indeed, the virtues of better managed guaranteed lines like EIR and GIPR were highlighted by the author, in contrast to the state-run North Western.[26] As in all areas of Indian rail development, the public/private sector management/ownership debate on military lines appeared irresolvable. Indeed, the extent to which railways were an effective defence against Russia's Central Asian Empire, under any economic method, was the subject of great debate.

Influence of the American Civil War and Franco–Prussian War on British Railway Strategy

The enormous costs incurred in military railways needed to be justified in a period of severe fiscal constraint. While some commercial benefits could be claimed for the state and guaranteed strategic lines, the military arguments were pre-eminent. Most of the historiography on Indian railways and defence policy in this period assumes complete consensus amongst intelligence officers on the primacy of new transport technology for fighting wars in general, and defending India in particular. While the observations of Karl Marx and W. P. Andrew seem plausible, the empirical evidence of railways delivering value for money in warfare was less compelling. The American Civil War and German Wars of Unification were two precedents, which might have provided evidence on the advent of 'railway wars'. In fact, the railway focus of both conflicts was linked. General Von Moltke dominated Prussian strategic thinking throughout the mid-nineteenth century. He had followed the US Civil War closely, sending a senior Prussian observer to America. Von Moltke's officer must have been impressed at the Union forces' capacity to move 80,000 men some 1,200 miles from Virginia to Tennessee in 1863, in only seven days.[27] The US Civil War ended only one year before the Austro–Prussian War began. Railways failed to make much impact in that conflict, but over the next four years Prussian rail capacity was built up for military purposes. By 1870 the Prussian railway force available for the assault on France consisted of some 3,881 locomotives, 6,151 passenger cars, 86,299 baggage cars, delivered over nine lines at up to seventy trains per day.[28] However, the hegemony of Prussian railways in the German wars of Unification was subsequently challenged by scholars. In fact by 1870, it was the superior French railway system which facilitated the Prussian encirclement of Paris, after victories at Sedan and Metz. Defensive railways were used by the offensive power in a precedent which should have worried railway 'forward-ists' in British India. After using French railways to surround Paris, the Prussians plundered the rich agricultural resources of France, which minimized the use of Prussian railways for supplies. Von Moltke's armies turned the outskirts of Paris into a 'gigantic food producing machine'.[29] This experience seemed to contra-dict the theory of Friedrich List, whose key work on military railways argued that high specification rail lines would advantage the defending power in whose terrain the investment was made, consistent with the British Indian strategy.[30] However, by 1903, in the context of Indian railways, Prime Minister Balfour was challenging List's assumption that railways benefited the defending power.[31]

Earlier, the British had sent military observers to America and France to analyse these mid-nineteenth-century 'railway' conflicts. National Archive records suggest that the significance of railway capacity for the American unionists and Prussians was understood in Britain. British military attaches, who accompanied the French and Prussian armies over 1870–1, reported back to the War Office with a balanced view of the potency of railway war. Prussian troop movements were constrained by civilian railway workers administering troop movements. Future India Coun-cil member, Lieutenant Colonel Chesney, criticized shortcomings in the Prussian Railway 'Abtheiling', which was not upgraded for the French campaign after the Austrian confrontation of 1866.[32] Where the Prussians had operated efficiently was in transporting their sick and wounded from the battlefield by train, but this was unlikely to be replicated in Britain or India since English rail carriages were inadequate.[33] List's promotion of strategic railways for defensive purposes attracted support from a British military observer at Metz and Strasbourg during 1870–1. The French railways might have been used to improve French troop mobility, and could have been sabotaged to prevent Prussian advances by the demolition of bridges as French forces retreated west towards Paris.

In fact, Prussian railway wars were said to display less impressive tactics than the American Unionists.[34] British military files refer frequently to the strategy of General Ulysees S. Grant. A later CID paper on the defence of India, for exam-ple, gave details of the remarkable Union achievement in supplying 100,000 men and 35,000 animals over 196 days during the Civil War, by way of the 5,000-mile Louisville to Atlanta railway.[35] Further, the Prussian and American experience was seen by General Frederick Roberts (Commander in Chief in India during the later nineteenth century) as relevant to India. He saw India as akin to con-tinental Europe rather than other British Empire theatres of war. Addressing an audience of army officers of the 'Eastern Command' in 1905, Roberts described the vulnerability of the North West Frontier from large land borders placing India 'in the position of a continental nation'. This necessitated a continental approach to warfare, with the army taking precedence over the traditionally dominant Royal Navy. However, even the pro-army Roberts failed to question whether the Royal Navy could deliver their part of Indian defence, in terms of seaborne troop reinforcements to Karachi. The lack of Royal Navy compatibility with an Indian railway war was a legitimate concern.[36]

While Robert's memoirs display no great strategic or technical insight comparable to Clausewitz/Moltke, his policy was borne of long experience in his rise 'from subaltern to commander-in-chief'.[37] He frequently displayed familiarity with the writings of Von Moltke, quoting from the German *Preuszische Zeitung* that 'railways are nowadays the life source of all "great military operations"'.[38] Equally, the exchange of information between Roberts and German counterparts is evident in his memoirs. In August 1881, for example, Roberts spent three weeks with Emperor William I of Germany, watching military manoeuvres at Hanover and Schleswig-Holstein. The invitation was reciprocated in 1885. As the annexation of Upper Burma was proceeding, Roberts invited two senior representatives of the German Emperor to watch British/Indian troop movements outside Delhi. The background to these war games was described by Roberts as a response to the 'many weak points in the Commissariat and Transport Departments' evidenced the previous year in a trial mobilization.[39] In short, while General Von Moltke's own accounts of Prussian railway achievements were questioned by the British, railways had become an accepted focus of Robert's strategy by the late nineteenth century, partly through observations in Prussia and the USA. In that sense, W. P. Andrew, in emphasizing the primacy of railway investment for the defence of India, was pushing at an open door.[40]

Russia's Transcaspian and Orenburg–Tashkent Railways as a Threat to British India

Van Creveld noted the early use of strategic railways by Russia. In 1846, they moved a corps of 14,500 men, together with all its horses, some 200 miles from Hradisch to Cracow in two days.[41] However, by the time of the Crimean War of 1854–6 the Russians still had no rail links between Moscow/St Petersburg and the Crimea, meaning they were unable to replenish supplies under siege from the British/French/Turkish forces. In a CID report, written much later in the context of Indian defence, Russia's defeat was put down to a combination of 'defective communications' and 'the state of her finances'.[42] The massive railway building programme undertaken by Russia over succeeding decades to supply Central Asia was viewed by the British as a response to the failures of the Crimea. However, there was little questioning by the British of the extent to which Russia's weak finances would constrain her aggression. The British in India continued to pursue an arms race focused on railway construction as the Tsarist economy fell further behind Western Europe in industrialization.

In March 1903, Roberts, by then Commander in Chief of the British Army, wrote a memorandum on the 'military defence of India' for the CID. He recommended changes in strategy resultant of Russian rail expansion and territorial incursions in Central Asia. The 'presence of Russian Emissaries at Cabul' had pushed Britain into two costly Afghan Wars. Like Macgregor, his deputy in the second campaign, Roberts saw Russia threatening through control of buffer states. However, in 1838 and again in 1878, Russian rail communications proved inadequate for facilitating troop and logistics movements. During the Second Afghan War, for example, it would have taken the Russian troops six months to reach Samarkind from their rail terminus at Orenburg. In contrast, by the time of Roberts's memorandum, the Transcaspian Railway, linking Russia with Samarkind via the Caspian Sea, had been open for seventeen years. In addition, the Orenburg and Tashkent Railway was to be completed within a couple of years, which promised access to the Oxus River. Roberts saw the former railway as a key strategic change in the region, and argued that through that construction effort Russia had 'overcome enormous difficulties far greater than any that now remain to be surmounted between the Oxus and the Indus'. The Russian confrontation with Afghanistan at Pendjeh had been a lost opportunity for Britain to finally displace Russia in the affections of the Afghan Amir. Had Britain confronted the Russians over their slaughter of several hundred Afghans, 'the Ruler whom we subsidize might be guided by our advice and welcome our assistance, if threatened by Russia.'[43]

The extent to which the later 1880s represented a point of inflection for British policy toward Russia was manifest in Curzon's 1889 analysis of Russia's Transcaspian Railway. His book amalgamated a series of newspaper articles written during a journey along the length of the railway the previous year. Its purpose, according to the book's dedication, was to forge a middle way between the 'Russophobes who mislead others, and Russophiles whom others mislead.'[44] Curzon claimed his book represented the first significant English language publication on Central Asia in five years. During that time the railway had 'modified if not revolutionised' the situation in the region. While Curzon (like Macgregor) remained unconvinced about the Russian appetite for incursions into British India, he saw that Russia might wish to secure a stronger position in Europe by weakening England in Asia.[45] He charted Russia's plans to build the Transcaspian Railway from its early occupation of Turkestan in 1865 through to the campaign against the Turkomans in 1877, at which point the centre of Russia's Asian focus shifted from Turkestan to Transcaspia. Work on the railway was planned over 1879–80 and locomotives were operating on the first section by December 1881. The Russians appeared to have noted the shortcomings in Prussian civil rail administration, centralizing control of all labour and materials for railway construction through their war ministry in St Petersburg.

Military dominance of the railway was overt, with engines 'driven by soldiers', and officers becoming 'station-masters', while soldiers made up most of the other railway staffing.[46] However, Curzon foresaw weaknesses in Russian railways for offensive purposes. Russian lines were mismatched with British Indian gauges. While European Russia used a 5 ft gauge, the British Indian 5ft 6 inch or metre gauge would have presented problems for Russian forces crossing the border, comparable to those encountered earlier in the Russo–Turkish confrontation. Against this, Russia was producing offensive capability at a fraction of the cost of the British defensive lines. Russian controls were impressive, keeping construction costs in Central Asia down to £4,500 per mile. The Transcaspian used second-hand rails from other regions and cheap labour, without the burden of English-style rail contractors. Curzon had no ideological attachment to private sector military railways, as pursued in India, and identified the excessive 'agency' costs incurred in the British 'mixed economy'. He correctly anticipated that the Russians would extend their cost effective railways to Pendjeh, but exaggerated Russian rail ambitions in predicting that many then living would see Russian rail termini deep inside Afganistan at Herat.[47]

The future Viceroy avoided detailed analysis of the sustainability of Russian military expenditure, given the Tsar's limited borrowing capacity. Precise economic analysis was never his strength, but he was able to see benefits outside Britain's free trade/laissez-faire culture. Curzon pointed to certain financial advantages in Russia's 'national economic policy'. Russia's trade protection 'from the Baltic to the China seas' formed a key component of what he viewed as a centralist/mercantilist state. These trade barriers to British goods could be expected to extend to Afghanistan, once Russia's rail links to the tribal region had enhanced Russo–Afghan trade further, in a land once seen as 'the private preserve of English traders'. In time the commercial links between the two countries would allow political dominance of Afghanistan by St Petersburg, affected through its railways. Further, Russian railway ownership avoided the uncomfortable hybrid private/public approach, which had evolved in British India. Private companies had been mooted in Russia as possible purchasers of strategic rail lines, particularly in view of the fact that the Transcaspian was profitable. However, the concept of private share issues, akin to the new generation of Indian-guaranteed rail companies was dismissed by Russians as being 'in direct conflict with the present imperial policy'.[48] In maintaining cost effective government control of railway development, the Tsardom was able to build prestige in the area through spectacular public works. The audience for this would be the Afghans and Persians, who were being courted by both powers. Curzon was fatalistic, concluding that Russia's 'railway in the deserts of Central Asia is a far more wonderful thing to the Eastern mind' than Britain's which ran 'through the teeming territories of Hindustan'.[49] In showing the achievements of Russian engineering to Persian observers, the architects of the Transcaspian would improve their chances of attaining rail concessions across Persia itself. While Russia had already made incursions into Northern Persia and Khorassan, her real ambition was to build railway lines all the way to the Straits of Ormuz or the Indian Ocean. Thus railways would secure for Russia another of its strategic aims: to develop great naval power status in the Persian Gulf, so threatening the Royal Navy. Curzon's wish to deter Russia from this prompted relentless British focus on strategic railways towards the Persian–Afghan frontier province of Seistan.[50]

Curzon's newspaper accounts were supplemented by other correspondents in *The Times*. A detailed description of the scale of the Transcaspian line was given by the St Petersburg correspondent at its opening in 1886. The journalist catalogued some sixty-three stations constructed from the Caspian Sea to Samarkind. He highlighted controversy within the Russian administration, where the ex-Governor General of Turkestan had been dismissed from military duties for criticizing the strategic qualities of the Transcaspian. The official had ridiculed Russian claims that they could transport 200,000 troops to Afghanistan in two years. While *The Times* correspondent dismissed Russian criticism of the railway as exaggerated, he had been advised not to travel on the line himself due to the 'single line' aspect, and the lack of irrigation and water supply at various stations.[51] Further criticism of the Transcaspian was given by intelligence branch observers in 1887. They argued that the railway route was 'strategically faulty' over at least 250 miles, where it ran parallel to the Persian border. The line was placed at the foot of a range of hills said to provide excellent cover for groups of tribesmen wanting to sabotage the line. Notwithstanding this weakness, the report concluded that the Transcaspian was 'a strategic success' in reducing the time taken to move a Russian division from the Caspian to within range of the Afghan border to only twenty days.[52] By 1891 Curzon wrote to *The Times* warning of further extensions of the railway from Dushak on the main line to the Afghan frontier at Sarakhs (70 miles from the border). Such a development could be expected to further threaten the key Afghan stronghold of Herat, near the Persian border. From there, Curzon suggested that the 'Persian and Afghan capitals are the real destinations'. Further evidence of Russian military aggression was clear in the 'exclusive control' of the Transcaspian by Russia's military department. Curzon's tone in the newspaper was altogether more alarmist than in his earlier book. He concluded that a 'little cloud is forming on the horizon ... Let us keep our eyes on it as it swells upon the heavens'.[53]

While Prime Minister Salisbury shared Curzon's concerns about Russian railways, he argued Britain might contain Russian rail expansion using London's potent influence in financial markets. Limited demand for Russian domestic funding, or 'Treasury money', might require Russia to fund internationally through 'the market'. Britain could portray such investments as implying 'a hostile act' and make plain that any future annexing of Russian railway lines by Britain in war would imply no compensation for shareholders. Salisbury assessed that this would 'prevent money being raised on any Bourse in Europe'. The Prime Minister's observations were a rare example of the British seeking to assess the constraints imposed on their regional foe, by the same financial limitations which had cost Russia dear in the Crimea.[54] The economic limitations of the Transcaspian were further emphasized by Captain A. C. Yale writing in 1891, who pointed out that the railway fell some 250 to 300 miles short of Herat or Balkh, as key strategic settlement points in Afghanistan. Meanwhile the railway transported little other than cotton, and the 'Turcomans' grew only enough grain for themselves, leaving Russian forces short of supplies on the route from Merv to Herat. Moreover, were Russians to reach Herat it would require a massive development of the area to sustain a repopulated military base. Herat's food supplies could support no more than 12,000 men. Yale contended that German observers had exaggerated the capacity of the Transcaspian to concentrate and maintain Russian troops at Herat. German claims that some 190,000 troops could be maintained in this manner were railway hyperbole worthy of Von Moltke himself.[55]

By 1900, the British focus was on the new Orenburg–Tashkent railway which was expected to transport troops to another part of the Afghan border, east of the Transcaspian termini.[56] This would threaten Kabul more directly and allow Russian incursions via Afghanistan without having to send supplies across the Caspian Sea. The railway brought the centre of European Russia some 2,000 miles closer to the Chinese border. Again, *The Times* followed developments closely, reporting that large parts of the railway line were subject to flooding by Central Asian rivers. This might have been expected to reduce concerns about the efficacy of large Russian troop movements. Nevertheless, by October 1904 *The Times* referenced articles from the *Moscow Gazette* pressing the strategic significance of the 1,900 kilometre line for Afghan, and possibly Manchurian, operations by Russia. China had by then become a key focus for railway related British Russophobia, notably concerning the Trans-Siberian Railway. *The Times* contended that Britain should localize any confrontation which threatened India. The obvious means of achieving this was new Indian railways, facilitating concentrated troop movements.[57] Significantly, the Orenburg–Tashkent line had been the focal point for a massive war game carried out by the Indian Army at Simla in 1903. Strikingly, the Franco–Russian military alliance was overshadowed in British thinking by concerns about Russian railways, in a detailed report of over 200 pages. Correspondence followed which showed poor British intelligence on the speed of Russian rail construction. The war game report concluded that Russia could rapidly move 100,000 troops across the Afghan border, with 300,000 in reserve, but the speed of rail construction implied was unrealistic. Again, the threat posed by Russian railways was exaggerated.[58]

With Russian railways creating heightened concern in British military circles, the CID meetings over the period 1900–7 focused on India. In particular, the Orenburg–Tashkent railway figured prominently in minutes. The line was due for completion by 1905. This led the British War Office to raise their estimate of Russian troops transportable to the Afghan front, within five months, from 150–200,000 to 300,000.[59] Accordingly, the size and speed of British troop concentrations needed to repel the Russians in Afghanistan had increased. An additional 100,000 British/Native troops would be required. The Railway arms race entertained by the British was far from achieving the troop reductions and military cost savings promised by W. P. Andrew and Marx.[60] This had important implications for Indian/Afghan/Persian rail construction by the British. Further, the Indian Commander in Chief Kitchener made criticisms of the War Office analysis of Orenburg–Tashkent. Kitchener posited an extension of the Russian railway from Samarkind to the Afghan border at Termez by 1905. In a wide-ranging critique of what was viewed as complacency by the War Office, apparently goaded on by Curzon's Russophobia, Kitchener argued that carrying capacity on all Russian railways had been underestimated.[61] The uncertainty on intelligence provided ammunition for both Russophiles and Russophobes. Kitchener appeared to exaggerate the rapidity with which Orenburg–Tashkent could be built. The threat posed by a Russian railway line to British India rested on the determination of the Tsar to press forward with aggressive troop movements. This was a dangerous policy for the Tsar, since it risked war with British and Native armies while potentially alienating Russia's sympathizers in Afghanistan and Persia. The sceptics on Kitchener's 'forward policy', notably the new secretary to the CID, Sir George Clarke, were corroborated when the Tsar pulled back from an experimental troop movement to Turkestan, via the Orenburg–Tashkent.[62]

Notwithstanding Clarke's scepticism and his 'peace at all costs' followers, the crude Russian rail capacity looked impressive. During Sergei Witte's period of financial hegemony in St Petersburg (1891–1906), the Russian network had grown from 18,000 miles to 37,000 miles. By 1903 some 70 per cent of that network was in state hands to allow efficient militarization of all railways. However, the extent to which these vast railway groupings translated into military strength, and a real threat to British hegemony in Europe was less clear. Many of Clarke's observations on Russian weakness became plain. Across Central Asia, Russian troop numbers fell in the year after the Russo–Japanese War, and the 1905 St Petersburg Revolution. The Cossacks in the region were loyal to Tsarist principles, but other races and military groupings were 'much contaminated with revolutionary principles'. Railway battalions were vulnerable to liberal teachings, as were civilians in the growing rail networks. Ironically, the large numbers of dissatisfied railway workers were undermining Russian security in Central Asia, which railways were designed to promote.[63] CID assessments of Russian strategic railways were problematical, given the qualitative aspects of their infrastructure and personnel, Russian financial limitations, and the persistent obfuscation of intent with the commercial façade given to them. Nevertheless, British alarm about the Russian railway threat was maintained at a high level, prompting the allocation of up to one third of resources to state-owned North Western after nationalization in 1886.

The British Reaction to Russian Railways: Kandahar Railway and the North Western Group

Macpherson noted that no purely military Indian railways had been built before 1870 (see Maps 3, 4 and 5 for key military railways). Thereafter, the Russian railway building programme was used to justify large expenditure programmes, even while government borrowing was stretched. This was sometimes in place of famine and commercial railways. The size and opacity of military railway budgets within and outside the North Western group became highly controversial over time. By 1884, before Pendjeh increased the demand for railways, Secretary of State Kimberley had prioritized the first £5 million of strategic railway expenditure above that of famine relief and commerce.[64] By the following year, Sir Theodore Hope, the public works member in Calcutta, pushed forward seven new 'strategic railways' and a total budget for 'frontier railways' of some £1.87 million out of an aggregate new government expenditure of £4 million, to be incurred over the following three to five years.[65] Hope pressed for this military expenditure to come out of borrowing rather than income (akin to 'productive' railways, but outside the £2.5 million annual borrowing ceiling), with such loans segmented from general railway requirements. Military protection was promised 'for one half the cost of this Afghan war'.[66] Further, the concept of Indian railway construction as a deterrent became the focus of much debate. What Sir Richard Temple termed 'the Pegasus that is winged with political power' could be used to simultaneously dazzle and frighten Afghan and Persian peoples.[67] This engendered resentment amongst the growing nationalist voices in India, which saw excessive defence expenditure paid from Indian taxes.[68] Indeed, Hope's assertions about strategic railways reducing Indian defence costs in Afghanistan were attacked a few years later in an Indian budget debate. An Oldham MP complained to the House of Commons that additional military expenditure since the Second Afghan War, over 1880 to 1891, had totalled £43.3 million, of which £9.5 million was 'strategic rail'. This was despite an initial £2 million saving on cancelled frontier lines after the war. In the MP's assessment, 'the armed peace' in India was nearly as expensive as mounting the war. While strategic rail expenditure declined after the war to almost nothing by 1883/4, it rose precipitously after Pendjeh to £1.63 million by 1885/6. The aggregate total over 1879/80 to 1887/8 was some £5.16 million, with a further £3.63 million on 'state' railways, of which a large percentage was military.[69]

Rail enthusiasts like Charles Marvin (a central Asian correspondent for the *Morning Post*) argued that these levels of strategic rail expenditure offered value for money, in comparison to the amounts squandered on the Second Afghan War. That confrontation had absorbed nearly £20 million of GOI expenditure. Meanwhile, the Russian's had constructed railways at between £4,000–5,000 per mile, to create the complete Transcaucasian network (connecting the Black and Caspian Seas) for less than £9 million. The Transcaspian at £6 million offered extraordinary value for money, leaving Russia able to exploit her new territories militarily and commercially. Like Curzon, Marvin was aware of the more disciplined cost control practised by the Russians, but was confident that problems of British 'outsourcing' of railway materials, and wasteful 'agency' costs could be curbed. Britain might construct railways from Sibi to Herat at £5,000 per mile, and ultimately challenge Russian dominance, with the entire International railway budgeted at £20–5 million. These investments would create for England the required 'counterpoise' to Russian rail investments, with commercial benefits for Britain and India. Marvin quoted from the regional Karachi Chamber of Commerce which pressed railways to Quetta, and probably as far as Kandahar. The lack of Afghan products reaching India was testimony to the failings of existing railways. Marvin condemned Viceroy Ripon over India's failure to match Russian investment, and mocked the Liberal government's weakness in facing down the threat. He called on readers of his pamphlets to lobby their MPs to take a more Russophobe stance than that pursued by the 'Baboo Viceroy' Ripon.[70]

Marvin's call for his Russophobe readership to press politicians on railway development was timely, given Russia's annexation of Merv and confrontation at Pendjeh. An important joint War Office/India Office memorandum of 1889 was co-authored by the head of military intelligence in the Indian army, Brackenbury.[71] The authors rejected calls to 'attack Russia at Herat' since, in inciting conflict so far from Indian railways, supply difficulties would leave the Indian Army disadvantaged. Instead a line from Kabul to Kandahar might be drawn, to defend the Amir's power base and maintain indigenous opposition to Russian incursions. Indian railway lines were only ninety-four miles from Kandahar, much closer than the Transcaspian, and provided a good base to defend Kabul. In general, the British benefited if confrontation was dragged into Southern Afghanistan, so stretching Russian supply lines further than British/Indian. However, it was understood that the requirement for supply lines could be overridden if the Russian troops were able to requisition food and materials from conquered territories. While Afghanistan was unlikely to yield the food supplies that the outskirts of Metz and Paris had allowed Von Moltke, the slow Central Asian incursions had shown the Russians to be adept at cultivating infertile land.

Brackenbury envisaged the development of roads, railways and telegraphs at Herat and Afghan Turkestan, allowing 'the resources of the new territories [to] be developed'. This would repeat 'that process of consolidation' which Russians had pursued in Central Asia. British Indian defence policy, facilitated by the Indian railways would then be reactive, but far from passive. Any Russian move to Herat/ Afghan Turkestan would prompt a British move to Kandahar, Jellalabad and Ghazni. This division of Afghanistan into occupied spheres of influence would necessitate Britain expanding its rail links in Southern Afghanistan to match any Russian rail-building in the North. In the meantime British resources might be focused on improving communications to the Afghan–Indian frontier.[72] Further, by 1891, in a secret military report, railway construction was prioritized in the defence of India over troop reinforcements from Britain and India. General Roberts used the precedent of Pendjeh in 1885 to demonstrate that troop recruitment would prove inadequate. While some 10,000 British and 20,000 native troops were enlisted at that time, most were sent to Upper Burma. Forces to confront the Russian menace on the North West Frontier were static. Without conscription, which remained politically impractical in Britain, troop numbers would be too low to enforce Brackenbury's 'forwardist' policy. In line with Robert's recommendations, the report pressed railways as the most practical method to 'compensate for our deficiency in British soldiers'. Railways would optimize troop distribution, meaning it was 'difficult to over estimate' their importance.[73]

This prioritization of strategic railways in defending India, pressed by Roberts, Curzon, Temple, Brackenbury, Chesney and Marvin implied a continuation of high government expenditure for years. Revenues from these railways were meagre, and the commercial potential remained uncertain. Guaranteed lines like Scinde–Punjab had taken funding off the balance sheet, but the size of funding for guaranteed interest payments was still substantial. The Punjab and North West territories contained several state and 'private' guaranteed military lines, which were designed to protect the most vulnerable mountain passes.[74] By 1886 the dual government's wish to control military assets and concern over financial scandals at military lines pushed the pendulum back towards state funding. In amalgamating several companies under the state-owned North Western, a consolidation of railways akin to that later pressed by Secretary of State Hamilton in the 'productive' sphere was achieved. However, within the North Western group, individual lines maintained great autonomy. The India Office promoted some competition within the state sector, allowing Theodore Hope to boast of his seven discrete strategic projects by the mid-1880s. Many of these were small local lines, and Indian strategic railways development focused on three parts of the North Western grouping. The Kandahar State Railway (later renamed Sind–Pishin) became the focus of debate between forwardists and 'wait and see' supporters. Kandahar State railway was intended to access Quetta, and beyond that Kandahar, by way of a broad-gauge line through Harnai. Secondly, the narrow-gauge Bolan railway was to traverse the Bolan Pass on a narrower gauge, creating a similar transport link for troops. The fate of this second railway was linked to strategic and engineering concerns on the Kandahar. Finally, the Khyber Railway was much delayed through engineering and political concerns, and was abandoned in 1909. It was finally constructed after the Third Afghan War of 1919.[75]

Notwithstanding the profusion of British pamphlets and intelligence material written in support of these lines, the practical development of the Kandahar and Bolan lines illustrated the extent to which British Indian railway policy was dominated by financial resources. Scarce funding led to a 'stop go' approach to construction. Building beyond the Indian border undermined the existence of Afghanistan as a 'buffer' state and risked conflict with fierce local tribes, many of whom lay outside the control of the Amir. The suspicion that military railways were being used to covertly expand military budgets was a preoccupation, highlighted in the Welby Commision's deliberations on Indian expenditure. The commercial and cultural potential of the railways was exaggerated to create consensus. However, the construction of the Kandahar and Bolan lines reflected above all a reaction to the proliferation of Russia's state-owned and managed military railways, and its growing influence in the buffer states. After the trauma of the Second Afghan War in 1879 Viceroy Lytton became committed to transporting British troops and commerce to Afghanistan. The Russians had built influence in Afghanistan under Tsar Alexander II, and had goaded the Afghans on in a manner warned of by Macgregor. Pushing Indian railways into Afghanistan implied a dismantling of Afghanistan as a 'buffer state' by British 'forwardists'. Separate British and Russian spheres of influence would be created, divided by a so called 'scientific frontier'. The British press, led by *The Times*, argued for railways to Kandahar, even without Russian incursions into Afghanistan. In 1879, Sir Richard Temple, with Lytton's support, received approval to extend the Kandahar State Railway to the key Afghan terminus.[76] However, the following year, with the return of Gladstone and his liberal appointee Viceroy Ripon at Calcutta, there was heightened opposition on economic grounds. Ripon could do little to constrain rail expenditure as far as Quetta, and on to the Afghan border at Chaman, but he found more support from those resisting extensions into Afghanistan.[77]

The Kandahar debate raged during the 1880s. Writing in *The Times* in August 1880 the prominent agent of the Governor General of Beluchistan, based at Quetta on the Bolan Pass, wrote a strongly worded defence of the railway extension from Quetta to Kandahar. He argued in prudent financial terms, likely to appeal to Viceroy Ripon, suggesting that the barren picture of Kandahar painted by opponents of the scheme failed to recognize fertile valleys surrounding the region, which could be used for crops to sustain an occupying force. He saw Sibi, at the southern end of the Bolan Pass, as a helpful precedent, where the building of the railway and the GOI's annexation of Quetta had doubled revenue from the region. Banditry in the Bolan Pass had almost disappeared, making the region 'almost as safe as an Indian highway'. The 'peace and prosperity' brought by the railway to Sibi could be repeated at Kandahar.[78] By October 1885, *The Times* reported the 'incredible' cessation of construction work beyond Sibi, which characterized the period up to the confirmation of Russian occupation of Merv at April 1884. While Lytton had pressed through railway orders of over £500,000, Gladstone's Secretary of State Hartington raised questions about whether a long-term occupation of Kandahar was feasible, and abandoned construction in the Bolan Valley. The cost of materials, already ordered in England, was charged to the 1881 GOI budget statement at £500,000. Sir Theodore Hope looked back on the delays to the Quetta line as having cost more than the 'entire capital cost' of the line.[79] With Merv annexed by Russia in 1884, the new Secretary Kimberley pushed through renewed parliamentary approval for construction to Quetta of a renamed railway. In this development he was supported by Roberts, who viewed the extension of a railway up the Bolan Pass to Quetta, and then to Kandahar, as central to his 'forward' defence policy. Roberts had relieved Kandahar during the Second Afghan War after his 'heroic' march from Kabul, only to see it handed back in 1881 to the Afghans as the Quetta Railway extension was abandoned. He was familiar with the technical challenges of railway construction and organizing troop movements across mountain passes. In demonstrating technical expertise and a preparedness to invest in a defence of the Quetta/Pishin region, Roberts argued that the Afghans would become more Anglophile. The use of railways to win greater Afghan and border tribe support was a prominent feature of Roberts's thinking.[80] However, when he rode on the Quetta and Bolan railway in 1886, Roberts was shocked to discover breaks of gauge made efficient military transport impractical. Before any further British investment in strategic railways was contemplated, existing routes must be surveyed and bolstered. While Roberts had persuaded Salisbury that Kandahar rather than Kabul held the key to Indian defence on the North West frontier, he had come to accept, by the late 1880s, that the railway must end at the Indian border town of Chaman, short of Afghanistan. Helpfully, the tribes of Kandahar were neither so 'warlike' nor 'fanatical' as those encountered by the British at the Khyber/Kuram.[81] The other end of the line would extend to Peshawar to meet the new threat of Russians moving south across the Pamirs. Karachi would provide the vital sea route for reinforcements via the Punjab railway to the North West Frontier.

Salisbury concurred with Robert's railway strategy, and attacked less focused 'forwardists' who lacked commitment to Kandahar's defence. However, the expense and troop diffusion in defending distant Herat made Roberts's approach less tenable. Many British thinkers were deluded by the 'friendly Afghan' theory which assumed that the Indian army would meet loyal Afghan support from tribesmen within the country in a combined anti-Russian consensus.[82] Further, the Pendjeh incident of the following year added impetus to the building process. By 1891 the British representative in St Petersburg was able to tell Foreign Secretary Salisbury that he viewed Pendjeh as a 'blessing in disguise' which had helped facilitate 'our whole system of railway construction up to Quetta' with flexibility to reach Kandahar.[83] The renamed Sind–Pishin Railway continued to extract funding from the defence budget of the GOI. While *The Times* documented challenges in transporting all the railway materials from England, and in the construction of bridges across valleys prone to flooding, by 1885 there was a general approval that the timidity of Secretary of State Hartington had been reversed.[84] An extension to Quetta appeared to satisfy the press's determination to face down Russia's gradualist railway annexations. At the same time the strategic question of Seistan against Kandahar was left unresolved, pending clarification of Russian actions, and the internal politics of the Amir.

With the hardening of British attitudes after Pendjeh and the profusion of strategic railway papers that followed, the House of Commons allocated time to discuss the Kandahar Railway in August 1891. Sir Richard Temple, now a Westminster MP, pressed his own contribution with Lytton in 1879 for advancing construction to Kandahar. He foresaw problems after Gladstone's re-election in 1880 in paying for the line. The GOI would be loath to fund an external line as a state railway or to provide a guarantee. Quetta was a base for delivering Indian troops to the Afghan border, but Temple resisted railways beyond the border. He was sceptical about Afghan reactions to 'forwardist' military railways. Temple saw the Afghans as less likely to fund the Kandahar extension than Indians (they had little choice). Further, any Afghan support in the construction effort would require a 'great alteration in the manners and customs' of the Afghans. The Amir would view the construction effort and 'the approach of the iron horse' with suspicion. Temple's scepticism was that of an Indian railway enthusiast, who in his Indian memoirs of 1880 had pointed to great (if unspecified) advantages for India from the use of railways in the recent Afghan War. Indeed 'the military advantage alone' justified all GOI funding and guarantees for the railways. In extremis, all Indian railways would expedite troop movements from outlying areas of India to the North Western Frontier. Temple echoed the Prussian commander of the 1830s who saw all commercial rail networks serving a military function.[85] Temple met support during the debate from George Curzon, then a Lancashire MP. Curzon saw the Amir as suspicious of Indian rail extensions from Quetta to Chaman, arguing that British efforts should be focused on opening Kandahar up to British exports rather than soldiers. This would tie the Amir and his subjects more closely to British interests. With the railway reaching Chaman, it would be used for its less controversial function of promoting commerce. Greater security might be expected to accompany trade. To achieve this, Afghanistan's domestic tariffs, devised by the Russians, must be dismantled. In Sibi, for example, the arrival of the Indian railway enhanced trading revenues of the town from Rs 10,000 to an impressive Rs 125,000. A similar pattern was anticipated at Kandahar, where wool, skins, nuts and dried fruits might all be exported. Moreover, Roberts felt confidence in the 'civilising influence' of the Indian railways, to allow substitution of English goods and traders for the dominant Russian exports.[86] Sir J. Gorst, Under Secretary of State for India, agreed that commerce and defence should develop in parallel with railways. Eventually Kandahar might be connected, but only by 'patiently waiting until the Ameer sees its advantages'.[87]

A vitriolic attack on the consensus 'wait and see' policy, agreed to by Temple, Curzon and Roberts, came from another Lancashire MP. As ever, Manchester MPs with their cotton exports to concern them were never far from the debate on Indians spending money on railways. Mr Maclean MP, of the weaving and dying centre of Oldham, argued that money had been wasted in arms to the border. He saw the development of rail links to Quetta and beyond in far less positive terms than the resident Sandeman had suggested. An expensive tunnel had been constructed to Chaman through the most demanding part of the terrain, but that money had been wasted since it fell short of Kandahar. The Quetta–Chaman railway ended in what 'is literally a hole in the wall'. India was spending comparable sums on Afghanistan to those incurred during the two Afghan Wars, and this railway expenditure could be expected to continue with railways to be built through all 300 North West mountain passes. The British nervousness about upsetting the Amir was partly to blame. There was unwarranted concern that railway materials stockpiled around Quetta were a direct threat to Afghan independence. Rather than presenting Kandahar Railway as 'a standing menace', the development potential of railways extended into Afghanistan should be stressed. The project would make the Amir richer and his people 'more prosperous and contented than they are now'. Like many Indian rail evangelists of the late Victorian period, the Oldham MP displayed a strong understanding of the development potential of railways in an under-invested region like India. However, there was a failure to confront the dissipation of railway's development impact, through the 'buy British' policy. Maclean emphasized the benefits of Russian railways in Merv, which had a comparable 'investment leakage' for the local Turkestan economy through a 'buy Russian' policy on rail materials. Nevertheless, he identified a dramatic increase in 'cultivation and population' through the Transcaspian, with enormous trading benefits to Russia. Kandahar could potentially receive cheap British goods (including presumably Oldham cloth) in the same way that the railways now benefited to consumers in Punjab. Like Curzon, he saw that trade restrictions from the Amir ('our subsidized ally') must be dismantled to facilitate a railway utopia.[88] None of the participants in the debate doubted that longer-term, Afghanistan could be brought under the commercial dominance of India, facilitated by railways which would bring trade and (if necessary) soldiers. The extent to which diplomacy with the Amir and his peoples was appropriate sparked controversy and determined the speed of construction beyond the Bolan Pass. Even railway enthusiast General Roberts foresaw problems in building to Kandahar. Without the capacity to deliver troops to within striking distance of the Kabul–Kandahar line, there were flaws in Britain's defence strategy of employing railways as a substitute for troops, and as a suitable method for 'containment' of Russia in Central Asia. In the meantime, the extent to which the GOI could be left to fill in railway lines over Maclean's 300 mountain passes was checked only by the monitoring of the British parliament. As Kaminsky has emphasized, this was an imperfect 'check and balance' on the India Office. The 'great bore' of parliamentary debate could easily be dominated by a handful of Lancashire MPs, as the Hansard record of strategic rail debate evidences. Indeed, by the time the House of Commons finished the debate at 8.45pm, only three MPs were left in the chamber.[89]

Military railway construction, by the British on the North West Frontier, slowed after 1891. When a detailed report and comments were produced by the War Office in 1904 on the defence of India, the progress made in the intervening years was said to be minimal. An extension of barely 11 miles of line from Peshawar to Jumrood, and the construction of a narrow gauge line to Kohat and Thall were highlighted. The military value of the latter was 'slight' and the Indian railhead remained at Chaman, as it had in 1891. In contrast Russia had completed lines to the Oxus River, and had 'doubled her power of offence against us'. With Russian rail-power stronger than thirteen years previously, the capacity to deliver British/Indian reinforcements must by 1904 have been inadequate.[90] Predictably Roberts adopted a hawkish approach to India's modest rail extensions. He complained to Secretary of State Hamilton that British policy since the Second Afghan War had been 'half-hearted' and had left India in a situation 'fraught with ruinous consequences'. The so called 'scientific frontier' at the Afghan border must be secured with railways, and any resistance from the Amir should prompt the Imperial government to remove his subsidies. At the Amir's death, Roberts hoped that the state of Afghanistan might be 'disintegrated' with a puppet ruler installed in a new city state of Kandahar. This would allow the final construction of the much delayed line to Kandahar.[91] Later, a more measured approach was adopted by Prime Minister Balfour, who requested a long-term comparison between the strategic position at the time of the Second Afghan War in 1878 and that existing in 1904. Over that period, the War Office reported, the Kabul rail line had seen significant extensions. The 70 mile extension from Rawlpindi and Jhelum had been completed, facilitating more rapid troop movements to the most difficult theatre of war. However, these reports pointed to a failure to carry through W. P. Andrew's strategic rail vision, driven by stretched financial circumstances in India, coupled with concerns about Afghan and Russian reactions to an aggressive railway arms race, on the North West Frontier. Moreover, the problem of distinguishing Russian military railway-building from commercial lines remained.

As British diplomacy with Russia continued, culminating in the 1907 accord, divisions between the Russophiles and Russophobes, when Curzon had sought to unite years previously, became more prominent.[92] This was manifest in British government comment on Russophobe contributions from Viceroy Minto and Indian Chief of Staff Kitchener in 1906. Minto concentrated his analysis of Indian defence almost exclusively on 'the railway question'. The Viceroy, like Dalhousie, presented railways as a convenient method for combining security with economic development. Any delay in rail construction, resulting from Russian 'entente', would 'grievously cripple' Indian defences, setting prosperity back ten years in large parts of northern India. In fact, according to the British Government critique, the two Indian railway lines that concerned Minto (the Kabul River and Kurram Valley Lines) were already sanctioned and would go ahead even with the entente. Minto had raised a consistent theme amongst the more 'hawkish' railway enthusiasts, that without aggressive Indian rail construction the Afghans would detect a British 'fear of Russia' and view Raj policy with 'the gravest suspicion'. However, building these two railways was likely to do little to quell the growing radicalism amongst Afghan tribesmen. In the event of a tribal uprising, Kabul itself could only be defended by at least 30,000–40,000 British and native occupying troops. Meanwhile, the report stated that Afghanistan was now 'as undesirable from the Russian point of view as from our own' since it would tie down resources while yielding little. If railways no longer deterred Russian aggression in Afghanistan, nor improved internal security with hostile Afghan tribesmen on the Indian border, it suggested that the external defence rationale for Indian railways was dead by 1906. In fact, the Russophile tone of the report went further in suggesting that a cursory glance at a map of Afghan railways in 1906 revealed Britain to be the railway aggressors on the North West Frontier. Lord Kitchener's Russophobe approach had misrepresented Russia's 'spur from Merv to Kushk' on the North West Afghan border, which was nothing other than a response to the Raj's rail extension to Chaman in 1892.[93]

By 1906 the British Government was frustrated at the complexity of decision-making on military railways. Westminster sought to undermine Calcutta, stating that 'the external policy of India can be directed by His Majesty's Government alone', and complaining Indian council divisions undermined firm policy.[94] Moreover, the shift from internal to external security concerns in India, after 1857, gradually made the GOI less central in military railway policy. Imperial policy in the region was controlled by the British cabinet, of which the Secretary of State for India was just one member.[95] Nevertheless, while new technologies would be developed to undermine railway warfare, the British focus on railway defence in Central Asia was maintained beyond the First World War.[96] As late as 1924, five years after the Third Afghan War, *The Times* reported on the opening of the Khyber Railway, built on General Roberts's preferred 5ft 6 inch gauge. It rose to some 3,500 feet, with challenging tunnels and bridges spanning ravines. At £50,000 per mile over some sections, it was one of the most expensive railways ever constructed. This was said to be a small price to pay in allowing the Indian army to suppress future Afghan rebellions speedily and firmly. However, *The Times* correspondent, reporting from Peshawar in 1924, commented insightfully that 'Afghanistan can easily be conquered' but 'it cannot easily be held own'. There were concerns that the British occupation of Kabul would encourage Bolshevik risings at Herat. The railway facilities reflected the tribal banditry of the region with fort like stations, steel shutters convertible into 'machine-gun loopholes'. It had taken the Great War to allow military 'forwardists' to press ahead with railways beyond Indian borders, but by that time railway technology for military purposes was becoming superseded by the aeroplane.[97]

British Railway Strategy on the Indian–Persian Border, Baghdad Railway and Germany

The diplomatic language used to encourage moves towards the 1907 entente was the culmination of years of concern about the dangers of building railways through Afghanistan. This encouraged a shift in strategic emphasis in the railway debate towards Persia. Persian railways had played a role in British strategic thinking since 1872, when Baron Reuter secured exclusive railway concessions in Persia for seventy years. Reuter, a British citizen by naturalization, looked to construct a line from the Caspian via Tehran to the Persian Gulf. He would own exclusive rights to mine all minerals in the area traversed, apart from gold and silver. It also offered rights to all irrigation works, state forests and control of customs for twenty years. The Persian government was given a meagre royalty of 15 per cent for surrendering these rights, and in return would guarantee a 7 per cent return on capital to Reuter's lenders/investors.[98] Reuter attempted to bring Bismarck and Lord Rothschild into the project to raise finance for railway construction, which would create a defensive shield against Russian incursions into Persia. Rothschild's response to Reuter's plan illustrated the extent to which British Imperial control of overseas territories was considered essential to derive value from sovereign guarantees. Persian guarantees on their own were worthless and required British guarantees on the concession: a guarantee of the integrity of Persia, with the Persian army officered by British or German commanders, and a force provided to protect customs houses.[99] Strategic railway construction inside the borders of British India was far easier for London financiers, since the control of Indian taxation was within the legal remit of London. Equally, this would have been a problem on railways in Afghanistan, if the 'forwardists' had stretched Indian networks that far.

There were differences between the Persia and Afghan railway projects. Captain Yule brought these out in a paper of 1891. Building Indian railway lines as far as Kandahar was impractical since it would probably involve a 'precipitous ... rupture of our relations with the Amir'. Instead, by building lines to the south east extreme of Persia at Seistan, bordering Afghanistan and Baluchistan, the indigenous opposition from the distant Kabul and Tehran troops would be more manageable. At Seistan, British troops would be only half the distance from the Russian threat at Herat than were they placed at Kandahar. While Yule's distinction between native opposition to Indian railways to Seistan and Kandahar was probably exaggerated, his preference for a Seistan railway was prominent in much British discussion over the ensuing period.[100] Salisbury suggested to his observer in Tehran, Sir H Drummond Wolff, that the GOI could be pressed into an extension from Chaman to Seistan once the Quetta railway was running properly to the other end of the Kohjak Pass. In general, he supported building Indian/Persian railways 'entirely on the defensive' from Russian construction, but saw that with Chaman up and running 'the absurdity of stopping there will force the Indian Government to go on' to Seistan.[101] Salisbury's room for manoeuvre on this point was limited by Russia's success in diplomatic overtures to the Shah of Persia. His language revealed significant autonomy for the GOI in 1890, even in regard to railways in Persia. This presumably reflected the source of funding for such exercises. Later in 1890, the Russians negotiated a moratorium for ten years on Persian railways with the Shah's government. Thereafter concessions to build could only be given with the mutual agreement of Russia and Persia. The Shah informed the British that this was beneficial to Persia since her government never intended to agree to any Russian-sponsored railway construction. He told a British representative in Tehran that he failed to understand the fascination amongst young Europeans for railways, and never considered himself 'delayed by the want of them'. Whether the construction was undertaken by 'English, Dutch, Americans, or others' the result of granting such concessions was always to say 'farewell to our independence'.[102] Salisbury had pressed the Russians the previous year to develop their own railways in northern Persia.[103] He objected to the ten-year moratorium, though it was arguably a more sensible approach than that pursued on and beyond the Afghan border, where an expensive railway arms race ensued. Against this, rail construction might have allowed more rapid economic development in the British sphere of influence in Southern Persia. The moratorium marked a reversal of the Shah's promises to Drummond Wolf of two years before.[104] The Shah had even toured the great financing houses of the City in 1889, to see financing possibilities for British/Indian railways in Persia.[105] Finally, the Russians were viewed by many British representatives as having achieved a significant propaganda victory over the British and GOI. As A. P. Thornton put it 'they had no capital themselves with which to build railways; therefore nobody should build them'.[106]

The Seistan Railway itself was included in the Persian railway moratorium, but had anyway been rejected by the political department of the India Office in 1893 as too costly. At £2 million for 400 miles (£5,000 per mile) this was cheap by Indian standards, but there were added military costs to protect the railway from native attacks. Salisbury railed against this decision to Sandeman and others, arguing that the absence of such rail links left Southern Persia, and Afghanistan as far as the Helmund, unprotected from Russians. The departure of Chesney and Roberts from India weakened support for the project.[107] By the 1890s, Thornton argued, Persia had 'lapsed out of diplomatic sight so that, even Persian specialists, came to see it as an aspect of Indian policy'.[108] However, by 1903, the Seistan strategic rail debate was again prominent in CID and other military correspondence.[109] Prime Minister Balfour drafted a long note on the subject as a dominant issue on 'Indian Defence'. Balfour dismissed all thoughts of a Russian invasion by way of the Hindu Kush, but in Eastern Persia he feared the combination of Russian rail extensions and the 'Russianising process' which had been used to make Central Asia culturally amenable to annexation by St Petersburg. From the relatively fertile region of Seistan, Russian rail links could step by step be extended to the key Kandahar region, although the lack of rail links in Beluchistan made this difficult.[110] Balfour was more sensitive than most British observers to the financial strains that railway development was impos-ing on Russia. Russian railway-building in eastern Persia was 'a very costly and unremunerative addition to a very costly and unremunerative railway system'.[111] If India resisted constructing her own railway west towards Seistan, Russia might conclude that she had little need to extend the Transcaspian from Askabad south through eastern Persia. Although there would be advantages in 'anglicizing' Seistan with railways, the risks of encouraging a through-rail link from Russia to India was too high. While there would be bridges which could be blown up to sabotage Russian troop movements to the Indian border (as had been done in the South African War) the Russians would be able to repair damage. Russian rolling stock could be adjusted to fit the wider 5ft 6 inch Indian gauge and the Indian railway system could become 'a potent military instrument in the hands of our enemies'.[112] Elsewhere doubt was cast on Balfour's pessimism about Russian use of Indian railways. In particular the ripping up of Indian iron sleep-ers of the wrong gauge was viewed as far more difficult in India, where wooden sleepers were used. Iron sleepers were chosen primarily to benefit Sheffield steel suppliers, but had these unforeseen additional benefits.[113]

Further analysis on the problem in 1904 reiterated that while any Russian rail extension from Askabad to Seistan would not provide huge 'strategic value' to St Petersburg, it would make Kandahar somewhat more vulnerable and could allow Russia to concentrate up to 100,000 more men on the Afghan border.[114] The response to Balfour's 'status quo' approach was ambiguous and unconvincing. In short, Balfour unlike Salisbury, decided to support the ten-year moratorium on foreign rail construction in Persia, and its extension to 1910. He concluded in favour of 'the status quo' but regretted the loss of commercial opportunities, through failing to construct a Nushki to Seistan railway. Balfour saw that the benefits, in terms of Indian defence, far outweighed the lost trade.[115] Of course his concerns about railways, as a weapon in the hands of the enemy, could have been used to undermine all railway-building in India. The GOI might have been accused of funding accelerated Russian troop movements, once they had crossed the border. Sadly, the concerns of the British Prime Minister do not appear to have been debated widely elsewhere, and as ever there was a failure to draw parallels with other experiences. The British appear to have been aware of the potency of French railways in the hands of Von Moltke's troops, for example, but nowhere are the similarities and differences of the two situations discussed. By the end of the extended railway moratorium on Persian construction in 1910, the Anglo–Russian Convention was three years old. Tensions were still clear in the discussions between the two regional powers. A letter from Sir G. Buchanan of the Foreign Office to the Russian Government in 1913 makes it clear that Russia was viewed as pressing rail concessions on the Persian Government, outside the spirit of the 1907 agreement. Instead, by constructing railways together in Persia the British/Indians and Russians might optimize the chance of 'the re-establishment of order in Persia'.[116]

Further west, the weakness of the Ottoman Empire made railway concessions up to the Persian Gulf a matter of concern for all the western powers. The British believed that German attempts, after the death of Bismarck, to build a line from Constantinople to Konia had implications for the defence of India. Railways through Mesopotamia might be linked to Persian routes, perhaps shadowing the route of Rowland Macdonald's 'International railway', to access British India. However, the so called 'Baghdad Railway' demonstrated again the low-risk nature of British international railway investors, and the permanent Russophobe aspect of British policy. While Curzon was concerned about the rise of Germany in Mesopotamia, complicating security matters in Central Asia, which had hitherto been the preserve of Russia and Britain, much of the British approach was concerned with Russian reactions to the construction of the railway. French investors were prepared to finance the venture with the support of a Turkish guarantee at a fixed amount per kilometre constructed (with Great Power control over Turkish customs duties). In contrast, the British Morgan and Barings houses were unsuccessful in attracting the required British government support and investor demand. *The Times* attributed the failure of British capitalists to support the project to British political overtures to Russia, Eastern shipping interests, and the courting of Germanophobe sentiment. Edward Sassoon, of the powerful Bombay managing agency grouping, in a letter to the paper the following day, congratulated the British government on scuppering a project which would have rendered British 'tenure of India as insecure as a publican's license' and made it 'subject to the 'whims and caprices of European alliances'. A. J. P. Taylor in contrast, put it down to 'British capitalists' discontent at the prospect of being outvoted by French/German shareholders, financing the import of non-British manufactured steel railway lines, and dislike for the 'house of Morgan'. These disadvantages did not apply to Indian rail finance and, curiously, at the India Office by this time, Secretary of State Hamilton was pressing the merits of J. P. Morgan as a suitable successor to Rothschild in Indian rail finance.[117] British financiers' ambivalence towards the German-led project was shared by Russian participants, who were equally keen to keep German industry out of Central Asia. Workings together, up to and beyond the Triple Entente, the British and Russians were able to preserve the railway 'cold war' for themselves. Lack of funding and construction difficulties meant that, even by 1914, Germany's Baghdad railway was only partially constructed.

Conclusion

Strategic railways dominated discussion of the Russian threat to India on both the Afghan and Persian Borders. This was so readily accepted that when the Simla war game of 1903 was carried out the General Staff at the War Office stated that 'questions of transport and railway construction ... for obvious reasons, form the most important factors in the problem'.[118] In fact there was nothing obvious about this. The difficulty in distinguishing strategic from commercial railway-building made the debate between Russophiles and Russophobes irresolvable. The press and the House of Commons highlighted the support lent to Russia's compelling 'step by step' imperialism by railway supplies and development. However, by the early twentieth century, railways were viewed by many as something of a 'blunt instrument' with termini in arbitrary locations and significant logistical problems to move soldiers to where they were needed. The Amir of Afghanistan and Shah of Persia both saw this symbol of modernity as threatening and sinister. Even Lord Roberts of Kandahar seemed to accept that the Kandahar railway would need to stop short of the Afghan border. The approach arrived at in Persia, where an early railway 'détente' with the Russians saved money for the GOI and maintained greater border stability, was arguably more sustainable than the constant panic and indecision over Kandahar, Kabul and Herat. While the Russophile grouping in Whitehall who had moved Great Britain closer to the Russian entente of 1907 sought to downplay the need to spend money on North West railways, the railway arms race was far from over. In a key Foreign Office memorandum of 1906 on the implications of the entente for British defence, Indian railway-building was pressed again. While the military planners had for long ignored the financial weakness of Russia, believing, like Curzon, that the centralist government could override economic backwardness, the report highlighted 'Russia's crippled state'. Presumably the military defeat by Japan, and 1905 'revolution' were too prominent to ignore. Of course Britain's own shortcomings, displayed in the South African War, played a role in prolonging Russophobia.[119] In fact, the Foreign Office report called for a step up in British Indian railway-building on the Afghan Border to Dakka and Peiwar Kotal, and a challenge to the rail moratorium in Persia. This additional investment was to be made on the assumption that British troops could be readily shipped from England to Karachi, to use the railways provided, and supplement Indian army reserves. In fact, this confidence in the Royal Navy was seen to be misplaced, when the Admiralty admitted in 1907 that a combined Russian/French enemy would be likely to block British troop carriers.[120]

Whilst the War Office and CID could increasingly marginalize the Viceroy and even the Secretary of State for India in railway planning, the funding of related deficits in India remained the responsibility of the GOI. Great Power politics, centralized in London, subsumed all matters of Indian defence. Meanwhile, the thinly attended Indian budget debates continued to be viewed by MPs as the 'great bore' of the House of Commons.

4 INDIAN RAILROADING: FLOATING RAILWAY COMPANIES IN THE LATE NINETEENTH CENTURY

Introduction

The flotation of a 'second wave' of guaranteed rail companies in the 1880s and 90s shows 'gentlemanly capitalists' of the City and commerce exerting great influence on the India Office, in a manner which challenges Macpherson's benign view of their activities.[1] They performed incompatible functions of principal investor and government advisor. This conflict was justified by India Office officials on the basis of the enormous financial burden of railways for commerce, famine relief and military transportation. Nowhere were those conflicts more apparent than in the informal advisory appointment of Lord Nathaniel Rothschild to a succession of Indian Secretaries of State, on the floating of Indian rail companies as joint stock companies on the London Stock Exchange. In analysing four specific Rothschild-led share floatations of the period, the mutual dependence of the City and government officials becomes clear. The government guaranteed securities were bought by City underwriters and MPs alike.

Macpherson observed that 'the profits of promotion' were 'not the motive' for pre-1875 railway promoters and financiers. However, the evidence from private papers of Kimberley, Cross, Hamilton and Fowler is that enormous pressure was exerted on the India Office after 1875 by the City and Calcutta/Bombay managing agents. The railway concessions granted facilitated profits for underwriters, traders, investors and suppliers.[2] For example, by the mid-1880s Secretary of State Cross was alert to aggressive lobbying by rail promoters, but was confident that he could avoid 'the abuses' which were 'so apparent in American "railroading"'.[3] Sir George Campbell MP, formerly Lieutenant Governor of Bengal, was less sanguine. He complained to the House of Commons in 1889 that the India Office was 'continually granting fresh railways at a time when they are buying back the old guaranteed railways at an enormous premium'. For City underwriters, the government buyback of EIR and GIPR stock left unsatisfied demand for Indian railway paper. Campbell explained the government's contradictory behaviour as reflective of the 'great financial syndicates in the City of London' who pressed the India Office in Whitehall to grant state support to equity and bond issues. This left underwriters and investors with a risk profile characterized by the epithet 'heads I win, tails you lose'.[4] Campbell was noticeably scathing about Secretary of State Randolph Churchill's willingness to divert famine insurance fund revenues, enhancing the revenues of Rothschild's Bengal–Nagpur railway. In fact, Rothschild boasted of a unique advisory relationship on railway matters with successive Indian Secretaries of State. This delivered continuous business for his bank, as his advisory and underwriting roles became self reinforcing.[5] Only when the shortcomings of the Rothschild group's risk appetite and management competence were pressed by Curzon was their monopoly financing role questioned. By that time, the Rothschild group suffered the indignity of seeing Ernest Cassel, J. P. Morgan and the revitalized Baring Brothers facilitate the huge funding requirements of the imperial government in South Africa.[6]

Bengal Central Railway Company

In 1881, after condemnation of the first generation guaranteed companies, Indian Finance Member Evelyn Baring pressed Nathaniel Rothschild to bring his Bengal Central Railway to market without government guarantees. According to an unnamed source at the India Office, close to Baring, this attempt was overturned by Rothschild. The latter persuaded Secretary of State Hartington that a guarantee was required, at least during construction.[7] The company was formed to construct a line from Calcutta to Kulna, and from Ranaghat to Bongbong. The Bengal Central issue was launched by Rothschild/Baring in July 1881, raising £1 million initially. It benefited from the guarantee secured by Rothschild during construction only up to £1.25 million at 4 per cent. The construction period was limited to 30 June 1886. Once up and running there was to be an equal division of excess profits above 5 per cent until aggregate guarantee payments had been reimbursed, after which shareholders of Bengal Central were to retain everything. The GOI had a repurchase option at 1912 or 1932, such that 125 per cent of the aggregate capital expenditure was to be paid subject to a generous maximum.[8] From the records at the Guildhall Library, which give details of the applications made for shares, and the BT31 records on dissolved companies at Kew, it is clear that the shares were popular and attracted the backing of Rothschild himself. Almost 500,000 shares were applied for against a volume offered of only 100,000, which must have left a large number of disappointed applicants who were presumably scaled back. Rothschild himself was allocated almost 5 per cent of the issue.[9]

The company was revealed to be a pure financing vehicle when, a matter of months after listing, the operations of the line were subcontracted to the wealthy Eastern Bengal Railway Company (EBR). The price of EBR's 5 per cent guaranteed shares reacted positively to this arrangement, rising from £148 to £157 over June 1881 to June 1882, shortly after which it was purchased by the GOI at a premium of over 50 per cent.[10] Bengal Central's management reverted to the GOI at that time, so that Rothschild was left to focus on financing. Financial performance disappointed, which must have alarmed investors, whose 'interest only' guarantee was due to expire in 1886. However, the contractual arrangements negotiated by Rothschild created off-balance-sheet treatment for the GOI on the debt principal, coupled with investor protection comparable to the discredited first generation of railway companies. While the principal amount was not formally guaranteed by government, the GOI foresaw having to exercise their prohibitively expensive call option some time in the future, to keep the operation afloat.[11] Had shareholder capital been at risk, the India Office should have let the operation fail, justified by the 'illusory' projections which Bengal Central's promoters and financiers had presented. Instead, the India Office foresaw that it would have to subsidize the operation through to 1912 before contributing an additional windfall of 25 per cent on shareholder moneys. The India Office was alarmed at the potential damage to railway finance in India, and the prospect of a worsening of GOI's own credit. Over 1885/6, the India Office intervened to guarantee all share capital in perpetuity and acquired the outstanding debentures.

Indeed, Secretary of State Randolph Churchill pressed to have his friend Rothschild treated generously over the failed Bengal Central. By 1885, Churchill blamed Evelyn Baring for having misrepresented the company's financial prospects to investors. The omnipresent Richard Strachey was keen to see the GOI repurchase Bengal Central stock at low prices to teach shareholders a lesson, but Churchill saw this as a 'shortsighted' policy. The City would retaliate by withholding all finance in future. Instead, government support for Rothschild's private-sector experiment should be 'genuine and liberal'.[12] Whitehall appeared to be reliant on the goodwill of City bankers. Surprisingly, given their role in Bengal Central's failed financing structure, Baring Brothers were retained as advisors to the company in a restructuring. The India Office pressed a familiar method for enhancing Indian railway companies by offering additional state railway assets at below market prices. Hence, Barings reviewed financing options for the transfer of suitable government railway lines to Bengal Central from the contiguous Eastern Bengal region. By 1885, all thoughts of non-guaranteed finance for the company had been abandoned, with Baring asked to place £3 million of fully government-guaranteed debentures in Bengal Central, to fund the purchase of new railway mileage at discounted prices. Richard Strachey continued to exert pressure in the background, concerned that the state was being under-paid for its railways. However, he had the short-term financial profile of the GOI to preoccupy him and needed to solve the Bengal Central problems rapidly. The company was running out of money and would struggle to make dividend payments without new financing. That necessitated an emergency fundraising by July 1885. Hence, Bengal Central shareholders had benefited from the GOI's financial crisis, as the expense of Pendjeh tensions and the annexation of Upper Burma loomed large.[13] Baring Brothers and N. M. Rothschild's brinkmanship on the refinancing paid off with additional layers of credit support for Bengal Central provided by government. Further capital calls followed, all guaranteed or directly funded by the GOI. Remarkably, given the operating performance of the railway, Bengal Central re-applied for the right to operate their lines by the 1890s, after the windfall nationalization of EBR.[14]

Bengal and North Western Railway Company

By 1882, based on the initial success of the Bengal Central issue, the India Office looked to float their first non-guaranteed railway without the construction guarantee offered to Bengal Central. This was to be the Bengal and North Western Railway (Bengal NW). Presumably alert to the protection given to shareholders, Rothschild pressed for comparable buyout conditions to those on Bengal Central. He asked for a minimum buyout price of 125 per cent of the capital expended on the project with the potential for significant gains through an earnings-related buyout price. In the end the earnings-related arrangement was granted without explicit downside protection by the Secretary of State.[15] As would become clear in future India Office support, this gave investors upside on the buyout price, with downside protection in all but name. Nevertheless, an India Office associate of Baring presented this as a disaster such that 'the financiers lost their money' and 'the policy of the India Office was discredited'.[16] This perception was echoed by Richard Strachey in his testimony to a later select committee on railways. Under questioning from Campbell, he argued that the Bengal NW issue had continued to perform badly in the secondary market up to 1884.[17] However, as with Bengal Central, the Guildhall data presents a different picture, with the 220,000 shares covered by orders for over 350,000 shares. Again, lead bankers Evelyn Baring and Nathaniel Rothschild were not scaled back in the manner suffered by other shareholders, and took 25,000 shares each.[18] If the share price performed badly in the secondary market, it was not because the Secretary of State drove too hard a bargain, but through a weak market.

Nevertheless, the company and its sponsors would have been conscious of the political embarrassment of a poorly performing issue. Success was crucial for attracting more private capital into the Indian railway sector, especially given the depreciating silver rupee. Most observers wished to avoid a return to the discredited guarantee system which had prevailed up to 1869. The India Office source, for example, complained that the guarantees implied huge 'lobbying' of the public works committee by 'enterprising interested promoters' who sought only to 'turn over a percentage'.[19] This determination of the GOI to make the issue successful was manifest in the Bengal NW prospectus of 1882. GOI support was assured with Viceroy Ripon offering to build the railway as 'a productive public works' were private enterprise inadequate.[20] When the Bengal NW share price fell, the company lobbied the Secretary of State for improved terms. The company's annual report of 1884 reported the decision made by Secretary of State Kimberley in January to abandon the government's claim to 50 per cent of excess profits on earnings above 6 per cent, so leaving upside with shareholders. Indian taxpayers had gifted land and a valuable regional monopoly to the company but would not share in the earnings. The same document complained that the buyout arrangements at a generous 25 times trailing net earnings would not include the now withdrawn 50 per cent government share in the calculation. As ever railway investors wanted to be paid twice, with an enhanced running yield coupled with generous buyout conditions, which capitalized such income.[21] The desire to recover the trading performance of the stock was explicit in a public works memorandum of January 1883, which stated that the floatation 'did not command the premium looked for by its promoters', but it was hoped that this would prove 'temporary' since changes could be made to the 'division of profits' or the 'purchase conditions'.[22] Kimberley's support for the Rothschild and Baring investments was seized on by the sceptical Campbell at the key 1884 'select committee on East India Railway Communication'. Campbell asserted that the risk for sponsors and investors was removed by their capacity to return to government and negotiate 'more favourable terms'. Further, Sir James Caird made the point that the line 'being in a rich and thickly-peopled country' could be expected to do well in the longer term, so recovering the banker's paper losses.[23] In fact, after the generous contract revisions, Bengal NW's share price bounced to close to 104 by January 1887. While it fell back in the late 1880s, by January 1894 the stock was trading at 118.5. Rothschild dumped his stock over the period 1888–93 at an average price above par, having enjoyed his 4 per cent coupon during construction.[24] By the early 1890s, shareholders were enjoying annuity-type returns from their valuable concession for a period of ninety-nine years, secure in the knowledge that the venture would not be allowed to fail. Like Bengal Central, further government inducements were offered to the company in 1890 when Tirhoot State Railway was leased on favourable terms to the company. The India Office provided flexibility on funding for the company by offering to fund further Tirhoot expenses on its own balance sheet. It also provided covert support for Bengal NW in offering additional free land on 'reasonable request'. By 1894, Auckland Colvin (ex-Finance Member) and Secretary of State Fowler were pressing to give Bengal NW a monopoly over all railways falling between the Ganges and 'Benares Corner', despite the public works committee's favouring of state railways. John Strachey observed that Fowler had 'committed himself ... to City people in the matter'.[25]

By that time Bengal NW had built up sufficient critical mass to be counted amongst a small group of Indian railway companies seen as having the scale and experience to command further government sponsorship and concessions. In 1895, Secretary of State Hamilton articulated a vision of a railway oligopoly to his Viceroy Elgin, whereby companies like Bengal NW were granted concessions to expand on a metre gauge (for economy). Bengal NW and other favoured railways offered 'resources greater and credit better' than those backed by less formidable promoters. Moreover, in a state of war it would be an advantage to call upon 'strong, rich, and well-organized Railway Associations' which could support the government's strategic requirements. This, presumably, meant that Rothschild and others might be expected to provide open access to the Indian Army when troop movements to the North West Frontier were needed.[26] Given the antipathy felt by the Rothschild group for the anti-Semitic regime in St Petersburg, the family would have been appropriate partners from a strategic perspective. Only the elite of gentlemanly capitalism could be expected to provide this level of mutual support for the GOI. Within a few years the candidature of even the Rothschild's was called into question by Secretary of State Hamilton in the context of Burma. Nevertheless, during the 1880s and 90s, the financial position of the 'non guaranteed' Bengal NW was protected robustly by the India Office. Strong criticism of Bengal NW from within the India Council by members like Hardie (Chairman of the Finance Committee) was resisted by Hamilton as being 'unreasonable and wild'. In short, Hamilton was more dependent on Rothschild sponsorship than they on him. India remained a relatively small part of the New Court business, dwarfed by the operations in the Americas and Middle East.[27]

Demonstrating his group's remarkable caution towards corporate risk, Rothschild himself missed out on much of the improved performance and concessions of the Bengal NW group, having exited most of his investment by 1893. While conditions in the London financial markets worsened over 1894 to 1907, Bengal NW's chairman Colonel Gracey was able to boast to the Mackay committee that his company's share price rose steeply from 114 to 148. This was driven by the generous government buyout provisions. Imitating Richard Strachey at EIR, Colonel Gracey had moved from the government side to the 'private' company after negotiating contracts beneficial to Bengal NW.[28] Sir George Campbell's assertion that the India Office was happy to sweeten terms for Bengal NW shareholders, leaving the market more mercantilist than laissez-faire, was insightful.

The later Acworth railway committee of 1921 did give representatives of Bengal NW a more demanding interview than Mackay had managed. Company Director and city stockbroker Lionel Cohen was made to defend the complicated and unduly generous contractual arrangements which his company had negotiated with the government in 1882. The contracts had since been renegotiated for a further twenty-five years, and were set in stone until maturity. In contrast, the French government, according to Acworth, reserved the right to renegotiate during the life of a railway lease. Cohen rejected the French system, arguing that the government was protected by their right to repurchase the stock at par at the end of twenty-five years. Cohen's colleague at Bengal NW, Colonel Gracey, asserted that the GOI's maximum/minimum fare structure placed reasonable limits on private-sector profits. In spite of his sympathies for private rail companies, Acworth seemed unconvinced with this defence. Acworth described Bengal NW in understated terms as being 'not an unprosperous company'.[29] While the Rothschild's had by this time withdrawn their sponsorship role for the company, in line with the diminished underwriting fees and potential for capital gain, they left an attractive legacy for risk-adverse London investors. Bengal NW had evolved into a risk-free annuity with government support, lacking only trustee stock status.[30]

Bengal–Nagpur Railway Company

Remarkably, the Bengal NW experiment with non-guaranteed rail finance was abandoned after 1882. Looking back on the Bengal NW private initiative some years later, finance member Sir Edward Law described the financing as a 'brilliant example' but complained about the lack of similar attempts. He blamed the return to an 'easy system of Government assistance' which had 'paralysed all independent financial initiative'.[31] In positing this distinction between early Rothschild ventures and later financings Law simplified matters. Nevertheless, soon after the Bengal NW floatation Lord Kimberley, Louis Mallet and Juland Danvers discussed the necessity for new guarantees. While Mallet (permanent undersecretary) and Danvers (public works) were philosophically opposed to government guarantees, the apparent failure of the Bengal NW issue damaged confidence in private enterprise. Danvers reluctantly concluded in a letter to Kimberley in July 1883 that the required Indian lines were unlikely to be constructed 'unless private enterprise is assisted in the shape of a moderate guarantee for a short period'.[32] His guarded support for more guarantees was given impetus by a vote at the Council of India in favour of the principal of state support. By 1884, the detail of such support was being put to the test in the context of what would become the Bengal Nagpur Railway Company (Bengal Nagpur). The proposal was controversial from the outset with a split on the India Office

Public Works Committee.[33] By June 1886, arguments were still raging, with the financial position of the GOI deteriorating and state support for railways more sensitive. Danvers assessed that four council members were now in favour of the Bengal–Nagpur line 'as an insurance against famine'. Finance Member Auckland Colvin was opposed, partly due to silver rupee depreciation and the rising cost of a sterling guarantee.[34]

The protective aspects of the line came to the fore in debate within parliamentary committees. In particular, Kimberley called a select committee on East Indian Railway Communication in 1884 to examine the funding dilemma on railways, with focus on the recommendations of the preceding Famine Commission of 1880/1. The 1884 committee produced detailed recommendations on railway building, including arguments for Bengal–Nagpur. The line was viewed as a vital part of a railway network which would eventually provide food distribution 25 miles either side of 20,000 miles of track, so covering India's 1 million square miles.[35] Amongst committee witnesses, Major Conway-Gordon emphasized the role played by railway promoters Hoare Millar and Co., who had been pressing for the concession to enhance and extend the line. The controlling partners in this firm, Samuel Hoare and Robert Millar, became key management and investors in Bengal–Nagpur when it was finally floated by Rothschild in 1887. They had been lobbying for the concession to extend the line for many years. As early as 1882, Secretary of State Hartington sent a telegram to Viceroy Ripon urging a rapid appointment of Hoare Millar. He stressed the 'protective urgency' of the railway. This followed a conference chaired by Sir Theodore Hope (Public Works Member) on the subject with all the interested Bengal parties.[36] By 1884, Conway-Gordon pressed Hoare Millar's credentials as 'backed by a very strong syndicate at home' (presumably N. M. Rothschild). However, these financial resources would not be available forever since such City investors 'will not keep that money available at call from year to year'.[37]

In fact Hoare and Millar were powerful City allies for the Rothschild railway groupings.[38] This choreographed City lobbying was supported by Bengal and Bombay Chambers of Commerce, whose managing agency representatives saw attractive trade-related business from the railway.[39] The scope for government lobbying potential for railways defined as 'protective' had been expanded in 1881, when the terms of the famine insurance fund had been altered. In non-famine years half the fund could now be expended on railway construction not directly linked to famine prevention. However, City and Chamber pressure was required to overcome objections set down by Indian Secretaries Kimberley and Cranbrook. Kimberley argued that Bengal Nagpur and Indian Midland railways (both Rothschild sponsored) 'appear to me to have no greater claim to this character [protective] than could be advanced in behalf of every railway'.[40] He resisted pressure to channel Indian taxpayers' money from the emergency famine insurance fund to the two railways. Nevertheless by 1885 new Secretary of State Randolph Churchill had re-characterized the two Rothschild-backed railways as protective rather than productive, giving them access to the fund. Churchill allowed interest on the debt of the two lines to be charged against the fund over 1885–1900, which arrangement was subsequently extended.[41]

Thereafter, in preparing to float Bengal Nagpur in London, with multiple levels of government support, the newly ennobled Lord Rothschild benefited from having a railway enthusiast at the India Office. Secretary of State Cross had little time for his predecessor Randolph Churchill, personally or politically, and was overlooked by Prime Minister Salisbury in favour of Churchill for the highest political office. However, the two shared a commitment to Indian railways. It is unclear to what extent Cross's Lancashire business and political background informed these views. When discussions ensued between Cross and his counsel on the financing of the railway in late 1886, he was prepared to challenge sceptics on the public works committee, such as Richard Strachey. He told Viceroy Dufferin that conditions had changed since Kimberley declined the insurance fund monies for the railway and declared progress on the terms negotiated with Hoare.[42] Cross's correspondence provides insight into India Office negotiations with the sole underwriter on the Bengal–Nagpur issue, N. M. Rothschild. Rothschild and Barings (earlier involved) had displayed brinkmanship in declining to accept fees of 1.25 per cent on underwriting and brokerage. The bankers pressed for improved terms, comparable to those available to the other beneficiary of famine insurance support, Rothschild's Indian Midland. In desperation Cross asked Dufferin if there were any chance to restructure the financing of Bengal Nagpur as a state railway, but ultimately agreed exclusive terms with Rothschild. He described the latter as 'very stiff as to terms'.[43] Dufferin for his part had pressed Cross not to give in to the doubters on his Council, and thanked his senior partner for his efforts in overcoming Whitehall resistance.[44]

While the market presented some difficulties due to the simultaneous efforts being made to convert existing Indian 4 per cent stock into lower coupon paper, the Bengal Nagpur issue was duly launched by Rothschild alone in February 1887 on Rothschild's terms.[45] The stock paid a guaranteed dividend of 4 per cent and entitled the shareholder to 25 per cent of 'surplus profits'. The government had no right to change any terms of the concession until 1913. The Rothschild share prospectus for the 1887 issue made the attractiveness of the proposition clear. The central province of Chattisgarh was described as 'a perfect granary' whose produce would now be transportable to the ports of Calcutta and Bombay. The density of population and available workforce in the region promised high potential economic growth. Migration of peoples within the region, to work on the railways and the 'cultivable wastes', was anticipated. Viceroy Ripon's earlier despatch on the subject was quoted at length, where Bengal Nagpur was said to have the combination of 'remunerativeness' and 'famine protective' qualities. In short, equity holders enjoyed the benefits of long-term contracts and gifted land from the GOI, coupled with a double protection through government-funded famine protection, supported by trading-related cash flows. The construction risks in the project were reduced, since the proceeds of the issue were being used partly to purchase the existing Nagpur–Nandgaon state line (150 miles). Investors took construction risk only on the conversion of this to broad gauge and the extension of the line.[46] The Bengal–Nagpur promotion and government negotiations displayed many of the characteristics critiqued by George Campbell. Later, Campbell recorded his opposition to the 'expensive' Bengal Nagpur line, constructed by the Rothschild syndicate, under a government guarantee which was 'too liberal'.[47]

Not surprisingly the Rothschild-led issue was hugely oversubscribed with 566,000 shares applied for and only 150,000 shares issued, partly paid at £20 per share. The satisfaction expressed by Cross that he had managed to press Rothschild for the best terms seems not to have been borne out in the level of excess demand. While there is a thin dividing line between share issues meeting excess demand and those failing to create sufficient interest, oversubscription by almost 400 per cent indicated that the terms were considered very generous in the City.[48] The breakdown of large shareholders subscribing at the time of issue, and subsequently, is even more revealing than the volume of demand. Davis and Huttenback carried out an exhaustive analysis of the backgrounds of early shareholders in a large sample of 260 domestic, foreign and Empire companies over the period 1883–1907. Their intention was to identify demographic patterns that would provide social and economic information on the motivation for investing at home or overseas, during this period of 'high Imperialism'. Strikingly, Bengal Nagpur was revealed to have attracted more high net worth investors than any other company in their sample. Of the thirty-five investments of over £100,000, across the universe of companies no less than eighteen were in Bengal–Nagpur. Most of these investors were characterized by the authors as 'peers and gents'. In fact a number of those titled investors could comfortably be described as Cain and Hopkins 'gentlemanly capitalists'. These included Thomas Sutherland (Chairman of P&O), Sir Everard Hambro (Director of Bank of England), Leonard Lionel Cohen (financier and prominent railway investor) and Nathaniel Rothschild himself.[49] Remarkably, a number of the MPs who had debated the ethics of dispensing famine insurance monies to Bengal–Nagpur with George Campbell, also subscribed for shares in the railway. Davis and Huttenback calculated that no less than £1,115,000 of MP's money was placed in the railway (37 per cent of the issue), including a number of industrialist/trade related MPs like Bernard Samuelson (steel) and W. H. Smith (railway books), who were outside the remit of Cain and Hopkins. Interestingly W. H. Smith (by then first lord of the Treasury), like Rothschild, combined a role of advisor to the government on railway matters with that of private rail investor.[50] Bengal Nagpur's financial backing straddled politics, commerce, finance and manufacturing. Rudyard Kipling was a minor shareholder. This reflected the importance of Bengal Nagpur's demand for British railway product, and the generously priced gold-plated arrangements.[51]

The wider focus of Davis and Huttenback's analysis prevented them from examining explanations for this deep-seated London confidence, in the distant Bengalese railway. In fact, parliamentary and Indian counsel debates would have made Bengal Nagpur more prominent than many comparable listed companies. The requirement for the Secretary of State to make the guaranteed company's flotation successful would have been widely understood. Moreover, Nathaniel Rothschild's ability to extract generous terms after the 'disappointment' of Bengal NW may have allowed him to present the investment to 'gents and peers' as remunerative and risk free. Certainly Rothschild was comfortable about making a large personal investment at the time of issuance. We are fortunate that the National Archives have retained all of the share registers for Bengal Nagpur from listing in 1887 to state acquisition in the 1940s. This allows us to follow the purchases and divestments of stock by Rothschild, and other key investors. Rothschild's negotiations to improve the Bengal NW terms necessitated a 'buy and hold' approach, until the further government concessions allowed an exit at a healthy profit. However, the Rothschild holding in Bengal Nagpur was more short term. With the stock price rising from par to 108.5 by January 1888, Rothschild sold approximately £180,000 of his stock over the period 1 December 1887 to 13 January 1888 generating an immediate profit of over £15,000, enhanced by the dividends and underwriting fees. This more 'speculative' behaviour was mimicked by Rothschild's close City associate and co-investor Lionel Cohen.[52]

Despite the protective and productive attributes of Bengal Nagpur the operational performance was disappointing. It was highlighted by Indian nationalist Dinshaw Wacha as one of the worst performing railways between 1881 and 1901, over which time it used £11.7 million of capital and lost in aggregate £1.3 million.[53] From an investor's perspective, those losses meant they were unable to benefit from surplus earnings but enjoyed the state-protected 4 per cent dividend on a growing principal outstanding. Moreover, the government support meant that Bengal Nagpur's operations were protected through generous famine insurance subsidies, and a valuable coal duopoly with Bengal's dominant EIR. Both these levels of 'gold plating' were controversial. The insurance fund suffered misappropriation of some £8 million out of a total of £24 million contributed by Indian taxpayers, over 1878–9 to 1894–5. Most of this went on military expenditure, but the interest charges on Bengal Nagpur/Indian Midland accumulated. By 1899 the fund followed advice from the previous year's famine commission and targeted some Rs 400,000 (approximately £30,000 per annum) of its anticipated Rs 1.5 million income annually to the two railway companies.[54] The budget for Bengal Nagpur alone in 1889–90 was some Rs 246,800 against a total irrigation budget for the whole of India of only Rs 80,000. By 18⁹⁹/₁₉₀0, the allocations to Bengal Nagpur interest payments had ceased, according to the fund's returns, while the effects of the 1900 famine in Central Province and Berar had made a significant impact on the company. Bengal Nagpur was able to transport some 356,965 tons of rice, gram, pulse and other non-wheat crops in the six months to 30 June 1900, compared to 99,582 the previous year.[55]

The railway was repaying subsidies provided by the famine insurance fund and transforming itself, as *The Times* observed, from 'an exporting railway' to provide 'inwards traffic into the Central Province'. The railway benefited directly from this shift to domestic business, reporting a large increase in profitability. Gross receipts per mile per week increased from Rs 157 to Rs 262 over 1899– 1900.[56] In short, Bengal Nagpur was bolstered by protective famine insurance subsidies and charged extra to transport grains when famine occurred. Later, Viceroy Curzon tried to reverse Churchill's decision, which he characterized as an attempt 'to squeeze them [railways] within the four corners of the Grant'. Curzon claimed Bengal–Nagpur and Indian Midland enjoyed the best of both worlds, in following government-guaranteed borrowing as 'productive' business, while absorbing fund monies as 'protective' construction.[57] Further, Secretary of State Hamilton accused his predecessor Churchill of 'mischievously' interfer- ing in the use of insurance fund monies by channelling them towards supposed 'public works' of 'doubtful utility'. Churchill had 'forced the council' into this arrangement. In the process he had alienated Indians, who 'not unnaturally allege that the fund is juggled with'. However, neither Hamilton nor Curzon was able to reverse the decision.[58]

The company's coal duopoly was equally unpopular. The Chambers of Com- merce, which had supported the Rothschild concessions, complained by 1890 about Bengal Nagpur's failure to open the region up to competition to exploit agricultural and mineral resources.[59] By the early twentieth century concerns about EIR/Bengal Nagpur's regional coal duopoly had heightened. Indian coal prices fell briefly in 1901, after Bengal Nagpur gained access to the EIR con- trolled coal fields but rose later with price manipulation.[60] In 1904 the Chairman of the Indian Mining Association wrote to Curzon complaining about the slow progress in instituting proper competition in these Jherria coal fields. In spite of Curzon's greater focus on industrial matters on taking up his position in 1899, little improvement was discernible in coal production or transportation.[61] The London Chamber of Commerce was affiliated with Bengal's Chamber through a joint chairman. As late as 1912/1913 the problem remained unresolved with the London Chamber and the Indian Mining Association pushing memorials on the subject to Secretary of State Crewe. At the same time things had improved.

Other members of the London Chamber could boast of the Bengal coal trade expanding from 1 million to 12 million tons over 1881–1911.[62] Inevitably, with the benefit of these multiple subsidies Bengal Nagpur became more profitable, creating returns above the guaranteed 4 per cent. Noticeably, in the company's annual reports for succeeding years there was no reference to the large insurance fund payments, or apparent requirement to justify the use of the fund's capital in improved famine prevention and protection.[63]

The legacy of Bengal–Nagpur was discussed at several parliamentary committees of the late nineteenth and early twentieth centuries on railway matters. At Mackay in 1908, Sir Samuel Hoare, chairman of the company, accused the Secretary of State for India of exercising anti-competitive power.[64] Hoare argued greedily for increased private involvement in Indian railways to lessen the 'monopolist' powers of the India Office. This was ungrateful, given the generosity shown to his company in securing consistent government support. Again, by Acworth in 1921, committee members were critical of the India Office's generosity to Campbell's 'city syndicates'. Acworth cross-examined the omnipresent Bengal Nagpur board member Lionel Cohen, expressing incredulity at the terms enjoyed for so long by he and fellow gentlemanly capitalists (Cohen had some £300,000 of his own money invested). By the 1920s, Bengal Nagpur had contracts to run the railways until 1950 with no government right to amend. Cohen defended the contracts by pointing out that the government was beneficiary of the company's handsome profits in sharing surplus earnings, though such earnings were only distributed after payment of the guaranteed dividend.[65]

Burma Railway Company

Secretary of State Cross declared to Viceroy Dufferin, after the successful Bengal Nagpur floatation of 1887, that he looked 'upon that and the Mandalay Railway as rather triumphs, and ships for other schemes in due time'. Dufferin was appreciative of Cross's efforts in overcoming the opposition of council members, including Strachey.[66] In Burma, Cross was dealing with the legacy of Randolph Churchill's period as Secretary of State when the annexation of Upper Burma was pressed through. The invasion of 1885 has attracted widespread attention from scholars seeking to understand the extent to which the last significant expansion of the Raj was driven by commercial or military/security requirements.[67] The invasion was important for Cross's tenure as Secretary since it imposed new pressures on the financial position of the GOI, with increased military expenditure and very limited additional revenues. Webster has dissected the role of Chambers of Commerce and companies, in pressing the India Office for annexation. However, the business opportunities in Upper Burma are far from evident in the Cross/Dufferin correspondence. Even Burma Ruby Mines preoccupied the dual government more as a source of scandal and difficulty in the House of Commons.[68] Ultimately, Calcutta and Whitehall were prepared to override MP's concerns, giving Rothschild's ruby mines consortium exclusive access to Upper Burma. Under government protection, Rothschild would assess mineral resources, and determine whether they wished to exercise a long dated lease over Burmese properties.[69] The Rothschild hold over Burmese business resembled something of a family fiefdom. Within a week of British annexation of Upper Burma, Rothschild offered to absorb all existing rail lines, and construct lines to the frontier of China. By 1889 N. M. Rothschild had floated Burma Ruby Mines stock at a 300 per cent premium, on a wave of speculation. However, the subsequent Burma Railway Company was only floated by Rothschild some ten years after initial approaches to the Indian finance committee had been rejected. The Westminster MP's concerns appear to have created some check to unbridled regional monopoly.[70]

Privatization of existing Burma railway lines was equally controversial. There was strong opposition to a widening of the Rothschild concession. Bernard, chief commissioner of Burma, was sympathetic to private capitalists owning new lines, but resisted handing over lines already developed by the state. He may have resented giving shareholders cash flows from existing lines in addition to government guarantees on new construction. However, by 1886 he had climbed down and generous underwriting fees of 2 per cent were being discussed to override investor apathy.[71] Cross pressed the military rationale for a railway which might move troops across the eastern extremity of India Office terrain. General Roberts, long a rail enthusiast on the North West Frontier had taken control of military matters in Burma. Cross was under pressure from some members of the India Council to construct 'a good military road' in combination with the existing river traffic, rather than incur further debts on expensive railways. He encouraged Dufferin to consider silver rupee borrowings as an alternative to gold sterling, but ultimately pressed the Viceroy to ensure 'that the railway should go on'.[72]

When the Rothschild-led Burma Railways issue was belatedly launched in October 1896, it attracted demand comparable to Burma Ruby Mines. The modest £2 million issue was oversubscribed more than eight times, though the Rothschilds were able to secure large amounts of the stock. Nathaniel, Alfred, Leopold and Walter together secured allocations of over 20,000 £10 shares to take 10 per cent of the issue.[73] The shares traded up from 100 to 108.5 by January 1899, generating a book profit for the family of some £17,000 in addition to the 3 per cent running yield over the first couple of years. This was supplemented by generous 'underwriting fees' of 1.5 per cent or, for Rothschild, £30,000.[74] Revealingly, Sir Theodore Hope is present on the share register for 1896, having served as head of the Viceroy's public works committee, gaining a reputation for being too close to railway promoters. Sir Auckland Colvin ex-finance member of the viceroy's council and rail enthusiast, and Robert Millar, promoter of Bengal Nagpur, sat on the board of Burma with shares. Indeed, the Strachey brothers, who had fought privatization of Rothschild's previous companies, hoped to exploit Colvin's position as Chairman of Burma Railways. They looked to secure employment for a 'young friend' at £500–600 per annum.[75] Finally, Wallace Brothers, lobbyists for the Upper Burma invasion in 1885 and thereafter Burmese rail extensions, found representation on Burma Railway's board through Alexander Wallace. The managing agent pressed Rothschild strongly to expand the lines to Mandalay in line with Cross's original plans. This impressive list of investors and sponsors for the Burma railways issue attracted support from Secretary of State Hamilton. He viewed Burma Railways as a worthy peer for Bengal NW. It sat in the cartel of strongly capitalized railway groups, again within the Rothschild orbit. Prior to the share placement, Hamilton professed that having the Rothschild's overseeing Burma Railway's management could be expected to 'give Railway enterprise generally in India a lift'. As with Bengal NW, Hamilton had seen off Council 'agitation against the transfer [of Burma's railway] to the Company'.[76] Of course, the Empire enthusiast/Russophobe profile of Lord Rothschild made the New Court group a suitable strategic, as well as financial partner for the India Office. In contrast their relationship with the other regional foe, France, was more ambiguous, with strains apparent between the Paris and London branches of the Rothschild group.

After Burma railway's floatation, the strategic and commercial attributes of Rothschild's railway were pressed to justify further guaranteed financings to link India with China via Upper Burma. Company representatives pressed for concessions to expand as far as Yunnan with a network linking Peking and Tonguin. The opportunity to construct rail links between the two most populous countries on earth with government funding or guarantees must have been attractive. Godley, as head of India Office administration, was supportive, and there was strong sponsorship from Prime Minister Salisbury, who feared French railway incursions into Burma.[77] However, with Curzon's accession to Viceroyalty, power shifted somewhat from Whitehall to Calcutta.[78] Curzon took a less positive view of Burma's military railways than Cross. He persuaded his Secretary of State Hamilton that railway extensions from Bengal deep into Burma risked the Burmese feeling 'over-swamped by the pushing multiplying Bengali'.[79] Curzon demanded that Indian taxes should not be used to expand railways outside 'Indian territories'. This made expansion from Burma into China problematical. Finally, despite the attention of Godley and Salisbury, and enormous Chamber of Commerce pressure from Sir James Mackay, Hamilton supported his Viceroy and rejected demands for GOI guarantees for Burma-China rail extensions. Hamilton concluded that 'if any guarantee is given it should be Imperial'.[80] The extent to which military purposes could be used to justify additional Indian railway related taxes was limited. Curzon demonstrated greater pragmatism in this approach to strategic rail construction than Cross or Roberts. Equally, he had shown himself, through opposition to the plundering by rail companies of the insurance fund, less prone to flattery from City of London syndicates than his colleagues in Whitehall. The share price performance of Burma Railways after Rothschild's initial 'stagging' of the issue disappointed. The stock market was weak by 1900, and Burma's prospects in particular looked uncertain.[81]

Certainly, by 1902, the legitimacy and sustainability of the partnership between Rothschild's railway vehicles and the India Office was openly questioned by Curzon in Calcutta. The Viceroy's criticism of the management of Burma Railways prompted Hamilton to doubt his own faith in the Rothschild's, Hambros and other sponsors of the railway. With railway profits beginning to exceed expectations, Hamilton questioned whether his 1896 negotiations with Nathaniel over Burma Railways had delivered to the India Office 'a sufficiently good bargain'. He still hoped that the Rothschild management team would deliver superior performance and override Curzon's concerns. However, by April 1902 Hamilton concluded that the problems in Burma were reflective of a deeper malaise in the Rothschild group. His strategy of working hand in hand with strong City sponsors appeared to lie in tatters with the admission that 'the Rothschilds ... are completely played out'. In contrast the new industrial power of the United States was manifest in the virility of Pierpoint Morgan who 'has the power of effecting great trade combinations'.[82] The rise of Morgan in London must have been greeted with particular concern by the English houses which had controlled Empire railway finance. By the following year, the London based business J. S. Morgan & Co., was playing a coordinating role in efforts to bring English capital into the Baghdad railway project. Morgan's potency was supported by their strength across both French and English markets. In the latter, the appointment of Curzon's confidante and ex-finance member, Sir Clinton Dawkins, as Morgan's lead banker on the Baghdad transaction may have been crucial. Dawkins played a key role in framing Curzon's India railway policy in previous years.[83] Rothschild's vulnerability in Europe was made greater as Lord Revelstoke and Pierpoint Morgan began merger talks for Baring/JP Morgan over 1904/5, though these were ultimately shelved.

This competitive threat from the USA extended to British interests in Burma and India generally, from service industries to manufacturing. When Burma Railway placed significant orders for railway materials and locomotives in the USA, a public controversy between Secretary of State Hamilton and British manufacturers ensued.[84] Hamilton called for greater standardization in British manufacturing to meet the economies of scale achieved by the US manufacturers. He seemed impressed by the cartel arrangements practised in the USA where locomotive manufacturers had 'brought to a fine art the power of combination'.[85]

Hamilton and Curzon together arranged meetings for UK locomotive builders to share designs and press for standardization to see off the American competition that was threatening the extent to which Burma and other railways were required to 'buy British'. While these efforts were partially successful in seeing off American competition in railway supplies, the Hamilton vision of an India Office/Rothschild 'combination' for railway finance had collapsed. Burmese mineral extraction had disappointed, and the commercial aspects of the railway looked less appealing. By 1908, the Rothschild family had sold most of their Burma Railways stock and further equity issues were underwritten by Cazenove and Akroyds, far less profitably than the earlier N. M. Rothschild issues with a disappointing level of investor demand.[86] Even with government guarantees and trustee stock status, the risk return on Burma railway business had by then become unappealing to New Court. The new City syndicates proved less capable of marketing the equity upside on the stock, and were thinly capitalized imitations of American underwriters like J. P. Morgan.[87]

Conclusion

Bengal Central was presented as a departure from the unacceptable first-generation Indian rail companies. It amounted to nothing other than a speculative financing vehicle for Rothschild/Baring. When the prospects were revealed to have been exaggerated, Churchill and other India Office friends stood by to offer further guarantees to Rothschild. Bengal NW was an experiment in private-sector capitalism which seemed an ideal candidate for non-guaranteed financing, based on strong local demographics and the promise of additional military-related revenues through facilitating troop movements towards the North West Frontier. While the original issue was oversubscribed, the stock's subsequent performance disappointed, in a poor market. However, unlike other investors, the Rothschild/Barings-led London syndicate who underwrote the issue benefited from a subsequent renegotiation of their government-controlled contracts and further concessions to facilitate a rapid recovery in the performance of the stock. Five years later, this experience was used to justify new levels of government support for Bengal Nagpur, which enjoyed generous government guarantees and access to a famine fund targeted at and paid for by the peasants of India. This subsidization of London-based gentlemanly capitalists by the poor was extended with the granting of duopoly control over Bengal coal reserves and a heightened fuel cost, ultimately paid for by Indian consumers. The India Office concluded that control of Indian railway companies needed to reside with financial groupings with the resources to provide support in the event of a foreign invasion of India. By the time Burma Railways was floated in 1896, after the bankruptcy of Barings, only N. M. Rothschild qualified. Lord George Hamilton posited a long-term partnership between his India Office and Lord Rothschild. N. M. Rothschild had consistently outsold Baring on their joint railway underwritings in India. However, when Burma failed to provide mineral resources comparable to South Africa, the bankers and their co-investors left to pursue more attractive investment propositions. The efforts made by Hamilton and his predecessors to attract London syndicates into the Indian railways were borne of necessity with a worsening financial position in Calcutta, and India Office officials were repeatedly out-manoeuvred by their opportunistic financial partners. Lord Rothschild demonstrated a strong insight into how revenues might be extracted from the commercial, famine-related and strategic aspects of the Indian railways. His contention that in Indian railway matters he was 'only a buffer' was self effacing and understated the influence he exerted over Cross, Churchill and Hamilton.[88] N. M. Rothschild skilfully originated guaranteed securities with trustee status tailor-made for the gentlemanly capitalist audience, while the India office struggled to remove similar securities from the secondary market. The low risk appetite of those London investors, comparable to the low risk/high return tendencies of the British locomotive builders, made gentlemanly capitalists unhelpful bedfellows for the India Office. 'Indian railroading' was pursued with the Indian taxpayer as lender of last resort.

5 NORTHERN WARS AND SOUTHERN DIPLOMACY: SIR DOUGLAS FORSYTH'S SECOND CAREER ON THE INDIAN RAILWAYS

Introduction

The Times obituary of Sir Thomas Douglas Forsyth in 1886 paid the former ICS representative a dubious compliment in placing him highly in the group of 'men of second rank' within the 'modern history of British India'. Forsyth was not unique in having combined a somewhat forgettable and modestly paid Indian government career with a move into the City. His boardroom appointments within Indian railways straddled several companies and geographical regions. The manner in which he promoted those companies, attracting public- and private-sector support, illustrates the division of power within Anglo-Indian commerce in the late nineteenth century. Forsyth used business, diplomatic and ICS/India Office contacts to negotiate advantageous arrangements on financings for companies representing the military, famine protective and commercial aspects of Indian railways. He forged close relationships with business mavericks in the Stafford House Committee (SHC), a charitable organization which transformed itself into a holding company for railway promoters. In the diplomatic arena he worked with ambitious and frustrated consular representatives to deliver combined British and Portuguese guarantees to a small Goa railway. Indian government guarantees were then negotiated to support funding for a contiguous railway, which stretched across large parts of the south. The Southern Mahratta promised to make the Deccan region free of famines, but failed to deliver famine protection. In the North, Forsyth promoted vast military expenditure in partnership with the Indian railway pioneer W. P. Andrew. Only when Lord Ripon took it upon himself to bring military railways back on balance sheet were these excesses brought under control. In short, Forsyth's 'second rank' ICS career could be viewed as illustrative of the quality of Indian rail management over the late nineteenth century. London boardrooms were dominated by well connected middlemen who performed an agency role between Indian government officials and City financiers, without obvious expertise in railway management.[1] Fortunately, Forsyth has left a range of valuable correspondence, and documents in several archives, providing a detailed narrative of his activities from the famine stricken south, to the military railways of the North West Frontier.

Earlier, Forsyth's career had promised a first-rank obituary. He left Hailey-bury in 1848, having topped the Bengal list, to join the Bengal Civil Service. As Deputy Commissioner of the newly annexed province of Punjab, he oversaw troop transport from Punjab to Delhi. During the Mutiny, Forsyth secured Sikh loyalist support under their chieftains, allowing Umballa's defence against rebel incursions. After the recapture of Delhi, he was asked to hunt down rebels, carry-ing through reprisals with enthusiasm and earning a CB. Indeed, violent reprisals were characteristic of Forsyth's ICS tenure and, by 1872, he played a central role in suppressing the Sikh Kuka rebellion in the princely state of Maler Kotla. For-syth and junior officers were harsh in their treatment of the rebels, executing sixty-five Sikhs with British cannon. As a result of his barbarism, Forsyth suf-fered short-term demotion, but his career was revived by Viceroy Northbrook. He was appointed KCSI by 1874 with later diplomatic postings to the Nepal border and Burma.[2]

Scinde, Punjaub and Delhi Railway

Like many former ICS representatives, Forsyth's pension proved inadequate for his retirement in England (which happened at the comparatively early age of fifty-five). Paid directorships at City-based Indian railway companies were an obvious means of supplementing pensions. Forsyth joined the strategic Scinde, Punjaub and Delhi Railway (Scinde, Punjaub) in 1878 to take advantage of his diplomatic and military contacts. He explained to an old Punjabi ICS col-league that he had been offered a couple of safe Conservative seats, which might have allowed him to attack Gladstone's despised foreign policies, but thought the salary unappealing. Instead, it was easy to 'extend one's hold on City busi-ness'. This went beyond Punjab with 'one or two other pleasant little seats' in Railway boardrooms.[3] However, as a first 'seat' Scinde, Punjaub offered Forsyth a generous salary, the opportunity to display his 'expertise' on Punjabi matters and to use friendships with ICS decision-makers in Calcutta and Punjab. The rest of the board offered similar advantages for the company, with a late judicial commissioner from Punjab, a Major General and a former Commissioner for Lucknow. Juland Danvers was the omnipresent India Office representative on the board, representing Whitehall's public works department. The intentions of the company were made plain in each annual report with the nineteenth-cen-tury equivalent of a 'mission statement'. A 'sure and speedy' rail link was to be completed from the port of Karachi to the interior of Punjab, coupled with a link between Lahore and the North West Frontier. This would facilitate troop movements across country from Calcutta to the west coast. Forsyth's Chairman was the omnipresent W. P. Andrew, who had long pressed the strategic importance of rapid troop movements to impede the Russian threat.[4]

However, Scinde, Punjaub met criticism from the outset for the generous level of state support negotiated by its directors. By 1882, W. P. Andrew and colleagues were beneficiaries of some £20 million of state guaranteed capital, but generated profits sufficient to pay only half the guaranteed 4 per cent. Additional GOI payments of £400,000 per annum were being made on interest alone. Finance Member Evelyn Baring reported to Viceroy Ripon on the prospects of a state acquisition of the company to stem government expense. Like most 'nationalizations' contemplated, any buyback would capitalize these losses and rumours of a government purchase would increase the share price above the already inflated £130 per share. In fact, to compensate shareholders (including buyouts and generous foreign exchange provisions) the price would be closer to £162 per share (or £17.82 million).[5] The unwinding costs on the foreign exchange arrangements alone were estimated at nearly £3 million, a cost which was not made public. This was too expensive to contemplate. Instead, the GOI focused on folding the underperforming Indus Valley railway into the group at a discounted price to bolster the operation (further enhancing the shares of Forsyth and colleagues). The social and economic benefits of all this were questionable. The Punjab's grain trade was growing with rail transport, supported by the government's 'bounty on all the import and export trade'. However, Scinde Punjaub, like all wheat-carrying railways, had encouraged peasants to abandon self insurance of foodstuffs. By 1885, critics of the state subsidized railway argued that this placed Punjab 'in danger of starvation if it had been visited by drought'.[6]

Andrew's links with Bombay Governor Sir Henry Bartle Frere allowed him to widen his transport interests. Frere placed Andrew on the board of Sir William Mackinnon's two Indian Ocean shipping lines: the British India Steam Navigation Company (B. I.) (focused on sea lanes around India), and Netherlands India S.N.Co (N. I.), responsible for island trade between Indonesian islands. Frere controlled stock in Mackinnon's businesses and used political influence within India and Africa to secure valuable postal franchises for Mackinnon. The Frere–Mackinnon relationship across India and East Africa was symbiotic. The pressures they exerted on the India Office/GOI to secure mail concessions were comparable to lobbying for railway guarantees.[7] Frere's political influence was supported by the financial resources of Mackinnon/Andrew. Between 1870 and 1876, for example, they jointly guaranteed loans to Sir John William Kaye, secretary of the India Office, at the political and secret department. Kaye had got into financial difficulties through his profligate sons in Australia. He expressed gratitude to the railway and shipping entrepreneurs for their generosity in guaranteeing his 5 per cent loan on £1500. Kaye offered to speak to Lord

Northbrook on Mackinnon's behalf, asking the shipping man to draw up a wish list of his needs in the Indian region. He was grateful for 'a mysterious chest of tea which arrived at my Penge bungalow'.[8] It is likely that co-guarantor W. P. Andrew would have forged the links between Mackinnon and Forsyth, who came together in later efforts to secure railway concessions in Goa.

Forsyth was given a directorship at the EIR at the same time. The Bengal railway was far more profitable over the longer term than Forsyth's Punjabi railway holdings. EIR controlled valuable trading links into Calcutta, while Scinde, Punjaub relied on government guarantees to meet dividend and coupon payments. However, as Forsyth joined the board of the Punjabi line, it was enjoying a mini-boom with troop and police conveyance revenues boosted by the Second Afghan War. The company's annual report for 1879 boasted of military revenues rising by 34 per cent over the previous year. This was the first time in the twenty-five-year history of Scinde, Punjaub that net revenues were sufficient to pay guaranteed interest (at 5 per cent and 4.5 per cent).[9] By 1881, as the war faded, returns had fallen to 3.2 per cent, necessitating renewed government funding. The company's financial viability depended on tensions on the North West frontier. This was evidenced by troop numbers using the railway during and after the Afghan confrontation. During late 1878 and early 1879, some 192,000 troops were moved against 41,000 during the first half of 1881. The company found new military revenues by 1882 in transporting Indian troops to the pier at Karachi for disembarking to the Egyptian war, and by 1885 with new tensions at Pendjeh.[10] Nevertheless, as a guaranteed joint stock company, Scinde, Punjaub needed diversification and, with the build-up of port facilities at Karachi, the company transported part of the Punjab's burgeoning wheat harvests for export. Again, this failed to produce satisfactory revenues. There were strong complaints about the efficiency of Scinde, Punjaub in food transportation. By 1883, Secretary of State Kimberley complained to the company about wheat tariffs being charged. The Liverpool Chamber of Commerce, the destination for much of the imported wheat, had lobbied aggressively on this subject. While labour costs at Scinde, Punjaub were a fraction of those in America, wheat was transported by the railway at a rate per ton mile which was 57 per cent higher than the USA. Punjabi farmers struggled to take British export business away from American mid-west wheat producers, who still dominated the British market. The reaction of Forsyth and colleagues to such criticism was to press for more GOI support and investment. They demanded government support for bridge building, and a completion of the Lahore–Karachi link.[11] Further, in 1884 W. P. Andrew, presumably with the support of William Mackinnon and the B. I. shipping group, was the first Indian railway executive to press for an integrated ticketing system for sea/rail journeys. This might have reduced some of the competitive advantage of the Americans, but discussions with the India Office became intractable and no such service was made available until after the railway was 'nationalized'. Given the close links between Mackinnon and Forsyth, evident in the latter's southern railway ventures, it was a wasted opportunity.[12] It is difficult to understand how after twenty-five years of GOI financial backing Scinde, Punjaub was still so inefficient in the provision of wheat transport and reliant on volatile military revenues. Equally, there was little evidence that the company had helped in Andrew's vision of drawing Central Asia into the commerce of the British Empire to create strong trading links. In fact, when Lord Roberts invaded Afghanistan in 1879 he was struck by the monopoly which Russian goods enjoyed. Rather, Scinde, Punjaub appears to lend support to Daniel Thorner's assertion that, with underperformance paid for by the GOI, Indian railways were run to pay their guarantees rather than to minimize costs and maximize revenues.[13]

In spite of this poor financial record and customer complaints, Forsyth could find nothing to criticize in his tour of the Scinde, Punjaub over the winter of 1883/4. Instead he gave a 'favourable account' of the whole network. His daughter later recounted that Forsyth had been mobbed by adoring Punjabis wherever he travelled on the railway, overtaken with nostalgia for their former commissioner. It seems unlikely that there would have been a large contingent of Sikhs amongst the crowds.[14] In Calcutta, there was less enthusiasm for the company. Viceroy Ripon was unconvinced of the Scinde, Punjaub model for financing strategic railways. He wanted a pooling of military lines, to be financed on balance sheet as cheaply as possible with long dated sinking fund debentures. This would ensure transparency in military expenditure, through public finance debates. Scinde, Punjaub's losses were buried in the detail of annual railway reports.[15] In fact, the Secretary of State had the right to repurchase Scinde, Punjaub in 1885, after twenty-five years. In line with their buyback of EIR stock and frustration at the management of the line, they informed Forsyth and his board of their intention to do so. The board promised to fight for the best deal possible from the India Office. By this time, they had been joined by the ubiquitous private rail company director, Lieutenant General C. H. Dickens. He had been secretary to the GOI in the public works department and, like Forsyth, had secured a number of valuable private postings. Dickens held chairmanships at Rothschild's ill fated Bengal Central railway and his 'private sector' Bengal NW. He later joined forces with Richard Strachey on the controversial Assam–Bengal line.[16] His appointment in 1885, while the buyback of Scinde, Punjaub was being negotiated, seems to have been intended to extract more generous terms from the Secretary of State. The India Office was keen to avoid the controversy of the EIR transaction where the requirement to have the Bank of England bless the arrangements had been ignored. This time the Bank oversaw the calculation of annuity payouts for Scinde, Punjaub shareholders. Nothing was left to chance in avoiding the furious arguments over annuities which had blighted parliamentary hearings on the EIR transaction. The existence of a 'ready reckoner' calculation table in the India office railway archives is a testimony to efforts made to make the process more transparent.[17] Encouraged by the board's aggressive stance on the repurchase, shareholder groups pressed for a wide range of exchange options including annuities, India long dated stock, and sinking funds. Given the 5 per cent guarantees enjoyed, it is unsurprising that the directors and other shareholders were reticent to part with their assets. Employees and management were also protected with employment secured for nearly all the 11,554 'officers and subordinates' in the new state railway.[18] Hence, the Ripon vision of a more integrated centrally funded strategic rail network, was partially fulfilled with the government takeover of Scinde, Punjaub and its merger with the contiguous military line, the Indus Valley State Railway. The resulting North Western Railway Company no longer provided so many boardroom benefits for the likes of Andrew, Dickens and Forsyth. However, little was done to prune management costs and North Western continued to represent a financial drain for the GOI. By 1896, military railways in India were still the second largest expense item in the cost of the Indian army.[19]

West of India Portuguese-Guaranteed Railway Company and Southern Mahratta Railway Company

Forsyth's role in Scinde, Punjaub diminished with state ownership, but the terms of the buyout were generous to replenish his pension. In the meanwhile, he had other railway interests to keep him busy, as director and investor. In 1879 he had been appointed to the board of the then state-owned and managed Southern Mahratta Railway. He was quickly made responsible for the construction of the company's harbour facilities at Marmagao in Portuguese India and for building a rail network linking Goa with the Southern Mahratta/Deccan counties. This was intended to connect Goa with Madras via the Madras Railway, and Bombay via the GIPR. In the biography of her father, Ethel Forsyth took a benign view of the purpose of these Portuguese/British India rail links. Like many private- and state-sector projects of the time, the mooted Goa Railway was said to be for famine protective purposes. The railway would provide enhanced food distribution to the Deccan and promote foreign trade through the expanding Goanese port of Marmagao.[20] In promoting the project, Forsyth found himself pushing at an open door. The British and Indian governments were pursuing closer trading links with Portuguese Goa. In 1878, the British had negotiated an initial Goa Treaty giving them a monopoly on salt production in the Portuguese protectorate. This was intended to prevent a flourishing salt-smuggling trade into British India, which was reckoned to be costing the GOI some £50,000–£75,000 in tax revenue.[21] The treaty was unpopular with Portuguese residents, for whom salt manufacture was the only large indigenous industry. Further, they resented the idea of a foreign-controlled monopoly as their main employer. The prospect of railway links to British India, with the possibility of foreign trade through Marmagao appealed as compensation for the loss of salt profits. On this basis early efforts were made by Frederick Campbell to win the rail concession and set up the 'Western Railway of India and Marmagao Harbour'. This was to be a joint venture with the profitable Eastern Bengal Railway (EBR) and English Great Eastern Railway. The Campbell letters to Secretary of State Lord Salisbury illustrate the compromises required to secure Whitehall support for an Indian railway concession in a mixed economy. The process also reflected the primacy of capital in the allocation of government business, which helped explain the City's dominant role. Campbell's railway was required to carry government mails free of charge, and officers, troops and military stores at subsidized rates. In times of war or 'internal disturbance', the railway would prioritize any military transport when the Indian army required it. In consideration for these India Office/GOI rights, the Campbell railway would receive free land and the right to excavate adjoining wasteland to the track. Salisbury personally pledged himself to help in raising capital and to pressure the Nizam of Hyderabad to grant access through his princely state. In turn, the GOI would be given powers to monitor the construction of Campbell's line to maintain cost controls.[22] Campbell understood that in negotiating with a Portuguese colonial counterparty, it was necessary to approach the Lisbon government centrally. He pledged to negotiate favourable terms for the India Office and to deliver free passage for goods through British India, and looked for Louis Mallet's (Undersecretary of State for India) backing in this. Campbell's Portuguese discussions had strategic importance for Whitehall since Murmagoa port had been used during the Mutiny. When the Indian army met problems at Belgaum, the Port of Bombay proved inadequate for landing relief troops. The south west monsoon was simply too strong. The British ignored Portuguese complaints and landed at Murmagoa instead to allow the relief of Belgaum and 'prevent a serious disaster'. With Murmagoa under British control through the railway, no such impediments would exist in the future. In the same way that enthusiastic India Office and ICS administrators sought recourse to multiple rationales for their railways, skilful promoters could do the same.[23] Equally, the India Office could present the railway as famine protective, while facilitating troop movements in southern India, without incurring Portuguese or local resistance.

Fortunately for Campbell, and subsequently for Forsyth, the British 'minister-plenipotentiary to King Luis I of Portugal' was an ambitious and imperially minded diplomat. Sir Robert Morier was a close Oxford associate of Benjamin Jowett and founder member of the free-trade Cobden Club. He entered the diplomatic service in 1852 with an initial posting in Vienna. While his political and cultural interests lay in Germany, his overt criticism of Bismarck meant that he was kept away from Berlin and sent to Portugal. It is fortunate that Morier bequeathed an extensive series of papers to Balliol College, which display an irreverence and tactlessness lending colour to the negotiations. Morier worked on the original Goa Treaty and, when Portuguese discontent risked an abandonment of the arrangements, he focused on securing rail concessions for credible promoters. In this he needed to balance the interests of Lisbon, London, Calcutta and Bombay, demonstrating great skill in cajoling the parties. However, even with Morier on side and with direct links into Lisbon, Campbell struggled to raise capital. The India Office needed to be ruthless in its approach to promoters who failed to provide scarce capital. In late 1877, Campbell was given a deadline to secure finance, and within a few months Whitehall was expressing scepticism on Campbell's negotiating ability with the City and Lisbon.[24] In desperation, Campbell brought in Robert Francis Fairlie, an inventor and patent holder in an innovative railway engine. Both failed to raise capital or secure the required Portuguese guarantee to cover financing for construction in non-Portuguese territory.

In the meantime, alternative schemes were presented to the India Office. John Fleming (of the City firm Smith, Fleming and Co.) pressed new Secretary of State Cranbrook on the merits of an alternative commercial and military port at Karwar on the west coast. This followed a concerted effort by Manchester MP Sir Thomas Bazley and the Bombay Chamber of Commerce to link the southern lines (in particular the Southern Mahratta) with Bombay. Bombay's standing had fallen after the cotton collapse of the mid-1860s, but Karwar was a sensible alternative to Murmagao. Fleming suggested that Murmagao would boost a foreign port at the expense of the British-controlled Karwar, and had support from powerful allies like Colonel Holland (future Chairman of GIPR) and Bartle Frere (ex-member of council for Bombay). However, he misunderstood the strategic ambitions of Salisbury, Cranbrook, Morier and others who sought rail expansion partly to control the Portuguese province of Goa.[25] There was nothing new in British efforts to control Portuguese-Indian territories. Morier's predecessor at Lisbon was Lord Lytton himself, who had been more transparent in 1875, offering to buy Goa, Damao and Dui from the Portuguese.[26]

By 1879 Campbell's consortium still struggled to raise finance and the alternative Karwar/Bombay projects failed to progress. The Portuguese minister in Lisbon, Corvo, informed Morier that any credible alternative must constitute a 'bona fide company' and must not be 'tainted' by association with the failed Campbell. Corvo had become sceptical about British methods of finance, which encouraged the setting up of 'bubble companies' in Portugal.[27] In some desperation, Morier lobbied Viscount Duprat to bring in the omnipresent Sir William Mackinnon. Mackinnon was pressing to set up monopolistic shipping links across the Indian Ocean, linking his East African hub at Zanzibar with the west coast of India. Morier pressed the possibility of using rail development in

Portuguese India to transform the 'medieval ruins of Goa' into 'an Indian Liverpool', and saw the political and economic advantages of the treaty as equally pressing for Britain. He pointed to an obscure clause in the existing Goa Treaty under which the GOI had pledged some Rs 4 lakhs (£40,000) to the Portuguese Government in consideration for treaty benefits, and suggested that these moneys might be used to secure any guarantees negotiated for a rail financing. He already had the attention of the wealthy Scottish landholder and railway enthusiast, the Duke of Sutherland, and pressed Duprat to deliver Mackinnon. This was an easy task since Mackinnon had, from 1874, been beneficiary of a contract allowing him to deliver mail on behalf of the Portuguese government between Lisbon, Goa and the port of Zanzibar. Moreover, Duprat assured Mackinnon that a beneficial Portuguese Treaty, concerning port and railway facilities in the Transvaal, would be advantaged if accommodation were reached with Lisbon over Goa. By 1879, Mackinnon's Asia/Africa shipping empire and Morier's diplomatic promotion from Lisbon were mutually dependent.[28]

Together, Sutherland and Mackinnon formed a wealthy Scottish grouping with a shared interest in railways. The former, also known as Lord Granville and Marquess of Stafford, had inherited his father's infamy for the excesses of Highland clearances at the family seat in Sutherland. Sutherland's ancestor, the first Duke, acquired the largest investment income in Britain, part of which was squandered by the second Duke. Sutherland was inspired by railway technology and built up a portfolio of overseas investments that reflected this and other Empire related concerns. Railways and coal mines, with their large land asset base, were natural targets for feudal capital in Britain and Empire.[29] Sutherland had promised to repopulate cleared Scottish lands after his father had replaced crofters with sheep, but instead invested scarce resources in his extravagant highland railway. At his Stafford House residence in London, Sutherland entertained prominent visitors from overseas and built up a charitable organization which sought to support servicemen and civilians in colonial encounters, falling within his areas of interest. By 1877, the Stafford House Committee (SHC) was sending surgeons to Turkey to support them in their war against Russia.[30] Shortly after, Sutherland partnered Mackinnon and Bartle Frere in attempts to use shipping-related customs revenue to finance rail concessions in East Africa, but the enterprise collapsed in 1878. This left SHC focused on shipping and guaranteed railways around the Indian Ocean, which required Indian railway 'talent' to appear credible in seeking concessions from Portuguese and British governments.[31] Forsyth (possibly through their mutual friend Andrew) was selected to improve SHC's railway expertise, notwithstanding his doubtful qualification for the role. Forsyth demanded rail guarantees 'analogous to those usual in British India Guaranteed lines' from Portuguese Minister Corvo. As a private-sector commercial organization negotiating with other governments on behalf of 'British interests', Forsyth's SHC had parallels with the earlier East India Company. However, even with the combined sponsorship of SHC and strong government links, Forsyth was battling against Viceroy Lawrence's shift to state funding. This made negotiations with the Portuguese and India Office in 1879 more problematical. London and Calcutta were contemplating the return of private-sector involvement, with reduced guarantees, but Forsyth demanded from Lisbon the traditional 5 per cent for the Goa line, with an equal share of surplus profits above 6 per cent. The Portuguese government was to be given the right, comparable to old guarantees, to purchase the business afterthirty years at the higher of market price or par (the arrangements which were simultaneously prompting such consternation over the EIR buyback in London). As a director of the EIR, Forsyth would have been aware of this, but perhaps saw his pension arrangements being enhanced by his windfall gain on EIR with the opportunity to repeat the trick on Goa.[32]

Morier's role as confidante of Corvo was crucial in the negotiations. He claimed no 'private interest in the project', but sought only to facilitate matters for his friends in Lisbon. Never one to understate his own contribution, he told Mackinnon that he was indispensable to the whole undertaking.[33] However, with a change of government in Lisbon, Morier's contacts had lost influence and he urged his SHC colleagues to quickly secure their concession. At the India Office, Louis Mallet was kept onside. He was assured that the whole enterprise would be paid for by the Portuguese, but primary benefits would accrue to the British. Mallet worked hard to persuade colleagues in Whitehall that the project was worth supporting. However, at the GOI in Calcutta there was scepticism, with the Goa railway being described as a 'chimera'.[34] GOI concerns about the railway appeared justified since the enterprise was not being financed exclusively by the Portuguese Government. The anticipated £40,000 of GOI cash flows pledged to Lisbon was targeted by the SHC as collateral for their equity and bond financing. Forsyth had failed to include this requirement in his written correspondence with Lisbon since he felt it would embarrass the Portuguese authorities. They would not wish to highlight that Portuguese government guarantees were of limited value without British Indian collateral. However, now that Lisbon was demanding 5 per cent money without an assignment of the GOI monies, Forsyth was forced to be more frank. While Great Britain could borrow at 3 per cent in London, Portugal's paper yielded closer to 6 per cent and the indicated 5 per cent guarantee was off market for the credit of the country. However, with interest payments fully collateralized, Forsyth foresaw that a 1 per cent reduction in rates was feasible.[35]

Morier pressed to have Forsyth visit Lisbon to help in face-to-face negotiations. A rarefied diplomat could be expected to mediate with his friends in Lisbon, but hardly discuss details of financings. Although Forsyth had only recently abandoned his ICS career and Tory politics, Morier described him as 'a real business man' who could be expected to 'fight it out'. Just as important was Forsyth's elevated ICS background in Punjab. According to Morier, he was 'a man of social status' who would impress the Portuguese. Indeed, Mackinnon had stressed Forsyth's experience, gained on other Indian railways, and his prestigious role as Chief Commissioner of Punjab.[36] However, with the impending collapse of talks over the demand for the GOI collateral, Morier railed against the greed of Forsyth and SHC. Worse, by mid-1880 Forsyth complained that a put option exercisable by investors at the end of the underlying Goa Treaty at twelve years would scare investors into believing their asset was short duration. Forsyth argued that this 'risk' (which was in fact protection) required an improved yield on the securities. Morier pointed out that the return over that twelve-year period was likely to be somewhere between 6 and 9 per cent, with the put at market value, enhancing the return further. Perhaps the EIR buyback process had spoiled Forsyth and other EIR shareholders, who had collected capital gains and were exchanged into generous annuity paper, to replace their asset. In the meantime, Mallet had lobbied GOI in favour of Forsyth and the SHC, to attain financial support from Calcutta. Crucially, Mallet was able to dispel GOI suggestions that, since the Viceroy Lawrence Minute, public support for private companies was non-existent. He used the recent precedent of handsome subsidies paid to the Assam Railway to gain backing for Goa. These subsidies implied a more discreet form of state support to Indian railways, before returning to transparent but controversial guarantees.[37]

In all the negotiations on railway guarantees in the 1870s and 80s, Sir Theodore Hope was never far from the centre.[38] Goa was no exception, and newly promoted Foreign Secretary Salisbury sent Hope to Lisbon in 1878 to gather information on the discussions. However, Hope was frustrated that he lacked the status of counsellor in Calcutta. He impressed on Morier that he could influence matters at the GOI more effectively if promoted from the level of legislative council member. He highlighted the impending retirement of council member Arbuthnot in 1879 and argued that, if he were to succeed to the position, he would control public works matters in Calcutta. Morier was close to Indian Secretary of State Cranbrook, and Hope asked him to lobby for his candidature. Morier was, according to Hope, 'a man of the world' and would understand the importance of personal lobbying.[39] Morier pressed Cranbrook to have Hope appointed as Public Works member on the Bombay Presidency council, arguing that fulfilment of both Goa Treaty and railway would be easier with Hope near the southern railways. Progress on such matters would expedite wider British ambitions in the region, which were that 'Portuguese India' be 'finally annexed to the Empire'.[40] Hope duly became a provisional member of the Council for Bombay and thereafter secretary to the GOI in finance and commerce.

The Mallet papers at Balliol show consistent lobbying for Hope's candidature to the Supreme Counsel, supported by ex Viceroys Northbrook and Hartington. Meanwhile, Hope was engaged by his other sponsor, Morier, in pressing the SHC's claims for the Goa concession to Calcutta. There was opposition from the GOI towards the SHC, but Hope promised Mallet that he would 'be on the look out to do anything I can'. He argued that the Goan Railway's costs of £1.5 to £1.4 million (nearly £12,000 per mile for 127–30 miles) were justified. Goa would achieve synergies with the contiguous Southern Mahratta Railway (also run by Forsyth), and the Mysore system, which Hope would invite Forsyth to purchase some years later. These costs were close to Lawrence's targeted £10,000 per mile. Hope's loyal service to Morier and SHC paid off and in 1882 he became Viceroy's Council member for public works, a post he retained until retiring under something of a cloud five years later.[41]

Equally omnipresent in late nineteenth-century railway discussions was Sir Richard Temple, then Governor of Bombay. Temple was concerned that the development of Murmagao as a port would threaten Bombay. Parochialism among Presidency officials was common, with Karachi also attracting opposition from Bombay representatives. Temple publicly opposed the activities of the SHC and criticized the underlying Goa Treaty. In the heat of negotiations, Morier wrote to Salisbury accusing Temple of encouraging the Karwar Chamber of Commerce in their lobbying against the SHC consortium, in favour of the Fleming-sponsored Karwar to Hubli line. Temple's indiscretions had led the Portuguese 'club' circuit to surmise that the SHC was merely a 'dummy put up by the Indian Government' to allow the Murmagao talks to fail and hence deny Portugal their Goan railway. Forsyth and Temple were accused of working duplicitously together to bring this about. The Portuguese were understandably confused by the British decision-making process, with the Government of Bombay, GOI and India Office all apparently overlapping. Behind the scenes, correspondence of the time suggests that the process was still more complicated. The British Foreign Office, Political Department and Railway Department all wished to have their say in Whitehall. Morier was frustrated by the impression left with the Portuguese. He quoted from the Lisbon publications '*Journal des Colonias*' and '*Diano Popular*' to Salisbury, identifying the worst of British imperial practice in the affair. Britain was accused of annexing Goa from the Portuguese for the paltry sum of £40,000 per annum (the pledged monies). This damaged Portuguese prestige. England was Portugal's 'ancient' and 'faithful' ally (an alliance which had its roots in a matrimonial arrangement in 1387), but practised 'systematic and tenacious aggressions' in east and west Africa. These activities, most apparent at Lourenco Manques and Angola, were aimed at promoting a rebellion of blacks against the Portuguese state. Significantly, Morier referred to earlier correspondence in his 'slave trade series' which had highlighted the role of the SHC in this matter. In fact, Sutherland and Mackinnon had anti-slavery as a guiding principle, placing them at odds with Portuguese colonial practice.[42] Meanwhile, Morier and Mallet opposed Temple's role as chief negotiator with Portuguese delegates in South India, which made matters worse. Temple was an opportunist and would simply back the winning position. In fact, Temple's intervention was more decisive. He tipped off Portuguese negotiators about the unfair terms being demanded by Forsyth and SHC. The 5 and 6 per cent guarantees of the 1860s were said by Temple to be gratuitous, and he urged the Portuguese to hold out for 3 per cent in line with British borrowing rates.[43]

The negotiations were made more difficult by the extent of regional partisanship displayed by the British. Talks had involved Portuguese, British and Indian governments, and the web of interested diplomatic, civil service and commercial interests. Evelyn Baring, never far from railway negotiations, was concerned that Mackinnon had pulled back from the enterprise, reducing the credibility of Forsyth's consortium. Forsyth pressed Baring directly for additional 3 per cent guarantees to support the Bellary line, in what he contended did not look like a 'strong' company 'from the City point of view'. However, Baring concluded that the demand for shares would be the real test, and the deal might be sweetened for SHC and fellow investors by 'handing over to them the whole of the Southern Mahratta system'.[44] In fact, by May 1881 Douglas Forsyth was able to boast to the loyal Morier that the prospectus for the 'West of India Portuguese Guaranteed Railway Company' (WIPGR) had been issued. With total orders for the securities at £6.6 million, the issue was oversubscribed by a remarkable 11 times. In Forsyth's opinion 'there never was such a success'. The papers at Guildhall Library confirm massive demand for the shares with 223,833 applications for the 20,000 shares offered to the public. Revealingly, the scale back suffered by most investors was avoided by Forsyth and management colleagues, whose allocation of 10,000 shares was protected. This gave them the full benefit of a partly paid share price which rose from $4\frac{5}{8}$ to $6\frac{3}{8}$ in the six months after issue.[45] With multiple levels of GOI and Portuguese Government support, and a coupon not seen on railway stock since the 1860s, such demand was wholly rational. It represented another high return/low risk security designed for a gentlemanly capitalist audience, which might be expected to facilitate the enhanced pension requirements of Forsyth and others. The final prospectus gave WIPGR authority to issue up to £800,000 of capital through a combination of common stock and debentures. Forsyth's brinkmanship on the assignment of GOI cash flows had been successful, with £40,000 of guaranteed interest on the WIPGR stock further collateralized by those moneys (originally assigned to Portugal under the 1878 Treaty of Lisbon). The company was able to boast in the offering prospectus that WIPGR credit was enhanced with a Portuguese government guarantee at 5 per cent on £800,000, with this full amount of £40,000 payable directly by the Imperial government under the treaty. This protected coupons with gilt-edged credit in the form of a joint and several guarantee of Britain and Portugal. Forsyth's other concern, for which he was berated by Morier, about requiring investor protection in the event of the exercise of Portugal's twelve-year cancellation of the treaty, was met with the granting of a twelve-year put at 110 per cent of cost, plus market value of all materials. In general, with the recent performance of British-Indian share prices, the security could be expected to perform well and benefit from future bond financings at very low rates of interest, reflective of the 'exceptionally safe character of the security'. However, with the Imperial collateral capped at Rs 4 lakhs any additional equity finance could not be raised at Portuguese guarantees below 6 per cent. The prospectus was accompanied by an impressive map showing the anticipated connections to be built beyond the Portuguese Indian frontier. Links were promised northwards via Belgaum with the GIPR, and southward via Bankapur through Mysore to Bangalore. Finally, links eastward would extend to the Madras Railway.[46]

Forsyth joined the board of WIPGR as Chairman, with every confidence that the network under his control would be allowed to grow under the patronage of Calcutta, Whitehall, Stafford House and Lisbon. Another SHC representative, Frederick Youle, gave Sutherland's group strong representation on a board of nine. All but one director was based in London. The sole Portuguese representative was expected to be Morier's trusted ally Corvo, but he took a more high-profile role in the Portuguese diplomatic service. Almost immediately, the trade-related advantages of the WIPGR to the British became obvious. In addition to the normal steel railway lines, locomotives, sleepers and coal that enhanced British manufacturing, the project involved the construction of a 1,200-foot quay and 1,800-foot breakwater at Murmagao port. By June 1883, the company's annual report pointed to almost 5,000 tons of Portland cement exported from Britain for this purpose. The same document pressed the importance of government concessions to Forsyth's Southern Mahratta for a further 450 miles of connecting line, coupled with large regional expansion on the Madras and GIPR lines. Overall, these developments were expected to open up 'fertile and well-populated country' to the Murmagao port.[47] By 1886, further debenture and common stock issues for WIPGR, guaranteed by the Portuguese Government, had been approved in Lisbon with guarantees ranging from 5 to 6 per cent. Outstanding issues traded at healthy premiums.

Temple's advice on the value of government guarantees had been ignored, and SHC delivered to shareholders a combination of explicit Portuguese support, coupled with GOI collateral, subsidies and the promise of off-market acquisitions.[48] Forsyth had played an active role in the enterprise after floatation, albeit without technical expertise. By late 1883, with the project proceeding at above budgeted cost and behind schedule, he travelled to Goa, and removed the existing contractor, to be replaced by a series of 'petty' contracts. As ever, the suspicion must remain that a London-based board was little qualified to oversee such a project, though more than qualified to channel orders to British cement manufacturers and other metropolitan suppliers.[49] The WIPGR was eventually completed three years behind schedule, so that Forsyth did not live to see his first southern railway. Lord Salisbury had warned in 1881 that the project was likely to lose someone money, and hoped it might be the Portuguese government rather than the 'much squeezed shareholders'. As usual, the level of guarantees and subsidies provided meant that London investors had more than enough protection from taxpayers, in Portugal and India. Salisbury's misplaced concern for Forsyth and fellow investors may have been informed by his own frustrations as a British railway shareholder, where he took real operational risk.[50]

Morier was honest in advising that he had no direct pecuniary interest in the company, but through the transaction he cemented valuable contacts with the SHC. By the time he moved to St Petersburg in 1884, as British Ambassador, he was able to pursue further projects with William Mackinnon where he would have capital at risk. By 1889, in Siberia, Morier pressed the opportunities for Russian sea connections to Mackinnon. The latter's shipping enterprise was promised trading access to 10 per cent of the world's annual output of gold. Morier sought to capitalize a company with £25,000 of initial funding, and anticipated that he and fellow investors would benefit from Siberian gold related business of £5 million. Notwithstanding their successful business dealings in Goa, Mackinnon was sceptical of the benefits of Morier's 'diplomatic commerce' further north, and Morier was compelled to beg him to provide his promised capital injection into the company. Even the leading railway contractor Lord Brassey held back his promised £1,000 investment.[51] Mackinnon and Brassey discovered that GOI-type guarantees were peculiar to enterprises within British India. Business without government guarantees required much more careful risk assessment. At the same time, the Mackinnon and Mackenzie trading company was refused Imperial or GOI guarantees for a proposed Persian railway system (the same answer had been given to Baron Reuter years earlier).[52] Indian railways had made genuine private-sector enterprises look unappealing even for Mackinnon, who could expect to derive more synergies than most.

In contrast to Morier, Forsyth's business ventures after the Goa 'success' were confined to India. He turned his attention to developing the Southern Mahratta franchise. Supporting both Forsyth and Morier from Calcutta, Theodore Hope was quick to congratulate the former on his Goa issue. He encouraged Forsyth that improved terms might be available on the WIPGR in due course, including a formal GOI guarantee at 3 per cent. This was a common approach in listing railway companies in the 1880s. Optimal terms were secured initially, while additional support was given to shareholders and bondholders after the company traded.[53] Behind the scenes, Hope pursued the Southern Mahratta extension with Mallet's support. Work on the railway had begun in April 1878 as a state line, and up to the end of 1881–2 some £394,000 had been spent on construction out of the GOI's 'protective grant' to support regional famine relief. A further £369,800 had been provided in cost estimates for the next financial year. From an internal accounting perspective, were the Southern Mahratta to be moved outside the 'protective grant' through a company structure, those moneys might be allocated elsewhere to other famine related railways.[54] In spite of this re-characterization, Southern Mahratta would continue to be seen internally as state-owned and managed, in line with the Lawrence minute. Off balance sheet treatment was possible, while seeking to keep the sceptics on private ownership/ guarantees at bay. While WIPGR had achieved de facto GOI support through the pledged cash flows, the India Office/GOI had not yet reversed the Lawrence decision, although the public funding situation was critical. Hence Richard Strachey reviewed the Southern Mahratta financing model at the Indian Railway select committee of 1884 as 'nothing more than a State agency for working the line'.[55] This was disingenuous since the Southern Mahratta had, from 1882, been London listed with a board headed by Forsyth and comparable financial incentives to those offered by the later 1880s guaranteed companies. Again, the relative generosity of the Southern Mahratta terms had much to do with Hope's lobbying. In late 1881, he had told Mallet that 'Forsyth's company' would allow 'pure economy' since it would improve food distribution and prevent the reoccurrence of a regional famine like that of 1876–7. Southern Mahratta's costs were expected to be less than GOI's famine expenditure in the Deccan during the crisis. Again, the assumption was that famine and related costs would disappear once railways were developed. Future experience showed this to be untrue.

The £3 million issue of Southern Mahratta stock in May 1882 was oversubscribed. It gave security which persuaded Stratchey and others that it was only a shell company, acting for the government, but with returns significantly above consols. The assets were owned by the GOI but leased over fifty years to the company. Land and the concession/ regional monopoly were gifted to shareholders, and a minimum coupon/dividend of 4 per cent was guaranteed for the initial five years of construction, falling to 3.5 percent thereafter to reflect the anticipated surplus profits. Those profits were to be shared 75:25 between GOI and the company, with government calls every ten years after twenty-five years. Put protection for shareholders was at par and exercisable annually after scheduled completion at June 1888.[56] Forsyth and co-investors benefited from the failure to deduct interest charges in calculating surplus profits for additional distribution. Hence no constraint was placed by the GOI on overspending for capital expenditure purposes.[57] This was understood at the time. In restructuring the Bengal Central Railway, the India Office public works member, Juland Danvers, spelt out the iniquities of the 'South Mahratta terms'. Such a calculation represented an 'undue indulgence' to railway companies which unfairly 'increase the charge upon the revenues of India'.[58] Characteristically, Randolph Churchill was unmoved by these complaints and offered Rothschild's Bengal Central comparable terms to Forsyth's company. In 1884, when Southern Mahratta's share price performed badly, reflecting depressed market conditions, the government 'came to the rescue' paying coupons on new debentures and leaving excess profits to shareholders. This was said to benefit 'the stock in the market considerably'.[59]

All negotiating of these Southern Mahratta terms was done by the India Office, without GOI input. As with the Goa extension, the GOI was simply kept informed. However, Hope was used as an enthusiastic intermediary in Calcutta to press Indian taxpayer support to Liberal Viceroy Ripon and others.[60] Mallet continued to be a proponent of all private companies and a key ally of Forsyth's in Whitehall, as Southern Mahratta terms were agreed. He told Secretary of State Kimberley that a co-existence of state- and private-sector railways was impossible longer term, since the greater efficiency of the latter breed would 'prevail' over the less efficient state railways. State support should be focused on profitable railways only to the extent that they needed help. The returns from private railways should be paid across to risk-bearing 'capitalists'. These targeted rewards were more defensible than distributing profits more widely over 'the whole of any particular community'. To impose more egalitarianism on the distribution of railway earnings risked moving to an ideology which had much in common with 'nationalization of the land, and other communistic theories'. While Southern Mahratta had required government guarantees, in an unfortunate departure from pure laissez-faire, Mallet considered the Southern Mahratta 'agency' approach superior to Lawrence's state railways. The company brought skill sets not possessed by government and reduced government overheads, segmenting the funding from pure GOI finance. As in the EIR annuity negotiations, Mallet's attention to detail on cost control for the railways left much to be desired. He would have viewed Danvers's complaints as minor in comparison with the benefits of such 'agents for the Government'.[61] Nevertheless, Mallet was prepared to concede to Hope, in private correspondence, how 'onerous' the terms of the Southern Mahratta settlement had been to the GOI. Even Hope himself expressed concerns about whether at £8,000 per mile for a narrow-gauge railway line, Forsyth's private-sector 'expertise' was really delivering the benefits of private enterprise.[62]

The ever vigilant Sir George Campbell highlighted the Southern Mahratta terms as an issue of concern to Parliament. He was one of the few MPs with a commitment to Indian matters who implemented the House of Commons intended role on Indian affairs-as check and balance on the India Office. Campbell complained that yields on stock and bonds for the Southern Mahratta were unduly generous. Investors took no start-up risk since they had a put at par onto government after five years. The investors were being generously rewarded for negligible risk. Moreover, the group of investors benefiting from these 'gentlemanly capitalist' arrangements was limited, and concentrated within Forsyth and his promoter friends. The promoters were offered at least 50 per cent of the shares on an exclusive basis, with the remaining half offered to the general public on a tender basis. The window for applications by the public was a token six-hour period over one day, meaning that the promoters were likely to buy up as much as they wished. Secretary of State Hartington did not dispute that the Southern Mahratta arrangements were generous, but presented the returns and conditions as necessary to coax Forsyth and partners into the connected Murmagoa project, which was inevitably loss-making. However, investors in WIPGR cared little about the operational risks of their railway given their gilt-edged joint and several guarantees from Portugal and the GOI. Southern Mahratta was said to be a key priority for famine protective reasons, meaning that the India Office was prepared to err on the side of generosity. The India office could exercise a call at par after twenty-five years, unlike the old guarantees at market price. In fact, this also benefited Forsyth and his board members. A twenty-five-year security provided long duration characteristics for the pension portfolio of Forsyth, and other ageing ex-ICS employees. Finally, Hartington assured Campbell that these arrangements were to be viewed as 'exceptional'. Campbell remained unconvinced and attacked the whole Goa/Southern Mahratta network arrangement, arguing that a British port in western India would have been preferable. Campbell's scepticism was well placed. He argued on the fundamental issue of value for money for Indian taxpayers, while India Office priorities lay elsewhere. Campbell may not have been aware of the diplomatic manoeuvrings of Morier and the SHC and the accounting advantages of the Southern Mahratta stock issue from the perspective of the GOI. In fact, the paid-up capital of £1.72 million raised in 1882 was applied to repay the GOI treasury sum already expended on the railway, and freed up GOI borrowing lines. Some £370,000 of 'protective grants' paid to the railway company were made available for other protective railways.[63]

As with the WIPGR, Forsyth took the chairmanship of Southern Mahratta. He was accompanied by another WIPGR director on the new board, Major General Sir Henry Green. The first annual report of Southern Mahratta made the links explicit, promising to complete line connections with WIPGR by early 1887. By 1884, the scale of the line was increased, with further government concessions allowing links to GIPR at Poona in the north and Belgaum in the south. The authorized capital of the company was accordingly increased to £5 million. Further help was provided by the India Office, with the minimum dividend of 4 per cent on common stock maintained for a further two years to June 1889, before falling to 3.5 per cent, as originally envisaged. New concessions were combined with more generous guarantee arrangements, proving again that whatever the performance of Indian rail companies, if they fell within an approved family of lines, the India Office would pay. Forsyth was fortunate in leading one of those groupings.

In fact, the performance of Southern Mahratta was poor, and by 1885 it was still significantly loss making. Even by 1897/8 the company was running a deficit of Rs 22.5 million lakhs (£220,000). Over the twenty years to 1901, Southern Mahratta absorbed £6.5 million of capital and produced losses of £2.9 million, creating costs for the Indian taxpayer of £9.4 million.[64] Moreover, Horace Bell's wide-ranging analysis of Indian railway policy showed the Southern Mahratta operating by 1892–3 at average earnings per mile per week of a paltry Rs 87 against Rs 580 for the EIR and Rs 513 for the GIPR. Even the Mysore section (see below) was outperforming the main portion of the line. The operating margin of 1.47 per cent was at the bottom of the Indian railway companies listed, representing a continuing fiscal burden on the GOI. Forsyth's military line, now renamed the North Western, with limited commercial potential, was outperforming the Southern Mahratta in terms of profitability.[65] The justification for poor operating results was the protective aspect of the railway, said to preclude a repeat of the catastrophic southern food crisis of 1876–8. Indeed, when Forsyth visited the Southern Mahratta rail workshops on the eastern side of the line in 1883 he was greeted with a 'triumphal arch' which bore the inscription 'welcome: no more famine'.[66] However, famine experience in the Deccan region in the 1890s suggested that such triumphalism was premature.

Further, the affectation of Southern Mahratta delivering minimum-cost rail services was maintained by Strachey at the select committee on Indian railways in 1884. According to Strachey, the GOI employed Forsyth's company to construct and manage the Southern Mahratta railway in a manner akin to employing a gardener to tend land for a homeowner. The person hiring the gardener declined to do the work, and a comparable rationale existed for private rail companies. As ever on such matters, Sir George Campbell provided healthy scepticism. He argued to Strachey that the GOI could more readily pressure engineers and subcontractors into bearing down on costs than could an appointed board of directors in distant London. The lack of rail expertise exhibited by Forsyth and colleagues supported Campbell's concerns. Moreover, the India Office/GOI control over technical and business competence at the London board of Southern Mahratta was questioned. Government played no role in choosing the board of directors (which cost at least £50,000 per annum per railway). The boards were composed mostly of enthusiastic promoters co-opted at the time of floatation, according to Danvers. Campbell further observed, perhaps with Forsyth in mind, that the same individuals sat on the boards of several such companies. These powerful directors were far removed from Strachey's metaphor of humble gardener, and perhaps more akin to wealthy landowners.[67] Unsurprisingly, given his active role in facilitating Forsyth's southern rail network, Hope joined Strachey in applauding the 'agency structure'. The off balance sheet treatment was seen by the public works member as a key advantage in freeing up state borrowing for his military railways.[68]

With the Goa–Southern Mahratta network securely under the same management, underpinned by various guarantees and levels of additional support, further extensions to Forsyth's regional railway empire were supported by Theodore Hope. By mid-1885 he had been negotiating on behalf of Forsyth's Southern Mahratta for many months, with the princely state of Mysore, to arrange a friendly takeover of Mysore's railway. In the same way that the Tirhoot State Railway acquisition helped the stock market profile of Bengal NW, the synergies available from merging with a contiguous line would benefit Forsyth. Hope pressed these advantages to Forsyth, suggesting that traffic on both lines would be expanded. The economic exploitation of Mysore was a controversial matter, raised in the House of Commons the previous year. Land with gold mining concessions was being sold off to British 'speculators' at a fraction of the real value by the government of Madras, and concern was aired about the defrauding of the Rajah of Mysore.[69] Similar concerns might have been raised about Forsyth's railway acquisition. Hope suggested that funding long-term at 4 per cent was practicable for acquiring Mysore, with retention of 25 percent of surplus profits. Southern Mahratta would be buying Mysore at cost price only, and would raise the additional capital required to complete the build out. Hope urged Forsyth to err on the side of caution in raising more for capital expenditure than was really needed, to maximize use of government guarantees. He hinted at a misconception on Strachey's part about real ownership of the property, using inverted commas to describe the extent to which a long term leasehold arrangement left the Mysore line as the 'property' of the princely state.[70] Presumably encouraged by the favours Hope was doing him, Forsyth wrote to Secretary of State Churchill boasting of his ability to sell 3.5 per cent guaranteed stock at a small discount. He would only be able to maximize such price, thus reducing the yield on the financing, if Churchill granted him further concessions on financing. For example, if they were issued as bearer bonds (without ownership listing) Forsyth's bankers might introduce 'some of the richest backers in India' to invest aggressively. Significantly, the ever-careful Juland Danvers wrote a note of caution to Churchill on the exaggerated claims of the intoxicated Forsyth. Churchill himself was keen to proceed with the transaction, ignoring warnings by Danvers and Strachey. He tied such 'private sector' acquisitions to his support for the 'annexation' of Upper Burma. Dufferin was told to feel optimistic about the chances of getting approval for the Mysore deal, since an expensive Burmese War would make all parties keen to pursue 'off balance sheet' rail financings.[71]

Later, the Southern Mahratta's annual report for year end 1885 described the advantages of the Mysore acquisition. The princely state's railway was already partially completed with surplus revenues of Rs 200,000 per annum from the 140 miles of line from Mysore to Bangalore. The capital was raised with an issue of long dated 4 per cent debentures at above par, to give attractive sub 4 per cent funding. These funds would be used to create synergies with the Southern Mahratta/WIPGR network by building from the company's terminus at Harihar to Gubbi. Shareholders in Southern Mahratta would have dependable guaranteed cash flows from the combined group, plus a 25 per cent profit share in the merged entity.[72] In private correspondence with Forsyth later that year, Hope made clear that as the GOI negotiator on the Mysore deal he had again secured a favoured promoter a generous deal. Southern Mahratta's shareholders would benefit from the 'irredeemiability' of the 4 per cent debentures for some fifty years, giving cheap financing. Those bond holders were earning guaranteed returns well above consol yields, and the GOI had given up any degree of flexibility on re-financing for the foreseeable future. Strachey's vision of passive agency amongst the management and owners of Southern Mahratta seemed a distant one.[73]

By 1900, at the thirty-third general meeting of Southern Mahratta, the company was able to boast of goods traffic up 21 per cent on the previous year, driven by the transportation of large grain supplies, to meet the demands of the most recent and acute famine in the region. The business was greater even than 1897, which had also been enhanced by the demands of food shortages. With the food crisis impacting trade, the exports of food to other railway lines had declined, but imports from other lines onto the Southern Mahratta had increased. This was an indication that the company was by then performing some of the role intended by Hope and Strachey in lessening the effects of famine on the Deccan region. Passenger traffic was volatile, but by 1900 at least showed an enormous improvement through the disappearance of the most recent plague epidemic in the region.[74] Nevertheless, the financial performance was still weak. Coal prices were high, increasing operating costs. In that respect Southern Mahratta continued to be dependent on the other Forsyth/Strachey vehicle, the EIR, which had maintained artificially high domestic coal prices. The company was required to access a reserve fund to pay the anticipated 5 per cent dividend, which reserve was depleting rapidly. The company anticipated that the government would exercise its right 'to purchase the line' at the end of the twenty-five-year contract in 1907, and emphasized that no payment in annuities would be allowed. Forsyth and his team had negotiated a favourable cash-only buyout in 1882 for shareholders. Again, the façade of state ownership with a hired 'gardener' tending the business was undermined. The buyout, like the ongoing subsidization of Southern Mahratta would have been an expensive undertaking for government. The company saw its responsibilities as primarily towards shareholders, like the audience at the results meeting, rather than famine relief or the GOI in general. As early as 1883, 'triumphal arches' had been erected at the company's offices declaring the end of famine, but almost twenty years later this had not been achieved. Indeed, the reversal of buoyant food exports, referred to at the 1900 meeting, might have simply returned Southern Mahratta to the position of 1883 in terms of supplies of food to combat drought.[75]

As the government call date approached, Southern Mahratta looked for new financing opportunities. Further GOI guarantees were constrained by Curzon after the vast overspend on Assam Bengal Railway. While Southern Mahratta was keen to construct three new branch lines for £500,000, the financial returns from the railway placed it outside the GOI's guarantee 'programme'. By 1904 Forsyth's successor as chairman was another ex-ICS representative, Sir William Bisset. He had first-hand knowledge of the intricacies of attaining off balance sheet treatment in the GOI's public works department. While GOI guarantees were placed under an overall ceiling, there appeared to be no such restrictions on regional or district guarantees. He approached Baring Brothers to arrange a financing with the offer of a four percent guarantee (plus ⅛ of surplus earnings) from the regional district board of Kristna. Generous GOI call provisions at twenty-five times net earnings were to be offered. It was clear that the promotion and financing costs would be high, with Baring and sub-underwriters demanding over 3 per cent. The transaction collapsed when it became clear that district boards did not have the legal right to pledge tax revenues against borrowings. This new off balance sheet funding was a step too far for Norton Rose and other city solicitors.[76]

Despite the financing difficulties, the company was left in private hands in 1907. Instead, the India Office moved to improve Southern Mahratta's critical mass and credit standing by affecting a larger rail franchise through a merger with Madras Railway Company. Madras Railway had been operating in private hands since 1852, but had been even less commercially successful than Forsyth's company. Gifting this business to Southern Mahratta with the anticipated synergies was the final leg of Forsyth's vision of a southern rail network, albeit realized posthumously. Indeed, at the 1914 general meeting, company secretary Colonel H. Bonham-Carter, anticipated a doubling of their closely related affiliate WIPGR in terms of line mileage. The façade of Strachey's 'agency' was maintained for shareholders until the eventual renationalization of the Madras and Southern Mahratta Railway Company in 1944.[77]

Conclusion

Sir Douglas Forsyth moved with ease from a controversial but elevated government career in British India to push private railway development in the Punjab and the southern states of the subcontinent in the 1870s and 80s. Strong relationships with W. P. Andrew in the North, and with SHC in the South, allowed him to use old Indian contacts profitably. Sir John William Kaye, as head of the political and secret department was described by his biographer in the *DNB* as having enjoyed a 'generous pension by the India Office' on retirement. However, his remuneration was insufficient to preclude the need for financial gifts from the likes of William Mackinnon and W. P. Andrew. Forsyth's enhanced pension arrangements were achieved in other ways, within the Indian railway sector, to give him a standard of living in later life which would have been impossible as a humble MP. Like Strachey at the EIR, on whose board he also resided, he negotiated in an efficient manner on behalf of his shareholders, and had strong ambitions for affecting a regional 'fiefdom' of Indian railways. The two ex-ICS men were successful in that respect and in the process secured their own retirement. However, both used military and protective rationales to further state support for their enterprises, while failing to ensure that the underlying social and security ambitions of these businesses were fulfilled.

6 EMINENT ICS VICTORIANS: RICHARD STRACHEY AND THEODORE HOPE AS POACHERS AND GAMEKEEPERS

Introduction

The role of Richard Strachey as Chairman of the EIR and Assam–Bengal Railway in the 1890s provides a good illustration of the thin dividing line between public servants and private industrialists in British India. In Theodore Hope, Public Works member of the Viceroy's Council, and later enthusiastic rail promoter, a cruder example of 'gamekeeper turned poacher' may be observed. In both cases, the detail of their negotiations with the ICS, India Office, and other private companies highlight the extent to which energetic individuals could influence GOI spending patterns. Strachey and Hope prospered under the unwritten constitution of British India, with weak checks and balances provided by Westminster. Parliamentary committees and commissions, designed to scrutinize ill-directed public-works spending and guarantees, were normally used as safety valves to relieve Indian public pressure, while failing to incorporate dissenting opinions in their recommendations and conclusions. Rare critical participants at these forums, like Henry Fawcett and Romesh Dutt, railed against private-sector lobbying activities, but could not hope to counterbalance the influence of energetic insiders.

Sir Richard Strachey was a model for the active and public-spirited 'eminent' Victorian gentleman. He would have made a suitable study for his fifth son Lytton's dissection of Victorian behaviour and ethics. Strachey's range of interests spanned military, scientific, horticultural, meteorological and public works matters, all in the context of India where he spent much of his life. While he appears to have been a somewhat distant and aged father to Lytton, the biographer had great respect for his father and appreciated Sir Richard's support in the face of early public school bullying.[1] In fact, Strachey and his family demonstrated a surprising combination of characteristics and pursuits. As a young officer in the Sikh campaign of 1846, his horse had been shot from under him and he survived heroically to rise to the position of General. Later, he catalogued countless new species of flora discovered in the regions of the Tibet plateau, and by 1888 had become president of the Royal Geographical Society. His wife, who was closer to Lytton, forged intimate links with the wife of one of Strachey's inquisitors on Indian railway committees, Milicent Fawcett. The two wives became active in the early feminist movement, with Jane Strachey being described as 'a disciple of John Stuart Mill and an ardent feminist'.[2] While Jane may have been persuaded by Mill's call for women's rights, her husband's appetite for the writer's 'laissez-faire' political economy proved to be tenuous in his career in public works.

The contradictions in Strachey's life extended to his approach to Indian railways. In 1858, he became consulting engineer in the GOI railway department in Calcutta and, for much of the next thirty years, played a leading role in the development of railways from within Calcutta and Whitehall. Strachey and his ex-military colleagues were the target of much private-sector criticism for their dominance of railway matters in India's Public Works Departments. Their tendency towards army bureaucracy and administration pushed up engineering costs and removed 'energy, zeal, and perseverance' amongst poorly paid engineers. The elite, of whom Strachey represented a prominent example, were cosseted with long employment (beyond the statutory retirement age of fifty-five) and relatively generous pensions (£1,100 for a senior Royal Engineer).[3] Strachey rejected these accusations but saw private-sector intrusions as unhelpful. He condemned the excesses of the early guaranteed railway companies in practising 'sham private finance', and negotiated the repurchase of the EIR on behalf of the Secretary of State to bring the profitable listed company back into majority state ownership. At the same time, he played a leading role in seeking to limit expenditure on military and other railways by pressing the adequacy of metre-wide gauges against aggressive commercial interests. He chaired vital government commissions on famine protection and irrigation. On the former subject, when not pressing the virtues of rail development as a panacea, he was able to produce learned meteorological studies on the monsoons of India.[4] However, by 1889, he had been appointed Chairman of the EIR in its new guise, with annuitants as quasi-shareholders to be protected. Noticeably, he moved from gamekeeper to poacher, pressing the EIR's regional monopoly through control of coal fields and limiting competition from new railways. His addresses to EIR annuitants were partisan, displaying little concern for the overall railway project in India. In fact, he and his brother John Strachey were significant annuity holders in the hybrid state/private EIR, with personal incentives to maximize monopoly profits. At the same time, he became Chairman of the Assam–Bengal Railway, which extended traffic connections north east toward Assam and Burma, and provided links to Calcutta via EIR. Assam–Bengal was condemned by Viceroy Curzon for its overspending and doubtful commercial value. Strachey and his Deputy Chairman at EIR sat with significant shareholdings in the GOI-guaranteed Assam Bengal, while Strachey's relation and namesake obtained employment at the company. Government-guaranteed dividends and capital gains from EIR and Assam–Bengal would have provided welcome relief for the cash-strapped Strachey family.[5]

Strachey's move from ICS to private-sector employment was paralleled at a less elevated level by Sir Theodore Hope. Hope had a distinguished early career in Calcutta and provincial government. He attained patronage from Viceroy Lytton, who appointed him as an Indian tariff board member supporting Manchester in their efforts to remove all trade protection for India's embryonic cotton manufacturing. By the early 1880s, Hope was courting controversy as the Viceroy's public works member. He encouraged Strachey in his attempts to wrest control of EIR, and worked closely with Strachey's junior colleagues in attaining guarantees for Assam–Bengal.[6] While Hope left the ICS under something of a cloud, Strachey moved to the private sector as the 'uncrowned king of the India Office' with influence in Whitehall and Calcutta. Nevertheless in their single-minded pursuit of government–protected earnings in the Indian railway system of the 1890s they both highlighted the conflicts and contradictions inherent in the peculiar blend of state and private ownership and management, which characterized Indian railways over the period. Both benefited personally in terms of salary and equity gains from the Assam–Bengal and EIR, transgressing the subtle bounds of acceptability in Victorian commerce. Both were immersed sufficiently in 'sham private finance' to warrant inclusion in Lytton Strachey's dissection of Victorian hypocrisy.[7]

Strachey's Buyback of EIR Stock and Later Chairmanship of the Company

The buyback of EIR stock, transacted in 1879 after a period of negotiations lasting several years, was the first state repurchase of a guaranteed private rail company in India. The purchase price of £125 per £100 of nominal stock followed the terms of the contract written in 1854. The repurchase price was the mean trading level of the stock for the preceding three years. Securities issued initially for £26.2 million were repurchased at £32.75 million. The original stock carried a 5 per cent guaranteed dividend, with shareholders enjoying 50 per cent of surplus profits above 5 per cent. This was replaced by a seventy-three-year annuity with a state guarantee at 4 per cent and 20 per cent of surplus profits. The original stock had enjoyed a guaranteed conversion of rupee earnings into sterling at an advantaged rate of 1s. 10d. This was dropped under the terms of the annuity, much to the annoyance of future Chairman Strachey.[8] Richard and John Strachey wrote a detailed defence of their policy of state support for railway and irrigation projects in 'the Finances and Public Works of India'. The government's decision to repurchase the stock of India's most profitable railway, the EIR, was estimated to have saved the GOI some £260,000 per annum on the repurchased sum of £26.2 million, given the funding costs of the new annuities compared to the original equity.[9] The Strachey brothers criticized the GOI's failure to exercise its repurchase option on three other railways, the GIPR, Bombay and Baroda, and Madras Railway. Those missed option dates meant guaranteed shares would be left outstanding for at least another twenty-five years, with a total cost which could 'hardly be estimated at less than several millions sterling'.[10] However, while the coupons attached to the EIR refinancing were lower, the overall transaction costs were generous to London investors. This was controversial and prompted a select committee investigation, chaired by Lord George Hamilton (future Secretary of State). Buyback costs were amortized through the accounts of the GOI, leading to a marked increase in the cost of 'productive public works'.[11] Strachey was in Calcutta at the time, finalizing negotiations with the company, so that much of the testimony in defence of Strachey's arrangements fell to Undersecretary of State at the India Office, Sir Louis Mallet. Mallet's testimony and correspondence reveal greater attachment to laissez-faire than Strachey, stretching to tolerance for private monopolies. He was a curious choice of negotiator for a 'nationalization' of India's largest railway company.[12] Unlike many parliamentary investigations of the time, the committee scrutinized the matter rigorously, through the questioning of Henry Fawcett, Professor of Political Economy at Cambridge (and predecessor to Alfred Marshall). Fawcett over time became known in the House of Commons for his engagement in Indian administrative matters as the 'Member for India'.[13] Mallet's defence of Strachey's EIR buyout negotiations did not rest on the argument that he was securing the best terms for the Indian taxpayer. The terms of the original EIR/GOI contract were said to be of such 'extreme obscurity' that the company could argue around ambiguous wording. Fawcett described the original contracts as 'the most extraordinarily unfavourable contracts that ever were entered into by Government'. However, the buyback deal negotiated between Robert Wigram Crawford (Chairman of EIR) and Strachey was offered on a 'take it or leave it' basis. Mallet believed that any attempt by Fawcett and the committee to alter aspects of the deal would prompt Crawford to reject the whole arrangement. While EIR shareholders had been enjoying government guaranteed dividends and a government-protected regional monopoly since start up in 1854, Mallet was now prepared to offer them 'liberal terms ... to ensure their cooperation'.[14]

Mallet argued that more strategic issues should override details of the buyback. The EIR franchise controlled the key Calcutta–Delhi line and could be expected to increase in value over time for the benefit of the GOI, as traffic increased. Moreover, there was a 'political motive' in the government exercising control over any 'great line'. Presumably this was the wish to use it for orchestrated commercial, military and famine-related purposes. In that sense Mallet's testimony was inconsistent with the India Office rhetoric generally which, after the state railways building of the 1870s, was moving back to state owned 'protective' lines leaving self financing projects to the private sector. It sat awkwardly with Mallet's own laissez-faire ideology.[15] Moreover, Lord Salisbury, as Secretary of State for India up to April 1878 had appointed Strachey to run negotiations. He took Mallet's arguments further, presenting a confused Tory 'laissez-faire' ideology to the committee. Government apparently required a portfolio of productive and protective lines to control borrowing requirements of the state. The state's loss-making branch lines fed the EIR, and government should be enjoying the benefits of these EIR revenues rather than simply supporting the smaller loss makers. However, Salisbury viewed ICS and public servants as less efficient than private-sector employees. State employees demanded long furloughs, leave and generous state pensions, which saddled railway companies with unnecessary costs. In using private management, with state ownership and ultimate control, the GOI would not need to pay across the 'political value' of civil servants to run the EIR, but would capture monopoly profits from the line. Further, Salisbury argued that the 'liberal terms' offered were necessary since without them EIR shareholders might have 'made themselves exceedingly disagreeable'. Viscount Cranbrook, Salisbury's successor at the India Office, was still more concerned about complaints from EIR shareholders. He worried about criticism that the India Office was trying to repurchase railways cheaply. This would be viewed generally as 'a very discreditable transaction'. There was no comparable level of concern expressed about the position of Indian taxpayers or consumers at the committee.[16]

Fawcett's critique of the Mallet/Salisbury/Cranbrook testimony, and Strachey's transaction, was wide ranging. He disagreed that EIR was well managed and criticized generous shareholder dividends and buyout windfalls as unreflective of management endeavour. Instead, EIR profits had risen dramatically in famine conditions when more foodstuffs were transported. In particular, food transported from the North, during the Madras famine, had made 1877 an extraordinary year for EIR dividends. Fawcett characterized the shareholders as benefiting from 'the misfortunes of India'.[17] Certainly EIR enjoyed great regional advantages, including rich soils in the Ganges Valley, high population density, commercial and pilgrim revenues, and economies of scale. Costs at EIR could be controlled since the engineering challenges were less than other lines. Gradients were slight, and fuel costs in the region were relatively low. A Parliamentary Rail Report of 1874 calculated EIR's ratio of expenditure to receipts at 41 per cent against an average for British railway lines at 48 per cent, allowing EIR to cover its 5 per cent guarantee as early as 1866/7.[18] Moreover, a report of the East India Finance Committee, in 1873, opined that EIR state support allowed overspending on construction of some £4 million.[19] Fawcett pressed this sceptical view at Hamilton's committee of 1881. Long-term efficiency at EIR was compromised by short-term dividend maximization aimed at stimulating the share price and buyout calculation, which was based on the mean three-year share price up to February 1879. Later complaints about shortage of rolling stock and general underinvestment, which scarred the reputation of the company, were consistent with capital expenditure being pruned for these short-term gains. High voting stock in the hands of senior management reduced any possibility of shareholder revolts over such behaviour. Shareholders controlling as little as £40,000 of a capital base of some £32 million could control shareholder 'packed' meetings, according to the Cambridge academic.[20]

However, Fawcett's most sustained criticism was reserved for the mechanics of the buyout price calculations. He was unconvinced by Mallet and Crawford's assertion that trust status investors required replacement long-duration assets for the disappearing EIR stock and debentures. Instead, EIR shareholders should be given cash or lower yielding GOI paper in exchange. This was allowable under the original contracts. An exchange for annuities was expensive and open to interpretation on Mallet's 'liberal terms'. In calculating the interest rate which applied to annuity payments, an implied interest rate was used which reflected the average coupon on old GOI paper (at 4.5 per cent) against the more relevant yield on such paper of 4 per cent. On the total buyout proceeds (£26.2 million of equity and £4.45 million of debentures), this translated to an overpayment of some £2 million.[21] Mallet had no defence against Fawcett's accusations. He could only respond that he had been burdened with 'an extremely complicated calculation to make' and was not in a position to calculate the precise annuity. Mallet's credentials for the role given to him by Salisbury were questionable.[22] Nobody else on the committee of investigation was mathematically alert enough to understand Fawcett's complaints. Further, the Cambridge academic highlighted the failure to attain Bank of England ratification on detailed buyback arrangements, which was engrained as a defence against improper practice in the original EIR contract. Either Mallet had made an unfortunate mistake or had decided to embellish his 'liberal terms', hoping nobody would notice. In fact, years later the Chairman of the committee, Lord George Hamilton, disclosed to Curzon that the annuity had proven still more generous to EIR shareholders by using GOI securities to calculate the discounted value of the buyback proceeds rather than the higher-yielding railway bonds. The terms of these annuities proved generous enough to attract significant City investors like Everard Hambro, who with four others was said to control shareholder meetings of annuitants.[23]

Strachey, like Mallet, had railed against the ambiguous wording in the EIR contract. Earlier, in 1877, in the midst of negotiations in Calcutta, he worried that without an 'amicable arrangement' with EIR shareholders, it was possible the buyback could 'land us in litigation'. While his boss Salisbury was still inclined towards the efficiency of private management, Strachey pressed the ownership question. He warned Salisbury that delays in the buyout arrangements risked a Whig government returning to Westminster, waiving the repurchase option and leaving private ownership at EIR. The Tory Secretary of State was more enthusiastic about partial 'nationalization' than his liberal opponents, who could be expected to support private initiative. Crucially, Strachey viewed his negotiations as setting a precedent for all government buybacks of Indian railways. With EIR's management on side, albeit under Mallet's 'liberal terms', other management groupings were expected to follow 'without trouble'.[24] Unfortunately, the precedent of government generosity in Strachey's EIR negotiations made the Eastern Bengal Railway (EBR) a still more expensive process for Indian taxpayers. The Stracheys were again prominent in early negotiations on EBR, with brother John supporting a buyback price of 150 for EBR stock in 1883. This process prompted wide criticism.[25] Perhaps Richard Strachey was aware that criticism of the EIR precedent would follow from Fawcett and others. He certainly felt compelled to give a lengthy account of negotiations with EIR's Chairman Crawford in 1880, highlighting that from July 1878 onwards Mallet had taken charge of negotiations with the company in London.[26]

Strachey's prominent role in Indian railway matters was consolidated with his presidency of the 1880 Famine Commission. He turned much of the commission's focus to railways, pressing for a further 10,000 miles of line for famine protection. His presidency was characteristically autocratic and attracted criticism. Even Louis Mallet accused him of 'hushing up' the extent of the famine in NW Provinces over 1877/8. Early reports, apparently suppressed by Strachey, had spoken of up to 6 million deaths in the region. Further, Sir James Caird, who sat on the commission, pressed Strachey to adopt a more consensual approach to the commission's findings. He forced Strachey to remove references to 'unanimous' support for the report's conclusions, noting his view that irrigation was being underemphasized. Reluctantly, Strachey agreed that the report's findings failed to represent even a 'majority' opinion within the commission, undermining credibility in the whole exercise. In defence, Strachey emphasized that Caird must not 'raise a controversy' which might destabilize matters. It was clear that Strachey's own pro-railway stance drove many of the findings.[27] Despite being immersed in the subject over the EIR buyback, Strachey failed to dissect the relative merits of state- against private-owned railway groupings. The EIR, which he had played such a prominent role in restructuring, attracted widespread criticism from Strachey's commission on famine relief and commercial practice. The private management/majority state ownership combination seemed not to have furnished the 'absolute control' from government, which Mallet had promised.[28]

Strachey's confused stance on private railway companies was again evident at the 1884 Select Committee on Railways. The EBR buyback, pressed by John Strachey using Richard's own EIR methodology, incurred Richard's pointed criticism. The 50 per cent premium to issue price at which EBR was repurchased represented, according to Strachey, a combination of the generous state guarantee which was funded 'from the taxes of India', and the 'action of a monopoly'. In general, Strachey saw the EBR's handsome profits and buyout premium as 'an entirely unjustifiable application of the resources of India for the benefit of private persons'. Under questioning, he refused to condemn outright the idea of private enterprise in the ownership and management of railways, but condemned guarantees for these companies as amounting to 'sham private enterprise'. Any state support for private-sector companies should be balanced by government call protection, to be exercisable at par rather than the inflated premiums paid in previous years.[29] While Strachey could not be blamed for the drafting errors of the original contracts, his enthusiasm for pushing through the EIR buyback as a precedent, to allow the EBR and other repurchases, made this attack on private-sector greed unconvincing. Further, Strachey's bias towards Bengal business interests, which he would evidence as Chairman of EIR in later years, was prominent in testimony. The lobbying activity of the Bombay Chamber of Commerce in pressing for £10 to £20 million of annual rail expenditure was condemned by Strachey, while aggressive lobbying by the Bengal Chamber went unnoticed. Finally, he displayed characteristic inconsistency in distancing himself from the recommendations of his own 1880 Famine Commission. Strachey declared that GOI enthusiasm for railways since that time had accelerated construction beyond prudent financial limits.[30]

By 1889, the Strachey family benefited directly from their involvement in part nationalization of the EIR. Early that year Chairman R. W. Crawford offered employment to one of Strachey's sons at the railway. He applauded Sir Richard on his thirty years of involvement in the company and argued that it would be appropriate to have one of the 'family' in the company. Later that year Crawford was dead, and Sir Richard himself was offered the chairmanship. He would be paid a salary of £1,000 per annum, plus substantial earnings derived from his management of a portfolio of EIR annuities.[31] However, Strachey was left in no doubt about the challenge he was taking on at EIR. The buyback might have been expected to increase the Indian public's confidence in EIR, given that most surplus earnings were now channelled to taxpayers. However, according to ex-Finance member Auckland Colvin, EIR was unpopular and required 'skilful piloting' by a new Chairman. Indian newspaper cuttings in Strachey's papers described the company as operating in a non-competitive manner, and raised concerns that Strachey was content to run a regional monopoly, depriving Bengal and the North West Provinces of the 'benefits of competition and private enterprise'. It was a common lament from nationalists that Indian business was being run by the British in a manner far removed from Mill/Smith laissez-faire.[32] Further, Strachey's move to EIR was regretted by Secretary of State Cross. Cross was an admirer of Strachey's efforts on the government public works, refuting accusations that he had constrained railway development. However, Cross was quickly made aware of a more assertive 'private sector' Richard Strachey, who pressed immediately to extend EIR mileage, while fighting 'to protect it from competition'. He warned his Viceroy that Calcutta would need to be vigilant in keeping Strachey's ambitions under control.[33] By the following summer Cross had lost any sympathy for his old colleague. Strachey had spent ninety minutes berating Cross on the iniquities of the Railway Traffic Act, threatening legal action against the legislation which served to maintain competition between lines. Cross was amused to witness the speed of Strachey's transformation from gamekeeper to poacher, evident in his ex-colleague's defence of 'a monopoly for the East India line'.[34]

We are fortunate in being able to chart Strachey's stewardship of the company from a complete set of his addresses to annuitants at the semi annual meetings of the company over the period 1890–1906.[35]Strachey moved effortlessly from India Office to spokesman and activist on behalf of the 'deferred annuitants' of EIR. He presented the company as part of a Calcutta taxpaying constituency required to redistribute wealth to a dependent Bombay Presidency. While the annuitants of EIR enjoyed a lesser profit share and no foreign exchange protection on guaranteed dividends/surplus profits, GIPR and Bombay Baroda, whose repurchase dates had been missed by government, were left enjoying generous annuity returns. The 1*s.* 10*d.* exchange rate in their contracts (against a market exchange rate of 1*s.* 4 ½*d.* by 1890) led to an exchange rate subsidization to the two Bombay railways of Rs 2.74 million and Rs 0.57 million respectively. The overall redistribution from Calcutta to Bombay was no less than Rs 4.79 million in the six months to June 1890. In partisan terms, Strachey described this as a 'bounty' to support low tariffs in Bombay, aimed at stealing business from the Bengal Presidency and improving the competitiveness of Bombay port against Calcutta. This had been a prominent rivalry since the opening of the Suez Canal in 1869. The Anglo-Indian 'traders of Calcutta' contributed to an overall 'bounty' of some Rs 50 lakhs (£300,000), paid across to Bombay's more diverse business franchise. This appeal by Strachey on behalf of Bengal business displayed pro-Anglo-Indian racial undertones.[36]

Strachey was equally preoccupied with accusations that EIR had overcharged for indigenous Bengal coal transportation, stifling economic development of the presidency. This was a recurring theme over the late nineteenth and early twentieth centuries, as Calcutta businessmen and London traders expressed frustration at railway fares. EIR was able to access coal reserves at a fraction of the price paid by other railway companies, giving Strachey's group an immense competitive advantage. There were accusations that EIR had overcharged other lines for fuel.[37] Even James Mackay, who joined EIR's board, criticized the company's practices, as President of the Calcutta Chamber of Commerce. Coal transportation costs towards Calcutta port, for transportation to other parts of India, were twice the cost per tonne charged on wheat. The latter fare structure included costs for tarpaulins and covered wagons, while any loading and freight protection on coal involved additional costs for customers of EIR. Mackay viewed this as an 'illiberal policy' by the EIR, damaging to both 'the port of Calcutta' and the railway, in the longer term.[38] By contrast, Strachey presented EIR as a force pushing Bengal towards industrial development with reduced coal tariffs, vertically integrated in coal mining through the rich Jherriah reserves. Wealthy coal entrepreneurs in Bengal owed their money to the activities of EIR. The railway had pushed up mineral property values through facilitating access to new markets. The inflated share prices of those collieries had been 'entirely' due to the 'initiative' of the railway. Strachey worried that EIR had helped create something of a speculative bubble in Indian coal mine shares. These arguments were akin to the ICS belief that railways increased the assessable land values for agricultural taxation, so benefiting rich zamindars. The analogy between coal and wheat price inflation was perhaps closer, with the common problems of 'exchange entitlement' engendered by frenetic railway development.

In sum, by 1904 Strachey calculated a balance sheet for the first twenty-four years of majority state ownership, and private management at EIR. The hybrid 'private/public' sector period for the railway had generated £3 million of 'surplus profit' to the company's shareholders, against £23 million to the GOI. Of course, this was a somewhat crude calculation since it ignored any consideration of economic externalities through the EIR's monopoly trading position and fare structure.[39] However, Secretary of State Hamilton viewed EIR's management and 'deferred annuitants' as performing sufficiently well not to justify replacing them with state management at the maturity of the deferred annuity contract at December 1899. Strachey, with enduring influence in Whitehall, was confident he would keep his job and valuable annuity securities, notwithstanding the level of criticism aimed at his management team.[40] Indeed, continuing links with the India Office kept him well informed of events within the EIR's 'regulator', and allowed him to react quickly to attacks on the company. By the turn of the century Viceroy Curzon had become irritated by Strachey's influence, and frustrated by the lack of controls exercised over the ex-ICS Chairman. In correspondence with Godley in 1901 the Viceroy highlighted a recent rail conference which had been critical of the EIR's service to the Jherriah Coal Fields. Curzon pressed that the company should be disciplined for unacceptable monopoly practices. Curzon had opposed the India Office's support for EIR as the company sought automatic access to Bengal Nagpur rail lines for Jherria coal transportation, serving to heighten EIR's coal monopoly. Curzon saw himself lined up with the trading community of the Bengal Chamber of Commerce and 'business community', against an alliance of Whitehall and EIR cemented by Strachey.[41]

The ownership structure of EIR was still sufficiently private sector to have the railway pursue profit maximization, above any development objectives of the GOI. Both Strachey brothers were annuity holders in hybrid EIR securities with incentives to maintain monopoly profits. Illustrative of their access to government circles, John Strachey wrote to Richard in 1894 with doubly pleasing news from the India Office. State financing limits for railways would be increased from Rs 2½ to 3½ lakhs to allow for additional support for Assam–Bengal Railway (Richard's other chairmanship). Meanwhile the India Office was examining the 'propriety' of using more 'cash balances' to fund EIR. Shortly afterwards John was able to boast to his brother that he was selling part of his EIR annuity portfolio at 136½ to book a handsome gain. Presumably he believed his India Office 'insider information' was now fully in the price.[42] Curzon linked Richard Strachey directly to these capitalist excesses, calling him 'a stormy and arrogant old man'. As the 'uncrowned king in the India Office' Strachey had 'ridden roughshod over the Government of India for years'. The EIR Chairman had forgotten his state-sector background and now criticized the indecision in GOI railway policy. Curzon, displaying great frustration, promised Godley that 'the man who cavils at our inertness will shortly be whimpering at our strength'. Strachey's EIR was condemned as 'a very selfish and not too scrupulous undertaking'.[43] By 1900 Curzon's relations with the India Office and Godley, as its chief civil servant, were strained over what the Viceroy considered to be excessive Whitehall interference in his administration. Strachey may have been viewed as part of this problem, and it is unclear where Godley's sympathies would have lain.[44]

However, within two years, Strachey incurred criticism from both sides of the dual government. In London, Secretary of State Hamilton was made to endure a lengthy monologue from Strachey on the unfair encroachment which Bengal–Nagpur Railway was making on the regional power of EIR. Moreover, the Secretary of State was getting early feedback from Thomas Robertson on his survey of the Indian railway sector, which was highly critical of management at Strachey's group. Congestion on EIR lines was publicly blamed on inadequate rolling stock, but Robertson pointed to a 'want of knowledge' at EIR on employing locomotives and carriages. EIR was unable to exploit the Jherriah coal field efficiently, and Bengal–Nagpur had been brought in to remedy the uncompetitive situation. However, while EIR had brought this action on itself, the India Office felt obliged to compensate Strachey's group with a new monopoly over the Burdwan–Howrah line into Calcutta. Hamilton was pleased that Robertson, his own appointee, had impressed Curzon (an unusual feat), and that he was prepared to attack EIR. While Hamilton described the franchise as 'the finest railway property in the world', it was dominated by Strachey who was a 'bully'. Like his peers

Hamilton viewed Strachey's tenure as chairman as characterized by 'great selfishness' on the part of the company.[45] The 'uncrowned king of the India Office' was by the turn of the century meeting opposition from his own constituency, through the resentment accumulated over ten years of partisan stewardship at EIR.

The Assam–Bengal Railway[46]

Strachey's other Chairmanship, attained shortly after, was even more controversial than his move to the EIR. The Assam–Bengal maintained private ownership and private management with a generous level of state support, more akin to the guaranteed rail companies of the 1850s and 60s, which Strachey had so roundly condemned. It was this project which brought Strachey together with Theodore Hope, as joint lobbyists and shareholders. This was an uncomfortable partnership since, in earlier years, Strachey had worked from the ICS side to curb what he saw as Hope's excessive government sponsored rail plans.[47] The guaranteed Assam–Bengal was one of the more extreme of such plans. Indeed, when early nationalist Romesh Dutt pointed to the unacceptable practices of private rail companies floated after 1878, he had Assam–Bengal as his most extreme example. Dutt told the Fowler currency committee of 1898 that the development of that railway had been pressed on the taxpayers of India without any concern for long term financial viability, despite its lack of protective qualities. The Bengal to Behar section of the line had done nothing for farmers or traders, and the extension from Assam to Chittagong traversed a 'very wild and hilly country' with no prospect of commercial success.[48] The Fowler Committee members presented Assam–Bengal as a company financed by risk-taking London investors, ignoring the existence of sterling government guarantees. Most unconvincing of these apologists for Strachey's 'sham private enterprise' was Sir John Muir (of James Finlay and Co., and Lord Provost of Glasgow) who feigned ignorance over the Assam–Bengal guarantee, while having been active in the lobby group, with Theodore Hope, which secured the guarantee in the first place.[49] Significantly, Dutt also highlighted the Burma Railway Company, which by 1898 was extending lines from Mandalay to the Chinese border for security reasons, again guaranteed by Indian taxpayers. This formed part of Viceroy Dufferin's grand military scheme to link Bengal with Burma via the Assam–Bengal. Dufferin's ambitious military network was ridiculed by Curzon, who also had little time for Dutt personally (whom he described as 'an unreliable, shifty, fellow'). However, Curzon and Dutt were united in their condemnation of Strachey's second great project. By 1900, eight years after Assam–Bengal's flotation, Curzon described the line as a 'horrible white elephant'.[50]

In fact, Curzon was sympathetic to private companies playing a role in rail development, even after the failings of the first guaranteed companies. In a rail despatch to Hamilton in 1899 he described the choice of state against private ownership as being only 'a matter of financial expediency rather than of fixed principle'. While he saw room for further buybacks of outlying lines by the state, he thought the government should sell off lines of sufficient maturity to fund themselves independently. Presumably EIR would have fallen into this category. Lord Dalhousie's original rail minute of 1853 had represented the high water mark for private-sector rail support, Curzon argued, while Viceroys Lawrence and Mayo had shifted policy to 'strict Governmental' and 'centralizing lines'. Curzon's sympathies lay more with Dalhousie, and he wished to avoid burdening the state with excessive ownership or managerial responsibility. At the same time he looked for a 'reasonable compromise' between the two.[51] In the context of Assam–Bengal this would have implied no government support, so that commercial failings would have precluded the line's construction. Curzon contrasted his own measured response with that of ICS predecessors in Calcutta. In particular, Sir Theodore Hope had been the Viceroy's Public Works member from 1884–9, attracting widespread criticism from all sides for his pursuit of dubious rail projects and his intimacy with promoters. Curzon highlighted Assam–Bengal as 'a monument to posterity of the confident incompetence' of Hope. The railway formed the mainstay of Indian rail construction by the mid-1890s, absorbing some £2.13 million of capital expenditure over 1895–7, more than double the next largest item.[52]

The construction of the railway was badly delayed by the 'kala-azar' and a severe earthquake in 1897. Meanwhile, the hill section of the line required construction of thirty-seven tunnels, aggregating over 15,000 feet in length. Cornish tin miners were consulted to advice on engineering aspects. At the peak of the construction effort, a labour force of 40,000 was employed on the project.[53] By 1900, building had been going on for twelve years and only 435 of the scheduled 735 miles had been completed. With costs way above budget and revenues disappointing, the line was yielding a derisory ¼ per cent against a sterling guaranteed return of 3 per cent, implying an annual deficit of some Rs 2.5 million (or £165,000) to add to the construction costs of £9 million. Much of the terrain crossed was jungle, with poor soil and negligible commercial potential. As ever, Curzon had looked into the matter personally by travelling vast distances on the Assam–Bengal. He assessed soil quality to be inadequate, demonstrated by the 'stunted appearance of the trees', which made opportunities for agricultural development limited. Curzon whimsically reflected that, in earlier centuries, blunders of the magnitude of Assam–Bengal would have led to Hope being 'hung or beheaded'.[54]

The overspend on the railway prompted the normally loyalist *Times* to publish a highly critical summary of the purpose and prospects of Assam–Bengal (though here pushing Curzon's viewpoint). The attempt to combine 'commercial' and 'strategic' aspects of the railway prompted building the line in unprofitable areas. In particular, a revolt in the princely state of Manipur in 1891 had been allowed to dictate the construction of 'a long unnecessary detour'.[55] The financial viability of Assam–Bengal's investment programme depended on the success of the port of Chittagong in diverting trade from powerful vested interests in Calcutta and river steamer companies. However, the analogy of the port of Karachi, which had failed to take business from Bombay and its powerful lobbyists, was viewed as ominous. Karachi was provided with railway links through Forsyth's Scind Punjaub, but failed to develop Punjab. Instead, the railway remained an overwhelmingly military undertaking. Chittagong's only chance to benefit from the new rail infrastructure would be under the administration of Assam, breaking free of unfavourable Bengal sponsorship. The Assam–Bengal was used by the paper as part justification for Curzon's efforts to partition Bengal three years later. However, *The Times* declined to condemn Assam–Bengal's government guarantees. Both government and shareholders were sufficiently motivated to maximize profits, and government support was not responsible for excessive construction costs. Rather, the partnership between Strachey's board and government had broken down through a restrictive regulatory environment which undermined private initiative. The Robertson committee, it was hoped, would free Richard Strachey to run the business in a more laissez-faire manner.[56] However, *The Times*'s image of Strachey being hamstrung by excessive government bureaucracy was not borne out elsewhere. By the time of Strachey's retirement from the Board in 1907, his successor chairman at Assam–Bengal praised Strachey's unique ability to overcome government intransigence, using his family name and prestige to press ahead with mostly state-funded development. Curzon's 'white elephant' grew partly through the unique lobbying position of Strachey, with his network of Whitehall and Calcutta links. Further, *The Times* failed to highlight Strachey's conflict of interest in protecting the EIR's monopoly Bengal trade, while encouraging development of Chittagong as a rival port through Assam Bengal.[57]

Curzon had a low opinion of the railway expertise of previous Viceroys. All Viceroys had avoided discussion of railway development. Even Curzon himself had focused on the problems of the railways over six years 'without any appreciable advance'.[58] In the Whiggish Lord Dufferin he saw a comparable level of ineptitude to that exhibited by Theodore Hope. Dufferin had dreamt of 'opening up communication with Upper Burma' through Assam–Bengal. Hamilton had a similar view of Dufferin's knowledge in these matters, suggesting that the former Viceroy would have waived the Assam–Bengal project through 'without looking at it'.[59] At the same time preparations were made for the 1896 floatation of Burma Railway, with a mandate to build beyond Lower Burma to Mandalay. Together Hope and Dufferin were responsible for the propagation of 'all sorts of military, political, and commercial fallacies' simultaneously.[60] The focus on Upper Burma-related railway building seemed out of kilter with the commercial prospects of the region, which had only been annexed in 1885, and had disappointed in terms of mineral-related resources. Hamilton had complained at the time of the Burma Railway floatation that Mandalay, Assam–Bengal and East Coast Railway lines made up the majority of new rail investment over the coming years, tending to crowd out more worthwhile investments.[61] Nevertheless, what Curzon termed the 'picturesque vacillations of Lord Dufferin' over Assam–Bengal was somewhat unfair. Dufferin was aware of the shortcomings of Hope's Assam–Bengal and other railway projects. The Viceroy elected not to extend Hope's term of Council membership for public works when it came up for renewal in 1887. Hope was considered to be 'not a favourite either here or at home'. He was seen as too close to a number of the railway promoters, bullying through selected projects. Dufferin had been close to lodging a formal complaint about Hope's 'vain ... arbitary, and so unscrupulous ...' behaviour.[62]

In fact, the archives suggest that Dufferin's correspondent, Secretary of State Cross, was closer to Hope in his evangelical zeal for railway construction. After securing finance for the controversial Bengal–Nagpur, and pressing the merits of the Mandalay line (both financed by Rothschild) Cross expressed to Dufferin that he viewed those projects as 'triumphs'. Perhaps giddy with success he asked 'what railways shall I take up next?' He noted Dufferin's warning that Hope was 'hardly the man to be trusted' for objective advice on rail extensions, but was keen to meet with Hope on his furlough in England.[63] Fortunately the Hope collection at the India Office Library has a comprehensive series of letter books charting his lobbying of Cross, Dufferin, Strachey and others involved in Assam–Bengal decisions. Dufferin was persuaded to keep Hope on over the summer of 1887 for 'sentimental' reasons. That would enable the public works member to tour his frontier railways one last time. Even at the end of his ICS career, with retirement beckoning within months, Hope concerned himself with his 'irons of more or less importance in this fire', of which Burma and Assam–Bengal were most prominent. By this time Hope was an isolated figure on the Council, having opposed all his colleagues over their support for the Ilbert Bill, and fought a long-running railway feud with Finance Member Colvin.[64] The aggressive internal marketing methods which Dufferin had criticized in Hope were manifest in his distributing files on the Assam–Bengal project to a number of influential Calcutta officials without his Viceroy's approval. General Roberts was brought into the discussion unnecessarily, with Hope presumably pressing the strategic links which Assam–Bengal would have with Burma.[65]

The end of Hope's ICS career in December 1887 did not remove him from a lobbying role in the Assam–Bengal financing. Like Strachey, he decided to move from government to private sector, using his knowledge and influence on behalf of Indian railway companies. Hope explained to his ICS successor at public works that he had already turned down two chairmanships of rail companies, since he was far from being a 'needy promoter'. Whether he had been offered either of Strachey's two railway chairs is unclear. In terms of his own investments, Hope intended to avoid all 'risky speculations' in the Indian railways, but to put himself and his friends into guaranteed or quasi-guaranteed ventures that he could 'honestly recommend'.[66] Among the projects which passed this test for Hope were the Burma Railway, and Assam–Bengal, which Hope played a leading role in launching as guaranteed vehicles, and in which he personally invested.[67] On the latter project he was constantly busy after official 'retirement'. In July 1888, Hope sent a draft prospectus for a £3 million capital issue for 'the Bengal–Assam Railway, Land and Minerals Company, Ltd' to the Under Secretary of State for India. He pressed the commercial, agricultural and military advantages of the proposed line, without outlining the specific advantages for the population of Upper Assam. With free land and permission to deduct interest from capital during construction, he argued that a guarantee might be avoidable. However, to place this investment within his universe of 'non speculative' investments he did ask for ten years' worth of exclusive rights to coal and other minerals, including all petroleum reserves.[68] His dialogue with both Strachey brothers appears to have been intimate over the period. John Strachey warned him that Cross was uncomfortable with giving private shareholders generous prospecting rights. Hope pressed these rights as 'a substitute for a guarantee' and highlighted the trading advantages of a railway which would increase the export of oil seeds, rice, cotton and tea. He understood that trade was more compelling than Indian development for the India Office. By late 1889, Cross complained to Viceroy Lansdowne that Hope was 'pressing' him on the railway and related mineral rights. Salisbury had agreed to look at the matter, but Cross feared it would be 'challenged in parliament'. Salisbury decided to have W. H. Smith, an unofficial Indian rail adviser, provide another opinion on the matter.[69]

Meanwhile, Hope pursued the alternative of Strachey's 'sham private enterprise' with the EIR Chairman's right-hand man, Craven Dickens. He urged Dickens to suggest guarantee arrangements which might meet the approval of the India Office. Dickens had been pressing for a 4 per cent sterling guarantee on Assam–Bengal, but Hope reminded him that the likely additional through-traffic for the Dickens/Strachey EIR was such that he might wish to compromise with a 3½ per cent guarantee. For Strachey and Dickens EIR/Assam–Bengal could be viewed as a contiguous interlinked network (again large enough to deliver the economies of scale favoured by Secretary of State Hamilton). Coal-freight business would be particularly profitable for the EIR/Assam–Bengal network. However, Dickens was greedily 'still dreaming of the EBR', whose buyout terms had been so generous to shareholders.[70] Hope now led the company's negotiations with the India Office, offering different permutations on state/private risk-reward profiles to Cross. He argued that mineral opportunities in Assam could only be exploited by 'private agency', offering to give up the first 7 per cent of surplus profits to government to secure upside for his co-investors (who would include Strachey and Dickens). Hope's anxiety was fuelled by reports in *The Times* that the GOI were looking at state funding for Assam Bengal.[71] Such an outcome would have precluded further employment and guaranteed investments, for Strachey and himself. In fact, his fears were misplaced since the India Office and GOI had their hands full with the ambitious East Coast Railway, which was expected to connect the Southern States with Bengal via the Madras–Calcutta link. Cross was getting pressure from Hope's successors in the Public Works Department over his apparent bias towards private companies, but tried to assure Viceroy Lansdowne that he was even-handed and had rejected Hope's more unreasonable requests.[72] Hope offered to bear construction risk with a 3 per cent guarantee, triggered only on completion of the railway. This seemed more reasonable to Cross and his council. By the end of 1890, Cross was confident that he could arrive at a financing package with Hope, working in concert with the contractors Matheson and Company.[73] By this time, however, the City was reeling from the effects of the Baring collapse, making access to any private sector finance problematical. When Cross's personal friend at Matheson's died, he was able to bring in another contractor and play off Hope against other promoters to attain agreement on all terms. Cross was confident that the rich mineral traffic in the region would provide ample returns for Hope and company when Assam was developed.[74]

The £1.5 million Assam–Bengal share issue was launched in 1892, with Baring investing. The issuing prospectus stressed potential trade at Chittagong, the fertile and densely populated Bengal lands around that port, and the prospects for access to new Burmese railways when opened. The sterling guarantee offered to shareholders was contrary to stated Whitehall policy in a climate of currency depreciation and budgetary concerns.[75] The dissolved companies' papers at Kew on Assam Bengal give a helpful insight into the extent to which the main protagonists in the story were able to benefit from the securities which they had 'gold plated'. Notwithstanding their financial difficulties, Francis and John Baring purchased 2,800 shares for £28,000. One of the largest share 'folios' was held under the intriguing title of 'Governor and Deputy Governor of the Bank of England, and Chairman and Deputy Chairman of East Indian Railway'. Either in a corporate or a personal capacity, Richard Strachey had direct financial links to the Assam–Bengal with a part share in a portfolio of 1,400 shares. Strachey also had a small portfolio in his own name. By 1897, the shared Bank of England/ EIR folio had been increased substantially to a value of £25,400.[76] For Strachey, this must have formed a large percentage of his personal net worth. Holroyd's biography of Lytton Strachey makes it clear that, by the late nineteenth century, the family's lifestyle at Lancaster Gate, London was far from opulent. The *DNB* states Richard Strachey's probate at death in June 1908 as a modest £6,470, and his personal papers include details of share certificates and litigation information on failed investments in the Metropolitan Coal/Consumers Association Ltd. It also shows Strachey selling part of his EIR deferred annuity holding in June 1892, presumably to switch into his other company.[77] While the Assam–Bengal may have offered some relief from the financial burdens of a long life without generous pension provisions, Strachey's ability to invest wisely appears open to some doubt. Lord Dufferin, also prominent in the promotion of the Assam Bengal, had similar problems. For ex-ICS men like Strachey and Hope, the absence of satisfactory pension provisions may have influenced their aggressive move from 'gamekeepers' to 'poachers'.

In fact, Hope and Strachey's optimism as promoters and co-investors in Assam–Bengal receded during the 1890s, as construction costs overran and revenues disappointed. By 1896 the agent for the railway at the Assam port of Chittagong was complaining that the India Office was withholding 'Imperial Funds' from a vital development of the port facilities. Without an expanding trade from the port, the Assam–Bengal freight business would stagnate. The government irrationally refused 'Imperial Funds in providing trade facilities at a port' while allowing 'them to be employed in the construction of a railway'.[78] By 1902, Strachey's namesake and relation Richard S. Strachey was ensconced in the role of Chittagong agent for the company. He pressed Strachey senior and other Assam–Bengal directors in London about the continuing failure to promote Chittagong trade expansion. A government report of 1892 had delayed investment in Chittagong port for five years and dampened government commitments to the Assam–Bengal project. He pointed out, presumably to the displeasure of his senior relation and EIR Chairman, that the report's authors had been Calcutta-based businessmen, with vested interests in seeing off any competition for the great Bengal port. Strachey Senior's position as Chairman of the Calcutta and Chittagong based businesses gave him a marked conflict of interest but, with his Assam–Bengal securities government guaranteed and foreign exchange hedged, his personal interest would always be primarily in the earnings upside of the EIR annuities. Further constraints on the capacity of Chittagong port and the Assam–Bengal to grow together were evident in R. S. Strachey's complaints about the lack of 'an adequate flotilla' of brigs to transport jute and other commodities from the port. Economies of scale for operations at Calcutta made Chittagong unattractive. Ralli Bothers, organizing the jute distribution (also Calcutta based), had seen a marked decline in jute trade from Chittagong over the period 1894–1902. Railways like Assam–Bengal had supposedly been built largely for trading benefits, while the economic development of the region itself was always likely to be modest. Although the potential of Assam–Bengal and Chittagong port was substantial for tea and coal, while jute was significant, Calcutta had a strong incumbent trading position. The role of Calcutta managing agents like Ralli Brothers and the Bengal-oriented Strachey in maintaining the status quo is not difficult to understand. By 1911 Chittagong exports of these products were normally targeted at Calcutta itself rather than London, appeasing the traders of Calcutta.[79]

The extent to which the Assam–Bengal constituted a financial burden on Indian taxpayers is clear in an ordering of the profitability of Indian Railways compiled for the GOI in 1900. During 1897/8 only four railways were making money, while Assam–Bengal was losing Rs 1.9 million (£127,000 per annum).[80] The GOI provided the usual additional levels of subsidy and support when trading conditions became difficult for the 'private' company. In 1902, for example, the government increased the rate on a £500,000 issue of debentures to persuade investors to lengthen maturity date, secure in the knowledge that payments were again guaranteed.[81] By February 1904, when Viceroy Curzon travelled to Chittagong to officially open Assam–Bengal, he was aware of the losses and the frustrations expressed by R. S. Strachey. He rebutted many of Strachey's complaints by pointing to government development of jetties, dredging services, warehouses, advantaged loans and debt forgiveness. Curzon pressed the opportunities provided by the new railway in terms of lower freight charges of tea, jute and rice to the port. These foreign earnings promoted import activity through 'piece-goods, salt and kerosine'. He was also sensitive to the uncertainties caused by his proposed Bengal boundary changes. It was not clear whether Chittagong would reside in the new province of East Bengal or Assam.[82] However, Curzon could not resist reminding his audience of the unfortunate background behind the Assam–Bengal Railway development. His public approach was consistent with his private complaints to Godley. The Viceroy looked back to the original cost estimates of £4 million at the time of floatation in 1892, and expressed astonishment that the budget had 'swollen' to some £9 million. Twelve years had passed since construction began, which had never been envisaged. Everyone needed to look to the future rather than worry that such monies could have been better expended elsewhere. Curzon had travelled over most of the line in preceding years and declared a 'personal interest' in the long-term success of the Assam–Bengal. Curzon's pragmatism in matters of laissez-faire capitalism was evident in his encouraging the railway to 'strive by combination' rather than competition to 'develop the joint interests of both'. The government would give whatever support for it could afford such a 'combination'. Assam–Bengal had been a misguided project, but now that it was constructed it needed to reside in India's mixed economy. With a lunch at the Chittagong Club hosted by the railway company, and the honour of driving a ceremonial 'spike' into the sleeper of the railway line, Curzon could not depart without thanking his guests. Much praise was heaped on the younger Richard S. Strachey for his 'long and devoted labours in the interests of this line'. Richard Strachey senior's labours as Chairman of Assam Bengal over fifteen years were also complimented. There was little to be said in favour of the company's cost control or revenue maximization, but at least Curzon could recognize longevity of service. Strachey was said to be without 'parallel' in the period over which he had continued 'to wear harness'.[83] Strachey lived to see the GOI/India Office effect another 'combination' to bolster the financial standing of his company. In 1905, the province of Assam was combined with part of Bengal, under Curzon's guidance, to form 'Eastern Bengal and Assam', and the same year the GOI bought out the Noakhali (Bengal) Railway, to merge it into Assam Bengal. Curzon's combination of provinces proved short-lived (only seven years), but the guarantees on the enlarged Assam–Bengal Railway continued to benefit shareholders until 1942.[84] The Acworth Committee reviewed the possibility of repurchasing Assam Bengal at the first call date of 1931 at par, but countenanced against nationalization given that the stock was trading by 1921 at only 45.[85] The financial performance of Strachey and Hope's 'white elephant' never recovered.

Conclusion

The Times obituary on Strachey presented his contributions as Chairman of both the EIR and Assam–Bengal as significant and poorly remunerated. In comparison to the Chairmanship of British or American railway companies, his salary was low and he was refused a pension entitlement. However, his role at the two railways was hardly a selfless labour on behalf of the Indian rail industry. Like Theodore Hope, Strachey was able to use government contacts to attain a prominent position in private/hybrid railway companies. He then pursued government-supported profits with little concern for commercial efficiency, famine protection or military security. In fact, Strachey boasted to his EIR annuitants that they were giving the minimal acceptable charitable contribution to late nineteenth-century Indian famine relief. This was from the former Chairman of the key 1880 famine commission. Accusations of improper lobbying of government representatives were levelled at both Hope and Strachey as they attained comprehensive gold plating from the India Office. However, while different Viceroys and Secretaries of State criticized the 'bullying' tactics of both men in private, they continued in elevated positions, with access to inside information from the public works committees in Calcutta and London. There was perhaps an understanding on the part of senior ICS and India Office members that the tenacity and energy of men like Hope and Strachey was required to get a railway system built, when nobody could quite decide on the balance of state and private sector. Unfortunately in the case of Assam–Bengal, and aspects of the EIR monopoly, these energies were directed in questionable ways.

7 BACKGROUND, PROCEEDINGS AND LEGACY OF THE MACKAY COMMITTEE OF 1908: GENTLEMANLY CAPITALISTS, INDIAN NATIONALISTS AND LAISSEZ-FAIRE

Introduction

The first parliamentary committee focused on Indian rail finance was assembled by Gladstone's biographer, Secretary of State Morley in 1907/8. Fifty-four years had elapsed since Viceroy Dalhousie's original minute. For a project which had already absorbed almost £300 million of mostly state-sponsored capital, this was long overdue. At Sir James Mackay's committee managing agents, City financiers, railway representatives and senior ICS mandarins pressed for increased GOI expenditure on railways to encourage the growth of the guaranteed companies and related trade opportunities. The representatives on Mackay were from trade, commerce and finance rather than manufacturing. This was consistent with Cain and Hopkins 'gentlemanly capitalism' paradigm. Their behaviour during the twelve days of testimony at Mackay highlighted the important lobbying role performed by 'expert witnesses' in matters of Imperial finance. With contracts and concessions at the behest of the GOI, it showed these gentlemanly capitalists practising selective laissez-faire.[1] The criticism which the Mackay Committee attracted from Indian nationalists showed disillusionment amongst even moderate Congress opinion at the time of the party's split in 1907. Revealingly, moderate liberal nationalists like Naoroji and Wacha displayed more deep attachment to laissez-faire than British 'gentlemanly capitalists'. While managing agents and financiers pursued direct and indirect government support, nationalists sought to use the market to promote more profound economic development.[2]

James Mackay and Indian Nationalists

Secretary of State Morley offered the Viceroyalty of India to Sir James Mackay at a country weekend they shared at Mackay's Essex estate in 1910. Morley had come to rely on the shipping and trading magnate for advice on India's financial affairs.[3] The offer was withdrawn after Prime Minister Asquith argued Mackay's business interests might compromise his position as the King's representative in India. As a consolation prize Asquith, under Morley's guidance, offered a peerage to Mackay on the latter's standing down from the India Council. The new Lord Inchcape of Strathnaver continued to build his business interests in India and elsewhere, which were seen as consistent with further political honours. After the Versailles Peace Treaty, the British Government even offered him the throne of the Balkan Kingdom of Albania. In 1907, at a less elevated point in Mackay's career, he had been appointed by Morley to chair the Parliamentary Committee on 'Indian Rail Finance and Administration'. Morley highlighted the 'enormous interest taken by traders in this country [England]' in Indian rail development at his budget address to the House of Commons. He contrasted this with the ambivalence of Indians and Anglo-Indians. Mackay, as senior partner of the shipping and trading concern Mackinnon Mackenzie and a former President of the Bengal Chamber of Commerce, would have been a leading London-based 'trader' in Morley's nomenclature. Naturally, Mackay's appointment as chairman of the railway committee met scepticism from the nationalist community. This followed criticism of his support for the gold standard on the 1893 Herschell currency committee, having been opposed previously. Wacha described Mackay as 'a sold man ... the arch agitator whom the Indian government put forward to pass their currency nostrum'.[4] Mackay had belonged to the City of London committee of the Bimetallic League but, with his conversion to gold, his social elevation had begun.[5] According to Wacha, Mackay had 'raised the banner of the gold standard' and was 'knighted and later ... smuggled into the India Council'.[6]

Mackay was described by Cain and Hopkins as 'a tireless and ubiquitous member of numerous Whitehall committees'.[7] His background was in non-manufacturing businesses in William Mackinnon's 'Mackinnon Mackenzie' group. These included shipping, trade, finance and diversified managing agency businesses, in line with the Cain and Hopkins archetype. A later biographer commented that his priorities were 'efficiency, economy and making the most of wealth generating opportunities' while he had 'little time for moral and diplomatic issues'.[8] This pragmatic outlook would have encouraged intellectual flexibility in arcane discussions on currency reform. While Wacha and other nationalists were concerned with the prospects for Indian industry, without the safety valves of currency depreciation or tariff protection, Mackay was convinced that a hard rupee currency would be good for inward British investors whose sterling assets needed protecting.[9] Nevertheless, Mackay had concerns about slow economic growth in India, which were expressed at the Herschell Committee. He complained that 'there is a very strong feeling that the country is getting into a state of great poverty'. His preferred route for remedying this situation was increased foreign trade with England rather than domestic investment and growth. The resulting 'deindustrialization' implied in India's free-trade exposure to British manufacturers became a prominent issue in nationalist discourse by the late nineteenth century. Writing later in the context Mackay's stewardship of his Indian railway committee, Wacha observed that 'because Free Trade has enriched England it cannot be categorically predicted that it has enriched India also'.[10]

Railways played a key role in the Mackay vision of free trade and the growth of Indian commerce. He had been active on the 1904 British Parliamentary Railway Rates Committee. This investigated the common practice amongst private sector English rail companies of applying preferential transport rates for certain customers. Mackay's laissez-faire sensibilities were prominent in his defence of private company's rights to maximize profitability, free from government regulation. This was consistent with Clive Dewey's characterization of Mackay as a 'rugged individualistic' entrepreneur who sought only government's 'non-interference'. However, by the time Mackay moved his attention to Indian railways, this fear of government intervention had disappeared. The Mackay Committee of 1908 pressed for greatly increased GOI expenditure and private sector spending (under a government-regulated ceiling) on railway's capital programmes. This was to support a transportation system that would facilitate free trade.[11] In both the British and Indian railway systems Mackay supported the interests of commerce, and private-sector management. British railway firms would apply lower freight charges to the dominant trading companies, with huge export and import quantities to transport. Meanwhile in India, increased government budgets for India's rail infrastructure involved the export of British steel, coal and locomotives to Bombay and Calcutta. This was transported by British shipping companies, and insured and financed within the City of London. The business was attractive for gentlemanly capitalists, who were able to operate outside more capital-intensive manufacturing. The service sector representatives, who dominated proceedings on the Mackay Committee, were condemned by Wacha as promoting unlimited rail expenditure so as 'to amass wealth without putting their hands in their pockets for a single rupee'.[12]

Background to the Mackay Committee: Herschell, Folwer, Welby and Robertson Committees 1893–1903

James Mackay joined a socially homogenous Herschell currency committee in 1892. Of the twenty-six representatives, there was only one native Indian (Naoroji). Mackay was surrounded by nine fellow Scots and six fellow managing agents.[13] This lack of Indian representation at Herschell was not surprising given the rising nationalist dissent during Lansdowne's viceroyalty. Indeed, Naoroji had made his objections to GOI currency and railway policy clear at the preceding Royal Commission of 1888. On being pressed by Sir David Barbour (a future committee member of Mackay) on why he held sceptical views on the benefits of British rail investment in India, Naoroji complained of 'the political drain ... which ... cannot be much compensated by the public works, because capital cannot accumulate [in India] ... it is all carried away by foreigners'. Later in his testimony, Naoroji pressed the links between the outflow of railway dividends and coupons to London, necessitating the sale of rupees for sterling, and the continued depreciation of the silver-based currency.[14] Barbour responded to Naoroji's critique by focusing on small ambiguities in his financial data. This was intended to undermine the integrity of nationalist discourse.[15] At the Herschell committee, classical economic confidence in gold-backed money could be reasserted by the assembled English bankers, Anglo-Indian merchants and managing agents. The problems of the depreciating currency for the railways were alluded to by some witnesses, but there were no direct representatives from the rail industry. Moreover sterling-based liabilities were treated as an unalterable attribute of the balance sheet of Indian railway companies. There was no discussion at Herschell of the capacity of Indian businesses to increase their use of rupee borrowings. Naoroji, who again appeared as a witness, demonstrated scepticism towards bimetallism.[16] The protection of London-based investors and British traders with exposure to the sterling/rupee foreign exchange risk was critical in Herschell's recommendations. Mackay and others moved rapidly to close the Indian silver mints in 1893 and stabilize the exchange rate. This might have pleased Naoroji in avoiding the bi-metallic approach which had once been pressed by Mackay and Barbour, but it did nothing to tackle the core problem of 'political drain' which lowered demand for rupees.[17]

The wider ranging Welby Royal Commission, which met in 1897 to discuss the 'administration of the expenditure of India' gave greater exposure to nationalist opinion. Railways were a prominent item in GOI expenditure and featured in the testimony of Indian witnesses who believed that tax revenues could be better spent elsewhere. Naoroji, as liberal MP and 'grand old man of India', had by then graduated from witness to committee member. He highlighted the extravagance of the government buyback programme for old guaranteed railway stocks and bonds at large premiums above par, which were 'to a considerable extent only artificial'. Moreover, the decision to waive the buyback right on GIPR stock in 1880, for a further twenty-five years, so building up greater liabilities, was 'very unfortunate'.[18] Naoroji gave a damning critique of the wastefulness and single mindedness of the GOI's railway programme over several years. He pointed to the influence of Anglo-Indian controlled Chambers of Commerce who would lobby all new Viceroys arriving in Calcutta to expand the infrastructure while 'there is no feeling in India that there should be these railways'. The recommended maximum borrowing limit agreed by Parliament in 1879 was being exceeded. This suggested that investment was 'in the interests of the commercial classes'.

In contrast, no significant forum for Indian popular opinion, including Congress, was in favour of this railway programme. Though cost per mile appeared low in relation to other countries, Naoroji correctly observed that the very low Indian labour and raw material costs should have allowed cheaper construction. Finally, he focused on the inability of English financiers to float non-guaranteed securities, which appeared 'astonishing' given the anticipated profits of Indian rail companies. Instead 'every new scheme proposes that all elements of risk and possible loss should be shifted on to the Indian taxpayer, securing an absolutely safe, clear percentage of profit for the English investor'.[19] This was far removed from Naoroji's vision of laissez-faire capitalism.[20] Naoroji was subsequently joined by fellow commission members Sir William Wedderburn and W. S. Caine in producing a minority report. They objected to the limited nature of the commission's official report which focused the 'mechanical working' of GOI expenditure. Within the wasteful expenditures were 'railway extensions forced on without due heed to the country's needs or means'.[21]

Wacha appeared at the Welby Commission only as a witness and so could not join the minority report. However, in his testimony he denounced the 'continuous drain' from India to England. This prevented the accumulation of capital sufficient to fund the railways in India. The effect of this failure to fund in rupees could be destructive with foreign exchange movements often outweighing the lower coupons paid in sterling. Such complaints were sidestepped by the former Treasury representative Lord Welby. He pointed out that Indian railway companies were given privileged access to 'the advantage of the English market', as though the quantification of such an arrangement were unnecessary. Further, Sir Stephen Jacob was recalled to undermine Wacha's credibility by questioning irrelevant details in Wacha's rail expenditure numbers.[22] This recurring British tactic was highlighted in contemporary correspondence between Wacha and Naoroji. Wacha complained of Jacob's attempts to 'controvert me' and suggested that Jacob had misled him on matters of detail.[23] Moreover, Wacha was suspicious of the substantial time delay between the gathering of the Welby evidence in 1897 and the report's eventual publication some three years later, which he called 'inexplicable'.[24] By 1898, Wacha asked Naoroji whether Welby was 'incubating on the evidence' or more accusingly perhaps 'the India Office' was 'intriguing with him [Welby] after the events that have occurred'.[25] Lord Welby himself was viewed by Wacha as well-meaning but pressured into following 'Treasury traditions'. On the belated appearance of the majority report, Wacha considered that the conclusions were so tampered with that it 'might have never been written'.[26] After Welby, Anglo-Indians closed ranks to prevent any further embarrassment from nationalist dissension. While Naoroji's minority report on Welby was being fretted over by the India Office, his name was being considered by Lord Fowler for membership of a new currency commission of 1898. However, according to Wacha, his nationalist ally Naoroji was 'already a red rag to the India office'. Fowler was described as a 'pompous sophist' and his currency deliberations were expected to be 'accursed' with 'no confidence in what it may propose'. The future Mackay member Sir David Barbour sat on Fowler and faced difficulties of credibility in needing to 'wriggle out' of his old [bimetallic] views.[27] The composition of Fowler avoided the risk of Welby-style dissent. Naoroji described the members and witnesses as representing only 'Anglo-Indians-official and non official – and British capitalistic, commercial and banking interests'.[28]

With the currency exposures of Indian railway companies apparently solved by the Herschell/Fowler moves to a Gold Exchange Standard, the Robertson Committee of 1903 concentrated on the 'administration and working of the Indian Railways.[29] Robertson's terms of reference were more widely drawn than those of Mackay but curtailed discussions on crucial financing and economic aspects. The focus of the committee was on the appropriate public/private balance of railway management, whether a 'systematic plan for railway development' was appropriate, and means of enhancing revenue from freight and passengers.[30] This encouraged further debate on the extent of laissez-faire in running the railways and the relative performance of railway development under 'state versus company management'.[31] Robertson noted that he had not observed 'any very marked superiority in practical management in the company-worked railways over those worked by the state'. This was not surprising given the shortcomings of the 'pure' private-sector model in Britain, where wasteful competition created overbuilding and a fare structure that sought to recoup these costs.[32] He went on to list in some detail the pros and cons of the two systems but concluded that 'disadvantages' of state lines 'outweigh any advantages'. The threat of political interference and the financial constraints which accompanied public-sector enterprises were uppermost in his mind. However, the worst outcome was the present 'duality' with public and private working in parallel. That 'duality' had given rise to immense complexity with thirty-three different railway administrations covering every conceivable gradation of state interference. Instead, the GOI should lease all rail assets to private companies, leaving the state to 'adjudicate' on conflicts and promote 'healthy competition'. Furthermore he recommended the setting up of a Railway Board outside the Public Works Department to focus exclusively on railways. Robertson's recommendations were broadly in line with Viceroy Curzon's recommendations for 'gradually restricting ... Government agency' while seeking 'a reasonable compromise' between state and private sector.[33] He was satisfied that the unacceptable 'old guaranteed contracts' had been largely renegotiated, leaving only Bombay, Baroda and Central, and Madras Railway outstanding. Here the Secretary of State had buyback opportunities over the next few years. Robertson pointed to Southern Mahratta and Assam–Bengal as being more recent guaranteed private floatations which presented difficulties. Southern Mahratta's distribution formula imposed little discipline on capital expenditure, while Assam–Bengal was so far off generating surplus earnings that it gave no incentive to management to operate efficiently. Meanwhile, the 'company-worked railways' (EIR, Bengal Central, Bengal Nagpur, GIPR, South Indian and Burma Railways) were seen more positively, notwithstanding their awkward hybrid status.[34]

Proceedings of Mackay Committee 1908

Lord Morley's approach to Indian representation on the Mackay Committee might have been expected to differ from that of Secretary of State Hamilton on Fowler. After all, Morley had arrived at the India Office with a 'liberal' reputation based on his support for Irish Home Rule and the pro-Boer movement in the South African War. He had condemned Salisbury's description of Naoroji, prospective Liberal MP for Central Finchley, as 'a black man' and welcomed the Parsi Indian nationalist into the Liberal fold.[35] Yet on taking up his role at the India Office, according to Stephen Koss, Morley had 'revealed scarcely more affection for the yellow race' to which 'he consigned the population of India' than had Curzon. Moreover, the liberalism and admiration of John Stuart Mill which appeared to bind Morley to Naoroji and Wacha was based on 'antithetical lessons from their common master'.[36] While Morley may have been untroubled by the prospect of all British representation on Mackay, the make-up of the committee was unlikely to have been all his own choosing. The India Office, headed by Sir Arthur Godley, was alert to changes in Congress party strategy. Congress's British-centred approach to lobbying, through Welby and other parliamentary committees, had delivered disappointing results. This culminated in the division between Moderates and Extremists in 1907 as the Mackay selections were being made. Arnold Kaminsky argued that during this time the India Office 'undermined the British Committee's [of Congress] efforts at lobbying by manipulating the composition of royal and parliamentary commissions'.[37] Moreover, once Mackay had been appointed chairman he would have enjoyed significant influence in bringing likeminded individuals onto the committee. Mackay and his EIR colleague Barbour would meet no Indian dissent in person.

The Mackay Committee set restrictive terms of reference. This allowed more focused discussion, but risked evading the wider issue of whether India was gaining much benefit from the tax burden implied by high railway expenditure. The specific aspects highlighted for discussion at Mackay were:

'1) Whether the amounts allotted in recent years for railway construction and equipment in India are sufficient for the needs of the country and for the development of its trade; and if not then

2) What additional amounts may properly and advantageously be raised for the purpose;
3) Within what limits of time, and by what methods they should be raised;
4) Towards what objectives should they be applied; and
5) Whether the system under which the Railway Board now works is satisfactory or is capable of improvement and to make recommendations'[38]

The focus of this guidance was on rail expansion. Complaints from nationalists that the GOI was pressing railways to the exclusion of sanitation, irrigation and education went unheeded. By framing the discussion in these terms any wayward witnesses who strayed from the consensus on railway growth as a priority could be accused of failing to direct themselves at the subject under discussion. To facilitate this, all witnesses were encouraged to provide a written summary of their answers to the questions posed, allowing committee members to use such text as the basis of cross examination. Nationalist observer Ghose had been complementary about the intentions of Robertson and his committee but saw little to applaud in the set up of Mackay. Only those in 'official circles' knew 'what the object and scope of the committee were'.[39]

The assembled committee members and witnesses were far removed from the background of the dissenting members of the Welby Commission. Minority reports were an unlikely outcome. John Morley appointed four other committee members to work with James Mackay on twelve working days between 23 May 1907 and 16 January 1908.[40] Sir Walter Roper Lawrence had an impressive academic background having entered the ICS in 1877 with the highest marks of his year. He served as private secretary to Curzon over 1898–1903. By 1909 he had resigned from the ICS due to a conflict of interest between business and politics.[41] There is no mention of the Mackay committee in Lawrence's memoirs or private papers at the IOL. However, his personal closeness to Mackay is clear in the correspondence between the two and the solicitation he received to join the main board of Mackay's P&O shipping line.[42] Lawrence's fellow committee member, Sir Felix Schuster, was from a more cosmopolitan background having emigrated with his family from Frankfurt in 1873. He moved into the family's banking business and rose to prominence at the bank's amalgamation with the large joint stock bank, Union Bank of London (UBL). UBL sat outside the elite merchant banks/accepting houses of the square mile since it relied on joint stock capital to make loans and investments. Nevertheless, by 1903 it had taken on a hybrid character with the acquisition of merchant banking businesses.[43] UBL was actively involved in Indian railway companies with formal advisory relationships with a number of companies.[44] Substantial sterling bond investments in Indian railways are shown in the balance sheet of UBL over the period 1891–1914, illustrating that banks performed a joint advisory and investment function.

Interestingly the only equity investments shown in UBL portfolios were two Rothschild sponsored investments. UBL held stock in the Burma (guaranteed) and the Bengal NW (government supported) railway companies for short periods.[45] Sir David Barbour also had an ICS background, moving early into the GOI finance department. He spent much of the next twenty years working on bimetallic matters and Indian currency questions. After leaving India in 1893, Barbour took up appointments in the City and industry. He was a director of the EIR from 1895 and some years after the Mackay Commission was promoted to be company chairman. Like Richard Strachey and Mackay himself, Barbour was able to serve in a government capacity under which decisions favourable to the EIR were made, and later enjoy a senior appointment at EIR.[46] The final member appointed by Morley played the role of technocrat. Lionel Abrahams did not fit comfortably into the gentlemanly capitalist and aristocratic civil servant mould of his compatriots. Abrahams had headed the ICS list in 1893 and, by 1898, became secretary to the Indian currency committee. The *DNB* described him as 'John Maynard Keynes's mentor on Indian finance' and an architect of the gold exchange standard for India.[47] Abrahams spent much of his time on Mackay pressing detailed and difficult questions to less accomplished witnesses.

The committee members would have been comfortable with the assembled witnesses. The thirty-five witnesses called were all British or Anglo-Indian and came from managing agencies, the City, the ICS and Indian railway companies. The managing agency group included commercial men who had served as Presidents of Indian Chambers of Commerce. Sir Ernest Cable, for example, had been President of the Bengal Chamber of Commerce over 1903–5 and was a member of the Viceroy's legislative council. He had been a partner of Bird and Company since 1886 which was a large agency with interests in coal mining, jute mills and labour contracting. The history of Bird's activities disclosed the importance of early contracts from the EIR for labour supplies. The profits from these EIR contracts were said to be 'substantial'. The EIR labour contracting 'demanded no capital' which fitted into the managing agency business culture. Further, Bird's 'never paid coolies until they themselves had been paid ...'[48] Another contract with the EBR state railway was described by Cable as 'the heart and core of our business'.[49] These labour contracts with railway companies and control of seven coal companies, which benefited from railway use and transport of coal, meant Cable favoured further rail expansion, particularly that benefiting EIR. He pressed the Committee on the need to construct another 15,000 wagons for the Indian rail service over eighteen months, arguing that insufficient rolling stock at EIR had cost his agency some £50,000 in lost revenue. If that meant increasing the rates of interest offered by Indian railway securities to raise the required sum, then Cable contended it was a price worth paying. While theoretically averse to state involvement in commerce, Cable was another managing agent who practised 'selective laissez-faire'. He was convinced that to achieve the required funding 'the Government credit' was necessary. Cable felt confident in speaking for 'the head man' of an Indian village who would want to see increased rail expenditure, to have crops transported efficiently. This would apparently be more popular than reductions in the regressive salt tax that were being lobbied for elsewhere. Despite Cable's paternalistic assurances, wasteful railway expenditure and the hated salt tax became prominent nationalist concerns.[50]

Cable's fellow witness Sir Patrick Playfair had a comparable business and social pedigree. He was senior partner of the leading agency Barry and Company and a former Chairman of the Bengal Chamber of Commerce. He similarly pressed for greater government expenditure on railways, particularly rolling stock. Playfair articulated a fatalistic view of Indian economic development pointing to India's 'almost total absence of accumulated capital'. He quoted Cromer's description of India as a country 'of unbounded material resources' populated by 'poor people'. Without capital to invest or the hope of improvement, India 'depends on its being able to secure a large and favourable outlet for its surplus produce'. For Playfair, the railways would accelerate the speed at which crops were transported. There was no question of India ever being able to shift to higher value-added industrial products. Instead, her trading activities were dominated by the merchant who was 'simply a middleman' who could shift agency function from wheat to other primary product as opportunities arose. However, Playfair demonstrated independence from the dominant EIR in complaining that rail rates had been reduced too slowly by the guaranteed companies. He pointed to the million pounds of net profit which the EIR was draining from 'the trade of Bengal, if not out of the ryots of Bengal.[51] By this time the EIR monopoly profits could be characterized as an additional tax paid to the GOI.

A third senior Chamber of Commerce representative was called as a witness. The grandly titled Honourable Mr M. de P. Webb CIE, had spent seventeen years in India, partly as Chairman of the Karachi Chamber of Commerce. Like his fellow commercial representatives, Montagu Webb demonstrated the tendencies, which Wacha and Ghose had warned of, in pressing for unlimited GOI railway expenditure. However, Webb's criticism was focused on Bengal NW, the Rothschild sponsored private railway. He wanted control devolved from London to the new Indian Railway Board to reduce bureaucracy and delays. Like many observers, Webb was unconvinced about the benefits of boards of directors operating from the metropole and supported selective state intervention.[52] There was a pragmatic acceptance by most at the Mackay Committee that government, either central or local, was welcome providing it encouraged trade. Indeed, the wrong sort of private involvement was to be discouraged. However, Barbour of the EIR mocked Webb's rejection of laissez-faire, which he interpreted as an allegiance to financiers and promoters. These agents were parasitic, in lobbying for government support 'to make a profit on it, to float it and then have done with it'. Further tensions between the metropolitan tendencies of ICS representatives, like Barbour and Abrahams, and the more devolved approach of provincial Anglo-Indians, like Webb, were clear from cross examination. Abrahams mocked the idea that Railway Board members sitting in Simla could assess funding opportunities in the distant City of London. The Secretary of State had the power to decide and would be advised by 'people of knowledge, like Sir James Mackay'. It seems likely that centralization of railway finance and expenditure through a few key London, Calcutta and Bombay individuals would have left Webb's Karachi without a voice in matters. The dominance of Bengal's EIR reflected that bias. The reliance on London rather than Webb's preferred rupee finance heightened the India Office control, and had earlier exposed railway companies to substantial foreign exchange losses. Nevertheless, Mackay told Webb that Indian banks would stay outside the realm of rail finance since they were 'pretty well occupied in financing the trade of India'.[53] For a Calcutta and London based managing agent with trade and shipping revenues that position suited Mackay perfectly.

The Mackay Committee testimony suggests that Wacha and Ghose's characterization of Chambers of Commerce exercising unlimited influence over the India Office was a simplification. Influence was exercised, as ever, through small elites with personal links into the India Office. It was possible for James Mackay or even Ernest Cable to lobby Lord Morley and others in the manner suggested by Ghose. However, for the Karachi chamber of commerce and its members there was a need to deal with small rail promoters and press for delegated power to Simla. Even L. R. W. Forrest, an early witness on Mackay, partner at the agents Killick, Nixon and Company, and Chairman of the Bombay Chamber of Commerce, complained that the Secretary of State needed to take financial advice 'in wider quarters'. Bombay links to the City of London were less well-defined than those of Mackay and the rival Bengal Chamber.[54] Certainly the breadth of City advice solicited by the Committee was limited. Only four City representatives were called as witnesses, two of whom gave narrow feedback on funding tactics. H. A. Daniell, for example, was a partner at Mullens, Marshall and Company. He quantified funding available over three years at about £30 million of which the vast majority would come from London and a small amount might be raised in rupees or from savings banks. Lord Swaythling brought sixty years experience from the City but his testimony was focused exclusively on the techniques for encouraging successful secondary market trading in securities. On Indian rail securities, he argued 'it is better to give a little advantage to the public in order to make them run after the stock'. Perhaps conscious of the past debacle over market-priced call options on guaranteed railway securities, he pressed that the Secretary of State could easily maintain a 'right of redemption at par'.[55] He was more optimistic than Daniell on amounts, arguing that up to £20 million per annum might be raised. Like Daniell he declined to comment on strategic matters, suggesting he lacked real advisory influence at the India Office.

The testimony of Lord Rothschild was different in style and content, as was his introduction to the committee. Unlike the other witnesses, Nathaniel Rothschild was given no formal introduction nor was he asked for any biographical details. Mackay addressed him in reverential manner. He thanked Rothschild for being 'good enough to send [us] in a note of your evidence'. Rothschild read out the full text of his written statement to the committee and was assured by Mackay that it would be included in the final report. The statement included a summary of the financial health of the GOI as a whole. Rothschild asserted that net profits from railways alone at £12.4 million were large enough to meet all interest payments on outstanding GOI debt (railway and non-railway related) at £8.8 million. Moreover, the total debt of the GOI which stood at £232.4 million was more than covered by the value of Indian railway assets at cost, which was £272 million. Using such evidence the India Office should be able to counteract accusations that railway borrowings represented a 'burden on the Indian people'. Valuing railway assets at cost, given the questionable controls on supplier prices, was debateable. Nevertheless, a number of aspects of future railway financings might be stressed to 'appeal strongly' to British interests. These would include 'the vista of employment for the native population in India' and the promise 'of large amounts of railway material being ordered in England'. The former promise was genuine in terms of mass low-paid employment, but it is unclear to what extent Rothschild was offering this as a gesture to nationalist sympathizers in England. The latter aspect was central to Rothschild and government thinking and the financier returned to the matter in explaining how large amounts could be readily raised for 'locomotives, wagons etc'. The London investors would be keen to buy these railway securities 'especially if you make it known that it is going to be spent in this country'.[56] Rentiers from the metropole thrived symbiotically with the British steel and locomotive manufacturers. Rothschild's underwriting activity was concentrated on the low-risk sovereign and guaranteed securities, but saw value in Indian taxpayers financing British manufacturers. He was able to move effortlessly between private and public sectors while retaining the veneer of laissez-faire.

Rothschild used considerable charm and manners to consolidate his hold over the committee. He disarmingly spoke of his 'small knowledge of Indian affairs' but in the next breath underlined his position of authority having 'had the honour of being consulted by various Secretaries of State as to the best means of raising capital for Indian railways'. The prominence of his role in floating Bengal Central, Bengal NW, Bengal Nagpur and Burma Railways, amongst others, illustrated the extent of this informal position.[57] Rothschild contended that the present Secretary of State Lord Morley, like his predecessors, was convinced that the development of railways would 'mean increased prosperity to the inhabitants' of India. He continued the 'gifted amateur' persona in describing himself as 'only a buffer' prepared to deliver unpleasant messages to the assembled committee. In this context, he advised against being less than generous with London rail investors and risking 'that nobody can make anything out of it'. While his main overseas businesses were in the USA and South Africa, India provided important opportunities for the Rothschild group. Notably, Burma Ruby Mines Ltd was focused on mining in the recently annexed Upper Burma. This sat comfortably with his South African mining interests. For a man who was so secretive in his dealings that he insisted on having all private papers burned on his death, the extent of his candour on his Indian dealings at Mackay was surprising. He spoke of his bank's underwriting function on the floatation of the Burma Railway Company, which was brought to the market with full government guarantees as late as the 1890s, by which time such support might have been felt unnecessary. This was the same stock which his interrogator Sir Felix Schuster had purchased within UBL. Moreover, Rothschild had a strong dialogue with Evelyn Baring, of the rival family, on the subject of Indian railways. He told Mackay that he worked with Baring and City financiers on railway acquisitions, including the Bengal NW. Having attained the concession financed with borrowed money, Rothschild and his fellow investors had found it to be 'a most promising business'.[58] The obvious conflicts of interest in Rothschild's role as an underwriter and investor in railway securities, against his 'informal' advice to a succession of Secretaries of State, were ignored by the committee.

Rothschild's City views were complemented by the testimony of A. F. Wallace, a retired Governor of the Bank of England. Like Rothschild, he also had direct involvement in the Indian railways as a director of the Bombay, Baroda and Central Railway Company. He shared his City compatriot's enthusiasm for the private-sector financing of Bengal NW. While Mackay reminded him that most of the rail system was operated on leased terms by private companies, Wallace contended that private ownership of assets rather than leasing of state-owned railway assets was necessary to achieve efficiencies and access to capital. Barbour pointed out that the vast majority of railway infrastructures had been constructed using state financial assistance. However, Wallace's 'laissez-faire credentials' were clear. He asserted that 'the business of a Government is to develop the country and not go in for industrial business'. Wallace sounded like another Briton or Anglo-Indian arguing in favour of India as a primary producer trading with Britain on declining terms of trade. More optimistically Wallace asserted that railway financing in India, denominated in the required rupees, was tenable 'if you gave them [Indian investors] a prospect of a fair return'. He cited the domestically funded cotton mills as a counter example to the assumption that India was chronically short of capital. Local finance would remove the problem of scarce government funding imposed by cautious finance members. Again Barbour of the ICS objected to this characterization of Whitehall control and asserted that, in his time as finance member, the exuberance of other board members in their spending plans held sway over the Secretary of State.[59]

While managing-agency and City testimony showed the opinions and influence of Cain and Hopkins's 'gentlemanly capitalists' clearly, the majority of testimony at Mackay was taken from representatives of the railway companies themselves. The largest and most profitable EIR was well represented, which was not surprising given the direct links with Mackay and Barbour. EIR still made up 18 per cent of total Indian rail earnings, albeit down from 34 per cent in 1881. Equally there was over-representation by the Rothschild-sponsored Bengal NW and Burma Railways which together sent five witnesses to testify, but represented less than 6 per cent of earnings.[60] The Chairman of EIR (Strachey's succesor BW Colvin) spoke confidently about the strength and profitability of his company. EIR was producing an extraordinary 55 per cent net profit margin, which meant they could raise capital readily, secured only on the excess profits of £1 million per annum and paying modest underwriting and brokerage fees of 1.25 per cent. Part of this strength was due to vertical integration into coal mining and electricity supply, which provided secure and cheap raw materials.[61] EIR also maintained high monopoly coal prices for other railways. This was a major controversy which went unexamined by the chairman of the committee. In fact, Mackay himself chaired the Eastern Coal Co. Ltd and English Coaling Co. Ltd, in addition to his boardroom responsibilities at EIR.[62] Even EIR admitted to inefficiencies due to the 'buy British' arrangements which characterized the industry and, according to Rothschild, kept the British investing. An agent of EIR complained that deliveries of materials took eighteen months since 'we have to get the bulk of our material from England'.[63] The natural enthusiasm of Mackay's colleagues for the EIR was not shared by all. A Government Director of the Indian Railways was pressed by Abrahams on the assertion that Richard Strachey's chairmanship had turned EIR into an 'extremely well managed' business. The witness responded sceptically that 'a company which spends so much money can get a lot of efficiency, and the great prosperity of the line holds many deficiencies'.[64] It was easier for EIR's duopoly partner, Bengal–Nagpur, to maintain the façade of private enterprise, given its conventional joint stock status. Chairman Sir Samuel Hoare blamed the Secretary of State for exercising anti-competitive power. Hoare argued for increased private involvement in Indian railways to lessen the 'monopolist' powers of the India Office, ignoring the frequently made assertion that his own institution practised uncompetitive behaviour. At the same time, the returns to railways like Bengal–Nagpur appeared to follow naturally. In Hoare's metaphor 'the railways of India may be compared to the drainage system of a country where rainfall increases year by year'.[65] Any business whose profitability follows a defined meteorological and gravitational path might prompt scepticism of management's contribution.

The final group of witnesses to Mackay came from an ICS background, and included the prominent ex-finance member of the Viceroy's Council, Sir Edward Fitzgerald Law. Law had an early association with the railways, having argued for British involvement in the Baghdad railway in the 1890s.[66] Revealingly, he spoke of the over-represented Bengal NW, contending that there were 'some very acute financial people connected with that railway'. He observed public suspicion about financial prospects for Indian railway companies since the 'government advertised all its troubles about [foreign] exchange'. London-based investors were shy of currency risk and had disposed of their small portfolios of rupee-denominated railway paper. This anxiety was prolonged even after the move to the fixed-rate gold exchange standard. Generous buyback arrangements like the government's purchase of the Bombay–Baroda stock at 160 per cent of issue price (another cost to the Indian taxpayer) failed to lure investors. Uncertainty was simply too great. Law preferred a more transparent approach to government financing with GOI borrowing in its own name rather than providing indirect support through guarantees and subsidies to private companies. Guarantees placed the state in the position of the 'gentleman who backs his friends bills as a mere formality'. Further, the British government's handling of its debt management was so poor that, according to Law, even consols had by 1908 become viewed as 'a speculative stock'. Deputy Accountant General at the India Office, H. W. Baddock, argued that railway stock buybacks had absorbed much of the GOI's time and money. Consequently, financing for railway capital expenditure had fallen short. Even excluding the cost of the buybacks themselves the delays incurred on the GIPR and other buybacks had cost £20 million.[67] The delays were incomprehensible to Badock, but the decision was made around 1870 when it was 'not considered convenient or desirable to buy'. Moreover, the whole policy of exercising buybacks was questioned by Colonel Sir William Bisset, Chairman of the Bombay, Baroda and Central Indian Railway. Bisset said it was driven 'from a sense of the obligation to take full advantage of the rights which the Secretary of State possesses'. There was an absence of 'any broad motive of high policy'.[68] The testimony by ICS representatives in general gave the impression that policy had no consistent economic ideology. Instead the 'official mind' mirrored the pragmatism of James Mackay.

Recommendations of Mackay Committee

The recommendations of Mackay were brief and fail to convey the subtlety of debate and social interaction which characterized the full testimony. While the committee concluded that most complaints about lack of GOI support for 'private enterprise' were unjustified, the recommendations focused on encouraging private companies. In fact, Mackay claimed that he was unfamiliar with any examples of 'true private enterprise' or 'construction of railways without financial assistance from the state' which had not benefited from GOI 'encouragement'. With this in view the capital expenditure budget (the budget for all railway spend private and public) for railways was increased from £10 million to £12.5 million per annum. With some variance on a year to year basis, this was intended to deliver at least £100 million over an eight-year period. The favoured instruments for raising this funding were a blend of direct GOI funding, railway company secured debentures and guaranteed railway company 'share capital'.[69] The model of Rothschild's Bengal NW would continue to be pursued without any significant analysis on whether the 'acute financial minds' involved were benefiting the development prospects of India or hindering them. Moreover, the rather ill-conceived ideas on raising finance against capitalized earnings from railway assets were encouraged. These schemes, much like modern PFI projects, were more expensive than direct government borrowing, but left the GOI ultimately liable. Structures akin to the Bengal–Nagpur with private leasing of assets over long periods were applauded. This was in spite of that company's anti-competitive practices in Bengal where, after 1901, the management pushed coal prices up again in duopoly with the EIR.[70] Mackay's enthusiasm for leasing structures, with government ownership of assets and minimal capital investment, was in line with his managing agency background. The committee found it impossible to place an upper limit on the maximum desirable rail mileage but highlighted that a number of witnesses had pressed for an ultimate network of some 100,000 miles. Mackay responded that 'even this estimate of mileage is short of what will ultimately be found necessary in India'.[71] Shortly after Mackay, Ghose commented that 'railway expenditure ... is heavy in every direction'.[72]

Legacy of Mackay Committee

Mackay, now elevated to Lord Inchcape, returned to India in 1911 to 'settle certain difficulties' between the London-based Indian railways and the Railway Board.[73] His visit raised significant resentment from the Indian contingent on the Viceroy's legislative council. While the Mackay Committee had been left without an Indian voice through Morley's appointments, his Morley-Minto reforms of 1909 had at least set up a forum for debate. In February 1912, the moderate nationalist Gokhale made objections to Inchcape's visit, which he contended was shrouded in secrecy. It appeared that the report produced had been sent direct to Secretary of State Crewe in London without any discussion in India.[74] The Indian press had been reporting the visit widely, with the *Times of India* describing it as Inchcape's 'mission' on Indian railways.[75] Gokhale pressed Inchcape's unsuitability for this follow up 'mission' and, by implication, for the

Mackay Committee itself. Inchcape was not 'an expert' on Indian railways and was conflicted as 'the senior partner of a big commercial house in this country, having extensive dealings with railway companies'. Even if Inchcape was not consciously partial, Gokhale argued for 'an unconscious bias from which even the most eminent of men are not free'.[76] Inchcape was accused by other Indian spokesmen on the council of returning to India to dampen the powers of the Railway Board. The Board was seen by natives as the guardian of the Indian taxpayer in its maintenance of fiscal controls over individual Indian railway companies, with which Inchcape was held to be in league. Indeed, the Mackay committee had concluded that the Board should be excluded from all 'matters of detail' affecting the companies.[77]

Inchcape's 'mission' to India raised fundamental issues about the balance of power between London and Calcutta in Indian administration. Sir Guy Fleetwood, as Finance Member of the Viceroy's council over 1908–13, found himself dictated to by Inchcape over the agenda and detail of the railway discussions in India. Inchcape had requested that members of the GOI sit under his chairmanship at the discussions, which Fleetwood argued raised constitutional issues about the balance of power in Indian government. Inchcape was not even a formal representative of the India Office, but was allocating himself powers that would have been inappropriate for even the Secretary of State. Fleetwood's papers display a barbed exchange between himself and the visiting businessman. Inchcape was forced to retract some of his demands and state formally that he had no executive powers over working expenses or capital expenditure budgets for the railway companies. These powers resided in Calcutta. The railway companies were objecting to the degree of influence exerted by the GOI-sponsored Railway Board, which placed them on the same side as Inchcape and his supporters in Whitehall. Inchcape described his own role as being to lessen the 'friction' between companies and Board, but managed to heighten tensions through his brusque approach. His colleague from the Mackay Committee, Lionel Abrahams, sought to pacify the GOI, but attracted criticism from Fleetwood. Abraham's letters illustrated how 'absolutely disingenuous' the India Office had been in their tactics. If the excesses of such middle-ranking India Office representatives were not curbed, the whole structure of government would be in danger of collapse. The Secretary of State would be encouraged to send envoys on foreign policy to run Indian policy on the 'two frontiers', so that Persian, Afghan and Tibetan policy would soon be controlled from Whitehall. Pointedly, Fleetwood held up the threat of joint stock bankers, like Inchcape's other Mackay colleague, Sir Felix Schuster, running exchange rate policy. The 'cult of the special advisor', and the extent to which Inchcape and friends posed a threat to the independence of the ICS motivated Fleetwood's criticism. This was not directed personally at Secretary of State Crewe, but at his successors who might press centralizing powers too far. Future incumbents of the India Office, and their advisors, might feel compelled to visit India for the pleasant winter months to 'settle matters for the Viceroy'. In the process they would open up fissures in the British administration which would be manna to the 'dissatisfied Indians'. The Inchcape experience highlighted the impossible dilemma in which ICS representatives found themselves. They were torn between the need to subdue Indian native criticism and to see off pressures from these 'emissaries' of the India Office.[78] Railways, as the largest item of domestic expenditure, had brought mounting political and economic problems to the surface.

Seemingly undamaged by nationalist criticism, Inchcape was thanked by the 1921 Acworth Committee for his intermediation between Railway Board and companies. Acworth contended that this disagreement was 'all smoothed out, thanks to you'. By the time he was invited to appear at Acworth in November 1920, he admitted that he had not thought about Indian railways since 1912. In spite of this, Inchcape asserted that his opinions on Indian railways had not changed since 1908. He continued to have faith in the capacity of London-based private companies to raise finance and construct railways, although mileage had grown only marginally over those years. This made the prospect of their anticipated 100,000-mile system unrealistic. He insisted on recording that the late Lionel Abrahams had restrained the other members of the committee in their ambitions.[79] In 1919, Mackay's EIR had moved domicile from London to India, but maintained the Board in London. This was window dressing for the nationalist audience since control remained in the metropole, consistent with the Mackay recommendations. Inchcape's confidence in Indians' capacity to run their businesses had not increased over the Great War. The Indian director had 'no experience whatever … he is a child at that sort of thing'.[80]

The other members of Mackay were still alive and were all called as witnesses to Acworth. Mackay's close ally at EIR, Sir David Barbour, concurred with his colleague's pessimism on the suitability of Indians for railway directorships. Barbour argued that only London could provide the quality of directors needed for EIR. It was important that these directors spoke personally for a significant percentage of the company's capital. This argument seemed to preclude a large number of candidates from senior roles at the EIR, both in England and India. Fellow Mackay member Sir Walter Lawrence had taken on direct involvement in railway companies by 1921, with new directorships at Foryth's Madras and Southern Mahratta Railway and Strachey's Assam–Bengal. He had also joined Mackay on the board of P&O (the surviving entity of the old Mackinnon Mackay business). Lawrence was united with his fellow Mackay members in believing that power needed to reside in London where capital was accessed. However, some advisory role for Indians on particular railways might be appropriate. Lawrence felt that giving Indians something to do on railways might distract them from politics.[81]

While respect was paid to the work of the Mackay Committee and his sub-sequent 'informal' railway mission to India, the Acworth Committee took a far more corporatist approach to railway development. Acworth abandoned his own laissez-faire inclinations and recommended the phasing out of guaranteed companies when their contracts expired. In the meantime these companies would be prohibited from raising additional capital themselves.[82] Acworth personally pressed for the existing contracts on expiry to be 'entrusted to the direct management of the State'. Other committee members rejected the public-sector approach and pressed for 'Indian domiciled companies' to takeover EIR, GIPR and over time other railways.[83] Wacha had applauded Acworth as the greatest railway economist of his time due to his strong adherence to private-sector principles. The Great War had shown that management 'even temporarily taken over by the Government in England of many an industrial and business concern proved a failure'.[84] Participating again as a witness, after his exclusion from Mackay, Wacha's proposal to Acworth was far from radical. Indian railway company boards should continue to reside in London with a local advisory board in India to 'inform' the main board 'of the needs and requirements of the public'. Meanwhile funding by the government where required, to supplement the main source of private sector finance, was to be in simple government bonds with a 30–40 year maturity and sinking fund provisions to promote fiscal prudence.[85] Ironically his beliefs were more in line with the ideology of the Mackay report than that of Acworth. However, Wacha had no suggestions on how to curb the excesses of private businessmen and financiers in a landscape of regional monopoly, while Mackay would have seen these profits as a fair reward for endeavour. Acworth and colleagues rejected the arguments for London boards. Proximity to financial markets were outweighed by 'the great disadvantages of absentee control' and the distance from 'social and trade conditions of India'.[86] Perhaps the performance of board members like Douglas Forsyth, Richard Strachey and the Rothschild railway boards had finally dampened enthusiasm for Strachey's 'sham private finance'. By the following year, even Mackay was calling for greater cost controls on state support for Indian railway companies, as he chaired the Indian Retrenchment Committee, charged with curbing large Indian government deficits.[87]

Conclusion

Like John Stuart Mill, who fifty years before had asserted that 'laissez-faire... should be the general practice', James Mackay, Dinshaw Wacha and Lord Acworth would all have condemned excessive state intervention in the Indian railways as a general principle. Mackay and his gentlemanly capitalist friends saw their Indian Chambers of Commerce as promoting free trade and raw capitalism but they pressed, like Bright and Cobden had done, for large government investment in the Indian railways. The Mackay committee gave them a forum to do this with minimal dissent, using the Indian taxpayer as the lender of last resort. The interaction between witnesses on Mackay much more than the rather tame conclusions and recommendations showed the contradictions in laissez-faire. Committee members presented themselves as upholders of ICS objectivity and free market ideology, while extending personal business interests whose success relied on the decisions of committees like their own. Financiers negotiated attractive concessions and long-term contracts for their rail companies, while advising the GOI on the provision of credit to the same companies. Managing agents pressed for 100,000 miles of rail infrastructure with foreign trade oriented freight tariffs, which accelerated India's 'deindustrialization'.

Dinshaw Wacha attacked the motivation and legitimacy of these gentlemanly capitalists, but even more objected to their departure from private-sector discipline. State financing to Wacha and other nationalists implied regressive taxation with Indian ryots paying for British locomotives, steel rail lines and coal through their land taxes. These taxpayers were disenfranchised and denied the level of scrutiny given to shareholders in Britain's private rail companies. Even the Railway Board set up by Thomas Robertson to improve regulation of Indian railway companies seemed to be threatened by the Mackay Committee and Inchcape's subsequent mediation. The worst case 'duality' system which Robertson had criticized, before coming down on the side of private companies, was ultimately rejected by Acworth. He discarded laissez-faire instincts to press for state ownership and management and an overhauling of Mackay's self serving 'duality'.

CONCLUSION

At the Select Committee on Indian Railways in 1884 the disappointing early performance of Bengal NW was highlighted. Edward Charles Baring (first Baron Revolstoke) as senior partner of Baring Brothers, director of the Bank of England, and later chairman of Lloyds held 25,000 shares (over 10 per cent of the issue). Alfred Charles de Rothschild, also a Bank of England director, had an equal investment. Edward Baring's brother, Evelyn, was instrumental in guiding Calcutta and Whitehall towards this new generation of joint stock railway companies without guarantees, but subsequently pressed Viceroy Ripon to offer guarantees and other government support for 'productive' as well as 'protective' lines.[1] Through government concessions, Bengal NW's unguaranteed stock was expected to recover. However, Bengal NW coupled with Baring/Rothschild family short-term investments in the Nizam of Hyderabad's guaranteed railway company prompted Richard Strachey to describe representatives of the banks as 'in a certain sense speculators' as was 'everybody who put his money in such an undertaking'.[2]

Use of the pejorative term 'speculator' to describe the two dominant banking families of late Victorian London caused consternation amongst committee members. In Victorian society, speculation was located somewhere between respectable investment activities and illegitimate.[3] In fact, the risk undertaken by Baring and Rothschild families was removed from conventional ideas of 'speculation'. The Baring family straddled the government and City divide in the context of Indian railways. Meanwhile, Rothschild, more than Baring, avoided all corporate risk, preferring to underwrite and invest in sovereign bond issues. Government-guaranteed and supported Indian railway securities offered legitimate 'investment' business for both firms. Furthermore, such 'investments' combined Cain and Hopkins's twin 'gentlemanly' characteristics-land and government risk.[4] This avoidance of corporate risk, consistent with the 'gentlemanly capitalist' paradigm, was readily achievable in India through the prominent role of government in a 'mixed economy'.

The use of the term 'mixed economy' for late Victorian British India is open to debate. By contemporary standards an economy with only 5 per cent of national income characterized as government expenditure would be viewed as overwhelmingly 'private sector'. However, the combination of railway and army expenditure, which made up half of such expenditure by 1890, placed government in a prominent position in allocating resources. While national income statistics are notoriously inaccurate for the Raj, the national debt of £224 million at 1900/1, compared to a national income of approximately £1,209 million, representing a significant 18.5 percent. This was high by comparison with other countries. Also understated was the role of the state in the dominant agricultural economy, which had been interventionist from Cornwallis's 'permanent settlement'. Strikingly, railway debt made up more than 50 percent of Indian national debt, and with off balance sheet techniques was under-represented.[5]

Furthermore, railway financing and construction sat within Adam Smith and J. S. Mill's malleable 'laissez-faire' doctrine.[6] The three rationales for Indian railway development corresponded with Smith's recommendations for active government involvement: 'defence', 'justice' and 'public works'.[7] Policy-makers maintained the façade of laissez faire but, by the Robertson Committee of 1903 (which supported private ownership/management), only 21 per cent of Indian railway mileage could be described as pure private sector.[8] Different gradations of state/private ownership and management were attempted over 1875–1914 before the Acworth Committee of 1921 finally came down in favour of state financing, ownership and management. This level of GOI and India Office involvement makes Indian railways somewhat unrepresentative as an industry, for the purpose of analysing the potency of Cain and Hopkins service-industry elite. In other forums of Empire finance, the 'gentlemanly capitalists' were able to operate with a more passive group of administrators, who lacked the authority of the India Office to dispense limited guarantees and direct funding. Nevertheless, Cain and Hopkins stressed that their work needed verification by Indian example. Indian railways, as overwhelmingly the largest user of Empire capital and employment, do provide a crucial test for 'gentlemanly capitalism'.[9]

Cain and Hopkins pressed the social homogeneity of the ICS, and its compatibility with the pervading middle-class, public school, gentlemanly capitalists. Certainly, Evelyn Baring as Finance Member in Calcutta pushed joint stock railways as part of a liberal experiment, with its roots in the pre-Mutiny regime of Viceroy Dalhousie. Financing this experiment through his brother illustrated that at a rarefied level there was such social compatibility. However, the different case studies of Indian railways highlight disparate preoccupations amongst British Indian policy makers. These included Russophobia, fear of internal revolt, social concern at peasant starvation, feudal preoccupations, land values, foreign-exchange stabilization, free trade, Ricardian comparative advantage, technophilia, enhanced pension opportunities or simply the pursuit of railway mileage for its own sake. These administrators immersed themselves in the commercial aspects of India's mixed economy in a manner removed from the Victorian foreign office.[10] Even senior representatives like Lord Salisbury, Viceroys Dufferin, Elgin and Curzon, Secretaries of State Cranbrook, Churchill, Cross and Hamilton were involved in detailed contractual negotiations. Equally, Generals Roberts and Rawlinson had strong opinions on the minutiae of Punjabi and North West frontier railway specifications and ownership/ management details.

In British India's mixed economy, military and famine-related rationales for railways provided underpinning for the commercial rationale, which was always present. Roberts and Minto were united in seeing the commercial benefits of military railways, across the North West Frontier into Afghanistan and Persia. Indeed, Roberts's memoirs promised trade and commerce in regions of Central Asia, which even the most recent phase of 'globalization' has left untouched. Salisbury, Temple, Lytton, Hamilton, Hope and Curzon professed horror at the disastrous famines of the late nineteenth century, but ridiculed financial returns on irrigation projects which might have provided a more balanced development and avoided 'exchange entitlement' difficulties. In fact, average returns on irrigation exceeded those on railways by the early twentieth century. Equally, the most direct forms of 'famine relief' absorbed only 2 per cent of famine protection by 1898, illustrating the emphasis placed on 'capital' items which would add to the asset base of British India facilitating benign accounting treatment, while generating British export orders.

ICS/India Office officials, like Sir Theodore Hope, Sir Richard Strachey and Sir Richard Temple, exerted great influence on where and how quickly railways were built. True, they operated within constraints laid down by the Secretary of State in terms of aggregate annual expenditure. Even the Mackay Committee, packed with a combination of active officials and managing agents, could do little to increase rail expenditure when overall budgetary concerns predominated. However, the accounting flexibility lent by 'off balance sheet' guarantees gave officials and their promoter/financier friends room to press particular projects with some hope of success. Excluding the principal amounts borrowed by companies like Southern Mahratta, Assam–Bengal, Bengal Central, Bengal North West, Burma and West of India Portugal Guaranteed Railway from overall borrowing limits made the investment proposition far more attractive to Theodore Hope in Calcutta and Juland Danvers in Whitehall. While financial specialists like Auckland Colvin could resist such investment propositions for a time, the excesses of early railway promotion were repeated in the 1880s and 90s. Guaranteed and subsidized companies were floated with the promise of rapidly paying their guarantees in full. This made them potentially budget neutral from the perspective of the GOI. In fact, large guarantee payments were made until well into the twentieth century and many of these companies displayed volatile earnings which rose in line with famine- and military-related business then fell back. The monopoly profits generated by large regional operators like EIR, GIPR, and

Bombay Baroda, cross-subsidized the 'white elephants' which had been brought to market through aggressive promotion and creative accounting.[11]

The overlap of three rationales made resistance within government to uncertain investment propositions more difficult, silencing more dogged proponents of laissez-faire. The opportunity existed for Hope, Strachey, Forsyth, Dickens, Sir William Bisset, Sir David Barbour and others to supplement their £1,000 per annum ICS pensions with profitable railway directorships or consultancy arrangements. This was a benefit which may not have motivated their role in setting up such enterprises, but must have made them more amenable to future support in the form of subsidies, land gifts and off-market acquisitions. Even Colvin was prepared to join Rothschild's controversial government guaranteed family vehicle, Burma railways, by the mid-1890s. The Victorian mixed economy, like the modern one, had numerous gamekeepers turned poachers. Ex-ICS and India Office officials enjoyed comfortable London directorships, 6,000 miles from their operating assets and managing railways in their domestic currency rather than that of the underlying business. They worked seamlessly with the Cain and Hopkins City and agency breed in Boardrooms and Bank Offices.

The balance of power between officials, City financiers and manufacturers in a mixed economy was more difficult to assess than some of the more static debates on 'gentlemanly capitalism' have suggested.[12] The 'dualism' highlighted in Cain and Hopkins's analysis between 'southern trade and finance' and 'northern industry' was fractured in the context of Indian railways.[13] Even Lloyd George understood that British export potential for locomotives, steel rails and construction contracts in India was growing up to 1914. These exports helped maintain the healthy trade surplus with India, creating the trade balance that S. B. Saul has emphasized. In the context of Goa and Southern Mahratta, for example, the annual reports boasted of large orders of steel rails and Portland cement. However, in the background, trade and commercial interests in liaison with motivated officials drove the concession negotiations. At the Stafford House Committee (SHC), the Duke of Sutherland exemplified aristocratic feudal concerns with land and railways, coupled with a decadent flirtation with steampower and philanthropic concerns for Portuguese African slaves. William Mackinnon sought contiguous sea and rail links between his East African and Indian Ocean businesses, while Robert Morier identified an opportunity to elevate his secondary diplomatic posting. Douglas Forsyth identified a more affluent retirement as Chairman of WIPGR and Southern Mahratta than that available at Westminster. SHC were able to use the manufacturing benefits of their concessions to heighten consensus in their favour. As with Manchester cotton the potent lobbying after 1870 emanated from London free-trade oriented commercial circles.[14]

The 'official mind' with which SHC had to grapple was difficult to characterize. Theodore Hope had confidence in railways as a panacea for famine in the Deccan region, and Morier was convinced that railways might strengthen Britain's hold over Portugal in Goa. Straddling different government departments, these officials operated with limited technical and financial expertise or, in Curzon's words, displayed 'confident incompetence'. Such government officials warrant a more prominent position in the 'gentlemanly capitalist' debate. India's mixed economy, with huge military and railway budgets, developed with the blessing of Benthamite officials like James Stephens.[15] State intervention made officials more vulnerable to manipulation by City technicians, in a business which had become more specialized by the late nineteenth century. The capacity to exploit the India Office productively was greater than other government departments in Britain where government debt was steadily repaid after 1815, state-run industry was minimal, and the all-powerful Treasury protected officials. In the railway industry, for example, Greene's characterization of gentlemanly capitalists hoodwinking officials seems more apposite than Daunton's view that City financiers were required to shield government on difficult decisions.[16] This prompts the opportunity for further research on how India's mixed economy altered the role of the service industry elite.[17]

The Haileybury experience had placed senior ICS and India Office officials in a different public-school cohort to the City executives who flourished as the new aristocracy, but the technocratic functions associated with the Public Works Department ensured greater overlap. Moreover, the profusion of ex-ICS/ India Office officials who had moved into the City through railway companies made these public/private roles socially interchangeable.[18] Theodore Hope and Douglas Forsyth negotiated the Southern Mahratta concessions from different sides but it was difficult to judge which individual had a more socially elevated position. Richard Strachey became a committed 'poacher' but his Bengal status arguably left him with more influence on Indian railway matters than Richard Temple, who had served in all presidencies in senior positions, and chose a retirement in the public sphere as a low-paid MP. Strachey was triumphant over Temple in the 'battle of the gauges' for example. Temple was frustrated in his attempts to block the Goa railway, from his seat in Bombay, while Strachey and James Mackay found their Calcutta power base secure for maintaining the EIR monopoly. Karachi's lesser status meant the complaints of Montagu Webb fell on deaf ears. While Bengal's James Mackay never held formal government office, he participated in a number of committees of the Council of India. He and his Mackay committee representatives had attained City boardroom postings on Indian railway companies shortly afterwards. They managed, invested in and regulated their own industry, making the business/government division problematical. They shared membership of currency, expenditure, trade and railway committees with elite financiers like Nathanial Rothschild, who attained social status comparable to the highest levels of government and aristocracy, and rose to prominence as informal advisors and expert witnesses on these commissions. The esoteric nature of the financial markets placed City representatives, in that context, in an advantaged position vis-á-vis manufacturers. Frequently in the negotiations followed in the case studies, City financiers and railway directors worked successfully to attain levels of gold plating comparable to the discredited early guaranteed companies. As Cain and Hopkins observed, financiers often benefited from the relatively small number of players, wielding great influence through the Bank of England/Treasury axis. In contrast manufacturing in England remained highly fragmented.[19]

Despite the time and resources directed at the Indian railway project from public and private sectors, there was a lack of consistency and accountability which stifled economic development. Government scrutiny through parliamentary commissions and the House of Commons was threadbare. Thinly attended budget debates provided a forum for those already persuaded of the problems, like Sir George Campbell and Henry Fawcett. Even the Indian nationalist critique of Nairoji, Dutt and Wacha was weakened by their attachment to laissez-faire capitalism, symbolized by the rising mill towns of the Bombay Presidency. They struggled to suggest non-sterling alternatives to the balanced budget financings favoured by the India Office and GOI. India's financial system was embryonic and undernourished. Even with effective British/Indian currency union from 1893 onwards (the gold exchange standard), India's banking infrastructure failed to offer alternatives to London's risk-averse investor base. Self professed amateurs on matters of Indian finance, currency and railways like Lord Rothschild were listened to in reverence at currency commissions and Mackay. Their obvious conflicts of interest were never called into question. Meanwhile, energetic data collection by Temple, and finely choreographed analysis by the Strachey famine commission, was accepted as an alternative to poverty relief and famine prevention. The half digestion of strategic thinking on military railways by the Indian army was no more impressive. The continental challenges of the North West Frontier placed military thinkers outside their comfort zone. While steamships to Karachi and Bombay might have facilitated the utilization of W. P. Andrew's military railway network, the coordination between General Roberts and the Royal Navy was never strong. Military railways were pursued, as in famine and commercial matters, in isolation as a self-contained solution. Even after Russia's railway failings in the Russo–Japanese War, the Anglo Russian accord of 1907 and the appearance of the aeroplane, military railways continued to absorb large spending by the Raj, at costs per mile that were a multiple of those achieved by Segei Witte. In Persia, where more cost-effective 'railway détente' was attempted, it was a product of the Shah's wish to keep both Central Asian powers out of his country.

The façade of competition was maintained across 'guaranteed' companies, and the 'agency' structure favoured by Richard Strachey. Louis Mallet pressed the efficiency of these companies and the requirement to avoid any 'communistic' thinking, reflecting the continued importance of classical economic orthodoxy, in theory at least. Meanwhile, the Indian government moved towards an acceptance of regional monopolies and 'combination' to rival the financial power of overseas groupings. This took government further into the mixed economy with Secretary Hamilton and Viceroy Curzon attempting to standardize locomotive design and forge financial partnerships with well-capitalized banking groups. The frustration with Rothschild over poor management in Burma was coupled with N. M. Rothschild's declining status and meagre capital base. Sir Clinton Dawkin's J. S. Morgan was viewed with envy by British officials short of capital, and willing to embrace 'monopoly capitalism' practices, under the pragmatic approach to laissez-faire. While Rothschild proclaimed the advantages of selling Indian railway securities with a promise that the monies would be channelled back to British manufacturers, his bank steered clear of any financing relationship with those manufacturers. The 'agency role' of British investment banks was paralleled in the powerful managing agents from Birds, Gillanders and elsewhere who joined Rothschild on Mackay. Indeed, the reticence to 'play principal' in Indian railway-building was shared by all participants, who preferred to intermediate 'other people's money'. Even manufacturers like Cammel Laird avoided risk on railway locomotive contracts, since they were placed by the India Office on a cost plus basis. Meanwhile, the directors of Indian railway companies performed their own 'agency' function between India and London, taking investment exposure on gold-plated/guaranteed securities.

With so much focus on curtailing GOI budgets, and enhancing the order books of British manufacturers, there was little room for longer-term development ambitions in India. Many scholars have argued that such ambitions lay outside the technical competence of late nineteenth-century officials. The witness statements and correspondence of the time suggest otherwise. Juland Danvers pressed early for greater indigenous manufacturing to support the railway system, and the economic benefits of large railway orders were understood by the different Chambers of Commerce that aggressively pursued the business. Alliances between Bengal and London Chambers of Commerce made the unanimity of purpose between trading and commercial interests in Britain and India manifest. Lord Rothschild's assertion that selling railway bonds and equities in London was easier if the proceeds were to be spent on British manufactures illustrated the cementing of links between City and manufacturers. After all, the complaints of Joseph Chamberlain about Britain's failings in utilizing Empire links for the benefit of British industry had struck a chord with Westminster opinion. Secretary of State Cross's self congratulations on realizing financings for Bengal–Nagpur, Burma and Assam–Bengal Railways are perhaps to be understood in this light. While he was mesmerized by the vision of modern Indian communications, he seemed disinterested in the detail of what these railways would achieve. The guaranteed financings removed any need to persuade an investor audience of the attractiveness of projected returns, while the development potential of more 'white elephants' was limited. Bengal–Nagpur failed to prevent famines or to open up competition with EIR. Burma Railways were constructed in a mania of ruby mine speculation, without consideration for links to the Indian network. Assam–Bengal straddled inhospitable territory which its derisory financial results showed few people wished to cross. The 'cult of agency' which characterized the financing and implementation of the railway project, consistent with Cain and Hopkins's emphasis on the commercial elite, made participants in Indian economic development detached onlookers. They were motivated by the availability of risk-free business, which placed them outside the stigma of Victorian 'speculators'.

No individual scandals on Indian railways occurred which were comparable to the building of the private-sector railways in Britain. However, as Dewey has highlighted, there was a lack of creative entrepreneurial corruption in British India, stifled by Raj officialdom.[20] The consensus on railway development amongst service industry, manufacturing and government officials was strong enough to prompt the construction of many 'white elephants' on the Indian rail network. These diffuse lobbying interests, without consistent market or government price guidance, or the existence of benign entrepreneurial corruption, made the implementation of the Indian railway project flawed. The cumulative effect of poor resource allocation over hundreds of millions of pounds of railway lines implied profound opportunity cost for India. Under the banner of free trade, the railways of British India accelerated de-industrialization, silenced Russophobic sentiment in Parliament and the press, and protected the GOI from accusations of negligence on famine and social policy. Amartya Sen's dismissal of crude economic imperialism as attributing 'to a nation a Hegelian personality that is rather difficult to give any precise content to' remains relevant for analysing late nineteenth-century Indian railways.[21] However, the ideology of malleable laissez-faire in India's mixed economy, supported by large numbers of willing and motivated players on either side of the state/private divide, gave room for something comparable.

APPENDICES

Appendix 1: Revenue and Expense for British India At 1890 (£ millions)

	Revenue		Expenditure
Land Tax	23.4	Army	22.1
Railways	16.7	Railways	18.7
Opium	8.3	Post Office	13.3
Salt Tax	8.0	Roads	5.5
Post Office	2.3	Irrigation	2.6
Irrigation	1.9	Debt	4.4
Sundries	22.3	Sundries	16.2
Total	**82.9**	**Total**	**82.8**

Source: M. Mulhall, *The Dictionary of Statistics* (London: 1892), p. 274.

Appendix 2: Capital Expenditure by Indian Railway Company

Company	Total Capital Investment
Bengal Central	£4.0 mill
Bengal and North Western	£ 5.6 mill
Indian Midland	£6.8 mill
Assam Bengal	£9.0 mill
West of India Portuguese	£3.0 mill
Scinde, Punjab and Delhi (including Indus Valley)	£20 mill
GIPR, Bombay and Baroda, and Madras	£41.5 mill
Eastern Bengal	£3.0 mill
Bengal Nagpur	£11.7 mill
Burma	£9.5 mill
East Indian Railway	£38.8 mill
Southern Mahratta	£6.5 mill
Total Investment	£159.4 mill

Notes: Capital expenditures for Bengal North Western (743 miles), and Burma Railways (1260 miles) are estimated on the basis of the expenditure per mile on Rothschild's Bengal Nagpur (£7,529 per mile on 1,554 miles). Bengal Central is estimated at £4 million, and

West of India at £3 million based on capital raisings. In aggregate GIPR, Bombay and Baroda, and Madras guaranteed companies absorbed an additional £41.5 million. Finally, the amalgamated North Western Railways (including Scinde, Punjab) which became the mainstay of anti Russian defence, involved investment of £33.4 mill. Hence, the strengths and weaknesses of Indian railways which are elucidated in the thesis are representative of a large percentage of the £300 million investment programme.* If government buybacks (at prices up to 160 per cent of par), foreign exchange hedges, land gifts, and other subsidies on these railways are included the total investment programme rises significantly above £300 million, but the percentage covered by these companies would rise.

Appendix 3: Imports of Railway Plant and Rolling Stock into British India, 1884–1913

Year	Value of Imports (£)
1884/85	1,592,620
1885/86	2,018,065
1886/87	1,435,125
1887/88	2,577,603
1888/89	2,493,239
1889/90	1,821,337
1890/91	2,001,853
1891/92	1,484,173
1892/93	1,032,989
1893/94	1,242,997
1894/95	1,556,969
1895/96	1,520,585
1903/04	3,758,000
1904/05	3,744,000
1905/06	4,493,000
1906/07	5,662,000
1907/08	6,592,000
1908/09	7,960,000
1909/10	5,594,000
1910/11	4,124,000
1911/12	4,638,000
1912/13	5,960,000
Total	**52,525,000**

Sources: *Parliamentary Papers*, Statement of Trade of British India, Review of Trade of India, for various years.

* Sources: D. Wacha, *Speeches and Writings of SirDinshaw Edulji Wacha*, Congress Presidential Address (Madras: G. A. Natesan, 1918) p46; J. Danvers, *Indian Railways: Their Past History, Present Condition, and Future Prospects* (London: Effingham Wilson, 1877) p. 34; *Parliamentary Papers, 1882* (181), Financial Statement of GOI, 1882–3, Evelyn Baring, para. 118.

Appendix 4: GOI's Capital Outlay (Not Charged to Revenue) on Railways and Irrigation, 1896–1907

Year	Railways (£ millions)	Irrigation (£ millions)
1896/97	2.730	0.595
1897/98	2.424	0.461
1898/99	2.844	0.436
1899/1900	2.438	0.598
1900/01	1.435	0.590
1901/02	3.524	0.547
1902/03	4.564	0.564
1903/04	4.535	0.508
1904/05	5.894	0.361
1905/06	9.410	0.556
1906/07	7.915	0.798
Total 1896–1907	**47.713**	**6.014**

Source: A. Webb, *The New Dictionary of Statistics* (London: 1911) pp. 266/7.

Appendix 5: Breakdown of Railways in India Between Sectors at 1903

Ownership/Management	Mileage	Percentage of Total Mileage
Pure Private Companies (no overt state support)	5,462	21
State Railways (owned and managed by government)	8,537	33
Hybrid Sale and Leaseback (state owned/private managed)	4,614	18
Government Guaranteed Companies	7,321	28
Total	25,934	100.00%

Source: *Parliamentary Papers, 1903* [Cd.1713], Robertson Railway Committee, Appendix B and C.

Appendix 6: Maps

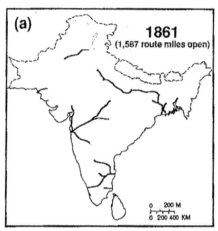

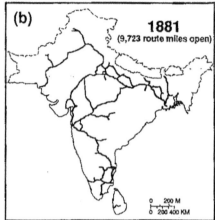

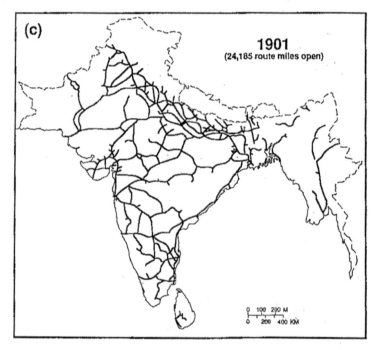

Map 1: Growth of Railways 1861–1901
Source: I. J. Kerr (ed.), *Railways in Modern India* (New Delhi: Oxford University Press, 2001). Reproduced with permission of the author.

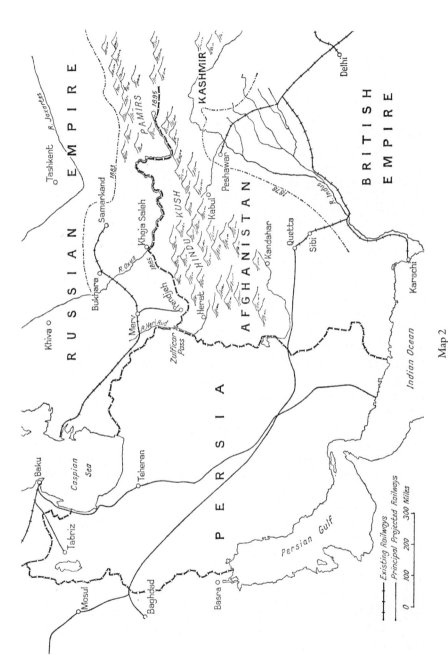

Map 2

SOURCE: C. Lowe, *The Reluctant Imperialists* (London: Routledge, 1967). Reproduced with permission from the publisher.

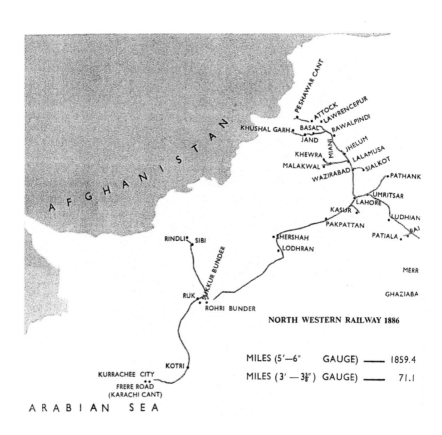

Map 3
Source: M. Malik, *Hundred Years of Pakistan Railways* (Kariachi: Ministry of Railways and Communications, Railway Board, Govt of Pakistan). Reproduced with permission from the publisher.

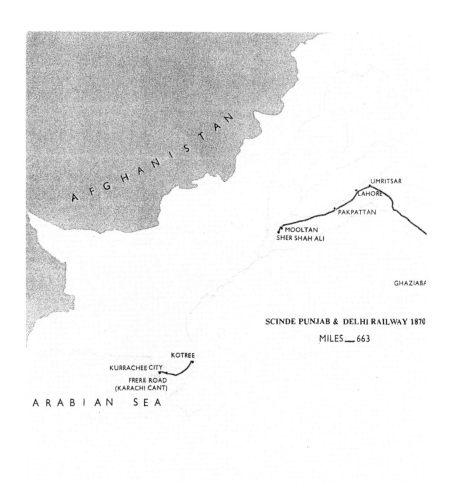

Map 4
Source: M. Malik, *Hundred Years of Pakistan Railways* (Kariachi: Ministry of Railways and Communications, Railway Board, Govt of Pakistan). Reproduced with permission from the publisher.

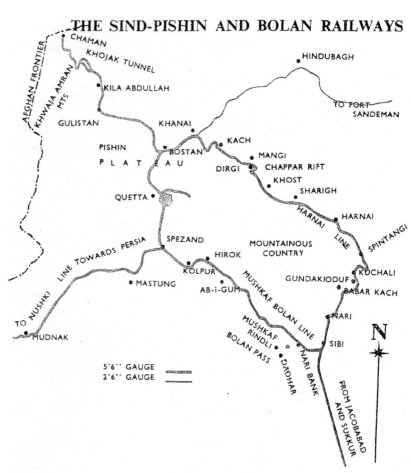

Map 5

Source: M. Malik, *Hundred Years of Pakistan Railways* (Kariachi: Ministry of Railways and Communications, Railway Board, Govt of Pakistan). Reproduced with permission from the publisher.

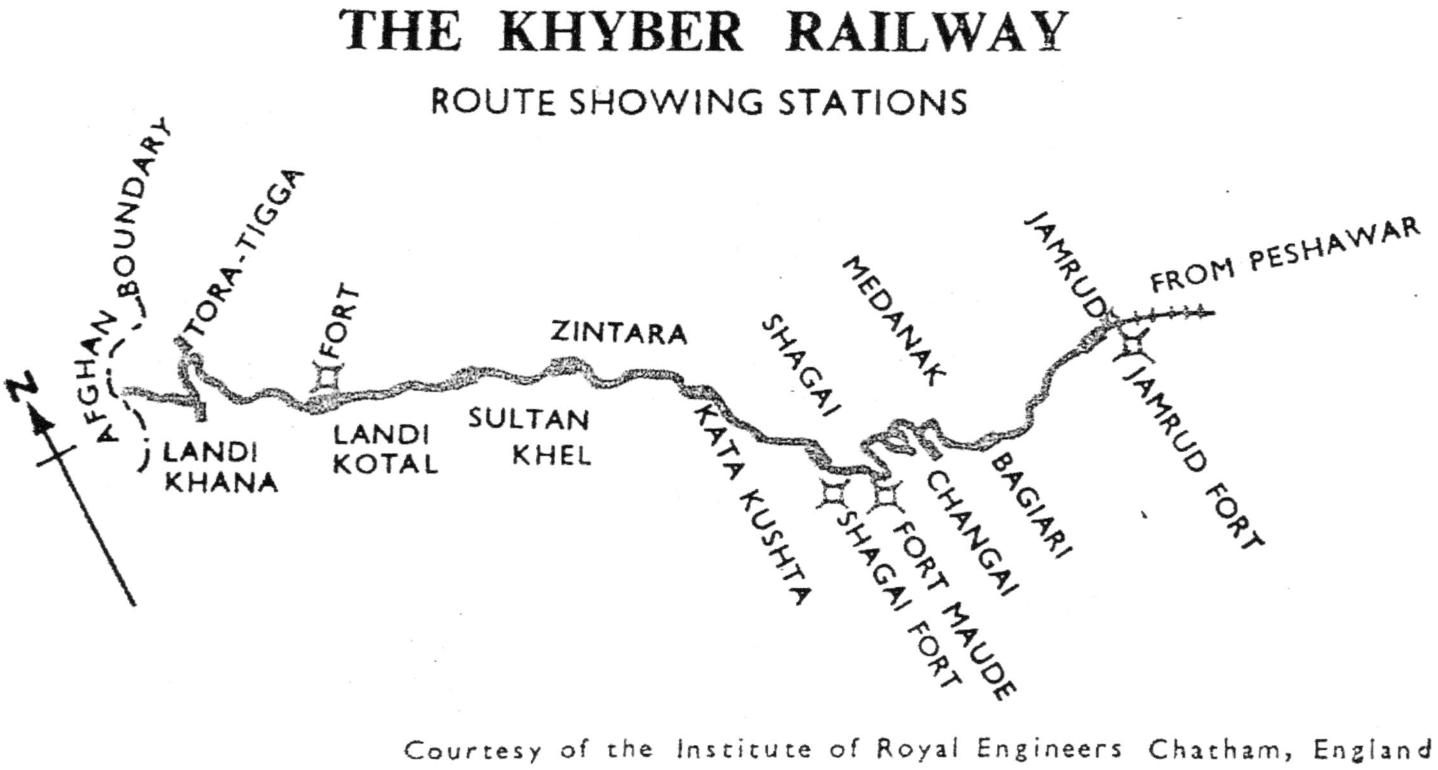

THE KHYBER RAILWAY

ROUTE SHOWING STATIONS

FROM PESHAWAR

JAMRUD — JAMRUD FORT

BAGIARI

MEDANAK

CHANGAI

FORT MAUDE

SHAGAI FORT

SHAGAI

KATA KUSHTA

ZINTARA

SULTAN KHEL

LANDI KOTAL

FORT

TORA-TIGGA

LANDI KHANA

AFGHAN BOUNDARY

N

Courtesy of the Institute of Royal Engineers Chatham, England

Map 6

Source: M. Malik, *Hundred Years of Pakistan Railways* (Kariachi: Ministry of Railways and Communications, Railway Board, Govt of Pakistan). Reproduced with permission from the publisher.

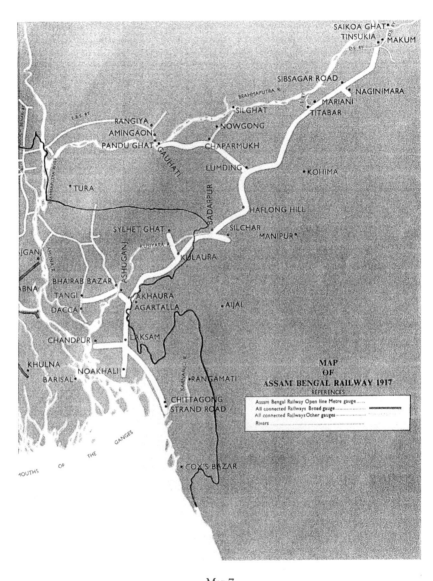

Map 7

Source: M. Malik, *Hundred Years of Pakistan Railways* (Kariachi: Ministry of Railways and Communications, Railway Board, Govt of Pakistan). Reproduced with permission from the publisher.

NOTES

Introduction

1. *Parliamentary Papers 1909* [Cd. 4956], Memorandum on Indian Administration , para. 39; D. Thorner, 'Capital Movement and Transportation: Great Britain and the Development of India's Railways', *Journal of Economic History*, 11:4 (Autumn 1951), p. 391 estimated capital invested of just £80 million up to 1868, implying almost £200 million over 1868–1908.
2. See B. Chandra, *Nationalism and Colonialism in Modern India* (New Delhi: Orient Longman, 2003), pp. 40, 44–5, for a Marxist/Nationalist attack on Morris D. Morris, Michelle McAlpin and the 'imperialist school'. Chandra ridiculed 'new imperialists' for asserting that 'India was growing more prosperous ... as a by-product of pax Britannica (ending 'a long anarchy')...' They shirked the question 'why did the Indian economy not generate economic development when USA, France, Germany, Canada, Italy, Russia, and even Japan did?'; L. Davis and R. Huttenback, *Mammon and the Pursuit of Empire* (Cambridge: Cambridge University Press, 1988), p. 101 saw per capita state public works expenditure (ex-railways) by the Raj as below other developing countries. Indian railways were pursued in relative isolation.
3. J. M. Keynes, *Economic Journal*, September 1911, p. 427; a view disputed in H. Singer, 'The Distribution of Gains between Investing and Borrowing Countries', *American Economic Review*, 40:2 (May 1950), pp. 473–85.
4. A. Maddison, 'A Comparison of Levels of GDP per capita in Developed and Developing Countries, 1700–1980', *Journal of Economic History*, 43:1 (March 1983), p. 28; In contrast, Argentina, which from 1863 raised British capital guaranteed by the independent government at 7 per cent in sterling achieved higher growth over the period. Argentina specialized in more profitable primary products-grain crops and meat, supported by 'unfettered rail promotion, speculation, and unrestricted foreign involvement' see R. Pulley, 'The Railroad and Argentine National Development, 1852–1914', *Americas*, 23:1 (July 1966), pp. 69, 71; W. Macpherson, 'British Investment in Indian Guaranteed Railways 1845–1875' (Cambridge Univ. Ph.D. thesis, 1954), p. 326 saw Indian rail development per capita as low compared to other countries. In rail-miles per square mile it was more comparable to the higher growth railway powers like Russia.
5. S. Pollard, 'Capital Exports, 1870–1914: Harmful or Beneficial?', *Economic History Review*, 38:4 (November 1985), pp. 513/14 ; W. Kennedy, 'Economic Growth and Structural Change in the United Kingdom, 1870–1914', *Journal of Economic History*, 42:1 (March 1982), p. 105 .
6. *Parliamentary Papers 1909* [Cd. 4956], Memorandum, para. 39/40.

7.   This approach is intended to avoid the 'seductive over-simplifications that India is poor because she was always poor, or because she has been robbed', see B. Tomlinson, 'Writing History Sideways: Lessons for Indian Economic Historians from Meiji Japan', *Modern Asian Studies*, 19:3 (1985), p. 698.

8.   Anon., *Railways in India: Their Present State and Prospects Considered with Reference to the Field they Present for English Capital* (London: 1855), p. 5; J. Danvers, *Indian Railways: Their Past History, Present Condition, and Future Prospects* (London: Effingham Wilson, 1877), p. 9.

9.   A. Porter, 'Gentlemanly Capitalism and Empire: The British Experience since 1750', *Journal of Imperial and Commonwealth History*, 18:3 (October 1990), pp. 271/2, questioned the capacity of the service industry elite to dominate manufacturers.

10.   P. Cain and A. Hopkins, *British Imperialism 1688–2000*, 2nd edn (Harlow: Pearson, 2002), p. 646 clarify the term 'gentlemanly capitalism' as representing 'a hitherto neglected theme in the historical transformation of British society ... centred upon the growth of the financial and service sector, an innovation which proved to be compatible with aristocratic power in the eighteenth century, supported a new gentlemanly order in the nineteenth century, and carried both into the twentieth century.'.

11.   R. Dumett (ed.), *Gentlemanly Capitalism and British Imperialism: The New Debate on Empire* (London: Longman 1999), pp. 7 and 10/11.

12.   C. Dewey, 'The End of the Imperialism of Free Trade: The Eclipse of the Lancashire Lobby and the Concession of Fiscal Autonomy to India', in C. Dewey and A. Hopkins (eds.), *The Imperial Impact: Studies in the Economic History of Africa and India* (London: Athlone Press, 1978), p. 56.

13.   S. Broadbridge, 'The Early Capital Market: The Lancashire and Yorkshire Railway', *Economic History Review*, 8:2 (1955) stressed the substantial Lancashire holdings, but over time London investors became more prominent; Davis and Huttenback, *Mammon and the Pursuit of Empire*, p. 51 pressed the high relative share of railway stocks amongst London investors Indian portfolios, the most relevant example of 'finance imperialism' on the subcontinent.

14.   R. Koebner, 'The Concept of Economic Imperialism', *Economic History Review*, 2nd series, 2:1 (1949), p. 10 stresses this implies 'the interests of trade, industry and finance' must be 'in the hands of discernible groups of capitalists' who exploit their influence; S. Swamy, 'The Response to Economic Challenges: A Comparative Economic History of China and India, 1870–1952', *Quarterly Journal of Economics*, 93:1 (February 1979), p. 26 dismissed the relevance of the 'drain' theory for either India or China arguing it relied on unanimity of purpose amongst 'Western imperialists' while the exploiters were 'an amalgam of heterogeneous interests'. The extent to which the British decision-makers on Indian railways were truly 'heterogeneous' deserves consideration.

15.   W. Macpherson, 'British Investment in Indian Guaranteed Railways 1845–1875' (Cambridge University Ph.D. thesis, 1954), pp. 101, 284, 122, 214, 243; F. Lavington, *The English Capital Markets* (London: Metheun, 1921).

16.   Railway construction over Macpherson's period of 1845–75 totalled 6,541 miles, against a staggering 27,000 miles over 1875–1914, see V. Anstey, *The Economic Development of India* (London: Longmans, 1931), p. 133 and I. Kerr, *Building the Railways of the Raj* (Delhi: Oxford University Press, 1995); Map 1 shows the extent to which construction after 1881 dominated; Davis and Huttenback, *Mammon and the Pursuit of Empire*, p. 76 saw little incentive for London investors in Empire railways, where average equity yields

over 1885–1912 were only 40 per cent of 'foreign' and 80 per cent of 'domestic'. In India this comparison is unfair since investors enjoyed GOI risk.

17. M. McAlpin, 'Railroads, Prices, and Peasant Rationality', *Journal of Economic History*, 34:3 (New York, 1974); and J. Hurd, 'Railways and the Expansion of Markets in India 1861–1921', *Exploration in Economic History*, 12 (1975); Hurd's conclusions were challenged by Bagchi who looked more closely at millet and more 'staple food of the poorer people'. The switch to higher priced grain amongst farmers through 'railway development' had left millet prices higher and more volatile for 'the poorer peasants', see A. Bagchi, *The Presidency Banks and the Indian Economy* (Calcutta: Oxford University Press, 1989), pp. 10/11.

18. M. McAlpin, *Subject to Famine: Food Crises and Economic Change in Western India, 1860–1920* (Princeton, NJ: Princeton University Press, 1983), p. 218. See also pp. 194–202 where R. Dutt, *The Economic History of India, Vol. 2* (Delhi: Government of India, 1960) is criticized for asserting that land taxes rose over the late nineteenth century, and for exaggerating the severity of the 1890s famines.

19. *Parliamentary Papers 1909* [Cd. 4956], Memorandum, para. 51 where officials boasted that over 1899–1900 railways carried 2 1/2 million tons of grain over a vast area, but omitted to mention the vast mortality .

20. McAlpin, *Subject to Famine*, p. 205 n. 24 saw Sen's market failure as 'just one special case of all those possible ways that a society can, through its social and economic matrix, distribute the effects of some initial decline in food supplies or rise in the prices of food across the population'. This seems Malthusian, and contrasts with the accepted role of government intervention through railways.

21. I. Klein, 'Population and Agriculture in Northern India, 1872–1921', *Modern Asian Studies*, 8:2 (1974), pp. 193, 202, 203.

22. *Parliamentary Papers 1909* [Cd. 4956], Memorandum, para. 51; more recent work on early 'globalization' in India also points to the benefits of rising prices for an overwhelmingly agricultural economy. For example K. O'Rourke and J. Williamson, *Globalization and History* (Cambridge, MA: MIT, 1999), p. 74 identified strong rental rises in Punjab over 1873–1906, as export targeted wheat production increased revenues, in line with Heckscher-Ohlin predictions of international specialization (increased reliance and prices of plentiful factors of production). Wages suffered relatively with the wage-rental ratio falling 68 per cent, confirming Indian nationalist complaints about persistent poverty and non-affordability of food.

23. S. Ambirajan, 'Malthusian Population Theory and Indian Famine Policy in the Nineteenth Century', *Population Studies*, 30:1 (March 1976), p. 9 highlighted JS Mill's emphasis on personal responsibility in family planning, and emigration, as an influence on Indian policymakers.

24. Macpherson, 'Investment in Indian Railways', pp. 186, 179.

25. North Western Railways absorbed £33.4 million of capital investment, see critique by D. Wacha, *Speeches and Writings of Sir Dinshaw Edulji Wacha*, Congress Presidential Address (Madras: G.A. Natesan, 1918), p. 46.

26. S. Ambirajan, *Classical Political Economy and British Policy in India* (Cambridge: Cambridge University Press, 1978), p. 230; Appendix 1 shows railways as the second largest revenue and expense item in the GOI's budget by 1890 .

27. Fortunately plentiful archival sources exist for these companies at Guildhall Library, India Office Library, and National Archives BT31 series. Companies aggregating more

than 50 per cent of the asset base of the Indian rail programme are scrutinized, see Appendix 2.

28. S. Saul, *Studies in British Overseas Trade* (Liverpool: Liverpool University Press, 1960); though K. Chaudhuri, 'India's International Economy in the Nineteenth Century', *Modern Asian Studies*, 2:1 (1968), p. 32 argued that by India's late nineteenth-century foreign trade was 'perhaps only a very small percentage of her total national income'.

29. D. Platt, *Finance, Trade, and Politics in British Foreign Policy 1815–1914* (Oxford: Oxford University Press, 1968) shows avoidance of guarantees elsewhere by Gladstone and Disraeli. India was unique. Argentinean railways, for example, had sterling guarantees from a non-dependent government.

30. P. Cain, 'Railway Combination and Government, 1900–1914', *Economic History Review*, 25:4 (November 1972), p. 625 argued that British railway companies operated in an 'oligopolistic or duopolistic' market characterized by damaging price competition up to 1870, and cartelistic behaviour thereafter.

31. Covert support for private companies was not unique to India, L. Jenks, 'Capital Movement and Transportation: Britain and American Railway Development', *Journal of Economic History*, 11:4 (Autumn 1951), p. 383 highlighted Argentina's 'government aid variously in the way of land grants, profit guarantees, stock subscriptions, and tax exemptions'; For the laissez-faire debate on India see J. Bartlet Brebner, 'Laissez Faire and State Intervention in Nineteenth-Century Britain', *Journal of Economic History*, 8 (New York, 1959), pp. 59–60 who characterized Bentham and J. S. Mill as 'formulators 'of state intervention for collectivist ends' rather than 'laissez faire'. E. Stokes, *The English Utilitarians and India* (Oxford: Clarendon, 1959), p. 145 focused on distinctions between traditional liberalism, and the more authoritarian and centralizing James Mill, J. S. Mill in Indian affairs; R. Collison Black, 'Economic Policy in Ireland and India in the Time of JS Mill', *Economic History Review*, 21:2 (August 1968), p. 336 argues that despite Mill's employment at the East India Company from 1823 he failed to guide policy makers in India/Ireland from 'vacillation and uncertainty' on matters 'of public versus private enterprise for railways'; S. Bhattacharya, *Financial Foundations of the British Raj* (Simla: Indian Institute of Advanced Studies, 1971), pp. 3/4 highlighted Haileybury College and Thomas Malthus, first professor of political economy, imbuing Finance Members in Calcutta with classical economics.

32. R. Tucker (ed.), *The Marx-Engels Reader* (New York: Norton, 1972), p. 586.

33. Ambirajan, *Classical Political Economy*, p. 228 and p. 266; and p. 265 where he observed that Smith's Wealth of Nations could be used to justify 'absolute non-interference, relative non-interference and even some sort of collectivism'.

34. D. Thorner, 'The Pattern of Railway Development in India', in I. Kerr (ed.), *Railways in Modern India* (New Delhi: Oxford University Press, 2001), pp. 94–5.

35. Ibid., p. 87; D. Rothermund, *An Economic History of India* (London: Routledge, 1993), p. 36 points to a rebate structure which at least until 1885 'encouraged linkages with the world market and worked against regional integration within India'; A. Bagchi, *The Evolution of International Business 1800–1945, Volume 5* (Cambridge: Cambridge University Press, 1972), p. 40 concluded that 'not very much progress was made in the direction of purchase of Indian materials for the railways until the [first world] war'.

36. T. Roy, *The Economic History of India*, 2nd edn (New Delhi: Oxford University Press, 2006), pp. 291, 86; and 323 where Indian national debt to GDP was estimated at a significant 26.5 per cent by 1900 driven by military expenditure and rupee depreciation bloating sterling debt. While Roy is unsympathetic with the nationalist complaints

about the colonial handicap of nineteenth-century India, he highlights India's poor performance against resource limited Japan after 1870, see p. 5; Tomlinson, 'Writing History Sideways', p. 690 suggested growth rates by the 1870s in Japan of 1.14 percent compared favourably to 0.4–.06 per cent in India.

37.   H. Ferns, 'Britain's Informal Empire in Argentina, 1806–1914', *Past and Present*, 4 (November 1953), p. 73 points out that after the Argentinean default of 1890, by which time British investment was £174 million (much of it in railways), the 'informally' constrained Argentina was able to inflate its way out of difficulties through lax monetary policy and 'abolish the evil system of guaranteed railway profits'; stretching the definition of 'informal' Empire see also Jenks, 'Capital Movement and Transportation', p. 375 estimated British investment in private US railways at $3 billion by 1914, supplying 15 per cent of capital for a network stretching 223,000 miles by 1906.

38.   See Chapter 1 for undermining of Danvers's ambitions; C. Dewey, 'The Government of India's 'New Industrial Policy' 1900–1925', in K. Chaudhuri and C. Dewey (ed.), *Economy and Society: Essays in Indian Economic and Social History* (Delhi: Oxford University Press, 1979), pp. 224–6, 246.

39.   Ibid., p. 252.

1 'Productive' Indian Railways, 1875–1914

1.   J. Seeley, *The Expansion of England: Two Courses of Lectures* (London, 1886), p. 263.

2.   J. Hobson, *Imperialism: A Study* (Ann Arbor, MI: University of Michigan Press, 1965), pp. 55, 57–8; the 'three conditions of a profitable [banking] business' as 'to create new public debts, to float new companies, and to cause constant considerable fluctuations of values...'.

3.   I. Kerr, (ed.)., *Railways in Modern India* (Oxford: Oxford University Press, 2001), p. 32 .

4.   IOR, V/4/Session 1853, volume 28: Fifth Report for the Select Committee on India Territories, 14 July 1853, p. 66.

5.   IOR, Mss Eur E234 18A (Chapman Papers), p. 12; Thorner, *Investment in Empire*, p. 55; emphasized the importance of precedent as a doctrine overriding laissez-faire inclinations at the Company; Ambirajan, *Classical Political Economy*, p. 19 commented that 'the administrative mind ... has an understandable preference for past experience in the form of precedents and conventions'.

6.   IOR, Mss Eur E234/106 (Chapman Papers), Private Note 'On the Question, Government versus Companies for the Construction and Management of Railways January 1849'.

7.   IOR, L/AG/46/42/14, Contract between the East India Company and the East India Railway Company 17 August 1845, p. 19.

8.   Kerr, *Building the Railways of the Raj*, p. 19.

9.   IOR, V/4/Session 1853, volume 28, p. 67

10.   IOR, L/PWD/3/69, Lawrence Minute, 9 January 1869, paras 3,15, 29–35.

11.   Ibid., para. 12, where 5 per cent GOI stock quoted at 116 versus 109 for EIR stock, implying a further cost of 7 per cent for the experiment in guaranteed railway companies; even rupee 5 per cent stock was priced at 106, allowing GOI funding in rupees without foreign exchange risk for only 3 per cent upfront.

12.   Ibid., para. 20–5.

13.   Ibid., para. 17–18.

14.   Kerr, *Building the Railways of the Raj*, p. 212.

15. Thorner, 'The Pattern of Railway Development in India', p. 86; and S. Checkland, 'The Mind of the City 1870–1914', *Oxford Economic Papers*, New Series, 9:3 (October 1957).

16. Ambirajan, *Classical Political Economy*, p. 264 pointed out that the minute had been drafted by Richard Strachey.

17. IOR, 8th Duke of Argyll papers, Neg Reel 4245, Rawlinson memo, 26 February 1869.

18. Ibid., E. Macnaghtan to Argyll, 15 December 1871; Halliday to Argyll, 19 January 1872.

19. Ibid., memo by Sir F. Currie, 22 February 1869.

20. See Chapter 5 on Southern Mahratta; IOR, L/PWD/2/96, EIR Report of Audit Committee, 1879.

21. Ibid., Sir C. Mills memo, 9 January 1869.

22. Ibid., Argyll note; French guaranteed private rail companies met criticism for locating boards as distant as Paris .

23. IOR, Mss Eur F90/28 (John Lawrence Papers), fo.16/17, Cranborne to Lawrence, 18 January 1867.

24. Anon, *Indian Railways: An Argument for a Government Monopoly in preference to Private Enterprise* (Calcutta: W. Newman, 1884).

25. BL, Ripon Papers, Ms 43,575, p. 497 Ripon to Baring, 21 May 1881, and p. 498 Baring Memo, 31 May 1881.

26. *Parliamentary Papers 1881* [205], Financial Statement of Government of India, 1881–82, para. 82–8, see para. 87 where Baring argued that as a result of the new guaranteed companies 'the value of land is enhanced, new markets are opened, an impetus is given to the export trade, and the greater power of transport and concentration affords a hope that military expenditure may be reduced'; and *Parliamentary Papers 1884–85* [151], Financial Statement of Government of India, 1885–86, para. 74–5.

27. IOR, V/4/Session 1888/volume 2 p. 526.

28. *Economist*, 30 July 1889; consols were yielding 3 per cent against a burdensome four percent for Indian Debentures, although India rivalled USA as a country 'which possesses so singularly all the requirements for great prosperity and rapid advance'.

29. IOR, V/4/Session 1896/Volume 15, paras 7715, 7717 .

30. IOR, V/4/Session 1900/Volume 29, para. 18,403.

31. N. Sanyal, *Development of Indian Railways* (Calcutta: University of Calcutta, 1930), p. 136.

32. IOR, V/26/720/7 Minutes of Acworth Commission, para. 5664.

33. Platt, *Finance, Trade, and Politics*, pp. 13–29. Imperial guarantees for foreign loans, and even loans 'tied' explicitly to British supply contracts were resisted by government. Indian guarantees were less controversial, creating no formal liability for the British Treasury, and being priced as a different credit to consols.

34. For government supported railway companies, sponsored by Nathaniel Rothschild see Chapter 4; IOR, Mss Eur F84/132c (Elgin Papers), fo.3–6, JW memo to Elgin, 16 February 1895.

35. Ibid., fo.3/4.

36. *The Times*, Horace Bell letter to editor, 6 January 1899, p. 8.

37. A. Kaminsky, *The India Office 1880–1910* (Westport: Mansell, 1986) examined Curzon's dominance over Hamilton.

38. A. Silver, *Manchester Men and Indian Cotton* (Manchester: Manchester University Press, 1966), pp. 266–8, and *Hansard*, CXCVIII, 1870, 23 July and 3,5 August.

39. IOR, L/PWD/2/176, Miscellaneous Railways 1877–9, John Fleming to Cranbrook, August 1878; even Bright and Cobden demonstrated ideological pragmatism in this context; see Chapter 5.

40. A. Taylor, *The Struggle for Mastery in Europe 1848–1918* (Oxford: Oxford University Press, 1954), p. 255 argued German and French tariff levels were barely higher than British. Russia and USA represented 'the only true protectionist countries'.

41. *Parliamentary Papers*, 1886, [c4715, c4715–1], Royal Commission to inquire into Depression of Trade and Industry Second Report, Minutes of Evidence, Appendix, John D.Ellis Testimony, Chairman John Brown & Co, and South Yorkshire Coal Association, paras 3213, 3217, 3254–8; Hobson, *Imperialism*, p. 49, linked Sheffield, Manchester, Birmingham manufacturers and the imperial railway projects of the Empire; Joseph Chamberlain, alarmed by the depression, pressed a £500 million twenty-ear loan programme to China for railway construction, see J. Garvin, *The Life of Joseph Chamberlain* (London: Macmillan, 1933), pp. 448–9; the term 'great depression' has been seen as problematical by some writers. W. Baumgart, *Imperialism: the Idea and Reality of British and French Colonial Expansion, 1880–1914* (Oxford: Oxford University Press, 1982). See Baumgart, *Imperialism*, p. 143 for increased real wages offsetting price deflation.

42. Ibid., Sir Lowthian Bell, paras 3540–1, 3758.

43. Ibid., J. Mawdsley, Amalgamated Association of Operative Cotton Spinners, paras 5103–4.

44. Ibid., G. Lord, Committee of directors of Manchester Chamber of Commerce, para. 5287–9, 5297–9, 5303, 5353; see Chapter 4.

45. Ibid., Appendix 1, Sheffield Chamber of Commerce and Manufacturers, p. 407, para. 13.

46. IOR, Mss Eur Neg 4352 (Dufferin Papers), Letter 10, Kimberley to Dufferin, 17 March 1886.

47. IOR, V/4/Session 1861/volume 43, p. 7.

48. IOR, V/4/Session 1860/volume 52, p. 42.

49. IOR, V/4/Session 1882/volume 49, p. 41.

50. IOR, V/4/Session 1906/volume 82, p. 13.

51. IOR, V/4/Session 1875/volume 54, p. 782; and *Andrew Yule and Company, 1863–1963* (Calcutta, 1963).

52. B. Kling, 'The Origin of the Managing Agency System in India', in R. Ray (ed.), *Entrepreneurship and Industry in India 1800–1947* (Delhi: Oxford University Press, 1992), p. 90; and IOR, V/4/Session 1902/volume 71, p. 483 Dubs and Co of Glasgow's bid on locomotives was 20% more expensive and twenty-five weeks slower than a German competitor; F. Lehmann, 'Great Britain and the Supply of Railway Locomotives of India: A Case Study of Economic Imperialism', *Indian Economic and Social History Review*, 2:4 (October 1965).

53. IOR, L/PWD/2/176, Miscellaneous Railways 1877–79, letters 9 September 1874, 14 September 1874, 4 June 1877.

54. Ibid., letters from E. Talbot, 29 January 1878, 16 may 1878, A. Rendel 22 July 1879, and AP Dunstan 24 October 1879; Cambridge University Library, Mayo Papers, Ms 7940/142/27 where Mayo declared 'I suspect all [British] iron makers are little above rogues'.

55. *Parliamentary Papers 1890* [c5965], Statement of Trade of British India, 1884–9, p. 29; and *Parliamentary Papers 1908* [cd 4390], Review of trade of India for 1907–08, pp. 19

and 78; *Parliamentary Papers 1907* [cd 3524], Papers laid before the Colonial Conference, p. 453–5 on tariff levels.

56. PRO, T171/20, Information provided for the Mansion House Speech, 1912, p. 3; in line with the theory of Saul, *Studies in British Overseas Trade*.

57. See Chapter 7 for Mackay lobbying; Appendix 3 shows the importance of plant and rolling stock imports over 1884–1913.

58. IOR, L/PWD/5/27, Contract, 19 December 1918; even by 1923, without overt compulsion 95 percent of Indian railway contracts were being placed in Britain, see Platt, *Finance, Trade, and Politics*, p. 29; Davis and Huttenback, *Mammon and the Pursuit of Empire*, pp. 225/6 pointed to the 'anomaly' of India, especially railways, where free trade was superseded by Whitehall's 'support [for] British commercial enterprises'.

59. Cambridge University Library, Randolph Churchill Papers, Ms 9248/9 fo. 1041.

60. IOR, Hamilton Papers, Mss Eur F123/51, April–June 1901, and Mss Eur F123/83 fo.79; see also F.Lehman, 'Great Britain and the Supply of railway locomotives of India: A case study of 'Economic Imperialism'', *IESHR*, October 1965, 2:4; Saul, *Studies in British Overseas Trade*, p. 200.

61. W. Birkmyre, *The Revival of Trade by the Development of India: Being an Address Delivered to the Members of the City of Glasgow Chamber of Commerce* (Glasgow: 1886), pp. 3–5, 16, 20.

62. Ibid., pp. 9–14, 19; A. Connell, 'Indian Railways and Indian Wheat', *Journal of the Statistical Society of London*, 48:2 (June 1885), p. 237 emphasized Birkmyre's role in lobbying to the East India railway Committee of 1884 'to cover India with a network of railways'; and pp. 238/9 summarized the combined pressures from chambers thus: 'Liverpool has been inspired with the hope of fresh freights, Middlesborough of a keen demand for rails, and London of investments for cheap capital; while Manchester ... has looked forward to' a time when 'every Hindoo and Mahomedan will swathe his body in twenty yards of Lancashire cotton.'.

63. A. Webster, 'Business and Empire: A Reassessment of the British Conquest in 1885', *Historical Journal*, 43:4 (December, 2000), pp. 1022, 1024 described the chamber as a mouthpiece for 'collective views' of the City, and 'gentlemanly capitalists'; IOR, Mss Eur F102/5 (Kilbracken Papers), 13 September 1899, fo. 15, H. Fowler to Godley, complaining of chambers lobby powers.

64. Guildhall Library, Ms 16, 532, London Chamber of Commerce: East India 1886–1926 and China 1886–1912 Trade Section Minute Book, pp. 9 and 44.

65. Ibid., pp. 25, 38, 67; Karachi itself was viewed as the key military port for any British troop reinforcements for the North West frontier, who would be transported by rail to the Afghan border; for Burma Railways controversy, see Chapter 4.

66. Ibid., p. 108.

67. Ibid., meetings, 12 March 1907.

68. Ibid., Deputation to Secretary of State for India from London Chamber of Commerce, 2 June 1913.

69. Ibid., H. M. Haywood, Secretary of Bengal Chamber of Commerce to Secretary to GOI, Calcutta, 7 February 1913.

70. M. Misra, 'Gentlemanly Capitalism and the Raj: British Policy between the World Wars', in R. Dumett (ed.), *Gentlemanly Capitalism and British Imperialism: The New Debate on Empire* (London: Longman, 1999), pp. 159–60 and note 9; Anstey, *The Economic Development of India*, pp. 502–4; Rothermund, *An Economic History of India*, p. 64 .

71. See Introduction, p. 3.

72. Ibid., letter to Chambers of Commerce, 1 January 1885.

73. Later director of Assam–Bengal Railway Company, and partner in their underwriter, Messrs Sheppards, Pellys, Scott & co, see IOR, L/F/8/13/974B, 21 March 1892.

74. Bodleian Library, Oxford, Kimberley Papers, Ms Eng c4285, fo 72–80, report of committee, Christmas 1884.

75. Cambridge University Library, Randolph Churchill Papers, Ms 9248/7 fo.850; RM Stephenson letter to *Times*, 3 April 1885.

76. R. Sulivan, *One Hundred Years of Bombay: History of the Bombay Chamber of Commerce 1836–1936* (Bombay: Times of India, 1938), pp. 226–38; Connell, 'Indian Railways and Indian Wheat', p. 237 saw the Chambers of Calcutta, Madras and Bombay competing for more railways, supported by the 'Anglo–Indian Press'.

77. G. Tyson, *Bengal Chamber of Commerce and Industry 1853–1953: A Centenary Survey* (Calcutta: Bengal Chamber of Commerce, 1953), pp. 47, 48, 73–80.

78. *Parliamentary Papers 1884* [284], Report from the Select Committee on East Indian Railway Communication, p. xxiv, para. 20–1.

79. IOR, Mss Eur F124/2146 (a); Report of Bengal Chamber of Commerce for 1908 Volume 1; pp. 60–62.

80. Trustee Act, 1893, Chapter 53, Part 1, Investments, p. 1.

81. However, the Indian securities often had put and call arrangements which effectively guaranteed principal while maintaining off balance sheet status.

82. PRO, T1/11391, memorandum from R. M. Kindersley, 23 February 1912, note from Lewis Harcourt, 25 July 1917; R. Dumett, 'Joseph Chamberlain, Imperial Finance and Railway Policy in British West Africa in the Late Nineteenth Century', *English Historical Review*, 90:355 (April 1975), p. 320 Colonial Stocks Act of 1900 gave 'colonial inscribed stock' in British West African railway companies trustee status. Guarantees were resisted due to uncertain commercial prospects; Davis and Huttenback, *Mammon and the Pursuit of Empire*, p. 145 compared India's spread to British Local Authority bonds of less than 1 per cent with those of developed countries (two percent) and underdeveloped countries (4 per cent), showing the advantages of the guarantees/trustee stock status.

83. Lavington, *The English Capital Markets*, p. 157 argued 'there is little scope for abuse in the marketing of highly reputable [Indian railway] stocks'. However, when government guarantees, put and call options, annuity related buybacks, and preference were considered Indian railway securities were bewildering even for professional investors. .

84. M. de Cello, 'Indian Monetary Vicissitudes: An Interlude', in G. Ballachandran (ed.), *India and the World Economy* (Delhi: Oxford University Press, 2003), pp. 228–231.

85. IOR, V/4/Session 1900/Volume 29 para. 17,572.

86. Ibid., para. 17573 .

87. Ibid., para. 20,207; see Chapter 8 on Wacha.

88. IOR, V/4/Session 1860/volume 52, p. 24.

89. Sanyal, *Development of Indian Railways*, p. 167.

90. Thorner, 'The Pattern of Railway Development in India', p. 93.

91. In contrast to Birkmyre's earlier assertions about currency strength through Indian railways.

92. *Parliamentary Papers 1888* [c 5512/c 5512–1], pp. 5, 62.

93. Ibid., Minutes of evidence, paras 9775–9808.

94. *Parliamentary Papers, 1893/94* [cmd 7060], Report of the Committee appointed to inquire into the Indian Currency, paras 28–32.

95. E. Green, 'Rentiers versus Producers? The Political Economy of the Bimetallic Controversy', *English Historical Review*, 53 (1988), p. 602.
96. *Parliamentary Papers 1898*, Indian Currency Committee, para. 247, 7614.
97. For Mackay committee see Chapter 8; *Parliamentary Papers 1914* [cd 7236], Final Report of the Royal Commission on Indian Finance and Currency, para. 35–6.
98. Ibid., paras. 14, 134, 305, 524, 526, 1337, 7113.
99. J. M. Keynes, 'The Economic Transition in India', *Economic Journal*, 21:83 (September 1911), p. 428.
100. I. Habib, 'Colonialization of the Indian Economy, 1757–1900', *Social Scientist*, 3:8 (March 1975), p. 39, the short staple problems of Indian cotton were recognized early in the nineteenth century, which makes the Bombay boom and bust engendered by the British more indefensible.
101. Kling, 'The Origin of the Managing Agency System in India', pp. 85, 88.
102. *Parliamentary Papers 1907* [cd 3524], Papers laid before the Colonial Conference, p. 455.
103. See Chapter 2.
104. T. Metcalf, *Ideologies of the Raj* (Cambridge: Cambridge University Press, 1995), p. 42.
105. D. Headrick, *The Tentacles of Progress: Technology Transfer in the Age of Imperialism, 1850–1914* (New York: Oxford University Press, 1988), p. 76, stated that Indian railways avoided the 'gross corruption' and 'financial scandals' of the British and American railway booms, but suffered from 'petty corruption'. This rather misses the point that agreed government policy in India was to run the railways for the benefit of a foreign power; for further British fatality on Indian economic development see PRO FO/233/78, p. 13, where the pressure group 'Friends of India' provided a memorial in support of Macdonald Stephenson's assertion that Chinese railways could achieve more than Indian through China's 'enterprising' and 'active' population, contrasted with the 'laborious' and 'thrifty' Indians.

2 Indian Railways and Famines, 1875–1914

1. IOR, Mss Eur F123/81 (Hamilton Papers) fo.126, 28 December 1899.
2. IOR, Mss Eur F111/266b (Curzon papers) fo. 307, Appendix 8, 25 April 1901.
3. Ibid., fo.183, 13 March 1901.
4. B. Chandra, *The Rise and Growth of Economic Nationalism in India* (New Delhi: People's Publishing House, 1966), ch. 5.
5. R. Dutt, 'The Currency Question', p. 99, and 'The Land Tax, Railways, and Irrigation', p. 31, in R. Dutt,(ed.)., *Open Letters to Lord Curzon* (Delhi: Gian, 1986).
6. R. Dutt, 'Famines in India', in *Open Letters to Lord Curzon*, p. 22.
7. M. Darling, 'Prosperity and Debt', in S. Bose (ed.), *Credit Markets, and the Agrarian Economy of Colonial India* (Oxford: Oxford University Press, 1994), p. 38 highlights that agricultural workers often had more food to buy than sell.
8. D. Naoroji, *Poverty and Un-British Rule in India* (New Delhi: Government of India, 1996), p. 160.
9. I. Derbyshire, 'Economic Change and Railways in North India', in I. Kerr (ed.), *Railways in Modern India* (New Delhi: Oxford University Press, 2001), p. 190.
10. J. Nehru, *The Discovery of India* (Oxford: Oxford University Press, 1985), pp. 495–499; I. Derbyshire, 'Opening up the Interior: The Impact of Railways on the North India Economy and Society, 1860–1914' (Cambridge University PhD. thesis, 1985), p. 219

argued that the 1943 famine proved the importance of railways, since Japanese blocking of rail routes caused famine.

11. IOR, Mss Eur F123/81 (Hamilton Papers) fo.126, 28/12/99; A. Loveday, *The History and Economics of Indian Famines* (London: G.Bell, 1914), p. 51.

12. R. Temple, *India in 1880* (London: Murray, 1880), p. 333.

13. IOR, Mss Eur E218/136 (Lytton Papers), p. 8: John Strachey speech.

14. Ibid., p. 33; W. Digby, *Prosperous British India: A Revelation for Official Records* (London: T. Fisher Unwin, 1901), pp. 111–112.

15. Loveday, *The History and Economics of Indian Famines*, p. 56 quoting John Strachey.

16. Temple, *India in 1880*, p. 332.

17. Ibid., p. 333.

18. *Hansard*, 4th series, 1897, 44:503, col 886.

19. Temple, *India in 1880*, pp. 335 and 337.

20. Ibid., pp. 333, 335/336; see for example *Parliamentary Papers 1899* [c9255] Report of Indian Famine Commission, 1898 Minutes of Evidence, Appendix Volume IV, Central Provinces and Berar, Bishop CF Pelvat testimony.

21. Ibid., p. 341.

22. *The Times*, 25 August 1877.

23. Ibid., 27 August 1877, p. 4.

24. Ibid., 25 and 27 August 1877.

25. Ibid., 25 August 1877.

26. IOR, Mss Eur F86/120 (Temple Papers), p. A2; Official Letters on Bengal Famine 1873/74; Anon., *The Political Economy of India Famines* (Bombay: 1877), p. 22.

27. Derbyshire, 'Opening up the Interior', p. 205.

28. Temple, *India in 1880*, p. 342.

29. *Parliamentary Papers 1880* [c2591], Indian Famine Commission Report, Part I, p. 50 para. 154.

30. IOR, Mss Eur F111/160 (Curzon Papers),p 241, letter 54, Curzon to Godley 7/8/01 dismissed Strachey's criticisms of GOI 'inertness' on railway policy from his corporate position. Strachey had been 'a sort of uncrowned King in the India Office' who had 'ridden roughshod over the Government of India for years…'.

31. *Parliamentary Papers 1880* [c2735] Indian Famine Commission Report Part II (measures of protection and preservation), p. 94, paras 3/4.

32. Ibid., pp. 171/2.

33. A. Cotton, *To The Edinburgh Literary Institute a Reply to Lord Napier's Address on the Indian Famine* (Edinburgh: Oliver and Boyd, 1878), p. 22.

34. *Parliamentary Papers 1880* [c2735] Indian Famine Commission Report Part II (measures of protection and preservation), p. 173/174 paras 22/3.

35. Ibid., p. 174 para. 26; Chapter 5 shows Bisset as Chairman of Southern Mahratta, benefiting from an amalgamated regional famine monopoly

36. *Parliamentary Papers 1880*, Report of the Indian famine Commission; Part I; Famine Relief, p. 200.

37. IOR, Mss Eur F86/176 (Temple Papers), Minutes of Madras Famine, 24 January 1877.

38. *Parliamentary Papers 1881* [c3036], Railway Organization by Captain Bisset, p. 200.

39. Ibid., p. 201.

40. IOR, Mss Eur D705/8 (Hope Papers), fo. 76, Hope to Miller 24 July 1886.

41. Cambridge University Library, Ms 9248/7 (Randolph Churchill Papers), fo.798, Hope to Churchill 15/8/85; for Bengal Nagpur see Chapter 5.

42. IOR, Mss Eur F86/114a (Temple Papers), p. A2, Argyll to Governor General 20/11/73.
43. H. Bartle Frere, *On the Impending Bengal Famine* (London: John Murray, 1874), p. 23;
    See Chapter 5 for Frere's (ex-Governor of Bombay) work on the Goa/Southern Mah-
    ratta concession.
44. IOR, Mss Eur F86/208a (Temple Papers), p. 30.
45. Ibid., p. 33.
46. *Parliamentary Papers 1881* [c3036], Indian Famine Commission Report Part III,
    Appendices, p. 45 q147, General Strachey Testimony.
47. Ibid., p. 45 q148.
48. IOR, F86/182 (Temple Papers), p. 23, Minute by Temple on Madras Famine, 14 April
    1877.
49. *Parliamentary Papers 1881* [c3036], Indian Famine Commission Report, Part III,
    Appendices p. 119.
50. Ibid., p. 449, Mr Buck Testimony.
51. Ibid., p. 213; Chandra, *The Rise and Growth of Economic Nationalism*, p. 209 .
52. Ibid., commission p. 212; S. Sharma, *History of the Great Indian Peninsula Railway
    (1876–1900), part II* (Bombay: 1990), p. 147 quoted from the *Economist* of July 1884
    which reserved special criticism for the GIPR's boasts that by maintaining low freights
    it had maximized wheat exports during famines; Sulivan, *One Hundred Years of Bombay*,
    pp. 228, 236 described the Bombay Chamber's lobbying of the GOI, Government of
    Bombay, India Office and London rail boards against the GIPR rail structure which was
    three times higher than the rival EIR. EIR's performance was flattered since it had flat
    terrain, cheap coal, and dependable traffic; In contrast, McAlpin saw little tendency for
    railways to shift production towards exports; see also IOR, Mss Eur F111/266b (Curzon
    Papers) fo.228, where GOI statistical officer argued that 'hardly more than one per cent
    of the food grain produced in India is exported....'.
53. *Parliamentary Papers 1880*, Report of Indian Famine Commssion, p. 1.
54. *Parliamentary Papers 1881* [c3036], Indian Famine Commission Report, Part III,
    Appendices, p. 214.
55. Ibid., pp. 475–485.
56. Ibid., p. 367.
57. *Parliamentary Papers 1893–94* [327], Despatch from Secretary of State, July 1889, p.
    58, Table 1.
58. J. Dacosta, *Fads and Fallacies regarding Irrigation as a Prevention of Famine in India*
    (London: W.H. Allen, 1878), pp. 8–10; H. Fawcett, *Indian Finance: Three Essays* (Lon-
    don: Macmillan, 1880), p. 54 expressed scepticism on 'speculative' railway projects .
59. *Parliamentary Papers 1883* [135], Financial Statement of Government of India, 1883–
    84, paras 174–90.
60. Connell, 'Indian Railways and Indian Wheat', p. 255; and p. 258 where the sensitivity
    of Indian rail company's profits to wheat prices is analysed. Strachey's EIR and Andrew/
    Forsyth's Sind, Punjab, Delhi suffered the largest profit falls over 1884/85 through fall-
    ing prices. In inflationary famine conditions they would have benefited.
61. *Hansard*, 4th series, 1897, 45:503, col 1530, 8/2/97.
62. Ibid., col. 1533, Earl of Onslow, Under secretary of State for India.
63. Ibid., 4:505, col 1124, 22 March 1897.
64. IOR, Mss Eur C125/1 (Hamilton Papers) fo. 439, Hamilton to Elgin, 4 December
    1896.
65. Chandra, *The Rise and Growth of Economic Nationalism*, p. 208.

66. P. Bandyopadhyay, *Indian Famine and Agrarian Problems* (Calcutta: Star Publications, 1987), p. 49.

67. *Parliamentary Papers 1899* [c9178], Report of Indian Famine Commission 1898, p. 357 para. 586.

68. Ibid., p. 328 para. 536.

69. *Parliamentary Papers 1899* [c9255], Report of Indian Famine Commission, 1898 Minutes of Evidence, Appendix Volume IV, Central Provinces and Berar, p. 102.

70. Ibid., p. 261, testimony of Rao Bahadar Rajaran Sitaram Dizit.

71. Ibid., p. 244 para. 283 and 283A, testimony of LS Carey.

72. Ibid., p. 106, testimony of Khan Bahadur Maulari Saiyyid Muhammad Husain, 11 March 1898.

73. E. Stokes, 'Peasants, Moneylenders and Colonial Rule: An Excursion into Central India', in S. Bose (ed.), *Credit Markets, and the Agrarian Economy of Colonial India* (Oxford: Oxford University Press, 1994), p. 73.

74. *Parliamentary Papers 1899* [c 9252], Report of Indian Famine Commission, 1898 Minutes of Evidence, Volume I, Bengal, p. 18, Testimony of Keural Chand.

75. *Parliamentary papers 1902* [c 876], Report of the Indian famine Commission 1901, p. 149, para. 17.

76. *Parliamentary Papers 1899* [c 9255] Report of Indian Famine Commission, 1898 Minutes of Evidence, Appendix Volume IV, Central Provinces and Berar, p. 10, testimony of Bishop CF Pelvert.

77. Ibid., p. 9 para. 1.

78. *Hansard*, 4th series, 1897, 45:503, col 897; the Madras famine of 1891–2, had seen philanthropists dump grain on the market to collapse prices, punishing speculators .

79. *Parliamentary Papers 1899* [c 9256] Report of Indian Famine Commission, 1898 Minutes of Evidence, Appendix Volume V, NW Provinces and Oudh, p. 273 paras 340–3 testimony of Lala Gomesh Prasad; *Parliamentary Papers 1899* [c 9255] Report of Indian Famine Commission, 1898 Minutes of Evidence, Appendix Volume IV, Central Provinces and Berar, p. 8 , testimony of Rev. J Lampard .

80. *Parliamentary Papers 1899* [c 9252], Report of Indian Famine Commission 1898 Minutes of Evidence Volume I, Bengal, p. 196, testimony of Babu Grish Chander Ghosal.

81. *Parliamentary Papers 1899* [c9256] Report of Indian Famine Commission, 1898 Minutes of Evidence, Appendix Volume V, NW Provinces/Oudh p. 168, para. 4 to 7, testimony of Revd JR Hill .

82. Ibid., p. 136, testimony of Raja Rampratap Sinha 26/3/98; and p. 151, testimony of Lala Baldco Navayan Singh .

83. Loveday, *The History and Economics of Indian Famines*, p. 65.

84. Ibid., p. 68/9.

85. *Parliamentary Papers 1899* [c9178], Report of Indian Famine Commission 1898, p. 327, para. 535.

86. IOR, Mss Eur F86/262 (Temple Papers), p. 1.

87. Bandyopadhyay, *Indian Famine and Agrarian Problems*, p. 16.

88. Ibid., p. 23 on charitable offers from USA, Russia and Germany etc; *Hansard*, 4th series, 45503, col. 1531 where Lord Kinnaird complained the government action in 'discouraging private charity had made it difficult to collect funds...'; L. Fraser, *India Under Curzon and After* (London: Heinemann, 1911), p. 287, Kaiser William's telegraph to Curzon in May 1900 betrayed Aryan sentimentality, saying his gift to India illustrated that 'blood is thicker than water'.

89. Ibid., p. 309.
90. Ibid., pp. 280/281.
91. Ibid., p. 284.
92. Bandyopadhyay, *Indian Famine and Agrarian Problems*, pp. 53/4.
93. IOR, Mss Eur F111/159 and 160 (Curzon Papers) on his thoughts over 1900–1.
94. *Parliamentary Papers 1902* [c 876], Report of the Indian Famine Commission 1901, p. 112, para. 349.
95. IOR, Mss Eur F111/709 (Curzon Papers), Report of the Indian Famine Commission 1901, p. 76, 8 May 1901.
96. *Parliamentary Papers 1902* [c876], Report of the Indian Famine Commission 1901, p. 76.
97. Ibid., p. 149 para. 19.
98. Loveday, *The History and Economics of Indian Famines*, pp. 71/2.
99. Ibid., p. 70.
100. *Parliamentary Papers 1902* [c876], Report of the Indian Famine Commission 1901 p. 112, para. 351.
101. Digby, *Prosperous British India*, pp. 143, 140.
102. *Parliamentary Papers 1899* [c9178], Report of Indian Famine Commission 1898, para. 585; IOR, Mss Eur F111/266b (Curzon Papers), fo. 213.
103. Ibid., fo. 216.
104. *Parliamentary Papers 1899* [c9178], Report of Indian Famine Commission 1898, p. 106.
105. Ibid., p. 248, Burma revenues converted at 1Rs=1sh 4d; see Chapter 5.
106. IOR, Mss Eur F111/266b (Curzon Papers) fo.221, and fo.225, there was prejudice against Burmese rice and grain.
107. Bandyopadhyay, *Indian Famine and Agrarian Problems*, pp. 31, 32, 34, Rally Bros are highlighted in this context.
108. IOR, Mss Eur F111/266b (Curzon Papers), fo. 213.
109. Hansard, 4th series, 1897, 47:505, cols 1347 and 1349.
110. Ibid., col 1349.
111. Hansard, 4th series, 1900, 81:539, col 1120.
112. Ibid., 4th series, 1897, 47:505, col 1398.
113. Ibid., 4th series, 1900, 81:539, cols 1086–1089; for continuing bias over 1896–1907 towards railways over irrigation see Appendix 4.
114. T. Roy, *The Economic History of India 1857–1947* (Oxford: Oxford University Press, 2000), p. 294; Digby, *Prosperous British India*, p. 134, even as railways were built, famine deaths increased from 1 million in the first quarter to 26 million in the final quarter of nineteenth century.
115. Kaminsky, *The India Office 1880–1910*.
116. Chandra, *The Rise and Growth of Economic Nationalism*, p. 192.
117. *Parliamentary Papers 1899* [c9254], Report of Indian Famine Commission, 1898 Minutes of Evidence, Appendix volume III, p. 243, testimony of Mr A Cumine.

3 Military Railways in India, 1875–1914

1. Macpherson, 'Investment in Indian Railways', pp. 186, 179.

2.   PRO, CAB 6/1/33, Defence of India: Memorandum, 28 November 1903, concluded that distances and climate made a French invasion unlikely, but with a simultaneous Russian incursion on the NW Frontier the French might attempt something.

3.   *Parliamentary Papers 1896* [c8258], Royal Commission on Administration of Expenditure of India. First Report Volume 1. Minutes of Evidence, para. 9618 on NW railways losses; para. 9681 and Appendix 26.

4.   PRO, CAB 18/24/17, para. 4; P. Berridge, *Couplings to the Khyber: The Story of the North Western Railway* (Newton Abbot: David and Charles, 1969), p. 54.

5.   IOR Mss Eur F132/44 (Sir Alfred Comyn Lyall Papers) fo. 123; the annexation of Upper Burma had been inevitable, according to Roberts, since Dalhousie's conquest of Lower Burma in 1852, implying that all contiguous states were 'fair game'; University of Cambridge, Randolph Churchill Papers, Ms 9248/9, fo. 990, Dufferin to Churchill, 19 October 1885, Viceroy Dufferin agreed, arguing Upper Burma could never act as a 'buffer state' for French Indo-China in the manner of Afghanistan, since Burma was 'soft and pulpy'.

6.   D. Dilks, *Curzon in India, Vol. 1* (London: Rupert Hart-Davis, 1969), pp. 171–2, Tsar Nicholas II's failure to capitalize on Britain's difficulties in the Boer War was due to Russia's uncompleted strategic railways into Turkestan; Curzon's downfall was partly explained by the construction of the Orenburg-Tashkent line.

7.   *Railways in India*, p. 5; W. P. Andrew (1807–87) variously described in C. Buckland, *Dictionary of Indian Biography* (London: Swan Sonnenschein, 1906) as 'an apostle of railways ... the railway statesman ... the pioneer of railway enterprise'; I. Kerr, *Engines of Change: The Railroads that made India* (Westport: Praeger, 2007), pp. 30–4 on minor scandals surrounding this company.

8.   W. Andrew, *The Indus and its Provinces* (Lahore: East and West Publishing Co, 1976), pp. 39/41, 220/221; see IOR V/4/Session 1857/8, Report of Select Committee on Railway and Canal Legislation, 12 July 1858, p. 228 para. 3276, Andrew mentioned Scinde railway's commercial attributes, while its military profile was of 'infinite importance'.

9.   Ibid., p. 14.

10.   *The Railway Times* (London), 10 October 1857.

11.   Andrew, *The Indus and its Provinces*; and W. Andrew, *The Punjaub Railway* (London, 1857), p. 8.

12.   Tucker (ed.), *The Marx-Engels Reader*, p. 585.

13.   *Parliamentary Papers 1884–85* (264): Report of 1879 Special Commission ... Organisation and Expenditure of the Army in India, para. 412.

14.   Ibid., p. 6,54,76.

15.   IOR, Duke of Argyll Papers, Reel 4245, Hon. A. Kinnard to Gladstone, October 1873, and W. P. Andrew, memorandum on the evils of the break of gauge in India, 14 October 1873; for famine aspect see Chapter 2.

16.   T. Otte and K. Neilson (eds.), *Railways and International Politics: Paths of Empire, 1848–1945* (London: Routledge, 2006), p. 13.

17.   PRO, CAB 37/25/43; 1889.

18.   A. Preston, 'Sir Charles Macgregor and the Defence of India, 1857–1887', *Historical Journal*, 12:1 (1969), p. 62, fear of Russian/Afghan 'sparks being thrown into the combustible material of northern India' was 'the core of British apprehensions ... until 1875'...

19.   M. Malik, *Hundred Years of Pakistan Railways* (Karachi: Ministry of Railways, 1962), p. 9.

20.   Wacha, *Speeches and Writings*, pp. 46–7, for NW Railway costing.

21. Malik, *Hundred Years of Pakistan Railways*, p. 40.
22. B. de Villeroi, *A History of the North Western Railway* (Lahore: 1896), pp. 7/8.
23. Ibid., pp. 9/10.
24. Ibid., p. 81.
25. J. Foreman-Peck, 'Natural Monopoly and Railway Policy in the Nineteenth Century', *Oxford Economic Papers*, 39:4 (December 1987), p. 714, average construction costs of Indian system at £8,800 per mile (versus £18,800 for 'Russia in Europe') hid important details.
26. Ibid., pp. 15,16,37,87.
27. A. Bucholz, *Moltke and the German Wars, 1864–1871* (Basingstoke: Palgrave, 2001), p. 72; M. Howard, *The Franco–Prussian War* (London: Collins, 1967), p. 2 .
28. Ibid., Moltke p. 163.
29. M. van Creveld, *Supplying War: Logistics from Wallenstein to Patton* (Cambridge: Cambridge University Press, 2004), pp. 101, 106, by 1836 the Bavarian minister of war pressed 'commercial' over pure military railways. Commercial lines would cover areas of dense population and hence strategic importance.
30. F. List, *Schriften, Reden, Briefe* (Berlin: 1931–5).
31. PRO, CAB 38/2/35 p. 6 Balfour worried that Russian rolling stock might be adapted to British Indian lines becoming 'a potent military instrument in the hands of our enemies'.
32. Prussian military influence on the defence of India in the 1860s and 70s, notably on Sir William Mansfield (Commander in Chief, Indian Army), Sir Henry Durand (Military Member) and Evelyn Baring (Military Secretary) is examined in Preston, 'Sir Charles Macgregor and the Defence of India', p. 65/6; PRO, WO 33/24, fo.276 .
33. Ibid., fo.19.
34. PRO, WO 13/22, fos.3, 19.
35. PRO, CAB 38/2/22; Otte and Neilson (eds)., *Railways and International Politics*, p. 10.
36. British India differed from European defence since buffer states of Afghanistan, Persia and Burma separated the Great Powers; W. Trousdale (ed.)., *War in Afghanistan, 1979–80: The Personal Diary of Major General Sir Charles Metcalfe Macgregor* (Detroit, MI: Wayne State University Press, 1985), p. 111, critiqued Roberts.
37. Otte and Neilson (eds.), *Railways and International Politics*, p. 13 on Roberts's failings on South African railway wars; F. Roberts, *Forty-One Years in India: From Subaltern to Commander-in-Chief* (London, 1898).
38. National Army Museum, Roberts Papers 7101/23 162/16 p. 15; and 7101/23 162/15 p. 10.
39. Roberts, *Forty-One Years in India*, pp. 497, 509 n2.
40. J. Gooch, *The Plans of War* (London: Routledge and Kegan Paul, 1974), p. 202, CID correspondence on Indian defence in the early twentieth century showed 'the British military had no clear concepts' of railway's military applications.
41. van Creveld, *Supplying War*, p. 82.
42. PRO, CAB 6/1/25, p. 110.
43. PRO, CAB 38/2/16; Pendjeh in 1885 prompted Gladstone's abandonment of Russophilia, creating Russophobe consensus in British politics, see A. Thornton, 'British Policy in Persia, 1858–1890 I', *English Historical Review*, 69:273 (October, 1954), p. 578; C. Lowe, *The Reluctant Imperialists* (London: Routledge, 1967), p. 93; Taylor, *The Struggle for Mastery in Europe*, pp. 299/300
44. G. Curzon, *Russia in Central Asia in 1889 and the Anglo-Russian Question* (London: Longman, 1889) dedication.

45. Ibid., pp. 12, 321, where Curzon declared Russia's 'object is not Calcutta but Constantinople ... the keys of the Bosphorus are more likely to be won on the banks of the Helmund than on the heights of Plavna'; PRO, CAB 37/25/43, para. 19.
46. Curzon, *Russia in Central Asia*, pp. 47/8.
47. Ibid., pp. 52, 267; an influential 'forwardist' strategist saw Herat as a Russian springboard for Indian offensives see C. Macgregor, *Narrative of a Journey through the Province of Khorasan and on the North-West Frontier of Afghanistan in 1875* (London: 1879) Volume II, Appendix VI, pp. 241–67.
48. Curzon, *Russia in Central Asia*, pp. 280–90.
49. Ibid., p. 275.
50. Ibid., pp. 377, 379.
51. *The Times*, 26 July 1886.
52. PRO, FO 248/451.
53. Curzon, *The Times*, 8 August 1891, p. 6.
54. PRO, CAB 37/27/33 Salisbury to Drummond Wolf, 19 May 1890. Russia railways relied on French capital .
55. PRO, WO 106/178, 'The Trans-Caspian Railway and the Power of Russia to occupy Herat', by Captain AC Yale, 29 April 1891.
56. Taylor, *The Struggle for Mastery in Europe 1848–1918*, p. 398.
57. *The Times*, 11 December 1903, p. 5; and 14 October 1904, p. 3; PRO, CAB 37/25/43, 19 August 1889, para. 20, where India Office/War Office pressed Anglo-Chinese alliance to 'compel Russia to retain troops in Turkestan...'
58. PRO, CAB 6/1/50, 5 May 1904, 'Defence of India ... war game played at Simla, 1903'.
59. Gooch, *The Plans of War*, pp. 202–3; PRO, CAB 6/1/6D, 10 March 1903, pp. 5/6.
60. Gooch, *The Plans of War*, p. 205; PRO, CAB 6/1/28, Memorandum from Balfour to Curzon/Kitchener, 3 July 1903.
61. Gooch, *The Plans of War*, pp. 211/12; and PRO, CAB 6/1/45D, 18 April 1904, p. 19.
62. Gooch, *The Plans of War*, p. 216.
63. IOR L/P&S/10/54, Railways: Central Asia: Orenburg-Tashkent Railway, Siberia-Tashkent; fo. 17, 15 June 1906.
64. Macpherson, 'Investment in Indian Railways'; and S. Gopal, *The Viceroyalty of Lord Ripon 1880–1884* (London, 1953), p. 184.
65. Cambridge University Library Ms 9248/7 (Randolph Churchill Papers), fo. 778, para. 12, Hope to Churchill 15/8/85, at 1 Rs=2s; Chapter 7 on Hope's career.
66. IOR, Mss Eur D705/7 (Hope Papers), fos. 1, 7, 317
67. IOR, Mss Eur F86/291(Temple Papers).
68. University of Cambridge, Randolph Churchill Papers, 9248/7, fo. 798, Hope to Churchill, 15 August 1885, government expenditure on protective/commercial railways was reduced, while military railway budgets rose to 47 per cent of railway spending; fo. 815 Dufferin to Churchill, 21 August 1885, railway revenues estimated at £500,000 by 1888, the largest revenue item for the GOI; IOR V/4/Session 1900/Volume 29 p. 709, para. 64 minority report to Welby Commission complained of additional military expenditure over 1885/86–1895/96 at Rs 47.6 million, with military railways second largest item at Rs 11 million; *Parliamentary Papers 1886* [172], Financial Statement of Government of India, 1886–87, p. 11, some £12 million of additional military lines were given precedence over £28.3 million for famine and commercial lines.

69. *Hansard*, 3rd series, 356, 4 August 1891 col. 1280; *Parliamentary Papers, 1893–94* [327], Despatch to GOI, July 1889, p. 58; I. Klein, 'English Free Traders and Indian Tariffs, 1874–96', *Modern Asian Studies*, 5:3 (1971), p. 266.

70. C. Marvin, *The Russian Railways to Herat and India* (London: 1883), pp. 16, 18, 27; and *The Railway Race to Herat: An Account of the Russian Railways to Herat and India* (London: W.H. Allen,1885), pp. 14 , 30.

71. PRO, CAB 37/25/43, 19 August 1889, paras 23, 31; Brackenbury professionalized Intelligence Division of War Office, following practices pursued by Berlin in Franco–Prussian War,; Waters, W., *Experiences of a Military Attache* (London: John Murray, 1926), p. 17.

72. Ibid., PRO, paras 23, 37/38, 33, 41, 46/47.

73. PRO, CAB 37/30/39 pp. 12/13; constraints on troop numbers were a perennial issue, with the British avoiding conscription until the First World War, see IOR Mss Eur D721/8 (Durand Papers), 15 June 1887, fo. 231/2, Durand, Indian foreign secretary, argued railways would allow as few as 60,000 Indian Army troops to hold Afghanistan, but in the final year of the Crimean War Britain recruited only 15,000 troops.

74. Malik, *Hundred Years of Pakistan Railways*, p. 40 highlighted seven key passes for Indian railway defences: Khyber, Kurram, Gomal, Zhob, Bolan, Harnai and Baluchistan.

75. Ibid., pp. 41–7; commented (p. 45) that 'each time the work stopped on the Sind–Pishin railway, the Bolan project moved forward'.

76. *Hansard*, 4th series, 1890–1, 356, 4 August 1891; and IOR, Mss Eur F86/291(Temple Papers); Temple's credentials for advising on strategic railways were questioned by military observer Sir James Browne, see J. McLeod Innes, *The Life and Times of General Sir James Browne* (London: John Murray, 1905), p. 232.

77. Gopal, *The Viceroyalty of Lord Ripon 1880–1884*, p. 184, expenditure on the Quetta railway in 1884 was £1,000 per day, crowding out famine railways.

78. *The Times*, 28 August 1880, p. 10; and Dilks, *Curzon in India* on Sandeman, British representative at Quetta; de Villeroi, *A History of the North Western Railway*, p. 45 blamed John Bright and his 'peace at any price party' for abandoning Kandahar Railway .

79. Cambridge University Library, Ms 9248/7 (R Churchill Papers) fo.798 para. 9.

80. Gooch, *The Plans of War*, p. 200; PRO CAB 6/1, Military defence of India, 24 December 1901, p. 19; Trousdale (ed.), *War in Afghanistan*, pp. 60, 62.

81. National Army Museum, Roberts Papers, 7101–23–95, p. 28.

82. B. Robson (ed)., *Roberts in India: The Military Papers of Field Marshall Lord Roberts 1876–1893* (Stroud: Alan Sutton, 1993), pp. xviii, 296, 323, 328, 344–346.

83. Thornton, 'British Policy in Persia', p. 578 n. 2; and PRO, FO 65/1415, Number 178.

84. *The Times*, 6 October 1885, p. 13.

85. Temple, *India in 1880*, p. 278; Hansard, 3rd series, 1890–1, Volume 356, 4 August 1891.

86. *Hansard*, 3rd series, 1890–1, 356 4 August 1891 col. 1294; National Army Museum, Roberts Papers, 7101/23–95 pp. 22/23; Roberts, *Forty-One Years in India*, p. 421 Roberts, entering Kabul in 1879 found 'Kabul much more Russian than English ... Russian money was found in the treasury, Russian wares were sold in the bazaars.'; *The Times*, 4 September 1880, p. 9, doubted Kandahar would become an 'emporium of commerce', ridiculing images of 'wild hillmen turning their spears into pruning-hooks, becoming peaceful traders, and going about in flowing garments of Manchester make ...'

87. Ibid., *Hansard* col. 1302.

88. Ibid., *Hansard*, cols 1279–85.

89. Ibid., *Hansard* col 1320; Kaminsky, *The India Office 1880–1910*; further Quetta rail extensions were too expensive, see National Army Museum, Roberts Papers, 7101/23, p. 19.
90. PRO, CAB 6/1/45, para. 27, 15 February 1904.
91. National Army Museum, Roberts Papers, 7101–23–106, Roberts to Hamilton, 12 September 1897, pp. 3/4.
92. Gooch, *The Plans of War*, p. 226.
93. PRO, CAB 18/24/17, paras 4, 6, 7, 9, 11, 16, 21; Sir Henry Rawlinson warned that Russian assaults on Herat and India would come from Merv, avoiding the Hindu Kush,; Lowe, *The Reluctant Imperialists*, p. 76. K. Meyer and S. Brysac, *Tournament of Shadows* (London: Little, Brown, 1999), p. 155; see Map 5 for Chaman link.
94. PRO, CAB 18/24/17, para. 21 .
95. Kaminsky, *The India Office 1880–1910*.
96. Otte andNeilson (eds), *Railways and International Politics*, p. 15 aeroplanes meant 'August 1914 was the last time that railways played a major part in the mobilization for war …'
97. *The Times*, 26 February 19 24, p. 13; In 1901 R. Kipling, *Kim* (Oxford: Oxford University Press, 1987), p. 26 described Lahore railway station as 'fort-like' whose 'gigantic stone hall' seemed to be 'paved … with the sheeted dead'.
98. Otte and Neilson (eds), *Railways and International Politics*, p. 138; PRO, FO 60/476 fo. 328; H. Rawlinson, *England and Russia in the East: A Series of Papers on the Political and Geographical Condition of Central Asia* (London: Murray, 1875), p. 129.
99. Ibid., fo. 484, Foreign Office to Salisbury, 14 August 1885.
100. PRO, WO 106/178, p. 10.
101. PRO, CAB 37/27/33, 23 May 1890.
102. PRO, FO 65/1395/133, 29 October 1890.
103. Thornton, 'British Policy in Persia', 70:274 (January 1955), p. 63; Otte and Neilson (eds), *Railways and International Politics*, p. 138.
104. Ibid., p. 60 n. 3, Drummond Wolff to Salisbury.
105. Ibid., p. 65.
106. Ibid., p. 69 n. 3.
107. FO 251/58, Persia minute 9 January 1893; R. Greaves, *Persia and the Defence of India 1884–1892* (London: Athlone, 1959), p. 212; IOR, Mss Eur E243/20 (Cross Papers) fo.201, 5 November 1891, even railway enthusiast Cross objected to Salisbury's efforts to fund Seistan costs from Calcutta .
108. Ibid., pp. 70, 67 'an anteroom to India whose keys we must keep'.
109. *The Times*, 14 January 1903, Persian/Afghan Seistan, spanning both sides of the Helmund, had worried Britain since the mid-nineteenth century.
110. Gooch, *The Plans of War*, p. 206, Curzon and Kitchener supported colonization and irrigation of the Seistan region to support troops; PRO CAB 6/1/30D, p. 6.
111. PRO, CAB 38/2/35 p. 8; Balfour rejected Curzon/Kitchener's assertion that the British could control irrigation of a Seistan region that would grow from 80,000 to 2 million people. Otte and Neilson (eds), *Railways and International Politics*, p. 144, starving 2 million people to death by cutting off the Helmund River water supply was impractical.
112. PRO,CAB 38/2/35, p. 6, 20 May 1903.
113. PRO, CAB 6/1/20, p. 95, 4 June 1903.
114. PRO, CAB 6/1/49, paras 1 and 6, 2 May 1904.
115. Ibid., pp. 6, 8.

116. PRO, CAB 37/114/13; 5 February 1913.

117. *The Times*, 24 April 1903, p. 14; Taylor, *The Struggle for Mastery in Europe 1848–1918*, pp. 410/411, 384/385; R. Kumar, The Records of the Government of India on the Berlin–Baghdad Railway Question, *The Historical Journal*, 5:1 (1962), pp. 76, 79; Chapter 4 on Rothschild.

118. PRO, CAB 6/1/50, para. 2, 5 May 1904.

119. IOR L/P&S/10/54, fo. 113, 18 February 1904, Russian defeat by Japan could prompt them to turn South to Afghanistan to 'retrieve some of her lost prestige'; National Army Museum, Roberts Papers, 7101/23 161/13, 17 November 1905, Roberts stressed the maintenance of British prestige with native Indians, avoiding reliance on the Japanese after their victory; Taylor, *The Struggle for Mastery in Europe 1848–1918*, p. 443, argued Russia and Japan resolved many differences by July 1907; P. Towle, 'The Russo–Japanese War and the Defence of India', *Military Affairs*, 44:3 (October 1980), pp. 111, 114, Russian military railways successfully maintained large troop numbers in Manchuria, a more difficult feat than Russian troops to India.

120. Gooch, *The Plans of War*; PRO CAB 6/3/99D, Transport of Reinforcements from the United Kingdom to India, 17 July 1907.

4 Indian Railroading

1. Macpherson, 'Investment in Indian Railways'; and Jenks, *The Migration of British Capital*; Sanyal, *Development of Indian Railways*, pp. 140–3.

2. Ibid., Macpherson, 'Investment in Indian Railways', p. 182.

3. Ibid., fo.18, 28 September 1886.

4. *Hansard*, Volume 340, 1889, cols 649/50: Indian Budget Debate, 27 August 1889.

5. IOR, L/Parl/2/439, para. 1115 Rothschild told the Mackay Committee in 1908 he 'had the honour of being consulted by various Secretaries of State as to the best means of raising capital for Indian railways'.

6. N. Ferguson, *The House of Rothschild* (New York: Penguin, 1998), p. 367.

7. Bodleian Library, Ms Eng c4283 (Kimberley Papers), fos. 34/5.

8. Ibid., Ms Eng c4299, item 12; IOR, L/F/8/12/898, Bengal Central contract, 26 July 1881; *Parliamentary Papers 1896* [c 8258], Royal Commission on Administration of Expenditure of India, First Report, Volume I, Minutes (Welby); para. 12,203, 1 July 1896.

9. Guildhall Library, 18000/4B/43, fo. 5; PRO, BT 31/2848/15664, fo. 3/231.

10. *The Times* 'stocks and railway and other shares', 2 June 1881 and 1882.

11. See Chapter 1, for estimate of this cost at almost 40 per cent above state financing.

12. IOR, Mss Eur Neg 4352 (Dufferin Papers), letter 67, Churchill to Dufferin, 28 August 1885.

13. ING Baring Archive, HC3.128, Bengal Central Railway Co Ltd to Colonel Ellis, Baring Bros, 22 May 1885.

14. *Parliamentary Papers 1896* [c8258], Royal Commission on Administration of Expenditure of India, First Report, Volume I, Minutes (Welby); para. 12,203, 1 July 1896.

15. Bodleian Library, Ms Eng c4283 (Kimberley Papers), fo. 36; IOR L/F/8/12/899, Company Indenture, 12 December 1882, where shareholders received earnings up to six percent and a 50 per cent share with GOI beyond that.

16. Ibid., fo. 37.

17. *Parliamentary Papers, 1884* (284), Select Committee on East Indian Railway Communication, para. 23: Strachey testimony, 21 March 1884.
18. Guildhall Library, 18000/6B/183, fo. 9b; PRO BT 31/30983/17441.
19. Bodleian Library, Ms Eng c4283 (Kimberley Papers), fo. 46/7.
20. Rothschild Archive, X 111/230/87.
21. Guildhall Library, Col/lib/pb02/70: First Annual Report of Bengal NW, paras. 8/10.
22. Bodleian Library, Ms Eng c4299 (Kimberley Papers), p. 2.
23. *Parliamentary Papers, 1884*, Select Committee on Indian Railways, para. 242 and 390; Chapter 6 for Caird's attack on Strachey's famine commission.
24. For share prices see for example *The Times*, 'Stocks and Shares', 4 January 1887 and 1894; for Rothschild share sales see PRO, BT 31/30983/17441.
25. IOR, L/F/8/13/955, Tirhut State Railway contract, 18 July 1890, paras. 6, 30; Sanyal, *Development of Indian Railways*, p. 143; *The Times,* 5 December 1900, p. 12 predicted that 'large amounts of Government capital would come in ...' to support '... Tirhut extensions'; IOR, F127/120 (Richard Strachey Papers) fo. 174 John to Richard 26 August 1894. While Colvin had demonstrated prudence over rail expenditure during the 1880s, by 1896 he became chairman of Rothschild's Burma Railway.
26. IOR, Mss Eur F123/77 (Hamilton Papers), fo. 15/16; this paralleled events in Britain where railway combination accelerated in the early twentieth century, see Cain, 'Railway Combination and Government', p. 636.
27. Ibid., fo. 29; Ferguson, *The House of Rothschild*, p. 292.
28. IOR, L/Parl/2/439 paras 1400, 1409, and J. Strachey and R. Strachey, *The Finances and Public Works of India from 1869 to 1881* (London: Kegan Paul, 1882) for an account of the EIR buyback negotiations.
29. IOR, V/26/720/4 paras 1119, 1168/1169; Chapter 8 for analysis of Mackay and Acworth committees.
30. J. Harrison, 'The Records of Indian Railways: A Neglected Resource', in I. Kerr, (ed.), *Railways in Modern India* (Oxford: Oxford University Press, 2001), p. 201 argued that Bengal NW up to its buyout by GOI in 1943 'was exceptional in receiving no government assistance ... beyond the grant of free land made to all railways in British India'. By the 1890s investors in the company would have disagreed.
31. IOR, Mss Eur F111/505 (Curzon Papers), para. 14.
32. Bodleian Library, Ms Eng c4242 (Kimberley Papers) fo. 61/63; Chapter 1, p. 9 for Baring/Ripon initiative on new guarantees.
33. Ibid., fo. 69–71.
34. Ibid., fo. 75/76.
35. *Parliamentary Papers, 1884*, Select Committee on Indian Railways, p. 578.
36. IOR, Mss Eur F130/8a (Dufferin Papers) fo. 131, Viceroy Dufferin by 1887 sought to block Hope's reappointment, concerned by his intimacy with Indian railway groups.
37. Ibid., para. 4090 and 5494; IOR, Mss Eur D604/6 (Hartington Papers), 631.
38. Rothschild Archive, 401/E 1887; *The Times* obituary 21 January 1915, noted Sir Samuel Hoare, Norwich MP, as Chairman of Bengal Nagpur, Lieutenant of City of London, president of Equitable Life Assurance Society. His son Samuel became Secretary of State for India in 1931, and later Foreign Secretary; Robert Millar was managing director of Bengal–Nagpur and director of Burma Railway .
39. *Parliamentary Papers, 1884*, Select Committee on Indian Railways, para. 25; IOR, Mss Eur 218/176 (Lytton Papers), p. 27.

40. Bandyopadhyay, *Indian Famine and Agrarian Problems*, p. 105 and Bodleian Library, Ms Eng c4283 (Kimberley Papers), para. 11.
41. Ibid., pp. 106/107.
42. IOR, Mss Eur E243/17 (Cross Papers) fo. 41: 25 November 1886; Kaminsky, *The India Office 1880–1910*, p. 69, Cross's enthusiasm for railways was an isolated passion. Godley viewed him as indolent.
43. Ibid., fos. 57, 65.
44. IOR, Mss Eur F130/8a (Dufferin Papers), fo.20.
45. IOR, Mss Eur E 243/17 (Cross Papers) fo. 43/44, and Rothschild Archive, 401/E 1887.
46. Ibid., pp. 2, 4.
47. C. Bernard (ed,), *Sir George Campbell: Memoirs of my Indian Career, Volume II* (London: 1893), p. 181.
48. Guildhall Library, 18000/16B/298, 18 March 1887.
49. Like Montagu, Lord Revelstoke (Baring), Cassel, Currie and Schuster, Hambro was a fierce rival to Rothschild's declining city hegemony, see Hambro, *DNB*, and K. Burk, *Morgan Grenfell 1838–1988: The Biography of a Merchant Bank* (Oxford: Clarendon, 1989), p. 58.
50. Davis and Huttenback, *Mammon and the Pursuit of Empire*, pp. 195, 206–8; IOR, Mss Eur E243/19 (Cross Papers) fo. 123; *Parliamentary Papers, 1886* [c 4715], Royal Commission to Inquire into Depression of Trade and Industry, para. 5297, where Manchester MPs pressed Bengal–Nagpur and Burma Railway claims for extensions into South West China via Siam.
51. See Chapter 1, n. 58; Kipling had 2,000 shares see PRO BT31/34255/23994, 13 November 1924.
52. PRO, BT 31/34240/23994, Volume 1, pp. 108, 26; R. Foster, *Lord Randolph Churchill* (Oxford: Clarendon, 1981), p. 203, described Cohen as '... a relation of the Rothschilds ... a close associate of Churchill's and a generous contributor to [Conservative] party funds...'
53. Large section of East Coast state railway was tendered cheaply to Bengal Nagpur in 1902, see IOR, L/F/8/16/1091; Wacha, *Speeches and Writings*, p. 46.
54. Ibid., pp. 110,112,115; Foster, *Churchill*, p. 194, Churchill had 'converted the Bengal-Nagpur Railway into an investment proposition ...'
55. *Parliamentary Papers, 1889* (231), Famine Insurance, p. 4; *Parliamentary Papers, 1906* (116), Return of the Net Income and Expenditure of British India, p. 66.
56. *The Times* 19 December 1900, p. 13.
57. P. Bandyopadhyay, *Indian Famine and Agrarian Problems* (Calcutta: Star Publications, 1987), pp. 116/117.
58. IOR, Mss Eur F123/82 fo.108, F123/83 fo. 39 (Hamilton Papers).
59. IOR, Mss Eur D558/50 (Lansdowne Papers), Volume 1, 21 January 1890
60. J. Hurd, 'Railways', in I. Kerr (ed.), *Railways in Modern India* (New Delhi: Oxford University Press, 2001), p. 169.
61. IOR, Mss Eur F111/505 (Curzon Papers), Appendix 73.
62. Guildhall Library, Ms 16,532, London Chamber Minute Book, Minutes 3 July 1913, 2 June 1913.
63. Guildhall Library, Col/lib/pb02/931, Reports 19 June 1906, 18 December 1906.
64. IOR, L/Parl/2/439, para. 1226.
65. IOR, V/26/720/4, para. 1121.

66. IOR, Mss Eur E243/17 (Cross Papers) fo.55; IOR, Mss Eur F130/8a (Dufferin Papers) fo. 20.

67. Webster, 'Business and Empire', pp. 1003–25; IOR Mss Eur F90/28 (Lawrence papers) fo. 120, Secretary of State Northcote warned in 1867 that state railway building in Burma could require annexation of Upper Burma.

68. IOR, Mss Eur E243/17 (Cross Papers) fo. 46; IOR, Mss Eur C144/5 (Northbrook Papers) fo.128, Dufferin to Northbrook, 26 September 1887; IOR, Mss Eur Neg 4352 (Dufferin Papers), Letters 60, 75, 77 for examples of Churchill lobbying Dufferin on behalf of English Chambers favouring acquisition of Upper Burma; R. Turrell, 'Conquest and Concession: The Case of the Burma Ruby Mines', *Modern Asian Studies*, 22:1 (1988), pp. 156, 158.

69. University of Cambridge, Randolph Churchill Papers, Ms 9248/11, fo. 1294.

70. Ferguson, *The House of Rothschild*, p. 332; Chapman, *Merchant Enterprise*, p. 255.

71. ING, HC3.127, letter dated 8 July 1886, financiers James Finlay (also prominent on the Assam Bengal financing), pulled Baring Brothers back into railway finance promising high remuneration.

72. IOR, Mss Eur E243/17 (Cross Papers) fo. 10; Cross's predecessor Kimberley had opposed any privatization of the Burma Railway assets, but told Dufferin that the need for off balance sheet military railways might make this necessary see IOR, Mss Eur Neg 4352 (Dufferin Papers), letter 18, Kimberley to Dufferin, 16 April 1886.

73. Guildhall Library, 18000/43B/530; PRO, BT 31/15646/48856.

74. IOR, L/F/8/15/1016, para. 6.

75. Ibid., Guildhall; IOR, Mss Eur F102/9 (Kilbracken Papers) f28, Colvin complained that Hope was 'too encouraging' to a 'mercantile community' who wanted 'to share in the profit' of railways but resisted any 'share in the risks', see Chapter 6; IOR, F127/120 (Richard Strachey Papers) fo.168.

76. IOR, Mss Eur F123/78 (Hamilton Papers) fo. 19, 57; Mss Eur C145/2 (Fowler Papers), Viceroy Elgin's told Secretary Fowler that Burma railways investments were huge necessitating 'cheap capital' since 'nothing is more important politically than the opening up of the country in all directions by railways', with a long term arranger of guaranteed funding required.

77. Ibid., letter 3 January 1902; IOR, Mss Eur F123/83 (Hamilton Papers) fos. 158/59.

78. Kaminsky, *The India Office 1880–1910*, pp. 139/140, the Council complained in 1902 that GOI was 'bypassing it on railway legislation'.

79. IOR, Mss Eur F123/84 (Hamilton Papers), fo. 5.

80. IOR, Mss Eur F123/84 (Hamilton Papers), fo. 179; Kaminsky, *The India Office 1880–1910*, pp. 14, 27, Salisbury resisted chamber of commerce pressure on guarantees on the Burma/Yunnan Railway, whereas the Japanese government guaranteed 5 percent returns on Manchurian railways by 1911.

81. *Economist*, 'London Stock', shows price moving from 103 to 105 1/2 over August 1901 to June 1914.

82. IOR, Mss Eur F123/84 (Hamilton Papers) fo.5, letter to Curzon, 24 April 1902.

83. ING, Baghdad Railway Files 201338 and 200248; the omnipresent Sir Ernest Cassel was involved; S. Jones, *Merchants of the Raj* (Basingstoke: Macmillan, 1992), p. 25, J. P. Morgan's Indian commitment increased in 1919 through acquiring Andrew Yule's Indian assets; *The Times*, 4 December 1905, p. 9, Dawkins's obituary described his shared Balliol and ICS background with Curzon; Ferguson, *The House of Rothschild*, p. 287, by 1901 Dawkins expected to see 'the Rothschilds thrown into the background and the

Morgan group supreme' within twenty years; IOR, Mss Eur F111/160 (Curzon Papers), Curzon to Godley, 3 January 1901, where Curzon complained of being 'ingeniously circumvented' by Dawkins over railway finance.

84.   IOR, Mss Eur F123/51 (Hamilton Papers), fo. 5.
85.   IOR, Mss Eur F123/83 (Hamilton Papers) fo. 79.
86.   Guildhall Library, 18000/115B/155; this was in spite of subsidized government loans, including, in 1907, Rs 85 lakhs (£850,000) at a rupee rate of 2.5 per cent on a perpetual basis, see IOR, L/F/8/16/1171, para. 2.
87.   Dumett, 'Joseph Chamberlain', p. 308, shows independent crown agents, elsewhere in the Empire, brokering railway loans for ½ per cent, while levying one percent commissions on British railway materials, without guarantees .
88.   IOR, L/Parl/2/439, para. 1169: Rothschild testimony to Mackay.

5 Northern Wars and Southern Diplomacy

1.   T. Gourvish, 'A British Business Elite: The Chief Executive Managers of the Railway Industry', 1850–1922, *The Business History Review*, 47:3 (Autumn 1973), pp. 315–6 saw greater professionalism in the British railway's management.
2.   *The Times*, 21 December 1886; *Sir Douglas Forsyth, DNB*; Metcalf *Ideologies of the Raj*, p. 39 argued Forsyth's 'vigorous defence of their actions marked out a path that was to lead in 1919 to the infamous Amritsar massacre'.
3.   G. Elsmie, *Thirty-Five Years in the Punjab* (Edinburgh: David Douglas, 1908).
4.   Guildhall Library, Railway Annual Reports, Col/Lib/Pb02/63, Scinde, Punjaub 48th annual report, dated 30 June 1880; see Chapter 4 for W. P. Andrew.
5.   BL, Ripon Papers, Ms 43,587, p. 156, Baring Memo, 26 August 1881.
6.   Connell, 'Indian Railways and Indian Wheat', pp. 252/3.
7.   J. Forbes Munro, 'Shipping Subsidies and Railway Guarantees: William Mackinnon, Eastern Africa and the Indian Ocean, 1860–93', *Journal of African History*, 28:2 (1987), pp. 213/214, described Mackinnon's B.I. as 'the maritime equivalent' of GIPR or Scinde, Punjaub; Cain and Hopkins, *British Imperialism*, p. 294 chart Mackinnon's shift to service sector representative with his firm's switch from Clydeside to London, and a directorship of the National Bank of India (recently moved from India to London).
8.   SOAS Archive, Mackinnon Papers, pp. MS 1/CORR 1/78 and 79, Kaye to Mackinnon 10 December 1870, 24 October 1870, 25 February 1872; For EIR see Chapter 6.
9.   Guildhall Library, Railway Reports, Col/Lib/Pb02/63, Scinde, Punjaub Report, 30 June 1880.
10.   Ibid., 51st, 53rd annual reports, 22 December 1881, 21 December 1882.
11.   Ibid., 54th Report dated 26 June 1883; see also comments on Bombay resistance to Karachi port development, *The Times*, 1 April 1902, p. 10.
12.   H. Bell, *Railway Policy in India* (London: Rivington, Percival, 1894), p. 223; Sharma, *History of the Great Indian Peninsula Railway*, p. 22.
13.   See Chapter 3 for cultural ambitions for railways in Afghanistan
14.   E. Forsyth (ed.), *Autobiography and Reminiscences of Sir Douglas Forsyth* (London: Richard Bentley, 1887), p. 280; and *Sir Douglas Forsyth, DNB*.
15.   Bell, *Railway Policy in India*, p. 47.
16.   see Chapter 4 on Dickens, Chapter 6; Dickens was illustrative of military dominance of early Indian railways, see Villeroi, *A History of the North Western Railway*, pp. 7–10.
17.   IOR, L/AG/46/17/27.

18. Guildhall Library, Railway Reports, Col/Lib/Pb02/63, Scinde, Punjaub, 29 June 1885, 22 December 1885.

19. IOR V/4/Session 1900/Volume 29 p. 709, para. 64 minority report to Welby; Chapter 4 on North Western Railway

20. Forsyth (ed.), *Autobiography and Reminiscences of Sir Douglas Forsyth.*

21. *The Times*, 30 September 1884.

22. IOR, L/PWD/2/176, Miscellaneous Railways 1877–9, Salisbury letter, 6 February 1877; Salisbury curbed speculation on Hyderabad railway paper by promoters, while silver Rupee depreciation strained financings see IOR, Salisbury Papers, Neg.11688, fo.100, Salisbury to Lytton, 16 June 1876; T. Sethnia, 'Railways, Raj, and the Indian States: Policy of Collaboration and Coercion in Hyderabad', in C. Davis and K. Wilburn (eds), *Railway Imperialism* (New York: Greenwood, 1991), p. 115.

23. Ibid., Campbell to Mallet, 18 and 25 October 1877; and Balliol College, Oxford, Morier Papers, Box 8, Item 3, Morier to Lord Granville 22 May 1880, Campbell to Morier 20 February 1879.

24. Ibid., India Office notes, 30 November 1877, 2 April 1878.

25. Ibid , Fleming to Cranbrook, August 1878.

26. A. Ramm, *Sir Robert Morier: Envoy and Ambassador in the Age of Imperialism 1876–1893* (Oxford: Clarendon, 1973), p. 27.

27. PRO, FO 63/1091, Morier to Salisbury, 7 June 1879; 'bubble' companies were perhaps more acceptable in British India (see Chapter 5 on Bengal Central).

28. Forbes Munro, 'Shipping Subsidies and Railway Guarantees', pp. 218–21; Balliol College, Oxford, Morier Papers, Box 8, Item 3, Morier to Viscount Duprat, 16 April 1879.

29. E. Richards, 'An Anatomy of the Sutherland Fortune: Income, Consumption, Investments, and Returns, 1780–1880', *Business History*, 21:1 (January 1979), pp. 48, 53, 54, 69; J. Beckett, *The Aristocracy in England 1660–1914* (Oxford, 1986), p. 243 observed in England that 'railways probably did more than ... other developments to raise land values'.

30. *Marquess of Sutherland*, *DNB* and *The Times*, 13 September 1877.

31. Forbes Munro, 'Shipping Subsidies and Railway Guarantees: William Mackinnon, Eastern Africa and the Indian Ocean, 1860–93', *Journal of African History*, 28:2 (1987), p. 221.

32. Balliol College, Oxford, Morier Papers, Box 8, Item 3, SHC to Corvo, 31 May 1879.

33. Ibid., Morier to Duprat, 16 April 1879; Morier to Mackinnon, 30 May 1879.

34. Ibid., Mallet to Morier, 20 October 1879.

35. Ibid , Forsyth to Portuguese Ministry, 12 August 1879.

36. SOAS Archive, William Mackinnon Papers, pp. ms1/corr 1/171; fo.6 note to Mackinnon, fo.19 Morier to Mackinnon, 8 July 1879; Balliol College, Oxford, Morier Papers, Box 8, Item 3, Mackinnon to Morier, 10 July 1879.

37. Balliol College, Oxford, Morier Papers, Box 6, Item (I) vi, Morier to Forsyth, 26 May 1880; and Forsyth to Morier, 22 April 1880.

38. See Chapter 6 on Hope.

39. Balliol College, Oxford, Morier Papers, Box 9, Item 3, Hope to Morier, 4 August 1879.

40. Ibid , Box 11, Morier to Cranbrook, 14 February 1880.

41. Balliol College, Mallet Papers, III (B), File 22, Hope to Mallet, 31 December 1879; File 23, Hope note dated 31 July 1880; Buckland, *Dictionary of Indian Biography.*

42. IOR, L/PWD/2/176, Morier to Salisbury, 21 September 1879; *DNB* on Sutherland/Mackinnon; Ramm, *Sir Robert Morier*, p. 36 ; PRO, FO 63/1091, Morier to Salisbury,

8 September 1879; Morier minute 29 November 1879 showing Portuguese discomfort at English capital punishment laws on railway lands inside Goan territory (Portugal banned the death penalty); *Parliamentary Papers 1900* [Cd.130], Royal Commission on Administration of Expenditure (Welby), para. 17,524–7 see Wedderburn on railways as part of the 'slavery' of Indian ryots, comparable to American negroes; PRO FO 84/1536 and 1594, Slave Trade Series, Morier on Portuguese slave trade.

43. Balliol College, Oxford, Morier Papers, Box 11, Item 3, Morrier to Cranbrook 22 August 1879; Item 4, Portuguese memo, 10 January 1880; given the collateralization, Temple's comments were fair.

44. BL, Ripon Papers, Ms 43,575, pp. 460/461 Baring Memo 24 May 1881; Baring calculated the cost of Forsyth's guarantee as three percent for ten years on Murmagao costs of £2.6 million, or £780,000 plus free land. Additional costs of government support were ignored.

45. *The Times*, 'stocks and railway and other shares' 2 July 1881, 4 January 1883.

46. Guildhall Library, Manuscripts, Ordered Application Listing of Shares, 18000/4B/119

47. IOR, L/AG/46/19, WIPGR File, 2nd Annual Report, 14 June 1883.

48. Ibid., 5th Annual Report, 30 June 1886.

49. Ibid., 3rd Annual Report, 26 June 1884.

50. Ramm, *Sir Robert Morier*, pp. 48/9; M. Bentley, *Lord Salisbury's World: Conservative Environments in Late Victorian Britain* (Cambridge: Cambridge University Press, 2001), p. 106; Beckett, *The Aristocracy in England 1660–1914*, p. 251, Salisbury was 'an active chairman of the Great Eastern between 1868 and 1872' where he 'grasped the fundamentals of railway operation'.

51. SOAS Archive, Mackinnon Papers, pp. ms 1/corr 1/174; fo. 28; Mackinnon to Morier 2 September 1889; *The Times*, 'The Sea Route to Siberia', 15 October 1889.

52. Platt, *Finance, Trade, and Politics*, p. 14.

53. IOR, Mss Eur D705/5 (Hope Papers); fo. 236 Hope to Forsyth 27/5/81; Chapter 5 describes a similar pattern for on Rothschild sponsored railways.

54. *Parliamentary Papers*, IOR, V/4/Session 1883/Volume 50, pp. 330–1, para. 139–139.

55. *Parliamentary Papers 1884* [284], Select committee on East Indian Railway Communications.

56. Bodleian Library, Kimberley Papers, Ms Eng c4299, Item 12; IOR, L/F/8/12/901 Southern Mahratta Indenture, 1 June 1882, para. 65; additional government support system was lent by giving more land when 'requisite for the construction', see para. 7.

57. H. Jagtiani, *The Role of the State in the Provision of Railways* (London: P.S. King, 1924), p. 135.

58. Cambridge University, Lord Randolph Churchill Papers, Ms 9248/9, fo. 1079; Danvers to Churchill.

59. *Parliamentary Papers 1884* [284], Select committee on East Indian Railway Communications; p. 421 para. 6556.

60. Ibid., Major Conway-Gordon Testimony, p. 254, para. 1120; Ripon's free trade enthusiasm included support for Indian tariff abolition and taxpayer funding for railways, see Klein, 'English Free Traders and Indian Tariffs', p. 264.

61. Bodleian Library, Kimberley Papers, Ms Eng c4277, Mallet memo 'Public works policy 1882, para. 26,30; Ms Eng c4283, Mallet to Kimberley, fo.8–10.

62. IOR, Mss Eur D705/6 (Hope Papers), Mallet to Hope, 23 March 1883; Balliol College, Mallet Papers, III (B), 24, Hope to Mallet, 5 August 1881.

63. *Hansard*, 3rd Series, 269, 25 May 1882, cols 1596–99; and 260, col.1818; IOR, V/4/ Session 1883/Volume 50, Financial Statement of the Government of India 1883–84, para. 138/139.

64. Guildhall Library, Indian Railway Annual Reports, Col/Lib/Pb02/63, Southern Mahratta, 1–3 Annual reports; and IOR, F112/445 (Curzon Papers), Note from GOI to Secretary of State dated 29 March 1900; Wacha, *Speeches and Writings*, p. 46. Southern Mahratta earnings converted at 1Rs=1s. 4d.

65. Bell, *Railway Policy in India*, p. 350.

66. Forsyth (ed.)., *Autobiography and Reminiscences of Sir Douglas Forsyth*, p. 278.

67. *Parliamentary Papers 1884* [284], Select committee on East Indian Railway Communications; Strachey testimony p. 20 para. 253–256; Danvers's testimony p. 445 para. 6961–6964.

68. Bell, *Railway Policy in India*, p. 43.

69. *Hansard*, 3 series, 289, 5 May 1884, col. 1329; Davis and Huttenback, *Mammon and the Pursuit of Empire*, p. 50 pointed to the prominence of Empire finance raised for the Indian 'extractive' sector over 1880–1905, notably 'Goldfields of Mysore' and 'Mysore Reef Gold'.

70. IOR, Mss Eur D705/7 (Hope Papers) fo. 291; fo.334; earlier Salisbury had mocked the 'several inchoate [rail] projects around Mysore see IOR, Salisbury Papers, Neg. 11688, fo.254, Salisbury to Lytton, 28 October 1876.

71. University of Cambridge, Randolph Churchill Papers, Ms 9248/11, fo. 1320, Forsyth to Churchill, 21 January 1886; and IOR, Mss Eur Neg 4352 (Dufferin Papers), Letter 76, Churchill to Dufferin, 16 October 1885.

72. Guildhall Library, Railway Annual Reports, Col/Lib/Pb02/63, Southern Mahratta 4th report, 30 June 1886.

73. IOR, D705/8 (Hope papers), fo. 91, Hope to Forsyth, 13 August 1886.

74. McAlpin, *Subject to Famine*, pp. 175, 185 argues famine relief by irrigation was difficult in Southern Mahratta/Deccan region, with the water table too low.

75. *The Times*, Southern Mahratta 33rd Ordinary General Meeting, 22 November 1900.

76. ING Baring Archive, HC6.3.27, dated 1904, fos.1,5,10,22,60.

77. *The Times*, 18 June 1914; IOR, India Office Records: L/AG/1–52 Part III, India Office: Accountant General's Records c1601–1974, Part III, L/AG/34–52 with Index, Summary on Madras an.

6 Eminent ICS Victorians

1. M. Holroyd, *Lytton Strachey, Volume 1* (London: Heinemann, 1967), p. 66.

2. *Sir Richard Strachey*, DNB, p. 5; Kaminsky, *The India Office 1880–1910*, p. 194 highlighted Strachey, with brother John and James Mackay as 'distinguished and capable men' who brought outside expertise to the Council .

3. A. Binnie, *Public Works in India: A Letter addressed to the Rt Hon. W.E. Gladstone, MP and the other members of Her Majesty's Government* (London: E. and F. N. Spon, 1881), pp. 5–19, railway engineering costs at the GOI were 25–30 per cent of investment (versus 5–6 per cent in private sector British railways).

4. IOR, Mss Eur F127/441 (R. Strachey Papers), fo.10, 'Royal Institution of Great Britain ... physical causes of Indian famines'.

5. Holroyd, *Lytton Strachey*, p. 26, Strachey's family were 'in decline' by the late 1880s.

6. Klein, 'English Free Traders and Indian Tariffs, p. 262; EIR communication see IOR, D705/7 (Hope Papers), fo. 53 and fo.114, 11 July 1884, 12 September 1884.

7. Meyer and Brysac, *Tournament of Shadows*, pp. 174/5, Lytton and fellow Bloomsbury members avoided observations on India, despite his godfather being Viceroy Lytton, and his father Richard 'an ornament of the Raj'.

8. Sanyal, *Development of Indian Railways*.

9. Strachey and Strachey, *The Finances and Public Works of India*, pp. 129–30.

10. Ibid., pp. 128–9.

11. *Parliamentary Papers 1881* [205], financial Statement of Government of India, 1881–82, para. 9 noted costs of £9.7 million, though by 1882/3 EIR had returned net profits of £4.1 million to GOI, since buyback at 1879.

12. Ambirajan, *Classical Political Economy*, p. 266 contrasted Mallet's 'cobdenite' ideology with Strachey's 'paternalistic ... liberal approach to the functions of government', after J. S. Mill; IOR, Mss Eur F127/150 (Strachey Papers) fo.13, 28 October 1881, ex-Viceroy Lytton railed to Strachey about Mallet's 'quack crotchet ... about the encouragement of private enterprise'.

13. *Henry Fawcett, DNB*, p. 7.

14. *Parliamentary Papers 1878–79* [c 226], Select Committee on the East Indian Railway Bill, p. xiv, p. 21; Fawcett, *Indian Finance*, p. 145 argued guaranteed companies profits were swollen by having the best trunk line concessions. By 1879 guaranteed lines had generated £96.7 million against only £ 21.3 million for state lines.

15. Ibid., p. 24.

16. Ibid., p. 53 and p. 60.

17. Ibid., para. 532.

18. Sanyal, *Development of Indian Railways* viewed EIR as the 'best managed line in many respects'; more recently this was challenged in University of London, SOAS, PhD Thesis, H. Mukherjee, *The Early History of the East Indian Railway, 1845–1879* (July 1966), pp. 104–5, and book of same title (Calcutta, 1994), pp. 50, 59.

19. Jagtiani, *The Role of the State in the Provision of Railways*, p. 101.

20. Parliamentary Papers 1878–9 [c226], Select Committee on the East Indian Railway Bill, paras 534 and 577.

21. Ibid., paras 455–8, and p. xii.

22. Ibid., para. 458; Guildhall Library, Col/lib/pb02/70: Report of EIR to Annuitants, 20/5/80; Chapter 5 for Hambro's role with Rothschild in Bengal Nagpur and Burma Railways

23. IOR, Mss Eur F123/81 (Curzon Papers) fo. 67/68, dated 30 May 1900.

24. IOR, Mss Eur F127/158 (R.Strachey Papers) fo. 12, Strachey to Salisbury, 2 April 1877.

25. IOR, Mss Eur F127/172 (R.Strachey Papers) fo. 33, 17 June 1878.

26. R. Strachey, *East Indian Railway Company Purchase Act, 1879: A Short Account of the preliminary negotiations* (London: 1880), p. 9.

27. IOR, F127/150 (Richard Strachey Papers) fo.86, fo.147, fo.210; J. Caird, *India, The Land and the People* (London: Cassell, 1883), p. 210, famine relief in India was less than two percent of the cost of British poor law.

28. *Parliamentary Papers 1878–79* [c226], Select Committee on the East Indian Railway Bill, p. 24 para. 382; G. Khosla, *A History of Indian Railways* (New Delhi: Government of India, 1988), p. 114, hybrid public/private ownership at EIR and GIPR/Madras Railway meant lost earnings for GOI.

29. *Parliamentary Papers 1884* [c284], Report from the Select Committee on East Indian Railway Communication, 18 July 1884, p. 4, paras 19 and 22.
30. Ibid., p. 4, paras 25–8.
31. IOR, Mss Eur F127/151(Richard Strachey Papers), fo. 98,104,106; Strachey's annuity earnings were allowable under the Companies Purchase Act 1879.
32. IOR, Mss Eur F127/178 (Richard Strachey Papers), fo. 30–1.
33. IOR, Mss Eur E243/19 (Cross Papers), fo. 89, 90, 131.
34. Ibid., fo. 168, Cross to Lansdowne, 10 July 1890.
35. IOR, Mss Eur F127/218 (Richard Strachey Papers).
36. Ibid., fo. 10 pp. 17/18.
37. A. Awasthi, *History and Development of Railways in India* (New Delhi: 1994), p. 139, coal price per ton in 1883/84 at EIR was Rs 2.19, against GIPR (Rs 13.1) and Sindh Punjab and Delhi (Rs 20.8).
38. Ibid., fo. 26 p. 13; Mackay retired from the board of EIR in 1897, see fo. 4 p. 4.
39. Ibid., fo. 196/7 pp. 8/9, and fo. 252 p. 11.
40. Ibid., fo. 132 para. 24.
41. IOR, Mss Eur F111/502 (Curzon Papers), para. 63.
42. IOR, Mss Eur F127/120 (R.Strachey Papers), fo. 172 and 173; John complained intermittently to Richard about inadequate dividends on his EIR annuities, see fo. 91 and 163.
43. IOR, Mss Eur F111/160 (Curzon Papers), letters 2 and 54, Curzon to Godley; and IOR, Mss Eur F111/159 (Curzon Papers), letter 20, p. 84, Curzon to Godley, 5 April 1900.
44. Kaminsky, *The India Office 1880–1910*.
45. IOR, Mss Eur F123/84 (Hamilton Papers), fo.19, 6 February 1909.
46. See Map 6.
47. IOR, Neg 4352 (Dufferin Papers), Letter 53, 10 September 1885, Dufferin to R. Churchill, said the Strachey's would oppose projects where Hope's was involved.
48. *Parliamentary Papers 1882* [181], Financial Statement of GOI, 1882–3, para. 105, Anglo Indians had lobbied for the Assam railway for years. In 1882 the Indian Tea Association, under J. Keswick, pressed rail links to Assam to bring in cheap plantation labour; Tyson, *Bengal Chamber of Commerce and Industry 1853–1953*, p. 72, migrant labour was controversial, with exploitation by Anglo-Indian tea planters. Recruits were ignorant of the terms of their employment, and by 1929/30 migrant employment was only 6 per cent of Assam's tea pickers, undermining the railway's rationale; Ambirajan, 'Malthusian Population Theory', p. 12, highlighted Assam and Burma tea plantations as destinations for Indian migrants from densely populated regions.
49. IOR, Mss Eur D705/11 (Hope Papers), memos 26 July 1888, 20 March 1890; C. Brogan, *James Finlay and Co Ltd: Manufacturers and East India Merchants 1750–1950* (Glasgow: Jackson, 1951), pp. 97, 102 on managing agency lobbying for tea plantations and related communications in Assam.
50. IOR, Mss Eur F123/82 (Curzon Papers) fo. 55 and fo. 36; whereas, *Parliamentary Papers 1896* [166], Financial Statement of Government of India, 1896–97, p. 139, described Assam Bengal as a 600 mile link which was bound to 'open up an entire province' and encourage rapid growth in tea exports.
51. IOR, Mss Eur F111/502 (Curzon Papers), para. 4, Curzon's Railway Despatch Number 66, 21 September 1899.

52. *Parliamentary Papers, 1896* [166], Financial Statement of Government of India, 1896–97, para. 50, Assam Bengal absorbed Rs 31.88 mill of capital expenditure (1898–1913 exchange rate 1 Rs=1s. 4d).

53. W. Gawthrop, *The Story of the Assam Railway and Trading Company Ltd 1881–1951* (London: 1952), p. 6; Malik, *Hundred Years of Pakistan Railways*, p. 19.

54. IOR, Mss Eur F111/159 (Curzon Papers); letter 41; Curzon to Godley, 4 July 1900.

55. IOR, Mss Eur E243/20 (Cross Papers) fo. 94,107,131, Cross wished to avoid military aggression, which had angered 'native chiefs' in Upper Burma in 1885. The Queen pressed to avoid any executions of native princes in Manipur .

56. *The Times*, 1 April 1902, p. 10.

57. IOR, F127/178 (Richard Strachey Papers) fo.60, 28 June 1907.

58. IOR, Mss Eur F112/445 (Curzon Papers); 'Note by Lord Curzon on the present position of the railway question', 17 June 1904.

59. IOR, Mss Eur F123/82 (Hamilton Papers) fo. 36, 5 April 1900.

60. IOR, Mss Eur F111/159 (Curzon Papers), letter 12, Curzon to Hamilton, 11 March 1900.

61. IOR, Mss Eur C125/1 (Hamilton Papers), fo. 439; Hamilton to Elgin 4 December 1896; Chapter 5 for Burma Railways.

62. IOR, Mss Eur F130/8a (Dufferin Papers) fo.11 and fo. 131; see also IOR Neg 4352 (Dufferin Papers), Letter 53, 10 September 1885, Dufferin observed that 'a more annoying, tricky, untrustworthy person in all matters of business than Mr Hope cannot be conceived'; Letter 54, 21 September 1885, Hope understated costs at Bolan military railway to gain approval, with an overspend of 200 per cent; Dufferin was ultimately disgraced by his chairmanship of London and Globe Finance Corporation which collapsed in 1900 through fraud, see Dufferin, *DNB*, p. 7, and IOR Mss Eur F123/83 (Hamilton Papers) fo.3, Hamilton to Curzon, 3 January 1901, described Dufferin's business practices as 'careless and reckless to the last degree'.

63. IOR, Mss Eur E243/17 (Cross Papers) fos. 55, 65, 26, 147 .

64. IOR, Mss Eur D705/8 (Hope Papers) fos. 135, 170, 171; Colvin accused Hope of misrepresenting approval of large government loans for the military Sibi-Quetta Railway to force the construction, see BL, Ripon Papers, Ms 43,587, p. 257, Memo by Colvin, 30 October 1884.

65. Ibid., fo. 316.

66. Ibid., fo. 492, Hope to Elliott, 28 June 1889.

67. PRO, BT31/15646/48856, Burma Railway, 1896, fo. 1015; PRO, BT31/31273/36029, Assam Bengal 'summary of capital and shares' at 13 July 1897, fo. 1093.

68. IOR, Mss Eur D705/11 (Hope Papers), Memo from Hope, John Muir, Bradford Leslie, 26 July 1888.

69. Ibid., memorandum titled 'Confidential: Bengal Assam Railway', 13 September 1889, pp. 1,4; IOR, Mss Eur E243/19 (Cross Papers), fos.102, 111, 123; Bentley, *Lord Salisbury's World*, p. 106, WH Smith's British kiosks sold books and newspapers on railway platforms.

70. IOR, Mss Eur D705/8 (Hope Papers), fos. 370, 347.

71. IOR, D705/11 (Hope Papers), Hope memo on 'Bengal–Assam Project', 24 March 1890.

72. IOR, Mss Eur E243/19 (Cross Papers), fos. 153, 155, letters to Lansdowne dated 23/9 May 1890.

73. This was part of the Jardine Matheson group who by 1876 had constructed the first railway in China; M. Daunton, *Wealth and Welfare: An Economic and Social History of Britain 1851–1951* (Oxford, 2007), p. 252 characterized them as emerging from the City's 'gentlemanly nexus of land and finance', and the trading interests of Liverpool and Glasgow, presumably a comfortable fit with Cross.

74. IOR, Mss Eur E243/20 (Cross Papers); fos. 13, 14, 28, 39; and fos. 28, 213, 258, 287.

75. Sanyal, *Development of Indian Railways*, p. 157; Bell, *Recent Railway Policy, papers before royal society of arts*, 4/98, pp. 15–16; while the initial share placement met problems from poor market support by brokers, the Assam price bounced to 108 by November 1895, before slumping again, see Economist, 16 November 1895, and IOR, Mss Eur E243/20 (Cross Papers) fo. 287; the choice of inexperienced underwriters Sheppards, Pellys and Scott may have been explained by Sir Lewis Pelly's position on the board, see IOR, L/F/8/13/974B for Assam–Bengal issuing prospectus, 21 March 1892.

76. PRO, BT 31/31273/36029 (Assam–Bengal Papers), Part 1, see share folios 150, 146, 2243, 1093; by 1902 Strachey's direct ownership portfolio was modest: £4,000 EIR deferred annuities D class, £10,500 EIR new debenture stock, and £1,000 Assam Railway stock see IOR F127/292 (Richard Strachey Papers) fo. 2; there was pressure on senior management to hold stock; IOR F127/152 (Richard Strachey Papers) fo. 5, 30 October 1891,where G. Chesney pressed Strachey for a job at EIR.

77. Holroyd, *Lytton Strachey*, p. 26; *Richard Strachey*, *DNB*, p. 6; and IOR, F127/293 (R.Strachey Papers) , Share Certificates .

78. IOR, Mss Eur C641 (Assam Bengal Railway Papers), fo. 7/8.

79. Ibid., fos. 27, 55, 56, 57, 65, 68.

80. IOR, Mss Eur F112/445 (Curzon Papers); note 112 of 1900, p. 17.

81. IOR, L/F/8/16/1103, where the coupon was raised from 3 per cent to 3.25 per cent and maturity seven years to 1899.

82. IOR, Mss Eur F127/270 (Richard Strachey Papers) fos. 3–5.

83. Ibid., fo.5; J. Hurd, 'A Huge Railway System but no Sustained Economic Development: The Company Perpectives, 1884–1939: Some Hypotheses', in I. Kerr (ed.), *27 Down: New Departures in Indian Railway Studies* (New Delhi: Orient Longman, 2007), p. 324, placed Assam Bengal bottom of all railway companies in track usage by 1914.

84. Gawthrop, *The Story of the Assam Railway and Trading Company Ltd*, p. 4; Malik, *Hundred Years of Pakistan Railways*, pp. 18–20.

85. *Parliamentary Papers 1921* [Cmd. 1512], Acworth Committee, para. 2.

7 Background, Proceedings and Legacy of the Mackay Committee of 1908

1. Chandra, *Nationalism and Colonialism in Modern India*, pp. 64–9 .

2. D. Wacha, *Indian Railway Finance being a revised reprint of a series of articles*, p. 37.

3. H. Bolitho, *James Lyle Mackay: First Earl of Inchcape* (London: Murray, 1936), p. 109.

4. R. Patwardhan, *Dadabhai Naoroji Correspondence, Volume II, Part I: Correspondence with DE Wacha* (Bombay: 1977) letter 443, 17 September 1898 .

5. Y. Cassis, *City Bankers 1890–1914* (Cambridge: Cambridge University Press, 1994), p. 300.

6. Patwardhan, *Dadabhai Naoroji Correspondence*, letter 443 .

7. Cain and Hopkins, *British Imperialism 1688–2000*, p. 295; Kaminsky, *The India Office 1880–1910*, p. 282.

8. Chapter 5 for William Mackinnon and Indian railways; S. Jones, *Trade and Shipping: Lord Inchcape 1852–1932* (Manchester: Manchester University Press, 1989), p. 31.

9. Ibid., p. 43.

10. Wacha, *Indian Railway Finance*, p. 19.

11. Jones, *Trade and Shipping*, p. 84; P. Williams, 'Public Opinion and the Railway Rates Question in 1886', *English Historical Review*, 67:262 (January 1952), pp. 37/38, deregulation of British railway rates was central to unionists split from Gladstone in 1886. Railways were said to charge lower freight rates for export/imports (similar to India); Dewey, 'The Government of India's "New Industrial Policy"', pp. 223/4.

12. Wacha, *Indian Railway Finance*, p. 24.

13. Jones, *Trade and Shipping*, p. 43.

14. PRO, T 168/ 85, paras 10,690, 10,700; Chapter 2 pp. 37/38 for Herschell/Fowler committees

15. Ibid., paras 10,701–5..

16. IOR, V/4/Session 1893–94/Volume 65.

17. PRO, T 168/ 85, paras 10,690, 10,700.

18. IOR, V/4/Session 1900/volume 29, para. 18,403.

19. Ibid., paras 18,407, 18,414, 18,416, 18,386–18,387, 18,390.

20. Chandra, *The Rise and Growth of Economic Nationalism*, p. 578.

21. IOR, V/4/Session 1900/Volume 29, p. 709 para. 3; Kaminsky, *The India Office 1880–1910*, p. 164.

22. Ibid., paras 17,548, 17,572, 17,573, 20,203. Jacob was controller/auditor general to GOI.

23. Patwardhan, *Dadabhai Naoroji Correspondence*, letter 392, 9 October 1897.

24. Ibid., letter 448, 22 October 1898.

25. Ibid., letter 415, 12 March 1898.

26. Ibid., letter 507, 5 May 1900.

27. Ibid., letter 425, 21 May 1898.

28. Chandra, *The Rise and Growth of Economic Nationalism*, p. 283 n. 41.

29. IOR, V/4/Session 1903/Volume 47.

30. Ibid., p. 489.

31. Ibid., p. 510.

32. Foreman-Peck, 'Natural Monopoly and Railway Policy in the Nineteenth Century', pp. 699, 717, the early appointment of a regulatory department in 1840 did little to curb private excesses, which the author estimated raised construction costs by 50 per cent and lowered per capita national income by ¾ per cent.

33. Ibid., pp. 510–13, 491, 513, 544; IOR, Mss Eur F111/502, para. 4 (Curzon Papers), 21 September 1899.

34. *Parliamentary Papers 1903* [Cd.1713], Report on the Administration and Working of Indian Railways, pp. 6/7; Chapters 5 and 6 on Southern Mahratta and Assam–Bengal.

35. S. Koss, *John Morley at the India Office 1905–1910* (New Haven, CT: Yale University Press, 1969), p. 125.

36. Ibid., p. 129.

37. Ibid., pp. 164/5.

38. Wacha, *Indian Railway Finance*, p. 5.

39. S. Ghose, *Indian Railway Finance and Indian Railway Rates* (Calcutta: H.K. Bose, 1912), p. 11.
40. IOR, L/Parl/2/439.
41. K. Prior, *Sir Walter Roper Lawrence, DNB.*
42. IOR, Mss Eur F143/31 (Lawrence Papers).
43. R. Davenport-Hines, Sir Felix Otto Schuster, *DNB*, p. 2.
44. These included Bombay, Baroda, and Central India Railway Company, Madras Railway Company, and South India Railway Company, see Guildhall Library Col/Lib/Pb02/70; Col/Lib/Pb02/62; Col/Lib/Pb02/63; Col/Lib/Pb02/1170.
45. C. Goodhart, *The Business of Banking 1851–1914* (Aldershot: Gower, 1986), pp. 505–507;Chapter 5 for Indian railway stocks as low risk/medium return assets.
46. Wacha, *Indian Railway Finance*, p. 47 .
47. G. Ballachandran, *Sir Lionel Barnett Abrahams, DNB*, p. 1.
48. G. Harrison, *Bird and Company of Calcutta* (Calcutta: Anna Art Press, 1964), pp. 30, 64.
49. Ibid., p. 36.
50. IOR, L/Parl/2/439, paras 96–8, 100–3, 143–5, 178, 238, 240, 208.
51. Ibid., paras 1017, 1030.
52. B. Tomlinson, *The Political Economy of the Raj, 1914–1947* (Basingstoke: Macmillan, 1979), pp. 21/22 highlighted Webb's campaign in 1912 to force the GOI to invest in domestic rupee assets as a precedent for other investors.
53. Ibid., paras 3417/19, 3536, 3512, 3511, 3478.
54. Sulivan, *One Hundred Years of Bombay*, pp. 241, 244 identified a Bombay and London Chambers initiative for rail companies to borrow in rupees at four percent, which lacked GOI support. Forrest used Bombay Chamber support to win feeder line concessions in the region, overriding financial restrictions.
55. Ibid., paras 273/4, 50, 4203, 4211.
56. Ibid., paras 1114/1115, 1148–9.
57. see Chapter 4.
58. Ibid paras 1115, 1169, 1165, 1159 and 1192. Guildhall Library Annual Report 1884 .
59. IOR, L/Parl/2/439, paras 1824, 1827, 1870.
60. Hurd, 'Railways', p. 162; Chapter 7 for EIR coal controversy .
61. IOR, L/Parl/2/439, paras 623/624, 642, 658.
62. Jones, *Trade and Shipping*, Appendix 2.
63. IOR, L/Parl/2/439, para. 723.
64. Ibid., para. 3337.
65. IOR, L/Parl/2/439, para. 1226; Chapter 4 for Bengal–Nagpur's disappointing performance.
66. F. Brown and H. Matthew, *Sir Edward Fitzgerald Law, DNB*, pp. 2/3; IOR, Mss Eur F111/505, Law's Indian railway minute, 21 December 1904 .
67. IOR L/Parl/2/439 paras 2535, 2549, 2517, 2524, 2439, 2447, 3060.
68. Ibid paras 3063, 3772; as Chairman of Southern Mahratta Bisset had benefited directly from waived buyback options and consistent government support, see Chapter 6.
69. Ibid., pp. 11, 29, 30.
70. Hurd, 'Railways', p. 169 .
71. In fact the maximum mileage reached was approximately 40,000 miles.

72. Ghose, *Indian Railway Finance and Indian Railway Rates*, p. 13; K. Shah, *Sixty Years of Indian Finance* (London: P. S. King, 1927), p. 352 argued the importance of Mackay lay in the removal of any upper ceiling on Indian rail mileage.
73. IOR, V/26/720/4, Acworth Report, para. 3862, Sir Henry Burt.
74. Anstey, *The Economic Development of India*, p. 135 n. 2.
75. IOR, V/9/38 volume 50, pp. 101/102.
76. Ibid., p. 103.
77. IOR, L/Parl/2/439, p. 31.
78. IOR, Sir Guy Douglas Arthur Fleetwood Papers, Mss Eur E224/19, The 'Inchcape Case', 1911/12.
79. IOR, V/26/720/4, paras 3862, 3757, 3000/3001
80. Ibid., para. 3771.
81. Ibid., paras 2229, 2385, 2459.
82. Ibid., p. 86 para. 23; W. Acworth, 'Government in a Democratic State', *Economic Journal*, 2:8 (December 1892), p. 629, 631 attacked Prussian and Austrian state models which implied covert tariffs through discriminating tariffs, and high construction costs.
83. Ibid., p. 88, paras 25, 25a and 26a.
84. Ibid., para. 9.
85. Ibid., para. 27; Anstey, *The Economic Development of India*, p. 138.
86. *Parliamentary Papers 1921* [Cmd.1512], Acworth Committee, para. 206.
87. IOR, V/26/300/6, Report of Indian Retrenchment Committee, 1922–3, pp. 291–2.

Conclusion

1. BL, Ripon Papers 85, Ms 43,575, p. 498.
2. *Parliamentary Papers 1884* [284], Report from the Select Committee on East Indian Railway Communication, para. 1203; PRO, BT31/30983/17441.
3. D. Itzkowitz, 'Fair Enterprise or Extravagant Speculation: Investment, Speculation, and Gambling in Victorian England', *Victorian Studies*, 45:1 (Autumn 2002), p. 124 defined 'speculation' in Victorian London as 'buying or selling of commodities in order to benefit from changes in price'.
4. R. Dumett, 'Exploring the Cain/Hopkins P', pp. 10–11 on shortage of case studies showing City influence in Imperial matters; Cain and Hopkins, *British Imperialism*, pp. 182–3, in fact the Indian railway land was gifted by the government to the guaranteed companies.
5. Roy, *The Economic History of India*, 2nd edn, p. 86; R. Goldsmith, *The Financial Development of India, 1860–1977* (New Haven, CT: Yale University Press, 1983), p. 6; A. Webb, *The New Dictionary of Statistics* (London: 1911), p. 267.
6. Ambirajan, *Classical Political Economy*.
7. A. Smith, *The Wealth of Nations* (London: Penguin, 1999) Book V, pp. 279–311.
8. Sanyal, *Development of Indian Railways*, pp. 142–3; See Appendix 5.
9. Dumett, 'Exploring the Cain/Hopkins Paradigm', p. 11 complained of insufficient test cases.
10. Platt, *Finance, Trade, and Politics*, p. xvii where Mallet and Morier were highlighted as exceptions to the rule.
11. Hurd, 'Railways', p. 162.

12. M. Daunton, 'Gentlemanly Capitalism and British Industry 1820–1914: Reply', *Past and Present*, 132 (August 1991), pp. 184/5; and W. Rubinstein, *Past and Present*, 132 (August 1991).

13. P. Cain and A. Hopkins, 'Gentlemanly Capitalism and British Expansion Overseas II: New Imperialism, 1850–1945', *Economic History Review*, 40:1 (February 1987), p. 3.

14. Dewey, 'The End of the Imperialism of Free Trade', p. 56.

15. Stokes, *The English Utilitarians and India*, p. 311 saw Stephens, legal member in Calcutta from 1869–72, as prominent in pressing 'close partnership' between state and companies to exploit India's resources.

16. E. Green, 'The Influence of the City over British Economic Policy *c.* 1880–1960', in Y. Cassis, (ed.), *Finance and Financiers in European History, 1880–1960* (Cambridge: Cambridge University Press, 1992), p. 202, argued Victorian bankers exploited technical 'knowledge is power'; while M. Daunton, 'Finance and Politics', in Y. Cassis, (ed.), *Finance and Financiers in European History, 1880–1960* (Cambridge: Cambridge University Press, 1992), pp. 284 and 289, dismissed Hobsonian 'demonology' of the City, identifying mutual exploitation with government using banks as cover for an 'unpopular decision'.

17. Dilks, *Curzon in India*, p. 90 'The [Indian] government, unlike its counterpart in Great Britain, undertook much commercial and industrial activity; built and ran railways; controlled the sale of opium and salt; manufactured its own warlike stores and was by far the largest employer of labour'.

18. Misra, 'Gentlemanly Capitalism and the Raj', p. 160 saw the 'unspoken alliance between gentlemanly capitalists and gentlemanly officials' unravelling by 1914.

19. Cain and Hopkins, 'Gentlemanly Capitalism', p. 5 n. 26.

20. Kerr, *Engines of Change*, p. 35, Sind Punjab came closest; Dewey, 'The Government of India's "New Industrial Policy"', p. 252.

21. A. Sen, The Pattern of British Enterprise in India 1854–1914, in R. Ray (ed.), *Entrepreneurship and Industry in India 1800–1947* (Delhi: Oxford University Press, 1992), pp. 116/117.

WORKS CITED

PRIMARY SOURCES
Manuscript and Archival Sources

Balliol College, Oxford
    Morier Papers, Box 6, 8, 9, 11.
    Mallet Papers, III (B), File 22, 23, 24.
Bodleian Library, Oxford
    Kimberley Papers, MS Eng c4285, c4283, c4299, c4242, c4277.
British Library, London
    Ripon Papers, MS 43,575.
Cambridge University Library
    Randolph Churchill Papers, MS 9248, 9249.
    Mayo Papers, MS 7940.
Guildhall Library, London
    London Chamber of Commerce: East India 1886–926 and China 1886–912 Trade Section Minute Book, MS 16, 532.
    Application for Shares, MS 18000/4B, MS 18000/6B, MS 18000/16B, MS 18000/43B, MS 18000/115B.
India Office Records, British Library, London
    Argyll Papers (eighth Duke), MS Neg Reel 4245.
    Assam Bengal Railway Papers, MS Eur C641.
    Chapman Papers, MS Eur E234.
    Cross Papers, MS Eur E243.
    Curzon Papers, MS Eur F111.
    Dufferin Papers, MS Eur F130 and Neg. Reel 4352.
    Durand Papers, MS Eur D721.
    Elgin Papers, MS Eur F84.
    Fleetwood Papers, MS Eur E224.
    Fowler Papers, MS Eur C145.
    Hamilton Papers, MS Eur F123.

Hartington Papers, MS Eur D604.

Hope Papers, MS Eur D705.

Kilbracken Papers, MS Eur F102.

Lansdowne Papers, MS Eur D558/50.

John Lawrence Papers, MS Eur F90.

Lawrence Papers, MS Eur F143.

Lyall Papers, MS Eur F132.

Lytton Papers, MS Eur E218.

Northbrook Papers, MS Eur C144.

Salisbury Papers, Neg.11688.

Richard Strachey Papers, MS Eur F127.

Temple Papers, MS Eur F86.

ING Baring Archive, London

HC3.128, Bengal Central Railway.

HC3.127, James Finlay.

ING, Baghdad Railway Files No. 201338 and 200248.

HC6.3.27, Southern Mahratta.

National Archives, London

Board of Trade Series

Dissolved Companies, PRO, BT 31/2848, BT 31/30983, BT 31/34255, BT 31/34240, BT 31/15646, BT 31/31273.

Cabinet Series

PRO, CAB 6/1, Defence of India.

PRO, CAB 6/3.

PRO, CAB 18/24.

PRO, CAB 37/25, India Office/War Office Memorandum.

PRO, CAB 37/27.

PRO, CAB 37/30.

PRO, CAB 37/114, Russia.

PRO, CAB 38/2, Balfour Memorandum.

Foreign Office Series

PRO FO 60/476, Persia.

PRO, FO 63/1091.

FO 65/1395, Persia.

PRO, FO 65/1415, Persia.

PRO FO 84/1536 and 1594, Slave Trade Series.

PRO, FO/233.

PRO, FO 248/451.

Treasury Series

PRO, T1/11391.

PRO, T 168/ 85.

PRO, T171/20, Information provided for the Mansion House Speech, 1912.

War Office Series
  PRO, WO 13/22, Prussian Railways.
  PRO, WO 106/178, Trans–Caspian Railway.
National Army Museum, London
  Roberts Papers, 7101/23.
Rothschild Archive, London
  File X 111/230, Bengal North Western.
  File 401/E, 1887.
SOAS Archive, London
  Mackinnon Papers, PP MS 1/CORR 1/78, 79, 171, 174.

Printed Primary Sources

Bodleian Library, Oxford
  Hansard.
Guildhall Library, London
  Col/Lib/Pb02/62, 63, 70, 931,1170, Indian Railway Company Annual Reports.
India Office Records, British Library, London
  IOR L/AG/46, 1–52, Accountant General Records.
  IOR L/F/8/12,13,15,16.
  IOR L/Parl/2, Parliamentary Records.
  IOR L/P&S/10, Private and Security.
  IOR L/PWD/2,3, 5, Public Works Department.
  IOR V/4/Sessions 1853,1857/58,1860,1861,1875,1882,1883, 1888, 1893/94,1896, 1900, 1902,1903, 1906, GOI Sessions.
  IOR V/9.
  IOR V/26.

Newspapers

Economist.
Railway Times.
The Times.

Parliamentary Papers, House of Commons Parliamentary Papers (online)

Parliamentary Papers 1878–79 [c 226], Select Committee on the East Indian Railway Bill.
Parliamentary Papers 1880 [c2591, c2735], Indian Famine Commission Report.
Parliamentary Papers 1881 [205], Financial Statement of Government of India, 1881–2.

Parliamentary Papers 1881 [c3036], Indian Famine Commission Report Part III.

Parliamentary Papers 1882 [181], Financial Statement of Government of India, 1882–3.

Parliamentary Papers 1883 [135], Financial Statement of Government of India, 1883–4.

Parliamentary Papers 1884 [284], Report from the Select Committee on East Indian Railway Communication.

Parliamentary Papers 1884–85 [151], Financial Statement of Government of India, 1885–86.

Parliamentary Papers 1884–85 (264): Report of 1879 Special Commission ...into the Organisation and Expenditure of the Army in India.

Parliamentary Papers 1886 [172], Financial Statement of Government of India, 1886–7.

Parliamentary Papers, 1886, [c4715, c 4715–1], Royal Commission to inquire into Depression of Trade and Industry Second Report.

Parliamentary Papers 1888 [c 5512/c 5512–1].

Parliamentary Papers, 1889 (231), Famine Insurance.

Parliamentary Papers 1890 [c5965], Statement of Trade of British India, 1884–9.

Parliamentary Papers 1893–94 [327], Despatch from Secretary of State.

Parliamentary Papers, 1893/94 [cmd 7060], Report of the Committee appointed to inquire into the Indian Currency.

Parliamentary Papers 1896 [166], Financial Statement of Government of India, 1896–7.

Parliamentary Papers 1896 [c 8258], Royal Commission on Administration of Expenditure of India (Welby).

Parliamentary Papers 1898, Indian Currency Committee.

Parliamentary Papers 1899 [c9255, c9178, c9252, c9256, c9254] Report of Indian Famine Commission, 1898.

Parliamentary Papers 1900 [Cd.130], Royal Commission on Administration of Expenditure (Welby).

Parliamentary papers 1902 [c 876], Report of the Indian famine Commission, 1901.

Parliamentary Papers 1903 [Cd.1713], Report on the Administration and Working of Indian Railways.

Parliamentary Papers, 1906 (116), Return of the Net Income and Expenditure of British India.

Parliamentary Papers 1907 [cd 3524], Papers laid before the Colonial Conference.

Parliamentary Papers 1908 [cd 4390], Review of Trade of India for 1907–8.

Parliamentary Papers 1909 [Cd. 4956], Memorandum on Indian Administration.

Parliamentary Papers 1914 [cd 7236], Final Report of the Royal Commission on Indian Finance and Currency.

Parliamentary Papers 1921 [Cmd. 1512], Acworth Committee.

SECONDARY SOURCES

Books

Ambirajan, S., *Classical Political Economy and British Policy in India* (Cambridge: Cambridge University Press, 1978).

Andrew, W., *The Indus and its Provinces* (Lahore: East and West Publishing Co, 1976).

—, *The Punjaub Railway* (London, 1857).

Andrew Yule and Company, 1863–1963 (Edinburgh: Andrew Yule, 1963).

Anstey, V., *The Economic Development of India* (London: Longmans, 1931).

Awasthi, A., *History and Development of Railways in India* (New Delhi: 1994).

Bagchi, A., *The Evolution of International Business 1800–1945, Volume 5* (Cambridge: Cambridge University Press, 1972).

—, *The Presidency Banks and the Indian Economy* (Calcutta: Oxford University Press, 1989).

Bandyopadhyay, P., *Indian Famine and Agrarian Problems* (Calcutta: Star Publications, 1987).

Banerji, A., *Aspects of Indo-British Economic Relations 1858–1898* (Bombay: Oxford University Press, 1982).

Bartle Frere, H., *On the Impending Bengal Famine* (London: John Murray, 1874).

Baumgart, W., *Imperialism: the Idea and Reality of British and French Colonial Expansion, 1880–1914* (Oxford: Oxford University Press, 1982).

Beckett, J., *The Aristocracy in England 1660–1914* (Oxford: Oxford University Press, 1986).

Bell, H., *Railway Policy in India* (London: Rivington, Percival, 1894).

Bentley, M., *Lord Salisbury's World: Conservative Environments in Late Victorian Britain* (Cambridge: Cambridge University Press, 2001).

Bernard, C (ed,)., *Sir George Campbell: Memoirs of my Indian Career, Volume II* (London: 1893).

Berridge, P., *Couplings to the Khyber: The Story of the North Western Railway* (Newton Abbot: David and Charles, 1969).

Bhattacharya, S., *Financial Foundations of the British Raj* (Simla: Indian Institute of Advanced Studies, 1971).

Binnie, A., *Public Works in India: A Letter addressed to the Rt Hon. W.E. Gladstone, MP and the other members of Her Majesty's Government* (London: E. and F.N. Spon, 1881).

Birkmyre, W., *The Revival of Trade by the Development of India: Being an Address Delivered to the Members of the City of Glasgow Chamber of Commerce* (Glasgow: 1886).

Bolitho, H., *James Lyle Mackay: First Earl of Inchcape* (London: Murray, 1936).

Brogan, C., *James Finlay and Co Ltd: Manufacturers and East India Merchants 1750–1950* (Glasgow: Jackson, 1951).

Bucholz, A., *Moltke and the German Wars, 1864–1871* (Basingstoke: Palgrave, 2001).

Buckland, C., *Dictionary of Indian Biography* (London: Swan Sonnenschein, 1906).

Burk, K., *Morgan Grenfell 1838–1988: The Biography of a Merchant Bank* (Oxford: Clarendon, 1989).

Cain, P., and A. Hopkins, *British Imperialism 1688–2000*, 2nd edn (Harlow: Pearson, 2002).

Caird, J., *India, The Land and the People* (London: Cassell, 1883).

Cassis, Y., *City Bankers 1890–1914* (Cambridge: Cambridge University Press, 1994).

Cello, M de., 'Indian Monetary Vicissitudes: An Interlude', in G.Ballachandran (ed.), *India and the World Economy* (Delhi: Oxford University Press, 2003).

Chandra, B., *Nationalism and Colonialism in Modern India* (New Delhi: Orient Longman, 2003).

—, *The Rise and Growth of Economic Nationalism in India* (New Delhi: People's Publishing House, 1966).

Cotton, A., *To The Edinburgh Literary Institute a Reply to Lord Napier's Address on the Indian Famine* (Edinburgh: Oliver and Boyd, 1878).

Creveld, M. van, *Supplying War: Logistics from Wallenstein to Patton* (Cambridge: Cambridge University Press, 2004).

Curzon, G., *Russia in Central Asia in 1889 and the Anglo-Russian Question* (London: Longman, 1889).

Dacosta, J., *Fads and Fallacies regarding Irrigation as a Prevention of Famine in India* (London: W.H. Allen, 1878).

Danvers, J., *Indian Railways: Their Past History, Present Condition, and Future Prospects* (London: Effingham Wilson, 1877).

Darling, M., 'Prosperity and Debt', in S.Bose (ed.), *Credit Markets, and the Agrarian Economy of Colonial India* (Oxford: Oxford University Press, 1994).

Daunton, M., 'Finance and Politics', in Y.Cassis, (ed.), *Finance and Financiers in European History, 1880–1960* (Cambridge: Cambridge University Press, 1992).

—, *Wealth and Welfare: An Economic and Social History of Britain 1851–1951* (Oxford, 2007).

Davis, L and Huttenback, R., *Mammon and the Pursuit of Empire* (Cambridge: Cambridge University Press, 1988).

Derbyshire, I., 'Economic Change and Railways in North India', in I.Kerr (ed.), *Railways in Modern India* (New Delhi: Oxford University Press, 2001).

Dewey, C., 'The End of the Imperialism of Free Trade: The Eclipse of the Lancashire Lobby and the Concession of Fiscal Autonomy to India', in C. Dewey and A. Hopkins (eds), *The Imperial Impact: Studies in the Economic History of Africa and India* (London: Athlone Press, 1978).

Dewey, C., 'The Government of India's 'New Industrial Policy' 1900–1925', in Chaudhuri, K., and C.Dewey (ed.), *Economy and Society: Essays in Indian Economic and Social History* (Delhi: Oxford University Press, 1979).

Digby, W., *Prosperous British India: A Revelation for Official Records* (London: T. Fisher Unwin, 1901).

Dilks, D., *Curzon in India, Vol. 1* (London: Rupert Hart-Davis, 1969).

Dumett, R., 'Exploring the Cain/Hopkins Paradigm: Issues for Debate', in R. Dumett (ed), *Gentlemanly Capitalism and British Imperialism: the New Debate on Empire* (London: Longman, 1999).

Dutt, R (ed.)., *Open Letters to Lord Curzon* (Delhi: Gian, 1986).

—, *The Economic History of India, Vol.2* (Delhi: Government of India, 1960).

Elsmie, G., *Thirty-Five Years in the Punjab* (Edinburgh: David Douglas, 1908).

Fawcett, H., *Indian Finance: Three Essays* (London: Macmillan, 1880).

Ferguson, N., *The House of Rothschild* (New York: Penguin, 1998).

Forsyth, E (ed.), *Autobiography and Reminiscences of Sir Douglas Forsyth* (London: Richard Bentley, 1887).

Foster, R., *Lord Randolph Churchill* (Oxford: Clarendon, 1981).

Fraser, L., *India Under Curzon and After* (London: Heinemann, 1911).

Garvin, J., *The Life of Joseph Chamberlain* (London: Macmillan, 1933).

Gawthrop, W., *The Story of the Assam Railway and Trading Company Ltd 1881–1951* (London: 1952).

Ghose, S., *Indian Railway Finance and Indian Railway Rates* (Calcutta: H.K. Bose, 1912).

Goldsmith, R., *The Financial Development of India, 1860–1977* (New Haven, CT: Yale University Press, 1983).

Gooch, J., *The Plans of War* (London: Routledge and Kegan Paul, 1974).

Goodhart, C., *The Business of Banking 1851–1914* (Aldershot: Gower, 1986).

Gopal, S., *The Viceroyalty of Lord Ripon 1880–1884* (London: Oxford University Press, 1953).

Green, E., 'The Influence of the City over British Economic Policy *c.* 1880–1960', in Y.Cassis, (ed.), *Finance and Financiers in European History, 1880–1960* (Cambridge: Cambridge University Press, 1992).

Greaves, R., *Persia and the Defence of India 1884–1892* (London: Athlone, 1959).

Harrison, G., *Bird and Company of Calcutta* (Calcutta: Anna Art Press, 1964).

Harrison, J., 'The Records of Indian Railways: A Neglected Resource', in I. Kerr (ed.), *Railways in Modern India* (New Delhi: Oxford University Press, 2001).

Headrick, D., *The Tentacles of Progress: Technology Transfer in the Age of Imperialism, 1850–1914* (New York: Oxford University Press, 1988).

Hobson, J., *Imperialism: A Study* (Michigan: University of Michigan Press, 1965).

Holroyd, M., *Lytton Strachey, Volume 1* (London: Heinemann, 1967).

Howard, M., *The Franco–Prussian War* (London: Collins, 1967).

Hurd, J., 'A Huge Railway System but no Sustained Economic Development: The Company Perpectives, 1884–1939: Some Hypotheses', in I. Kerr (ed.), *27 Down: New Departures in Indian Railway Studies* (New Delhi: Orient Longman, 2007).

—, 'Railways', in I. Kerr (ed.), *Railways in Modern India* (New Delhi: Oxford University Press, 2001).

Anon., *Indian Railways: An Argument for a Government Monopoly in preference to Private Enterprise* (Calcutta: W. Newman, 1884).

Jagtiani, H., *The Role of the State in the Provision of Railways* (London: P. S. King, 1924).

Jenks, L., *The Migration of British Capital to 1875* (New York: A.A. Knopf, 1927).

Jones, S., *Merchants of the Raj* (Basingstoke: Macmillan, 1992).

—, *Trade and Shipping: Lord Inchcape 1852–1932* (Manchester: Manchester University Press, 1989).

Kaminsky, A., *The India Office 1880–1910* (Westport: Mansell, 1986).

Kerr, I., *Building the Railways of the Raj* (Delhi: Oxford University Press, 1995).

—, *Engines of Change: The Railroads that made India* (Westport: Praeger, 2007).

— (ed.)., *Railways in Modern India* (Oxford: Oxford University Press, 2001).

Khosla, G., *A History of Indian Railways* (New Delhi: Government of India, 1988).

Kipling, R., *Kim* (Oxford: Oxford University Press, 1987).

Kling, B., 'The Origin of the Managing Agency System in India', in R. Ray (ed.), *Entrepreneurship and Industry in India 1800–1947* (Delhi: Oxford University Press, 1992).

Koss, S., *John Morley at the India Office 1905–1910* (New Haven, CT: Yale University Press, 1969).

Lavington, F., *The English Capital Markets* (London: Metheun, 1921).

List, F., *Schriften, Reden, Briefe* (Berlin: 1931–5).

Loveday, A., *The History and Economics of Indian Famines* (London: G. Bell, 1914).

Lowe, C., *The Reluctant Imperialists* (London: Routledge, 1967).

Macgregor, C., *Narrative of a Journey through the Province of Khorasan and on the North-West Frontier of Afghanistan in 1875* (London: 1879).

Malik, M., *Hundred Years of Pakistan Railways* (Karachi: Ministry of Railways, 1962).

Marvin, C., *The Railway Race to Herat: An Account of the Russian Railways to Herat and India* (London: W.H. Allen, 1885).

Marvin, C., *The Russian Railways to Herat and India* (London: 1883).

McAlpin, M., *Subject to Famine: Food Crises and Economic Change in Western India, 1860–1920* (Princeton, NJ: Princeton University Press, 1983).

McLeod Innes, J., *The Life and Times of General Sir James Browne* (London: John Murray, 1905).

Metcalf, T., *Ideologies of the Raj* (Cambridge: Cambridge University Press, 1995).

Meyer, K and Brysac, S., *Tournament of shadows* (London: Little, Brown, 1999).

Misra, M., 'Gentlemanly Capitalism and the Raj: British Policy between the World Wars', in R. Dumett (ed.), *Gentlemanly Capitalism and British Imperialism: The New Debate on Empire* (London: Longman, 1999).

Mukherjee, H., *The Early History of the East Indian Railway, 1845–1879* (Calcutta: Firma KLM, 1994).

Naoroji, D., *Poverty and Un-British Rule in India* (New Delhi: Government of India, 1996).

Nehru, J., *The Discovery of India* (Oxford: Oxford University Press, 1985).

O'Rourke, K and Williamson, J., *Globalization and History* (Cambridge, MA: MIT, 1999).

Otte, T and Neilson, K (eds.), *Railways and International Politics: Paths of Empire, 1848–1945* (London: Routledge, 2006).

Patwardhan, R., *Dadabhai Naoroji Correspondence, Volume II, Part I: Correspondence with DE Wacha* (Bombay: 1977).

Platt, D., *Finance, Trade, and Politics in British Foreign Policy 1815–1914* (Oxford: Oxford University Press, 1968).

Anon., *The Political Economy of India Famines* (Bombay: 1877).

Anon., *Railways in India: Their Present State and Prospects Considered with Reference to the Field they Present for English Capital* (London: 1855).

Ramm, A., *Sir Robert Morier: Envoy and Ambassador in the Age of Imperialism 1876–1893* (Oxford: Clarendon, 1973).

Rawlinson, H., *England and Russia in the East: A Series of Papers on the Political and Geographical Condition of Central Asia* (London: Murray, 1875).

Roberts, F., *Forty-One Years in India: From Subaltern to Commander-in-Chief* (London: Bentley, 1898).

Robson, B (ed.)., *Roberts in India: The Military Papers of Field Marshall Lord Roberts 1876–1893* (Stroud: Alan Sutton, 1993).

Rothermund, D., *An Economic History of India* (London: Routledge, 1993).

Roy, T., *The Economic History of India 1857–1947* (Oxford: Oxford University Press, 2000).

—, *The Economic History of India*, 2nd edn (New Delhi: Oxford University Press, 2006).

Sanyal, N., *Development of Indian Railways* (Calcutta: University of Calcutta, 1930).

Saul, S., *Studies in British Overseas Trade* (Liverpool: Liverpool University Press, 1960).

Seeley, J., *The Expansion of England: Two Courses of Lectures* (London, 1886).

A.Sen, The Pattern of British Enterprise in India 1854–1914, *Entrepreneurship and Industry in India 1800–1947*, Edited by R.Ray (Delhi: Oxford University Press, 1992).

Sethnia, T., 'Railways, Raj, and the Indian States: Policy of Collaboration and Coercion in Hyderabad', in C. Davis and K.Wilburn (eds), *Railway Imperialism* (New York: Greenwood, 1991).

Shah, K., *Sixty Years of Indian Finance* (London: P.S. King, 1927).

Sharma, S., *History of the Great Indian Peninsula Railway (1876–1900) Part II* (Bombay: 1990).

Silver, A., *Manchester Men and Indian Cotton* (Manchester: Manchester University Press, 1966).

Smith, A., *The Wealth of Nations* (London: Penguin, 1999).

Stokes, E., *The English Utilitarians and India* (Oxford: Clarendon, 1959).

—, 'Peasants, Moneylenders and Colonial Rule: An Excursion into Central India', in S.Bose (ed.), *Credit Markets, and the Agrarian Economy of Colonial India* (Oxford: Oxford University Press, 1994).

Strachey, J and Strachey, R., *The Finances and Public Works of India from 1869 to 1881* (London: Kegan Paul, 1882).

Strachey, R., *East Indian Railway Company Purchase Act, 1879: A Short Account of the preliminary negotiations* (London: 1880).

Sulivan, R., *One Hundred Years of Bombay: History of the Bombay Chamber of Commerce 1836–1936* (Bombay: Times of India, 1938).

Taylor, A *The Struggle for Mastery in Europe 1848–1918* (Oxford: Oxford University Press, 1954).

Temple, R., *India in 1880* (London: Murray, 1880).

Thorner, D., *Investment in Empire* (Philadelphia, PA: University of Pennsylvania Press, 1950).

—, 'The Pattern of Railway Development in India', in I. Kerr (ed.), *Railways in Modern India* (New Delhi: Oxford University Press, 2001).

Tomlinson, B., *The Political Economy of the Raj, 1914–1947* (Basingstoke: Macmillan, 1979).

Trousdale, W (ed.)., *War in Afghanistan, 1979–80: The Personal Diary of Major General Sir Charles Metcalfe Macgregor* (Detroit, MI: Wayne State University Press, 1985).

Tucker, R (ed.), *The Marx-Engels Reader* (New York: Norton, 1972).

Tyson, G., *Bengal Chamber of Commerce and Industry 1853–1953: A Centenary Survey* (Calcutta: Bengal Chamber of Commerce, 1953).

Villeroi, B de, *A History of the North Western Railway* (Lahore: 1896).

Wacha, D., *Indian Railway Finance being a revised reprint of a series of articles.*

Contributed ... to the Wednesday Review 1908 (Madras: G.A. Natesan, 1912).

—, *Speeches and Writings of SirDinshaw Edulji Wacha*, Congress Presidential Address (Madras: G.A. Natesan, 1918).

Waters, W., *Experiences of a Military Attache* (London: John Murray, 1926).

Webb, A., *The New Dictionary of Statistics* (London: 1911).

Articles

Acworth, W., 'Government in a Democratic State', *Economic Journal*, 2:8 (December 1892).

Ambirajan, S., 'Malthusian Population Theory and Indian Famine Policy in the Nineteenth Century', *Population Studies*, 30:1 (March 1976).

Bartlet Brebner, J., 'Laissez Faire and State Intervention in Nineteenth-Century Britain', *Journal of Economic History*, 8 (New York, 1959).

Broadbridge, B., 'The Early Capital Market: The Lancashire and Yorkshire Railway', *Economic History Review*, 8:2 (1955).

Cain, P., 'Railway Combination and Government, 1900–1914', *Economic History Review*, 25:4 (November 1972).

Cain, P., and A. Hopkins, 'Gentlemanly Capitalism and British Expansion Overseas II: New Imperialism, 1850–1945', *Economic History Review*, 40:1 (February 1987).

Chaudhuri, K., 'India's International Economy in the Nineteenth Century', *Modern Asian Studies*, 2:1 (1968).

Checkland, S., 'The Mind of the City 1870–1914', *Oxford Economic Papers*, New Series, Volume 9, Number 3 (October 1957).

R.Christensen, 'The State and Indian Railway Performance 1870–1920', *Journal of Transport History*, 3rd Series, 3:2 (March 1982).

R.Collison Black, 'Economic Policy in Ireland and India in the Time of JS Mill', *Economic History Review*, 21:2 (August 1968).

Connell, A., 'Indian Railways and Indian Wheat', *Journal of the Statistical Society of London*, 48:2 (June 1885).

Daunton, M., 'Gentlemanly Capitalism and British Industry 1820–1914: Reply', *Past and Present*, 132 (August 1991).

Dumett, R., 'Joseph Chamberlain, Imperial Finance and Railway Policy in British West Africa in the Late Nineteenth Century', *English Historical Review*, 90:355 (April 1975).

Ferns, H., 'Britain's Informal Empire in Argentina, 1806–1914', *Past and Present*, 4 (November 1953).

Forbes Munro, J., 'Shipping Subsidies and Railway Guarantees: William Mackinnon, Eastern Africa and the Indian Ocean, 1860–93', *Journal of African History*, 28:2 (1987).

Foreman-Peck, J., 'Natural Monopoly and Railway Policy in the Nineteenth Century', *Oxford Economic Papers*, 39:4 (December 1987).

Gourvish, T., 'A British Business Elite: The Chief Executive Managers of the Railway Industry, 1850–1922', *The Business History Review*, 47:3 (Autumn 1973).

Green, E., 'Rentiers versus Producers? The Political Economy of the Bimetallic Controversy', *English Historical Review*, 53 (1988).

Habib, I., 'Colonialization of the Indian Economy, 1757–1900', *Social Scientist*, 3:8 (March 1975).

J. Hurd, 'Railways and the Expansion of Markets in India 1861–1921', *Exploration in Economic History*, 12 (1975).

Itzkowitz, D., 'Fair Enterprise or Extravagant Speculation: Investment, Speculation, and Gambling in Victorian England', *Victorian Studies*, 45:1 (Autumn, 2002).

Jenks, L., 'Capital Movement and Transportation: Britain and American Railway Development', *Journal of Economic History*, 11:4 (Autumn 1951).

Johnson, R., 'Russians at the Gates of India? Planning the Defence of India, 1885–1900', *Journal of Military History*, 67:3 (July 2003).

Kennedy, W., 'Economic Growth and Structural Change in the United Kingdom, 1870–1914', *Journal of Economic History*, 42:1.

Keynes, J. M., 'The Economic Transition in India', *Economic Journal*, 21:83 (September 1911).

Klein, I., 'English Free Traders and Indian Tariffs, 1874–96', *Modern Asian Studies*, 5:3 (1971).

—, 'Population and Agriculture in Northern India, 1872–1921', *Modern Asian Studies*, 8:2 (1974).

Koebner, R., 'The Concept of Economic Imperialism', *Economic History Review*, 2nd series, 2:1 (1949).

Kumar, R., The Records of the Government of India on the Berlin–Baghdad Railway Question, *The Historical Journal*, 5:1 (1962).

Lehmann, F., 'Great Britain and the Supply of Railway Locomotives of India: A Case Study of Economic Imperialism', *Indian Economic and Social History Review*, 2:4 (October 1965).

Macpherson, W., 'Investment in Indian Railways, 1845–1875', *Economic History Review*, 2nd series, 8 (1955).

Maddison, A., 'A Comparison of Levels of GDP per capita in Developed and Developing Countries, 1700–1980', *Journal of Economic History*, 43:1 (March 1983).

McAlpin, M., 'Railroads, Prices, and Peasant Rationality', *Journal of Economic History*, 34:3 (New York, 1974).

Pollard, S., 'Capital Exports, 1870–1914: Harmful or Beneficial?', *Economic History Review*, 38:4 (November 1985).

A. Porter, 'Gentlemanly Capitalism and Empire: The British Experience since 1750', *Journal of Imperial and Commonwealth History*, 18:3 (October 1990).

Preston, A., 'Sir Charles Macgregor and the Defence of India, 1857–1887', *Historical Journal*, 12:1 (1969).

Pulley, R., 'The Railroad and Argentine National Development, 1852–1914', *Americas*, 23:1 (July 1966).

Richards, E., 'An anatomy of the Sutherland Fortune: Income, Consumption, Investments, and Returns, 1780–1880', *Business History*, 21:1 (January 1979).

W. Rubinstein, *Past and Present*, 132 (August 1991).

Singer, H., 'The Distribution of Gains between Investing and Borrowing Countries', *American Economic Review*, 40:2 (May 1950).

Swamy, S., 'The Response to Economic Challenges: A Comparative Economic History of China and India, 1870–1952', *Quarterly Journal of Economics*, 93:1 (February 1979).

D. Thorner, 'Capital Movement and Transportation: Great Britain and the Development of India's Railways', *Journal of Economic History*, 11:4 (Autumn 1951).

Thornton, A., 'British Policy in Persia, 1858–1890 I', *English Historical Review*, 69: 273 (October, 1954).

Tomlinson, B., 'Writing History Sideways: Lessons for Indian Economic Historians from Meiji Japan', *Modern Asian Studies*, 19:3 (1985).

Towle, P., 'The Russo–Japanese War and the Defence of India', *Military Affairs*, 44:3 (October 1980).

R.Turrell, 'Conquest and Concession: The Case of the Burma Ruby Mines', *Modern Asian Studies*, 22:1 (1988).

Webster, A., 'Business and Empire: A Reassessment of the British Conquest in 1885', *Historical Journal*, 43:4 (December, 2000).

Williams, P., 'Public Opinion and the Railway Rates Question in 1886', *English Historical Review*, 67:262 (January 1952).

Unpublished Theses

Burdett Smith, S., 'British Nationalism, Imperialism, and the City of London 1880–1900' (University of London, Ph.D thesis, 1985).

Derbyshire, I., 'Opening up the Interior: The Impact of Railways on the North India Economy and Society, 1860–1914' (Cambridge University PhD. thesis, 1985).

Macpherson, W., 'British Investment in Indian Guaranteed Railways 1845–1875' (Cambridge University Ph.D. thesis, 1954).

Mukherjee, H., 'The Early History of the East Indian Railway, 1845–1879' (University of London, SOAS, Ph.D thesis, 1966).

Thompson, A., 'Thinking Imperially? Imperial Pressure Groups and the Idea of Empire in late Victorian and Edwardian Britain' (Oxford University D.Phil. thesis, 1994).

Verhese, K., 'The Development and significance of transport in India 1834–82' (Oxford University D.Phil. thesis, 1963).

INDEX

For Product Safety Concerns and Information please contact our EU
representative GPSR@taylorandfrancis.com
Taylor & Francis Verlag GmbH, Kaufingerstraße 24, 80331 München, Germany